EARLY CHILDHOOD EDUCATION
94/95

Fifteenth Edition

A Library of Information from the Public Press

Editor

Karen Menke Paciorek
Eastern Michigan University

Karen Menke Paciorek is an associate professor of Early Childhood Education at Eastern Michigan University. All of her education has been in the field of early childhood, with a B.S. from the University of Pittsburgh, an M.A. from George Washington University, and a Ph.D. from Peabody College of Vanderbilt University. She is president of the 4,500-member Michigan Association for the Education of Young Children. Her presentations at local and national conferences focus on teacher preparation, quality programming, and establishment of the learning environment.

Editor

Joyce Huth Munro
Centenary College

Joyce Munro is chair of the Education Division at Centenary College. In addition to administration and teaching, she oversees The Children's Center at Centenary, which serves 200 children. Regionally and nationally, she presents seminars on curriculum design and teacher education. Currently, she is coordinator of a research project on case-method teaching for the National Association for Early Childhood Teacher Educators. Dr. Munro holds an M.Ed. from the University of South Carolina and a Ph.D. from Peabody College at Vanderbilt University.

Cover illustration by Mike Eagle

The Dushkin Publishing Group, Inc.
Sluice Dock, Guilford, Connecticut 06437

The Annual Editions Series

Annual Editions is a series of over 60 volumes designed to provide the reader with convenient, low-cost access to a wide range of current, carefully selected articles from some of the most important magazines, newspapers, and journals published today. Annual Editions are updated on an annual basis through a continuous monitoring of over 300 periodical sources. All Annual Editions have a number of features designed to make them particularly useful, including topic guides, annotated tables of contents, unit overviews, and indexes. For the teacher using Annual Editions in the classroom, an Instructor's Resource Guide with test questions is available for each volume.

VOLUMES AVAILABLE

Africa
Aging
American Foreign Policy
American Government
American History, Pre-Civil War
American History, Post-Civil War
Anthropology
Biology
Business Ethics
Canadian Politics
Child Growth and Development
China
Comparative Politics
Computers in Education
Computers in Business
Computers in Society
Criminal Justice
Drugs, Society, and Behavior
Dying, Death, and Bereavement
Early Childhood Education
Economics
Educating Exceptional Children
Education
Educational Psychology
Environment
Geography
Global Issues
Health
Human Development
Human Resources
Human Sexuality
India and South Asia
International Business
Japan and the Pacific Rim

Latin America
Life Management
Macroeconomics
Management
Marketing
Marriage and Family
Mass Media
Microeconomics
Middle East and the Islamic World
Money and Banking
Multicultural Education
Nutrition
Personal Growth and Behavior
Physical Anthropology
Psychology
Public Administration
Race and Ethnic Relations
Russia, Eurasia, and Central/Eastern
    Europe
Social Problems
Sociology
State and Local Government
Third World
Urban Society
Violence and Terrorism
Western Civilization,
    Pre-Reformation
Western Civilization,
    Post-Reformation
Western Europe
World History, Pre-Modern
World History, Modern
World Politics

Library of Congress Cataloging in Publication Data
Main entry under title: Annual Editions: Early Childhood Education. 1994/95.
        1. Education, Preschool—Periodicals. 2. Child development—Periodicals. 3. Child rearing—United States—Periodicals. I. Paciorek, Karen Menke, *comp.;* Munro, Joyce Huth, *comp.* II. Title: Early Childhood Education.
ISBN 1–56134–270–X   372.21′05   77–640114
HQ777.A7A

© 1994 by The Dushkin Publishing Group, Inc., Guilford, CT 06437

Fifteenth Edition

Printed in the United States of America

Printed on Recycled Paper

To the Reader

In publishing ANNUAL EDITIONS we recognize the enormous role played by the magazines, newspapers, and journals of the *public press* in providing current, first-rate educational information in a broad spectrum of interest areas. Within the articles, the best scientists, practitioners, researchers, and commentators draw issues into new perspective as accepted theories and viewpoints are called into account by new events, recent discoveries change old facts, and fresh debate breaks out over important controversies.

Many of the articles resulting from this enormous editorial effort are appropriate for students, researchers, and professionals seeking accurate, current material to help bridge the gap between principles and theories and the real world. These articles, however, become more useful for study when those of lasting value are carefully *collected, organized, indexed,* and *reproduced* in a *low-cost format,* which provides easy and permanent access when the material is needed. That is the role played by *Annual Editions.* Under the direction of each volume's *Editor,* who is an expert in the subject area, and with the guidance of an *Advisory Board,* we seek each year to provide in each ANNUAL EDITION a current, well-balanced, carefully selected collection of the best of the public press for your study and enjoyment. We think you'll find this volume useful, and we hope you'll take a moment to let us know what you think.

Early childhood education is an interdisciplinary field that includes child development, family issues, educational practices. behavior guidance, and curriculum. *Annual Editions: Early Childhood Education 94/95* brings you the latest information on the field from a wide variety of recent journals, newspapers, and magazines. In addition, this edition gives special attention to national and international developments in early childhood education. It concludes with significant information on child care, including the recent results of a long-term study of child care effects and a state-by-state survey of child care availability and quality.

Three central themes are evident in the articles chosen for this fifteenth edition of *Early Childhood Education.* The first theme is *children at risk.* In our nation today, far too many children are born into poverty, with little prospect of ever breaking out of the desperate cycle poverty causes. Even with significant changes in welfare, many poor families are unable to remain together. Children often end up living with mothers, while fathers are absent from the family. Today, the leading cause of death of small children in urban areas is shootings. Violence on the street and in the home is increasing, with deadly effects on our youngest children. The rising number of infants and toddlers with HIV/AIDS is particularly disturbing. Their care and support needs must be addressed by our nation. Other risk factors for young children include prenatal cocaine exposure, abuse, and homelessness. Children are extremely vulnerable in dysfunctional environments. Needed more than ever are teachers and other professionals who will dedicate themselves to improving the quality of life for children at risk.

The second theme is *diversity.* Teachers today need to acknowledge differences in children's cultural and ethnic heritage. They can begin by learning about and understanding how family customs and interactions differ. The diversity of heritage can also be incorporated into the curriculum. A global perspective is vital to today's early childhood educational experiences, because the children in our programs will one day work and interact in an international economy. Articles with diversity as a theme are included in each unit. A special section of Unit 1: *Perspectives* gives in-depth information on child care and children in a wide variety of countries. These articles, while informative of other places, can also enrich early childhood practices in our own nation.

Special needs children is the third theme evident in many of the articles. With recent legislation emphasizing the inclusion of children with special needs in regular programs, teachers need information and support for adapting their classrooms and activities. They will be working in collaborative teams with special needs children, which calls for increased communication for the delivery of educational services. Teamwork will require negotiation of new roles for teachers and will also provide them with opportunities for professional development.

Given the range of topics included in *Early Childhood Education 94/95,* it may be used with several groups: undergraduate or graduate students studying early childhood education, professionals pursuing further development, or parents seeking to improve their skills.

The selection of articles for *Early Childhood Education 94/95* has been a cooperative venture between the two editors. The production and editorial staff of The Dushkin Publishing Group ably supports and coordinates our effort. We especially appreciate the insight and assistance of members of the advisory board who share with us in the selection process.

We are grateful to readers who have corresponded with us about the selection and organization of previous editions. Your comments are welcomed and will serve to modify future volumes. Please take the time to fill out and return the article rating form on the last page.

Karen Menke Paciorek

Joyce Huth Munro
Editors

Contents

Unit 1

Perspectives

Eleven selections consider both the national and international development of early childhood education.

Unit 2

Child Development and Families

Seven selections consider the effects of family life on the growing child and the importance of parent education.

Unit 3

Appropriate Educational Practices

Eleven selections examine various educational programs, assess the effectiveness of some teaching methods, and consider some of the problems faced by students with special needs.

Unit
4

Guiding Behavior

Six selections examine the importance of establishing self-esteem in the child and consider the effects of stressors and stress reduction on behavior.

The concepts in bold italics are developed in the article. For further expansion please refer to the Topic Guide and the Index.

Unit 5

Curricular Applications

Seven selections consider various curricular choices. The areas covered include creating, inventing, emergent literacy, motor development, and conceptualizing curriculum.

Unit 6

Reflections

Four selections consider the present and future of early childhood education.

The concepts in bold italics are developed in the article. For further expansion please refer to the Topic Guide and the Index.

Topic Guide

This topic guide suggests how the selections in this book relate to topics of traditional concern to students and professionals involved with early childhood education. It is useful for locating articles that relate to each other for reading and research. The guide is arranged alphabetically according to topic. Articles may, of course, treat topics that do not appear in the topic guide. In turn, entries in the topic guide do not necessarily constitute a comprehensive listing of all the contents of each selection.

TOPIC AREA	TREATED IN:	TOPIC AREA	TREATED IN:
Advocacy	1. World's 5 Best Ideas 8. When Parents Accept the Unacceptable 33. Supporting Victims of Child Abuse 46. Child Care Workers	Diversity	21. Good Prekindergarten Programs 41. African American Children
		Divorce	7. Crisis of the Absent Father 15. Separation and Divorce
Aesthetic Development	37. Creative Arts Process	Drugs	10. Helping Crack-Affected Children Succeed
Affective Development	31. Tasks of Early Childhood	Dual-Income Families	8. When Parents Accept the Unacceptable
Assessment	22. Collaborative Training 27. Trouble with Testing 28. Assessment in Context 29. Assessment Portfolio as an Attitude	Emergent Literacy	18. How Schools Perpetuate Illiteracy 23. Preschool Classroom Environments 38. I Can Write!
Child Abuse	32. Helping Children Cope with Violence 33. Supporting Victims of Child Abuse	Emotions	27. Trouble with Testing 32. Helping Children Cope with Violence 34. How Kids Survive Trauma 40. All about Me 45. Head Start
Child Care	1. World's 5 Best Ideas 4. Where Did Our Diversity Come From? 8. When Parents Accept the Unacceptable 25. Place for Marie 43. 10 Best States for Child Care 44. Head Start's Big Test 46. Child Care Workers	Equipment/ Materials	21. Good Prekindergarten Programs 23. Preschool Classroom Environments 35. Early Childhood Classroom 39. Integrating Technology into the Classroom 42. Grounds for Play
Child Development	12. Amazing Minds of Infants 29. Assessment Portfolio as an Attitude 38. I Can Write!	Families	5. Preventing Early School Failure 7. Crisis of the Absent Father 9. Homeless Children 15. Separation and Divorce 17. Beyond Parents 26. Infants and Toddlers with Special Needs 34. How Kids Survive Trauma 41. African American Children
Collaboration	1. World's 5 Best Ideas 5. Preventing Early School Failure 9. Homeless Children 17. Beyond Parents 25. Place for Marie		
Creativity	2. Reggio Emilia Approach 37. Creative Arts Process	Federal Government	5. Preventing Early School Failure 44. Head Start's Big Test 45. Heart Start
Curriculum	2. Reggio Emilia Approach 20. Developmental Continuity 22. Collaborative Training 28. Assessment in Context 36. Curriculum Webs 37. Creative Arts Process 39. Integrating Technology into the Classroom	Gender Differences	13. How Boys and Girls Learn Differently
		Guiding Behavior	30. Positive Approach to Discipline 32. Helping Children Cope with Violence 33. Supporting Victims of Child Abuse 35. Early Childhood Classroom 40. All about Me
Developmentally Appropriate Practice	19. Essentials of Developmentally Appropriate Practice 20. Developmental Continuity 21. Good Prekindergarten Programs 24. Preschool Mainstreaming 25. Place for Marie 26. Infants and Toddlers with Special Needs 27. Trouble with Testing 28. Assessment in Context 29. Assessment Portfolio as an Attitude 38. I Can Write!	Head Start	44. Head Start's Big Test
		Health and Safety	1. World's 5 Best Ideas 11. Serving Children with HIV/AIDS 26. Infants and Toddlers with Special Needs 43. 10 Best States for Child Care 45. Heart Start
		History	4. Where Did Our Diversity Come From?
		HIV/AIDS	11. Serving Children with HIV/AIDS
Discipline	30. Positive Approach to Discipline	Homeless	9. Homeless Children

Perspectives

- **International Perspectives (Articles 1–3)**
- **National Perspectives (Articles 4–11)**

As editors of *Annual Editions: Early Childhood Education*, one of the exciting aspects of the job has been finding increased coverage of children's issues in magazines and journals aimed at individuals outside of the education profession. This is certainly true for the 1994/1995 edition. Several of the numerous sources for this edition are not education publications, yet they contain articles relevant to our examination of young children. The lead article is from a source aimed at the general public, but it is very appropriate for a discussion of early childhood issues. *Money* researched the world's five best ideas. Not surprisingly, four of the best ideas directly benefit young children and their families.

For some, domestic issues and problems surrounding early childhood are overwhelming, and it is difficult to look beyond our own country. Yet what is happening internationally will affect us and the ways we interact with children. By studying others, we can often learn more about ourselves. The world is changing rapidly, and the numbers of children from other cultures into our country increase daily. Recognizing the value of diversity in the classroom will enable knowledgeable teachers to provide antibias curricular experiences that meet the needs of all the children in the class.

As we examine the living and learning conditions for children today we see many problems, but there are educators, parents, and community groups ready to assist children and their families. Unfortunately, the numbers of people requiring assistance are growing at a rapid pace. Preventing problems from occurring in the first place seems to be the one key to ensuring a safe, nurturing, and successful educational experience for all our country's children.

The vast numbers of young children being born into and raised in environments where poverty, drugs, abuse, homelessness, and lack of medical care are prevalent pose special challenges for early childhood educators. The 26 percent of American children under the age of 6 living in poverty (Children's Defense Fund, 1993) are denied medical care, proper nutrition, shelter, and educational opportunities necessary for survival in America today. Families living in poverty are faced with a multitude of concerns, but few resources. They must find a safe place to sleep for the night or a church offering a meal and a box of used clothing. The children receive so little of quality. Often their lives are affected by the constant turmoil of moving from one temporary housing setting to the next.

Each year as articles are chosen for *Annual Editions: Early Childhood Education*, the editors make a list of current trends and issues and conduct an exhaustive search for a high-quality article covering each issue. One unfortunate trend listed for this year is the increase of absent fathers in families of the nineties. Two excellent articles were located, and "The Crisis of the Absent Father" from *Parents* was chosen. (For additional reading the editors can recommend "Bringing Up Father" from *Time*, June 28, 1993.)

The President's National Drug Control Strategy Report estimates that 100,000 cocaine-exposed children are born each year. After their birth, these children live in environments where drugs are an everyday part of their lives. Within a few years, they enter preschool and public school settings, and very few professionals are ready to meet their special needs. Children born exposed to crack are challenging for even the most experienced and seasoned professionals, yet they leave the hospital and enter homes often headed by poor, drug-addicted young mothers who are not able to cope with the demands of their own care, let alone the needs of a high-strung, difficult to soothe, unhealthy infant.

Teachers are looking for ways to help crack-affected children and HIV/AIDS children succeed in their classrooms. Two good articles are included, with specific suggestions for teachers working with children affected by drugs.

Community groups and business leaders are now collaborating with early childhood professionals in calling for greater funding and the establishment of partnerships among varied constituencies to ensure high-quality programs for America's young children. The reasons for these collaborative efforts are inadequate support during the 1980s from the federal government, greater numbers of families living in poverty, and an increase in the percentage of working mothers and dual-income families who need quality child-care services that they can afford. Successful government, business, and educational collaboration has occurred in the past during the Depression, World War II, and in the 1960s when Head Start began. The lessons learned from those interagency efforts have clearly shown both the necessity and effectiveness of early childhood programs that are comprehensive and high quality. In "Where Did Our Diversity Come From? A Profile of Early Childhood Care and Education in the U.S.," Patricia Olmsted traces the history of programs offering care and education to young children in America.

Public perceptions about our investment in young children in general, and at-risk and minority children in particular, are gradually changing. Today, millions of working parents need quality child-care programs that are consistently and adequately funded, comprehensive in nature to meet the basic needs of children and families, and operated by dedicated and specially educated staffs of professionals. The day-to-day stress that parents face in their jobs has become more intense and complex, and they often have to cope alone due to lack of support from employers, colleagues, family, and friends. This is where alliances formed among home, school, and business can be extremely helpful and comforting.

Looking Ahead: Challenge Questions

In what ways are other countries addressing the needs of families with young children?

Describe the beginnings of programs for young children in this country.

What strategies have proved to be most successful in preventing early school failure?

How are children from families headed by young, poor, and single parents at jeopardy for failure in school and society in general? What steps can be taken to assist these children who face poverty every day of their lives?

How has television affected the social interaction and academic performance of children who watch it excessively?

What can schools do to assist children and their families as they struggle to walk the thin line between economic disaster and a safe and secure life?

With so many children living in families with absent fathers, what affect does the lack of a male figure have on the lives of young children?

What unique qualities are present in the preschool programs of Reggio Emilia?

What is the role of the teacher in developing a curriculum that is antibias and relevant to the family composition, race, and ethnic background of each child?

How can teachers best serve children with HIV/AIDS in the classroom?

THE WORLD'S 5 BEST IDEAS

Other countries are doing a better job of caring for their infants, educating their children and tending to their sick than we are. Here are the lessons we can learn. In some cases, we could save money by adapting their ideas for use here.

Denise M. Topolnicki

1 LEAVES AND AF-FORDABLE DAY CARE THAT HELP PARENTS IN SWEDEN

Imagine an America where: ■ *All parents could take time off from their jobs with pay until their children were beyond infancy and enrolled in high-quality day care.* ■ *All children could attend free preschools.* ■ *All grade schoolers would have to master a rigorous core curriculum.* ■ *All young people entering the labor force would have a chance to be groomed*

2 FREE PRE-SCHOOLS THAT ACCOMMODATE NEARLY ALL OF THE YOUNG IN FRANCE

for highly paid, skilled jobs. ■ *All people would have equal access to first-rate health care. Each of these programs is a reality somewhere else in the world. And each could be adapted to work here, assuming there was a national consensus to improve*

3 GRADE SCHOOLS THAT HOLD KIDS TO HIGH STANDARDS IN JAPAN

child care, education, job training and health care. Now that Congress and the nation are debating President Clinton's ambitious domestic agenda, the time is right to identify the best ideas from other countries that America might borrow and modify. To that end, MONEY *reporters spent three months and traveled 22,500 miles to scrutinize social and educational pro-*

4 TRAINING THAT READIES TEENS FOR WORK IN DENMARK

grams that experts identified as the world's most effective. We cast critical eyes on parental leave, day care and welfare in Sweden, preschools in France, grade schools in Japan, job apprenticeships in Denmark, and health care in Canada—and found much worth imitating. We also learned that these programs aren't necessarily expensive; some actually cost less than the deeply flawed patchwork plans we now have in place.

5 HEALTH INSUR-ANCE THAT COVERS EVERYONE FOR LESS IN CANADA

SWEDEN
How to care for our young ones

MINIMUM AMOUNT OF LEAVE TIME THAT
EMPLOYERS MUST GIVE NEW PARENTS:

SWEDEN	**15 MONTHS, PAID**
U.S.	**3 MONTHS, UNPAID**

Compared with other wealthy democracies, our country does little to help parents cope with new babies or pay for child care. Granted, the Family and Medical Leave Act that President Clinton signed last February lets parents of newborns and newly adopted children take as much as 12 weeks off from their jobs. However, the law excludes the 61% of workers whose companies employ fewer than 50. The leave also is unpaid, making it a luxury few low-income families can afford. In addition, the dearth of inexpensive day care swells our welfare rolls because many single mothers can't find work that pays enough to support child care, so they go on the dole.

Contrast our miserly system with the more generous benefits in Sweden, where parents get 15 months of government-paid leave to divide between them as they wish during the first eight years of a child's life. For the first 360 days, a parent on leave receives a munificent 90% of salary, up to a maximum of 258,000 Swedish kronor (about $35,300 per year; all subsequent figures are in U.S. dollars using the exchange rates prevailing in late April). The last 90 days are paid at a flat $8 a day. Eighty-five percent of the $2.4 billion annual cost comes from Sweden's social insurance fund, which also pays for universal health insurance and other benefits and is financed by an employer-paid payroll tax of 31% (ours is 7.65%); the other 15% comes out of general tax revenues.

Then when Swedish mothers like Ulla Nord, who is profiled at left, return to work, they can enroll their preschoolers in city-run day-care centers that are 89% funded by local and national tax dollars. The rest comes from parents, who pay only $135 to $250 a month, depending on their incomes. By contrast, the average monthly cost of day care in the U.S. is $277, and only 3.3% of all families get direct government aid to cover fees.

Sweden's social policies are not without drawbacks, of course. Its day-care centers cost more to run ($10,730 a year per child, on average) than similar facilities in other countries (in the U.S., the cost is about $3,330 per child). Apparently, there's little incentive for the government to increase the efficiency of its day-care monopoly. And Sweden's parental leave policy fosters rampant discrimination against women in the private sector. Says Hansi Danroth, a male 27-year-old real estate broker in Stockholm: "Prospective employers have asked my sister if she plans to have kids. If I'm competing for a job with an equally qualified girl my age, it's an unwritten rule that I'll get it." Result: More than half of the working women are employed in the public sector, vs. only 22% of men.

But though no budget-minded American politician would advocate adopting the Swedish system wholesale, child development experts argue persuasively that some aspects of it are worth borrowing. First, we would not reduce our global competitiveness by making parental leave a universal, paid benefit, as it is in nearly every industrialized nation. Susanne A. Stoiber, director of social and economic studies at the National Research Council, argues that the burden needn't be overwhelming even for small companies if the leave is relatively short—say, six months. "That's about as far as you can push it without hurting employers and damaging women's chances of getting hired," concludes Stoiber, who has studied parental leave in three European countries. She also advocates paying parents on leave 50% to 60% of their after-tax incomes. Estimated annual cost: $8.3 billion to $10 billion, based on the U.S. General Accounting Office's assumption that 908,000 Americans would qualify for such leave under the Family and Medical Leave Act.

As for child care, studies show that we would be wasting tax dollars if we gave subsidies to the affluent, as Sweden does. According to a 1990 Urban Institute survey, the 32% of families who earn more than $50,000 a year devote a manageable 6.2% of their income to child care. In sharp contrast, the 17% of families making less than $15,000 pay a debilitating 25%. Though families can claim a tax credit of as much as $1,440 for these expenses, the poor are less likely than others to do

so, often because they are ignorant of the law. The best way to provide affordable high-quality child care, say many child-care experts, is to subsidize the enrollment of poor children in day-care centers operated by religious or non-profit groups, which figure to run them more efficiently than the government would. To qualify, centers would have to meet higher staffing and safety standards than they do now. Interestingly, the Swedes themselves, who replaced a socialist government with a right-center coalition in 1991, are leaning toward privatization. Says vice prime minister and minister of social affairs Bengt Westerberg: "In the next decade, I would like to see parents have more freedom to choose between state-run and private day-care centers."

Guaranteeing decent child care to low-income parents would do much to fulfill President Clinton's campaign promise to end welfare as we know it. And rather than encouraging single mothers to go on the dole, our welfare system could do as Sweden's does—provide incentives to postpone childbearing (teenagers account for only 6% of all unmarried mothers there, vs. 33% here) and keep working. Consider that a 25-year-old Swedish woman earning $20,000 a year who bears a child out of wedlock can collect a total of $21,200 in

Reporter associate: Baie Netzer

government benefits for the first 12 months she's on leave, while an unmarried teenage mother who doesn't work gets only $3,200. Says Martin Rein, professor of social policy in the Department of Urban Studies and Planning at the Massachusetts Institute of Technology: "Single mothers in Sweden can't afford not to work."

FRANCE

How to prime kids for school

PERCENTAGE OF THREE- TO FIVE-YEAR-OLDS ENROLLED IN PRESCHOOL:

FRANCE	98%
U.S.	43%

While Americans proclaim the social and academic benefits of early-childhood education, the French deliver it: Virtually all children attend preschool, and eight of 10 go to free, government-run institutions. By contrast, fewer than half of American kids attend preschool. Even the federally funded $2.8 billion-a-year Head Start program, which aims to offer children from families below the poverty line solid pre-elementary training, reaches only 34% of the 2.1 million preschoolers whom the federal government aims to serve.

President Clinton has proposed to spend $10 billion over the next four years to expand and improve the 1,370 Head Start projects, but before he does so, he might ask First Lady Hillary Rodham Clinton about the French preschools she visited on a French-American Foundation study tour in 1989. Unlike Head Start, French preschools are demonstrably effective: A 1983 study by the French National Ministry of Education found that children from families of all socio-economic levels greatly increased their chances of passing first grade if they attended preschool for the maximum three years. Even boosters of the Head Start program, on the other hand, admit that its effectiveness varies widely from project to project. Yale psychologist Edward Zigler, one of Head Start's founders, estimates that 25% of the projects are "poor in quality."

Disturbingly, it costs more than twice as much to enroll a child in Head Start ($3,720 a year) than in a French preschool (about $1,600), according to economist Barbara Bergmann of American University in Washington, D.C., who is writing a book on French child welfare programs. Yet French preschools are open 4½ days a week vs. only 2½ days (actually, five half-days) for Head Start. A typical eight-hour day for a French preschooler like the one profiled opposite includes stories and songs, art, reading- and math-readiness exercises, gymnastics, two to three recesses and a four-course hot lunch (cost: about $4 a day, depending on family income). Only the food isn't top quality; a typical lunch of beef patties, glutinous vegetables and supermarket cheese stops just short of sullying France's reputation as the culinary capital of the world.

The key reason why the French schools accomplish more than Head Start, yet spend less, is that the national government hires highly trained teachers who are capable of handling large classes. Says Colette Durand, a preschool inspector in Paris: "We are running pre-elementary schools, not nursery schools. Our teachers are not glorified babysitters; they are educators, like primary and secondary school teachers, and so they are paid on the same scale." Preschool instructors, who are required by the national Ministry of Education to have the equivalent of a master's degree, earn $19,500 to $37,300 a year, whereas Head Start teachers, 85% of whom never graduated from college, earn as little as $9,000. On average, there are 28 kids in a French preschool class, compared with 18 in Head Start.

Despite the class size, French teachers, who create lessons within a curriculum established by the Ministry of Education, seem able to command their students' attention. Says Françoise Rollet, director of a preschool in Paris' Montparnasse district: "It would be ideal to have only 20 to 25 students in a class and to employ a teacher's aide as well as a teacher for each group. But educators here are not convinced that such changes are required for academic success." American critics who argue that the French system of larger classes wouldn't work in the U.S. because of the greater ethnic diversity of American schools aren't paying attention to their own country's research. When the U.S. Department of Education studied elementary schools in 1988, it found no clear relationship between class size and student achievement.

WHY THIS FAMILY GLADLY PAYS TAX: FREE NURSERIES

Every morning at 8:15, François Gond drops his son at a taxpayer-supported nursery preschool, one of more than 18,000 such schools serving 1.9 million French kids. Pierre-Adrian, 6, and 150 others spend the day in its six large, brightly lit classrooms and rooftop playground. He enjoys it so much that he often hates to leave when his mother Celine, 37, fetches him at 4 p.m. The Gonds pay a mere $3 a day (which covers lunch), compared with the $6,000 a year some U.S. parents would have to shell out for similar schooling. That's one reason sales executive François, 39, doesn't complain about the income tax that claims 48% of his $60,000-plus salary. "When my money is well spent, as it is here," he says, "I don't mind."

—Elif Sinanoglu

The cost of Head Start is also driven up by the fact that, like many antipoverty programs that date from the 1960s, it is run to benefit the poor financially and psychologically by giving them jobs in the agencies that aid them. As a result, many Head Start payrolls are padded with positions for students' parents, most of whom have no expertise in early-childhood education.

If Congress expanded the Head Start program to cover all 11.2 million three- to five-year-olds in the U.S., it would cost a whopping $41.6 billion a year. But the same number of kids could be educated in French-style preschools for $17.9 billion—only $8 billion more than President Clinton proposes to spend to educate just the underprivileged.

JAPAN

How to fix our grade schools

AVERAGE NUMBER OF DAYS IN THE SCHOOL YEAR:

JAPAN	240
U.S.	180

If you live in a suburban U.S. school district that isn't plagued by violence or a high dropout rate, you may think that only our inner-city schools need improvement. Test statistics say you're wrong. The results of exams given in 1991 to kids around the world by the Educational Testing Service show that our top 10% of students compare favorably with other countries' brightest boys and girls. However, the other 90% don't even reach the *average* score attained by their foreign counterparts. When compared with their peers in 14 other countries, American 13-year-olds rank next to last in math and just one notch better than that in science.

How can we ensure that all students, not just the gifted, learn the skills necessary to compete in the global economy? One idea is to get kids off to a better start by revamping our grade schools along the lines of Japan's. (We should not look to Japanese high schools for inspiration, however, since they overemphasize rote learning to prepare students for multiple-choice college entrance exams.) Japanese grade schools don't owe their success to lavish funding (per-pupil expenditures average just $2,243 a year, compared with $4,083 here), technological gimcrackery or trendy theories about empowering teachers, parents or students. Instead, Japanese elementary schools work for three simple reasons:

■ **They are open more days a year.** By the time Japanese kids leave high school, they have spent the equivalent of two more years in school than American students have. Yet their daily schedules are actually less grueling than those of our kids. Japan's elementary school students get four or five 10- to 30-minute recesses and a 40-minute lunch period daily. Ours rarely get more than one recess and usually have half an hour or less to eat lunch.

■ **They follow a national curriculum.** By setting uniform, minimum standards for learning during each grade, Japan's national Ministry of Education ensures that all students—rich or poor, urban or rural—are exposed to the basics. By contrast, the education plan President Clinton proposed in April would set only *voluntary* national goals, not mandatory ones, and even that modest proposal faces stiff opposition from state and local school officials intent on preserving their fiefdoms.

■ **They don't segregate students by ability.** All Japanese grade schoolers are encouraged to master the same curriculum, even though some don't perform as well as others. Says Hiroko Oohisa, a

fourth-grade teacher in Sendai, Japan: "About a third of my students seem slower than the rest, so I work with them after school because I want all of them to understand." In the U.S., on the other hand, gifted kids take advanced classes—often taught by the most imaginative teachers—while other students

---

THESE KIDS CRAM BUT STILL HAVE TIME TO RELAX

If you've ever wondered why Japanese kids beat Americans on achievement tests, consider the schedules of Yoko Asano, 11, and her brother Haruhiko, 8, of Sendai. They are in class 240 days a year, vs. 180 for the average U.S. grade schooler. Yoko attends a juko, or cram school, five afternoons a week; Haruhiko goes on Saturdays (cost: $275 a month). Their father, Toshihiko, 46, a high school chemistry teacher, worries about the strain: "Nowadays children are expected to learn too much too soon," he says. Student life isn't all bad: Kids get plenty of recesses, and the jukos teach many non-academic subjects like piano, swimming and volleyball. Haruhiko even manages four hours of TV a day, about an hour more than American kids watch.

—Baie Netzer

---

are relegated to "dumbed down" lessons that are less demanding. "The Japanese don't undermine their educational system by holding some kids to a lower standard," concludes James W. Stigler, co-author of *The Learning Gap: Why Our Schools Are Failing and What We Can Learn From Japanese and Chinese Education* (Summit Books, $20). Stigler found no evidence that the brightest Japanese suffer as a result; 88 of the 100 fifth-graders who scored highest on tests he administered were Japanese. Only one was an American. One caveat: Whether we dismantle our tracking system or not, we should continue to provide extra help to students with serious learning disabilities. Indeed, the Japanese are studying our schools to determine how they might better serve children with special needs.

Since Japan now spends 45% less on grade schools than we do, it shouldn't be expensive to adopt their ideas. Lengthening the school year will require more money, but those costs could be offset by increasing our class sizes. The number of students per class averages 40 in Japan

vs. 24 in the U.S. Like the French, the Japanese don't think large classes impede learning.

A final word to the unconverted: Despite extensive publicity about pervasive and sometimes fatal bullying in Japanese schools, student violence is far less common there than here, where one student in 20 claims to carry a gun. And contrary to popular belief, Japan's rigorous educational system isn't driving students to suicide. In fact, the suicide rate for 10- to 14-year-olds is more than twice as high in the U.S. as in Japan.

DENMARK

How to train teenagers for real jobs

PERCENTAGE OF HIGH SCHOOL GRADUATES WHO SERVE APPRENTICESHIPS:

DENMARK	**50%**
U.S.	**3%**

Six in 10 U.S. high school students prepare to attend college, while the rest lay the foundations for nothing in particular and too often wind up in low-pay, low-status jobs. Many European nations avoid this waste of human potential by channeling students who aren't headed to college into apprenticeships after the ninth grade. In Denmark, for example, about a third of students attend college-prep high schools called gymnasiums starting in the 10th grade, but the others (including the teen profiled at right) enter commercial or technical schools that train them to become bank tellers, bookkeepers, clerical workers, toolmakers and the like. In the U.S., critics complain that training programs slot kids into lower-paying careers without giving them the opportunity to make more of themselves. However, that's simply not true in Denmark, where vocational students continue to take liberal arts courses and can get back on the college track if they wish.

President Clinton, who created a European-style youth apprenticeship program as governor back in Arkansas, now proposes to spend $1.2 billion over four years on high school apprenticeships nationwide. If Congress approves, the plan could initiate a sea change in U.S. job training. Our training now focuses on older, laid-off workers and welfare recipients rather than on teenagers; as a result, only 3% of high school graduates serve apprenticeships and a minuscule 0.08% of students do so while still in school.

Under the Danish model, a typical technical course lasts four years—80 weeks of classwork and 128 weeks of on-the-job training at private companies. Employers pay apprentices only 30% to 50% of what skilled workers make and are partially reimbursed from funds contributed to by all companies. Net cost to employers: an average of $8,900 per apprentice a year. At that price, it would cost about $26.6 billion a year to create apprenticeships for our 3 million 10th-, 11th- and 12th-graders who aren't college-bound.

At its best, the Danish system pushes such students to work hard so that they can step into skilled jobs. At worst, it provides cheap labor to employers. Of course, apprenticeships aren't a cure-all for the blue-collar blues. Denmark's unemployment rate is 12%, compared with Europe's 9.8%, and employers are creating only 35,000 full apprenticeships a year—forcing some 10,000 kids either to accept shorter training programs or to get their vocational training in the classroom. Still, enlightened educators and employers note that some kind of program inspired by the Danes would be a

---

WITH SCHOOL LIKE THIS, WHO NEEDS A SHEEPSKIN?

Unlike most young Americans who aren't college-bound, 19-year-old Hanne Madsen of Nordborg, Denmark, is on her way to a lucrative career. A third-year computer science student at technical school, Madsen earns $7.42 an hour as an apprentice at Danfoss, a heating and refrigeration manufacturer that is Denmark's largest employer. She landed one of 75 apprenticeships last year after daylong tests that eliminated 80% of the applicants. Since then, she's spent six months in on-the-job training. Even if Madsen isn't among the 40% Danfoss ultimately hires, she has a fallback plan: "I wouldn't mind becoming a computer technician," she says. Indeed, 20% of Danfoss' apprentices attend college or continue education in technical schools after the apprenticeships end.

—D.M.T.

---

vast improvement over our current system, which leaves so many high school graduates floundering.

CANADA
How to get medical care for all

PERCENTAGE OF GROSS DOMESTIC PRODUCT SPENT ON HEALTH CARE:

CANADA	**9%**
U.S.	**12.4%**

Although President Clinton appears to be ignoring Canada's universal health insurance system as he pushes for medical reform, Congress need not make the same mistake. After all, our neighbors to the north spend less on health care than we do and yet get better results than we and most other countries do.

When Canada first implemented government-sponsored coverage for all residents 21 years ago, it devoted about as much of its GDP—7%—to medical care as we did. Today, we spend the most in the world (12.4%, or $2,566 per person per year), yet 17% of Americans under age 65 lack insurance. By contrast, Canada expends only 9% of its GDP on medicine and spends just $1,730 per person a year.

Canadians enjoy better health for their money too. They boast the eighth highest life expectancy in the world, 77.03 years, while Americans, at 75.22 years, rank 33rd, behind even Jamaicans and Dominicans. Canada's infant mortality rate of 7.9 per 1,000 live births is the 10th lowest in the world; our rate of 10 per 1,000 births ranks 21st.

The Canadian system, which is regionally, not nationally, controlled, also seems particularly adaptable to our nation of 50 states. Canada's 10 provinces and two territories make their own rules within a broad, national framework. Most cover mental health services and prescription drugs for hospital patients, welfare recipients and anyone over age 65. Private insurance, which most Canadians have through their jobs, covers only items that government plans exclude, such as private hospital rooms, outpatient drugs, and dental and vision care.

Under this so-called single-payer system, the government—not hundreds of private insurance companies—pays for health care with dollars raised by federal and local taxes. The provinces, which actually send checks to doctors and hospitals, also negotiate fee schedules with provincial medical associations to hold down costs. Although physicians are Canada's highest-paid professionals, they earn an average of only $87,000 a year, vs. $170,000 for American doctors. And hospitals must obtain provincial approval to buy expensive, high-tech equipment. One result is that such gear is scarcer: The U.S. has nearly eight times more magnet-

---

WHY CANADIANS SAY THEIR HEALTH PLAN IS TO DIE FOR

Although the Warners of Hamilton, Ontario, have enough maladies to fill a medical text, they have been well served by Canada's tax-supported universal health-care system. Gary, 52, a French teacher at McMaster University, sees physicians twice a year for his glaucoma and as often as once a week for his high blood pressure. Wife Joy, 48, has had operations for colon polyps and hearing loss. Daughter Clare, 21, suffers from asthma; son Kassim, 13, has Osgood-Schlatter disease, a joint ailment; and daughter Jody, 23, gave birth to a son last year and had all but prescription drug costs covered. (Only son Remi, 19, hasn't needed much doctoring—yet.) Comments Joy: "The one thing Canadians would die defending is their health-care system."

—D.M.T.

---

ic resonance imaging (MRI) and radiation therapy units per capita than Canada, for example. Medical researchers have yet to show, however, that lots of high-tech wizardry improves our health. Canadians admit that they sometimes have to wait for nonemergency heart surgery, organ transplants, radiation therapy and the like. But they rarely queue up for run-of-the-mill services. In fact, a 1991 survey of 11,924 people by Statistics Canada, the government's statistical branch, found that 95% get the care they need within 24 hours (see the profile at left).

When there is a waiting list, a patient's spot on it is determined by doctors' ongoing evaluation of his condition. Delays vary by province and procedure, but to cite one example, there are usually 100 to 120 patients awaiting heart surgery in Ontario's central-west region (which includes Hamilton), where one cardiac surgery unit serves 1.8 million people. Waits average eight to 10 weeks, and some patients have to travel as far as 90 miles to the hospital. Americans with health insurance, by contrast, can shop for a doctor who will schedule them for tests or surgery immediately. But Americans who lack insurance often delay treatment until their deteriorating condition finally lands them in either the emergency room or the morgue.

Clearly, Canadians who have to wait for treatment are inconvenienced. But are they harmed? Research is scanty, but a 1992 study by doctors at the University of Manitoba and Dartmouth Medical School in New Hampshire reported mixed results. When the researchers compared postsurgical mortality rates in Manitoba and New England, they found that the immediate outcomes varied little for low- and moderate-risk procedures but that the survival rate after three years was better in Manitoba. For high-risk procedures, short-term results were better in New England, but the survival rate three years after surgery was similar.

Contrary to what many Americans believe, few Canadians cross the border to get care they would have to line up for at home. Of 7,654 Ontario residents having heart surgery in 1990 and 1991, for example, only 533—or 7%—went to the U.S. or other nations. And most (59%) of those who did were emergency patients who were stricken abroad and wouldn't have had to wait in Canada anyway.

Would Americans trade our system, which rations care based on ability to pay, for a Canadian-style plan where medical necessity is what counts? They might, but only if they understood that they wouldn't have to fill out another insurance claim form nor have limits placed on their choice of doctors, as happens under the increasingly popular managed-care plans in the U.S. Replacing our 1,300-company health insurance industry with a Canadian-style, single-payer system could even save as much as $3 billion a year, according to a 1991 report by the U.S. General Accounting Office. Up till now, fervent opposition by doctors and health insurers—who stand to earn less under a Canadian-style system—seems to have quashed public discussion of that option. But some health-care experts believe it's time to reopen the debate.

Fundamentals of the Reggio Emilia Approach to Early Childhood Education

Lella Gandini

Lella Gandini is liaison to the United States for the Department of Early Education, Reggio Emilia and Adjunct Faculty, School of Education, University of Massachusetts, Amherst.

Editor's note: *The early childhood programs in Reggio Emilia, Italy, have captured the attention of the world. More than 10,000 international educators have visited the schools. The exhibit, "The 100 Languages of Children," that describes their educational approach and documents the learning process through children's work and educators' reflections, is currently touring throughout North America.* Young Children *previously published articles describing the Reggio Emilia approach (New, 1990) and comparing it to practices in the United States (Katz, 1990). The three articles that follow further extend our understanding of the Reggio Emilia approach and its implications for early childhood practices in the United States.*

In June 1993 the founder of the Reggio schools, Professor Loris Malaguzzi, and several of the key pedagogical leaders, Sergio Spaggiari, Carlina Rinaldi, and Tiziana Filippini, visited the United States and were honored guests at NAEYC Headquarters. We invited Professor Malaguzzi to share some of the most important aspects of his philosophy, in his own voice, with the readers of Young Children. *We are indebted to Lella Gandini for her translation of Professor Malaguzzi's writing and for her succinct description of the fundamental principles of the Reggio Emilia approach, which provides a framework for understanding Malaguzzi's philosophy. Finally, NAEYC's director of professional development, Sue Bredekamp, reflects on her recent visit to Reggio Emilia and the implications of the work done there for revising NAEYC's position statements on developmentally appropriate practice.*

All photos are courtesy of Assessorato Scuole Infanzia e Asili Nido, Reggio Emilia, Italy.

In Italy both municipal and national programs for young children have been in place for about 25 years, since the enactment of a law establishing that children between the ages of three and six are entitled to free education. This law was followed in 1971 by a law establishing infant/toddler centers that also receive parental financial contributions. In each case, women were especially active and effective advocates for the legislation.

Of special note is that in these programs, both education and care are considered necessary to provide a high-quality, full-day program. These programs combine the concept of social services with education, an approach that is widely accepted in Italy. What, then, is so unusual or special about Reggio Emilia, a town of 130,000 inhabitants in northern Italy?

In Reggio Emilia the city-run educational system for young children originated in schools started by parents, literally built with their own hands, at the end of World War II. The first school was built with proceeds from the sale of a tank, some trucks, and a few horses. From the start, Loris Malaguzzi has guided and directed the energies of parents and educators.

The city now runs 20 schools for children ages three to six years, as well as 13 infant/toddler centers for children four months to three years of age. Children from all socioeconomic and educational backgrounds attend the programs: 47% and 35% of the two age groups are served, respectively. In Italy about 90% of children three to six years old attend some kind of school, whether municipal, national, or private; in Reggio Emilia 95% of preschool-age children are enrolled in school. Children with disabilities are given first priority for enrollment in the schools.

Through many years of strong commitment and cooperation, parents and educators in Reggio have developed the present excellent program that, in turn, has become a point of reference and a guide for many educators elsewhere in Italy, in various European countries, and—in the last 10 years—in the United States. Thirty years of successful experience with schools for about half of the children in a city of 130,000 inhabitants has created

From *Young Children*, Vol. 49, No. 1, November 1993, pp. 4-8. Reprinted by permission of the publisher, the National Association for the Education of Young Children. © 1993 by NAEYC.

powerful results and generated much interest, as evidenced by the number of international visitors, the number of articles and conference presentations describing the work, and the large number of people viewing the Reggio Emilia exhibits that are touring Europe and North America.

Child, parent, and teacher—the three subjects of the learning experience: a three-year-old arrives for her first day of school, accompanied by her father. The teacher welcomes them in front of the school.

Educators in Reggio Emilia have no intention of suggesting that their program should be looked at as a model to be copied in another country; rather, their work should be considered as an educational experience that consists of practice and careful reflection that is continuously readjusted. Nevertheless, the Reggio educators are pleased to share their experience with other educators in the hope that knowledge of the Reggio Emilia schools' experience will stimulate reflections on teaching, helpful exchange of ideas, and novel initiatives in other schools.

An examination of some of the basic principles that have inspired the experience in Reggio Emilia immediately reveals that these concepts are not new to American audiences. Indeed, many of the basic ideas that inspired the work of educators in Reggio Emilia originated in the United States and are, in a sense, returning to their point of origin. From the beginning of their unique school program, the educators in Reggio Emilia have been avid readers of John Dewey, and over the years, in addition to studying Piaget, Vygotsky, and other European scientists, they have continued to keep abreast of the latest research in child development and education in the United States. The following principles, or fundamental ideas, are presented one by one for the sake of clarity, but they must be considered as a tightly connected, coherent philosophy, in which each point influences and is influenced by all the others.

The image of the child

The educators in Reggio Emilia speak first and foremost about the image they have of the child. All children have preparedness, potential, curiosity, and interest in constructing their learning, in engaging in social interaction, and in negotiating with everything the environment brings to them. Teachers are deeply aware of children's potentials and construct all their work and the environment of the children's experience to respond appropriately.

Children's relationships and interactions

Education has to focus on each child—not each child considered in isolation but each child seen in relation with other children, with the family, with the teachers, with the environment of the school, with the community, and with the wider society. Each school in Reggio Emilia is viewed as a system in which all of these relationships,

A comfortable place to meet with their children in the entrance of the school is set up to welcome parents.

which are all interconnected and reciprocal, are activated and supported.

The three subjects of education

For children to learn, their well-being has to be guaranteed: the well-being of children is connected with the well-being of parents and teachers. Children's rights should be recognized, not only children's needs. Children have a right to high-quality care and education. By recognizing that children have rights to the best that a society can offer, parents and teachers gain recognition of their rights as well.

The role of parents

Parent participation is considered essential and takes many forms: day-to-day interaction during work in the schools; discussions of educational and psychological issues; and special events, excursions, and celebrations. Parents are an active part of their children's learning experience

Children play in the main space, or **piazza,** *at Diana school.*

and, at the same time, help ensure the welfare of all children in the school.

An amiable school

The layout of physical space in the schools encourages encounters, communication, and relationships. The arrangement of structures, objects, and activities encourages choices, program solving, and discoveries in the process of learning. In preparing the space, teachers offer the possibility for children to be with the teachers

Children take time revisiting the many reflections of their images in a mirrored structure built by parents and teachers in Diana School.

Children and the **atelierista** *discuss the plans they have drafted for constructing an amusement park for small birds in the LaVilletta schoolyard.*

and many of the other children, or with just a few of the children, or even alone. Teachers are aware, however, that children also learn from their peers, especially when they can interact in small groups.

The time not set by the clock

Children's own sense of time and their personal rhythm are considered in planning and implementing activities and projects. The leisurely pace that an observer notices is facilitated by the full-day schedule. Such a schedule, rather than overwhelming the participants, seems instead to provide sufficient time to complete projects and activities with satisfaction. Teachers get to know the children's personal timeclocks because children stay with the same teachers

and the same peer group for three-year cycles (infancy to three and three to six). Each year the group changes environments because their developmental needs and interests change, but the re-

Teachers and the atelierista *discuss and interpret the children's dialogs together to plan the next steps in their work with the children.*

The cooperation between teachers and parents and among teachers is reflected in the way the children work together.

lationships with teachers and peers remain consistent.

Teachers as partners

To know how to plan and proceed with their work, teachers listen to and observe children closely. Teachers use the understanding they gain to act as a resource for the children. Teachers ask questions; discover the children's ideas, hypotheses, and theories; and provide occasions for discovery and learning. In fact, teachers consider themselves partners in learning and enjoy discovering with the children.

Cooperation as the foundation of the system

Cooperation at all levels in the schools is a powerful mode of working that makes possible the achievement of the complex goals that Reggio educators have set for themselves. Teachers work in pairs in each classroom (not as head teacher and assistant but at the same level); teachers maintain a strong collegial relationship with all other teachers and staff and engage in continuous discussion and interpretation of their work as well as of the work of and with children. Those exchanges provide permanent, ongoing training and theoretical enrichment. Teachers see themselves as researchers, preparing documenta-

tion of their work with children, whom they also consider researchers. The system is further supported by a team of pedagogical coordinators, called *pedagogisti,* who also support the relationships among all teachers, parents, and community and city administrators.

The interdependence of cooperation and organization

Cooperation needs much support; in Reggio Emilia schools, cooperation is supported by a careful, well-developed structure or

This is an episode within a long project about shadows. After exploring their shadows outside, the children drew their hypotheses about the placement of the sun and the resulting shadows. Here a teacher poses a provocative question.

organization. From the details of each teacher's schedule to the planning of meetings with families to the children's diet, everything is discussed and organized with precision and care. In fact, the high level of cooperation is possible precisely because of such thoughtful organization; likewise, the organization is achieved because of the conviction by all concerned that by cooperating they will be able to offer the best experience to the children.

The atelier *at Diana School invites children to express themselves through many languages.*

The emergent curriculum

The curriculum is not established in advance. Teachers express general goals and make hypotheses about what direction the activities and projects might take; consequently, they make appropriate preparations. Curriculum emerges in the process of each activity or project and is flexibly adjusted accordingly.

Projects

Teachers facilitate children's exploration of themes and work on short- and long-term projects. Project ideas originate in the continuum of experience of children and teachers and in their practice of constructing knowledge together. Projects may start either from a chance event, an idea or a problem posed by one or more children, or an experience initi-

ated directly by teachers; for example, a study of crowds originated when a child told the class about a summer vacation experience, while a project on fountains developed when children decided to build an amusement park for birds. Projects can last a few days to several months.

Atelierista *and* atelier

A teacher who is trained in the visual arts works closely with the other teachers and the children in every preprimary school (and visits the infant/toddler centers). This teacher is called *atelierista,* and a special space, workshop, or studio, called *atelier,* is set aside and used by all the children and teachers. The atelier contains a great variety of tools and resource materials, along with records of past projects and experiences. The educators in Reggio Emilia prefer to speak of many different languages off children (in fact, 100 languages) rather than art. In their view, children's expression through many media is not a separate part of the curriculum but is inseparable for the whole cognitive/symbolic expression in the process of learning.

The power of documentation

Finally, transcriptions of children's remarks and discussions, photographs of their activity, and representations of their thinking and learning using many media are carefully arranged by the atelierista, along with the other teachers, to document the work (and the process of learning) done in the schools. This documentation has several functions: to make parents aware of their children's experience and maintain parental

Clay work portrays a mother pushing an infant in a stroller.

A teacher observes and supports the children's discussion, while the tape recorder and camera document the process of this exploration.

Documentation through a panel of photographs, transcripts of children's dialogs, teachers' notes, and clay work serves as a record of four-year-old children's explorations of mothers pushing infants in strollers.

involvement; to allow teachers to understand children better and to evaluate the teachers' own work, thus promoting their professional growth; to facilitate communication and exchange of ideas among educators; to make children aware that their effort is valued; and to create an archive that traces the history of the school and of the pleasure and process of learning by many children and their teachers.

The Reggio Emilia schools and their approach to early childhood education are not considered "experimental." These schools are part of a public system that strives to serve both the child's welfare and the social needs of families while also supporting the child's fundamental right to grow and learn in a favorable environment with peers and with caring professional adults.

Early Childhood Education in China

JoAn Vaughan

JoAn Vaughan is a Teacher in the Child Study and Teacher Education Department, Stephens College, Columbia, Missouri.

Traditional early childhood education in China currently faces both internal and external challenges—changing family structures and increased influence of foreign ideas and values. The one child policy in the People's Republic of China is altering family roles and childrearing practices, raising concerns about the possible harmful effects of too much attention and pampering. A study of single child families in the Beijing area found that these "little emperors and princesses" were more egocentric, less persistent and less cooperative than children with siblings (Jiao, Guiping & Qicheng, 1986). How have these children adjusted to schools? Or have the schools changed to accommodate them?

As China becomes more open to outside contact and influence, traditional teaching comes into conflict with Western ideas about "developmentally appropriate practices" and goals of creativity, autonomy and critical thinking. Have these goals and practices, which are so prevalent in the United States today, influenced Chinese early childhood education?

In 1991, I had ample opportunity to explore such questions when I spent seven months teaching in

China. I drew much of my information from observations of early childhood programs in Xi'An, where I taught at Xi'An Foreign Languages University. My conclusions are consistent with what I observed and heard in interviews with teachers, parents and teacher educators throughout China.

It is difficult to observe the ordinary functioning of a typical school in China because officially approved and arranged visits for foreigners are usually made to "model" programs and involve special arrangements and performances (Gentry, 1981; Shepherd, 1991). I was able, however, to arrange more informal visits through Chinese friends and travel companions. My most exten-

sive experience was as an English language teacher in a Xi'An child care center, which was considered a typical rather than a model center. My role as a participant-observer allowed me to witness the center's normal functioning over a period of time and gain deeper understanding of the children through personal interaction.

Three Types of Early Childhood Programs

Children enter elementary school at age 6. There are three types of early childhood programs for children under 6: nurseries, kindergarten and pre-primary programs.

Nurseries serve children under age 3. Small group size and many

From *Childhood Education*, Summer 1993, pp. 196-200. Reprinted by permission of JoAn Vaughan and the Association for Childhood Education International, 11501 Georgia Avenue, Suite 315, Wheaton, MD. © 1993 by the Association.

caregivers assure prompt, abundant care. Since physical care and nurturing are the primary goals, the caregivers are trained as "nurses" rather than teachers. Programs for 2-year-olds are often combined with kindergartens.

In China, the term "kindergarten" refers to full-day programs serving children from age 3 to age 6. About 20 percent of the 3- to 6-year-olds attend kindergarten (Zhong, 1989). The programs serve the twofold purpose of child care and educational preparation. The troublesome dichotomy between these two functions often found in the United States (Caldwell, 1990) is not an issue in China. There is no history of a dual development of one type of full-day program to provide care for children of working mothers and another type of half-day program to provide education for children of nonemployed mothers.

A variety of sources provide kindergarten programs—the government, government-licensed private individuals and neighborhood committees, and work units. Work units are government-operated comprehensive communities in which workers and their families work and reside, such as those organized around a college or factory.

As China becomes more open to outside contact and influence, traditional teaching comes into conflict with Western ideas about "developmentally appropriate practices" and goals of creativity, autonomy and critical thinking.

Photos courtesy of author

Singing and dancing occupy an important place in the curriculum.

Children are generally grouped by age in kindergarten. Government regulations in 1981 recommended three groupings: juniors (3-year-olds), middle (4-year-olds) and seniors (5-year-olds) (Cleverley, 1985). Education replaces physical care as the primary emphasis in this program. Class size increases with age, ranging from 20 to 40 children. Each group typically has two teachers and a nurse.

Large, affluent centers also often have one or more doctors on the staff to care for sick or injured children. They also provide other health-related services, such as performing health screenings, giving immunizations and planning nutritious meals.

An alternative type of early childhood program is the pre-primary classroom, which is a part of the elementary school. It is typically a half-day program serving children the year prior to 1st grade. Comparable to U.S. public kindergartens, these classes usually place greater emphasis upon academics and use teaching methods similar to those of the Chinese elementary classrooms.

Curriculum
The nationally prescribed curriculum includes language, math, art, music, physical education and gen-

eral knowledge, which is a combination of science and social studies (Spodek, 1988). Each class session focuses upon a particular curriculum area. In the language classes, children learn to read and write simple Chinese characters, plus pinyin (the phonetic romanization of Chinese). In math classes, they learn number concepts, numeral recognition and addition; manipulatives are frequently incorporated into the lessons.

The emphasis upon academic work varies with the school and the age of the children. Academics are generally not given major emphasis until children reach age 5. The pre-primary classrooms associated with elementary schools stress academic goals more than do the kindergartens. Parents often want their children to begin academic work early, believing it will give them a head start in the competitive struggle for scholastic success—considered the major route to future opportunities. The competitive and selective entry procedures to "key" and many better neighborhood schools heighten this perceived need for an early start (Hawkins & Stites, 1991). Key schools are highly selective schools designed for academically superior students.

Singing and dancing occupy an

important place in the curriculum. Even 2-year-olds may participate in well-rehearsed public performances of song and dance routines.

The following sections describe the physical environment, schedule, curriculum, teaching methods and discipline of the Chinese kindergarten centers, where most of my observations took place.

Physical Environment

A kindergarten often has several classroom buildings surrounding an enclosed courtyard. This courtyard serves as the playground and is used extensively between classroom lessons. The playground contains equipment for large motor activities, including slides, merry-go-rounds, climbers and swings. Bright colors and dragon or elephant shapes provide added appeal. The ground cover is usually a sturdy brick or concrete, with no sand, grass or dirt to soften falls. A few trees, bushes and flowers do, however, beautify the environment. Children are generally free to choose their own activities, with little teacher-directed activities or even supervision.

Each group of children has its

A child folds and twists tissue paper into butterflies.

own large classroom, plus a separate room with beds for afternoon naps. Several groups of children generally share toilet facilities and washrooms. Each group in the model school at the Xi'An Teachers College has a self-contained space, complete with classroom, sleeping room, toilet and washroom. The younger children even have their own playground.

The classrooms contrast sharply with a typical American preschool. The space is not organized into special interest areas and equipment is scarce or not easily accessible to children. American preschools are supplied with unit blocks, dramatic play centers, open shelves filled with art supplies, sand and water tables. In China, however, small tables and chairs for each child occupy much of the room. A large open space may be set aside at one end for group activities, such as dancing.

The better equipped centers may possess one shelf of toys and books available for children's use during their free time. Elaborate, artistic, teacher-made decorations and children's work brighten up otherwise drab rooms. One artistically talented teacher painted large murals of children and animals in the hallways. Another placed a large, colorful clown on the wall as part of a weather wheel. Children's work varied greatly and included such items as mobiles, math papers, crayon drawings and paper foldings.

Typical Daily Schedule

The length of the school day reflects the needs of working parents. At the Xi'An Foreign Languages University, kindergarten children begin arriving around eight o'clock. Class sessions alternate with free-play time. The length and number of these classes increase as children grow older, varying from six 15-minute sessions per week for the youngest to fourteen 35-minute sessions for the oldest (Lystad, 1987). Following a hot, nutritious lunch, children take

All children are expected to proceed at the same pace. The child is responsible for keeping up and poor performance is usually attributed to "not working hard enough." The solution is to admonish the child to work more diligently.

a long nap, eat a snack and then have free-play time. Families, often grandparents, pick up the children after work at about five or six o'clock. Instead of riding home in the family car, these children either walk to their nearby homes or ride on the back of the family bike.

Learning social skills is also considered an important part of the curriculum, particularly for younger children. Along with respecting the teacher and obeying school rules, children learn to help others and solve disagreements constructively. One teacher expressed concern about a common problem, the shy child. She described her efforts to help these children feel comfortable and speak up more.

Teaching Methods

While much of the curriculum content is similar to a typical American program, the teaching methods are quite different from the "developmentally appropriate practices" advocated by early childhood educators in the United States (NAEYC, 1986). Children seldom work independently or in small groups on self-selected tasks. Instead, the emphasis is upon teacher-directed, total group instruction. All children are expected to do the same thing at the same time. For example, in a typical art lesson the teacher demonstrates how to fold and twist tissue paper into butterflies. She then gives guidance to those children doing it incorrectly before proceeding to the next step of pasting the butterfly onto paper and drawing antennae. Drawing lessons often consist of children copying an object drawn by the teacher.

Even when using manipulatives, all children use the same kind at the same time. For example, one class of children might play independently with Legos, each child using just a few pieces, while in another room each child plays with a tiny portion of Playdough. The importance of the whole group instructional approach appears to outweigh the limitations of minimal supplies. Even such practices as going to the bathroom are often done in a group, with the explanation that "It's good for children to learn to regulate their bodies and attune their rhythms to those of their classmates" (Tobin, Wu & Davidson, 1989, 105).

I was surprised at the independence and lack of peer interaction in these group activities. Since China has a socialist ideology, I expected more lessons to use co-operative interactions and teamwork, in order to emphasize group rather than individual achievement. The encouragement of group rather than individual goals *was* evident, however, in the emphasis on teaching children altruistic and nurturing behaviors. Children helped one another with dressing and often gave up a prized toy to a playmate with no prodding by the teacher.

All children are expected to proceed at the same pace. The child is responsible for keeping up and poor performance is usually attributed to "not working hard enough." The solution is to admonish the child to work more diligently.

The teaching method and the

available materials limit opportunities for creative expression or pursuit of individual interests. Ample materials necessary for open-ended, unstructured exploration are seldom available. Sand and water play, blocks and woodworking equipment are rare. Art supplies are typically used for teacher-directed, rather than child-initiated, activities.

Guidance and Discipline

What is considered acceptable school behavior? During group activities, children are expected to give their complete attention to the teacher and participate fully. Talking or playing with other children is not allowed during this time. Respect for the teacher and prompt, unquestioning obedience

are expected. During free-play time, however, noisy and active social interactions are quite acceptable. Teachers encourage harmonious peer relationships, in which children respect the rights of others and help each other.

I was impressed with how well the children meet these expectations. They generally appear to be orderly, attentive, hard-working and eager to please the teacher. I saw very few incidents of peer conflict or inattentive or disruptive

behavior during group activities, and no cases of disrespect or lack of prompt obedience to the teacher's requests.

Some of the guidance and discipline methods differ from standard practices in the United States. A widely used technique is public correction and criticism, not just for misbehavior but also for poor performance. Children who are not doing well or have made a mistake are commonly singled out in public. One teacher removed two young girls from a group practicing a dance, asking them to sit down and watch the others because they were "not trying hard enough." In a pre-primary class where children completed a phonics task on the chalkboard, the teacher required those who had

In the playground, children are generally free to choose their own activities.

made a mistake to stand up and acknowledge their error.

Teachers do not appear concerned about any possible psychological harm resulting from these practices, such as lowered self-esteem. Rather, they believe such corrections will help the child work harder so as to avoid future mistakes. The threat of a public reprimand and "loss of face" appears to be a strong, pervasive influence upon children's behavior. The importance of "face" has a long history in Chinese culture. Loss of face results from public embarrassment and failure to meet group expectations. The child learns early to keep the approval of the social group, for loss of face is a reflection upon the whole family (Hu, 1944).

Positive reinforcement for good behavior is also used extensively. Teachers praise and recognize children who are doing well, often pointing out "the best ones" in class. Children receive rewards, such as red stars, for helping another child, answering questions in class or doing well on written work.

Effect of One Child Policy

Does a difficult transition occur for the only child who goes from being the center of attention at home to being part of a large group expected to obey and conform? Both parents and teachers told me that children may experience a difficult time at first, crying and wanting to go home, but usually they accept the situation and quickly adjust to school routines. Teachers try to comfort and distract such children by interesting them in new toys. Teachers seldom have a problem getting new children to participate in group activities. As one teacher stated, "When they see all the others participating, they do not want to be different." The schools assume that these only children will adapt to the traditional school expectations and, in most cases, this adjustment appears to occur without undue stress or rebellion.

The one child policy has, however, affected the schools in another way. It has strengthened the emphasis upon education for young children and the families' strong involvement and investment in their only child. Teachers report that not only are parents very interested in their child's school success, but they are also very quick to criticize teachers if they feel their child has been treated unfairly or too harshly.

Conclusion

Early childhood education programs in the People's Republic of China differ significantly from those in the United States, particularly in teaching methods. Both its socialist ideals and Confucian traditions may help explain the persistence of the whole group, teacher-directed emphasis, rather than the use of individual choices and creative self-expression. This emphasis may be changing, however, as a current reform movement works to foster more creativity and autonomy (Spodek, 1989).

My experiences in China confirm the view that the Chinese greatly love and value their children, regarding them as family and national resources. In spite of limited resources, they make major investments in their children and the education system. Through these investments, they effectively provide an early childhood education system that fosters obedient, hardworking children.

References

Caldwell, B. (1990). "Educare": A new professional identity. *Dimensions, 18,* 3-6.

Cleverley, J. (1985). *The schooling of China.* Sydney, Australia: George Allen & Unwin Australia Ply Ltd.

Gentry, J. (1981). Early childhood education in the People's Republic of China. *Childhood Education, 58,* 92-96.

Hawkins, J., & Stites, R. (1991). Strengthening the future's foundation: Elementary education reform in the People's Republic of China. *The Elementary School Journal, 92,* 41-60.

Hu, H. (1944). The Chinese concept of "face." *American Anthropologists, 46,* 45-64.

Jiao, S., Guiping, J., & Qicheng, J. (1986). Comparative study of behavioral qualities of only children and sibling children. *Child Development, 57,* 357-361.

Lystad, M. (1987). Children of China: A commentary. *Children Today, 16,* 20-22.

National Association for the Education of Young Children. (1986). Position statement on developmentally appropriate practice in early childhood programs serving children from birth to age eight. *Young Children, 41*(6), 3-19.

Shepherd, G. (1991). A glimpse of kindergarten—Chinese style. *Young Children, 47*(1), 11-15.

Spodek, B. (1988). Conceptualizing today's kindergarten curriculum. *Elementary School Journal, 89,* 203-211.

Spodek, B. (1989). Preparation of early childhood teachers in the People's Republic of China. *Childhood Education, 65,* 268-273.

Tobin, J., Wu, D., & Davidson, D. (1989). *Preschool in three cultures: Japan, China, and the United States.* New Haven, CT: Yale University Press.

Zhong, S. (1989). Young children's care and education in the People's Republic of China. In P. Olmsted & D. Weikart (Eds.), *How nations serve young children: Profiles of child care and education in fourteen countries.* Ypsilanti, MI: High/Scope Press.

See also:

Chen, J. Q., & Goldsmith, L. T. (1991). Social and behavioral characteristics of Chinese only children: A review of research. *Journal of Research in Childhood Education, 5,* 127-139.

Where Did Our Diversity Come From?

A Profile of early childhood care and education in the U.S.

Patricia P. Olmsted

Senior Research Associate

In 1838, *Letters to Mothers* by Lydia Sigourney was published in the United States. It was a book giving the following advice to mothers about early childhood care and education:

Who can compute the value of the first seven years of life? Who can tell the strength of impressions, made ere the mind is preoccupied, prejudiced or perverted? Especially, if in its waxen state, it is softened by the breath of a mother, will not the seal which she stamps there, resist the mutations of time, and be read before the Throne of the Judge, when the light of this sun and moon, are quenched and extinct? (p. 89)

The industry displayed in the various trades and occupations, should be a stimulant to the mother, who modifies a material more costly than all others, more liable to destruction by brief neglect. . . . Is the builder of a lofty and magnificent edifice, careless of its foundations, and whether its columns are to rest upon a quicksand, or a quagmire? (pp. 90–91)

Sigourney's advice clearly reflects the attitudes of that period in America—attitudes about the critical nature of a child's early years, the important role of religion in childrearing, and the pivotal role of the mother. It is perhaps no coincidence that around the year of publication of Sigourney's book, *out-of-home child care by groups and institutions* was just beginning in the U.S.

Any history of early childhood out-of-home services in the United States must trace two major strands of activity. The first strand, with roots in a social welfare tradition, has been associated with the provision of *care* for young children, particularly for those from poor and troubled families. The second strand, with roots in Friedrich Froebel's kindergarten movement, has been associated with the provision of early *education*, especially for children from affluent families. To understand the major events forming these two strands, it is helpful to first consider American attitudes towards childrearing and personal fulfillment.

ATTITUDES FORMED BY OUR HISTORY

The history of the United States has contributed in a unique way to a national set of attitudes including beliefs about the primacy of the family with regard to childrearing and beliefs about the value of personal fulfillment through work. Cochran (1982) discussed the former beliefs by noting that "There is a strong feeling that childrearing is a family affair, to be carried out by the mother, with help from the father, separate from public life. A national commitment to pluralism, stimulated by successive waves of immigration, has carried with it an agreement that different peoples rear their children differently, and reinforced the belief that childrearing practices are the private province of family members" (Draft, pp. 3–4). Regarding beliefs about personal fulfillment through work, Cochran pointed out that both church and state have promoted the value of work throughout the history of this country. Furthermore, with the industrial revolution, work has increasingly implied paid employment, for both men and women, away from home.

The historical movement of American women (including mothers of young children) into the labor force can be related to the combination of the growing mechanization of household tasks, the desire for more consumer goods, and a desire for personal fulfillment through paid employment. Cochran stated, "The tension created by combining the belief that childrearing is a private affair, to be carried out primarily by the mother, with a desire to maximize human potential, individual freedom, and socioeconomic participation through work for pay, is being felt both inside the family and at every other level of American society" (pp. 4–5). This tension manifests itself both in the individual arrangements made by families for child care (often informal, family-based arrangements)

"Where Did Our Diversity Come From?" by Patricia P. Olmsted, *High/Scope ReSource*, Vol. 11, No. 3, Fall 1992, pp. 4-9.
Reprinted by permission of High/Scope Press, Ypsilanti, MI.

and in the diverse views found among people in the United States about who (family, community, or government) should be responsible for child care.

THE CARE STRAND

The care strand of early childhood services began with **day nurseries,** the original social welfare day care centers. These first appeared shortly after the flood of immigration that brought more than 5 million foreign families to the United States between 1815 and 1860 (Clarke-Stewart, 1982; Kahn & Kamerman, 1987). As Kahn and Kamerman stated, "The early cases . . . involve instances of 'day orphans' who were to be protected while their mothers worked or of charitable groups that were responding to alleged or potential child neglect" (p. 121). During the 1870s and 1880s philanthropic agencies began sponsoring day nurseries, seeing such child care assistance for poor or immigrant mothers as the best way to help preserve the family (Steinfels, 1973).

THE EDUCATION STRAND

The beginning of the second strand, early childhood education, can be traced to the nineteenth-century development of the kindergarten. "The idea that some form of education outside the home might be appropriate for children before they entered the first grade paved the way for the later development of nursery schools" (Almy, 1982, p. 479). Specific elements of early childhood education in the United States can be traced to earlier programs developed in Europe by Friedrich Froebel and Maria Montessori (Spodek, 1973). For example, Froebel's ideas that the role of education was to support the child's natural development and that play was an essential part of the educational activity of childhood have been maintained in many U.S. early childhood programs. Similarly, such U.S. program features as prescribed sequences of activities, self-correcting materials, and indirect teaching styles can be traced to the work of Montessori.

During the 1930s middle-class families began to enroll their children in early childhood education programs in large numbers (Clarke-Stewart & Fein, 1983). Most of these early education programs were based on Froebel or Montessori or were derivatives of the nursery school programs developed in England by such educators as Robert Owen and Margaret McMillan.

COMBINING THE STRANDS—THE GREAT DEPRESSION AND THE WAR YEARS

The first large-scale early childhood care *and* education programs occurred in the 1930s, when such programs were authorized under the federally sponsored Work Projects Administration (WPA) to provide jobs for unemployed professionals. (Clarke-Stewart, 1982; Scarr & Weinberg, 1986). By 1937 there were 1,900 programs established and approximately 40 thousand children being served. Located mainly in public schools, the year-round, all-day programs were basically viewed as child care, although they clearly had educational components. With the demise of the WPA, most of the programs were phased out because of a lack of funds.

The variety of care and education settings available is a direct reflection of the variety of needs of families.

During World War II, early childhood care again attracted public attention as many women went to work in defense-related industries. In 1941 Congress passed the Lanham Act, which provided matching federal funds for states to establish day care centers and nursery schools. In 1945 between 105,000 and 130,000 children were enrolled in Lanham centers (Zigler & Goodman, 1982). Following the end of World War II, the Lanham centers and other wartime child care programs were dismantled everywhere except in California and New York City. As men returned from the battlefield, there was a general assumption that women would return to the home. For the most part they did—but not for long.

THE 1960S AND 1970S

In the 1960s women began participating in the labor force in large numbers once again, and thus the need for child care increased—for all families, not just for poor or troubled families, which was the earlier focus of the social welfare movement (Kahn & Kamerman, 1987). This brought renewed interest in early childhood care and education, with one result being a closer meshing of the two strands, child care and early education programs.

There was also an academic rediscovery of early childhood education during this time, as evidenced by the increased interest in the work of Jean Piaget, Jerome Bruner, J. McVicker Hunt, and others (Almy, 1982). More families began to see early education programs as helpful for their children, as a routine part of children's experience. During the 1960s several studies of the effectiveness of early childhood education, particularly for children in low-income families, were launched. Examples of these studies include the High/Scope Perry Preschool study (Berrueta-Clement, Schweinhart, Barnett, Epstein, & Weikart, 1984), the Early Training study (Gray, Ramsey, & Klaus, 1982), and the Mother-Child Home program (Levenstein, O'Hara, & Madden, 1983).

In 1965 the Head Start program, which is still the largest national effort in the area of early childhood education, was initiated. One important aspect of the Head Start program is that its development is based on the premise that early education and enrichment are important for *all* children, not just for children from affluent families (such as those served by the nursery schools of the 1930s). Also, Head Start has a strong educational emphasis, and therefore it has continued the trend (started in the Lanham centers) towards the provision of early education as well as daytime supervision for children from low-income families.

During the 1970s family use of early childhood care and education programs increased still more as American mothers entered the labor force in even greater numbers and as more families saw early education programs as beneficial for their children. During this period different models of early childhood education were tested in the national Head Start Planned Variation program. Most of the models being tested had been developed by child development scholars or early childhood education researchers at universities or research institutions (Miller, 1979). Some examples of planned variation models were the Behavior Analysis Model (University of Kansas), the Cognitively Oriented Curriculum (High/Scope Educational Research Foundation), and the Bank Street College of Education Model (Bank Street College of Education, New York).

In the area of child care during the 1970s, many professionals in the field consider the major event to be President Richard Nixon's veto in 1971 of the Comprehensive Child Development Bill. This bill, sponsored by Senator Walter Mondale and Congressman John Brademas and passed by both houses of Congress, would have established a national child care program for the first time in the United States. In vetoing the bill, President Nixon stated that the legislation "would commit the vast moral authority of the National Government to the side of communal approaches of childrearing over against the family-centered approach" (Nixon, 1971). Government policy since this watershed event has indeed steered a course far shy of any national child care program.

THE BEGINNING OF DECENTRALIZATION, PRIVATIZATION, AND DEREGULATION

According to Kahn and Kamerman (1987), "**Decentralization, privatization,** and **deregulation** became the guiding principles in federal child care policy in the 1980s" (p. 3). The **decentralization** occurred through a combination of federal funding cutbacks and the elimination of matching-fund requirements for states. Federal funds for child care services (Title XX) were converted into Social Services Block Grant funds in 1981 and were passed through to the states. Under this latter funding mechanism, policy and program decisions were made by the individual states. **Privatization** included open support for a diverse child care market: providing incentives to employers,

easing requirements regarding for-profit providers, and giving tax benefits to families. These forms of support were accompanied by a decrease in federal funding and policymaking.

The major instance of **deregulation** involved the failure to enact the Federal Interagency Day Care Requirements. These regulations, developed by federal agency experts and child development advisers in the late 1970s and based on research, would have established minimum standards for child care services, at least for those receiving federal funding, and would have served as general guidelines for all child care services. However, Congress has never adopted these standards, and consequently U.S. child care services are subject only to state standards. These standards vary considerably from state to state, and in some states certain forms of care (for example, family day care homes or church-based programs) are subject to *no* licensing requirements.

With decentralization, privatization, and deregulation characterizing the federal involvement in child care during the 1980s, the roles of state and local agencies became increasingly important. Some states created new child care programs, generally targeted to serve the children of special populations (such as low-income working families or adolescent parents), with state or combined state/local funding. Other states allocated no additional state or local funds for child care, and the federal funds (Title XX through Social Service Block Grants to states) failed to keep pace with inflation, resulting in the provision of services to fewer children each year. During 1988 twenty-nine states provided some funding for early childhood education programs (Children's Defense Fund, 1990). Some states made concerted efforts to integrate early childhood education and child care into one system, while others continued to have the two parallel strands. The resulting overall picture of early childhood care and education was one of great variation from state to state.

Today the United States continues to have a highly decentralized system of early childhood care and education services. The *federal government* does provide funding, organization, and guidelines for some special programs (Head Start, for example). Other federal financial support for the provision of child care comes in the form of tax credits for families, tax incentives for employers, and block grants for states. However, *state* governments set general policy, regulations, and licensing standards for most services and programs. Individual providers—for-profit as well as nonprofit, center-based as well as home-based—organize, administer, and operate their own programs. As a result of this decentralized system, various forms of early childhood care and education exist.

THE FORMS OF EARLY CHILDHOOD CARE AND EDUCATION

Child care arrangements for America's preprimary-aged children (3 to 6 years old) vary widely and may involve one or more of the following types of care. (Families in which all adults are employed often use multiple care-arrangements.)

• *Care in the child's own home, by a relative or nonrelative.* In this arrangement, an adult comes into the child's home to provide care and supervision. The in-home sitter is often a relative who may or may not be paid.

• *Care in another home by a relative.* A common child care arrangement is care of a child by a relative in the relative's home. In some cases, these services are provided without cost, while in others, money, goods, or an exchange of services may be involved.

• *A family day care home.* This arrangement involves care of one or more children on a regular basis by a nonrelative in a home other than the child's home. Family day care home arrangements can vary from an informal, shared-caregiving agreement between friends to a highly formal network of licensed homes.

• *A part-day educational program.* These programs, which can be under private or public sponsorship, are housed in a variety of settings, such as community centers, public schools, churches, and buildings specifically built for this purpose. Educational programs generally consist of a large group of children with two or more adults and are traditionally concerned with children's growth in several areas (social, cognitive, creative). There are likely to be scheduled activities, clearly defined play areas with associated routines, and a specific curriculum (for example, Montessori or High/Scope). Most educational programs for 3- to 5-year-olds, including public programs, are limited to half-day sessions, usually 3 hours a day on weekdays during the school year. However, there are many institutional efforts currently under way to coordinate educational programs with other child care arrangements, to better meet the child care needs of families throughout the entire working day and throughout the entire year.

• *A child care center.* In this arrangement, care is provided either full- or part-time, by groups or by individuals, in facilities devoted to child care. The average number of children served by a center is 50, but the number may range from 15 to 300. In large centers, children are usually divided into groups according to age. There are several types of centers, including: (1) *private for-profit,* (2) *private nonprofit,* (3) *publicly operated,* (4) *parent cooperative,* and (5) *employer-provided.*

Private for-profit centers may be either proprietary or commercial. Proprietary centers are usually small, serving approximately 30 children, and are typically family-run. They are often located in converted shops or homes and may accept only children within a specified age-range (for example, 3- to 5-year-olds) whose families can pay the fee. Commercial centers are generally operated as franchises: A specific program is developed and replicated on a large scale, which results in uniform facilities and procedures. Such centers may accommodate as many as 70 to 100 children in groups of approximately 20.

Private nonprofit centers are usually operated by churches or by private community or charitable organizations and are often located in churches, schools, or community halls.

Publicly operated centers serve children from low-income families who receive government subsidies for child care, as well as children whose parents pay for child care. Because they receive public funding, these child care centers must meet required standards that insure adequate physical facilities, equipment, staff, and educational programs. For many centers, adequate parent-involvement is another requirement.

Parent cooperative centers are those in which parents play a major role in providing child care, management, and decision making, usually with the guidance of a paid director and teachers. As a result of this in-kind service by parents, fees tend to be lower than those for other types of centers, but cooperative centers tend to attract high-income families because the parents must have the time flexibility to work at the center. Parent cooperative centers typically offer part-day programs for young children.

Employer-provided centers are offered by a small number of corporations, factories, hospitals, universities, and trade unions to provide child care as a fringe benefit for their employees. These centers are typically large (approximately 80 to 100 children, divided into appropriate groups) and are usually located close to the parent's workplace.

WHAT EARLY CHILDHOOD SERVICES DO FAMILIES USE?

In 1987 approximately 80 percent of America's 5-year-olds attended public or private kindergarten programs (National Center for Education Statistics, 1990). Data on child care arrangements for 5-year-olds not attending kindergarten is limited. Therefore our analysis here of the children's services that American families use covers only services for children 3 and 4 years of age.

Willer et al. (1991) reported on a survey that provides the most-recent information about the use of various types of early childhood services. Although the survey had two drawbacks (it was conducted by telephone, thus excluding families without telephones from the findings, and its response rate was lower than that usually obtained in surveys), the resulting information is useful in a general way. The survey found that families in which the mother is employed are most likely to choose child care centers for their 3- and 4-year-old children (43 percent use this type of care). This type of family less frequently chooses care by a parent with no supplemental care (21 percent), care in a family day care home (17 percent), and care by relatives (16 percent).

Families in which the mother is not employed most frequently (58 percent) choose care by a parent in the home and less frequently (30 percent) choose care in a center. These families use the other forms of early childhood services (such as family day care or relative care) infrequently.

HOW AVAILABLE ARE SERVICES?

A family's choice of a care or education setting for their child seems to be the result of several factors, including parents' income and education levels, parents' preferences about setting characteristics, and availability of care and education settings within a community. The variety of settings available for child care and early education in the United States is a direct reflection of the variety of needs of families.

When we examine changes in the availability of various types of child care settings over the past 10 to 15 years, we find a large overall increase but variations in size of increase among the different settings. We can provide data for two major settings, both of which are licensed— family day care homes and child care centers. In 1978 there were over 100,000 licensed or regulated **family day care homes** with an estimated total capacity of 400,000 children, based on an estimate of 4 children per licensed home (Ruopp, Travers, Glantz, & Coelen, 1979). By 1990 the number of licensed or regulated family child care homes had increased to approximately 118,000 (Willer et al., 1991) with an estimated total capacity of 860,000 children. Exact figures were not available, but Willer et al. gave indirect estimates of nonregulated family day care homes, which they based on parental reports of child care arrangements and on respondents identifying themselves as family day care providers. These estimates suggest the total number of non-regulated family day care homes to be between 550,000 to 1.1 million. This child care setting typically serves both preschool-aged children (full-day or part-day) and school-aged children (before and after school).

In 1978 the number of licensed or regulated **child care centers** was estimated to be 18,300 with a total capacity of 1.0 million children (Ruopp et al., 1979). By 1990 the number of licensed centers had increased to an estimated 80,000 (Willer et al., 1991) with a total capacity of 4.2 million children.

STATE LICENSING OF CARE AND EDUCATION SETTINGS

As mentioned earlier, in the United States, regulation of early childhood care and education is a *state* rather than a *federal* responsibility. All states have regulations for child care centers and regulations for preschool educational programs that are part of the public school system. The latter are typically included under regulations for regular public school programs. For child care centers, a typical

licensing procedure consists of an initial inspection visit and additional visits prior to renewal of the license (the license period may be 1, 2, or 3 years).

The states vary widely, however, in their licensing of family day care homes. Eight states do not regulate homes or regulate only for subsidized care; 3 states have voluntary registration; 13 states register but do not license homes; and 26 states license homes. The minimum enrollment requiring a family day care home to be licensed also varies among states, with half the states requiring licensing when one or more children are enrolled and the other half requiring licensing when from three to six children or more are enrolled (Morgan, 1987).

By 1995 an estimated 66% of children under age 6 will have mothers in the labor force.

Also, individual states have various categories of settings that are exempt from regulations. Twelve states exempt all church-sponsored day care centers; 21 states exempt all nursery schools and other part-day or full-day educational programs other than those affiliated with the public schools. Additional examples of settings that one or more states choose not to regulate include programs run by private colleges and universities, programs in which the parents are on the premises (parent cooperatives), and programs run by the military (Morgan, 1987).

Regulation of settings typically involves requirements concerning these program characteristics:

• **Child-staff ratios and group size.** Research has indicated that staff-child ratio and group size are strongly related to program quality (Ruopp et al., 1979; Whitebook, Howes, & Phillips, 1989). Guidelines for staff-child ratios and group sizes for children of different ages were developed from the National Day Care Study (Ruopp et al., 1979). For 4-year-olds, according to the study, group size should not exceed 20 children, and there should be at least 1 staff member for every 10 children. However, 32 states do not regulate group size at all for preschool children, and of the states that do regulate it, only a small number fall within the range recommended by the research study. For 4-year-old children, only 1 state sets the child-staff ratio at 7 to 1 or 8 to 1; 16 states set the child-staff ratio at 10 to 1; 10 states set a 12 to 1 ratio; and the remaining states set ratios ranging between 13 to 1 and 20 to 1 (Morgan, 1987).

• **Space requirements for centers and family day care homes.** Most states require centers to have 35 square feet of indoor space and 75 square feet of outdoor space. For family day care homes, 21 states have no space requirements. In states with space requirements for day care homes, the minimums are generally similar to those for centers (Morgan, 1987).

• **Age-appropriate program content.** Nearly every state requires centers to provide a written plan for a developmental program, and 34 states have similar requirements for family day care homes. In addition, 24 states require centers to express their educational philosophy in writing (Morgan, 1987).

STATE EDUCATIONAL QUALIFICATIONS FOR EARLY CHILDHOOD STAFF

Educational requirements for early childhood staff are another part of state regulation. Tied in with those requirements is the issue of the salaries of those who work with young children, which is an issue now receiving great attention in the United States.

Although there are large variations among states, salaries of teachers in public school pre-school programs are basically equivalent to those of other teachers in the school system. (For state-funded preprimary programs, the 1988 salary range for a beginning teacher was $12,000 to $20,000; the range for an experienced teacher was $16,000 to $24,000; Mitchell, 1988.) Salaries of teachers in private preschool programs are generally about half of what is earned by public school teachers. Salary levels and certification procedures are related; that is, for public school preschool programs, a college-educated, certified teacher is required, whereas for private preschool programs, certification requirements are a program-specific decision (Morgan, 1987; Schweinhart & Mazur, 1987). At present, some states have a separate certification for early childhood education; other states have programs for this specific certification under development (Seefeldt, 1988).

States tend to have two basic types of educational requirements for staff in child care centers: education prior to employment (preservice) and ongoing training (inservice). In addition, many states recognize the Child Development Associate (CDA) credential, which is a national competency-based credential that usually involves a training program and a competency assessment. The duration of CDA training ranges from 2 months to 2 years, but it is generally 1 year. States differ greatly in the educational qualifications they require for directors, teachers, and assistants in child care centers. For center teachers, 24 states have preservice qualifications, while 26 states do not. Among the states with preservice qualifications, there are 4 different patterns of college course work or previous experience requirements. Among the 26 states with no preservice qualifications, 17 require inservice training, while 9 do not. A few states have entry-level educational requirements for center classroom assistants: Some require a high school diploma; others, only basic orientation given by the center (Morgan, 1987).

For family day care providers, 27 states require neither experience nor any form of education; 13 states require at least preservice training; and 8 states (including 4 of the 13 just mentioned) require some inservice training. The remaining states do not regulate family day care homes and thus have no educational requirements for day care providers (Morgan, 1987).

Considering the minimal educational requirements for child care workers in centers and family day care homes, it is not surprising that they receive very low salaries. According to the Bureau of Labor Statistics, two out of every three child care workers earn wages below the poverty threshold, regardless of their education, training, or experience. In 1988 the median annual income of a full-time child care worker employed in a center was $9,363 (Whitebook et al., 1989). Willer et al. (1991) reported the following hourly wage rates: $7.49 for a preschool teacher, $4.04 for a regulated family day care provider, and $1.25 for a nonregulated family day care provider. Roughly 2 million persons, mostly women, are employed as child care workers. Related to their low salaries are their high turnover rates, in both centers and homes. Whitebook et al. found that annual *staff* turnover in child care centers averaged 41 percent, while Willer et al. (1991) found that annual *teacher* turnover in centers averaged 25 percent.

The issue of staff salaries cannot be addressed, of course, without also taking into account what parents have to pay for early childhood services. With salaries as they are, and with government support as it is, the estimated typical cost to parents for a child's full-time care is $3,000 a year. In a survey of child care professionals in seven major U.S. cities, the yearly cost for a 3- to 5-year-old in a child care center was found to range from $2,600 to $5,200, while the yearly cost for a child in the same age-range in a family day care home was found to range from $2,000 to $6,000. It is reasonable to assume that U.S. child care costs are slightly lower in rural areas than they are in major cities (Children's Defense Fund, 1987).

ISSUES FOR THE 1990S

The information presented in this profile helps to define the early childhood issues that policymakers face in the 1990s. These issues are defined by projecting trends and examining the implications of these trends. For example, although a stable birthrate is predicted for the United States in the near future, the number of 3- to 6-year-old children who will need care will continue to increase as more and more mothers of young children enter the labor force. If recent trends, such as the increasing number of single-parent and "working poor" families, continue, by 1995 the proportion of children under age 6 with mothers in the labor force will reach an estimated 66 percent (Hofferth & Phillips, 1986). This accelerating demand for early childhood services, the complex nature of the present system of services, and the historical roles of federal and state governments in early childhood care and education together raise questions in several areas:

Staffing Concerns

Considering past national policies, we can assume it is unlikely that government will provide substantial support for early childhood services for the majority of families in the United States. When this assumption is combined with the increasing need for child care, the following questions must be asked: Who will pay for these services (that is, for the salaries of providers, since staff salaries constitute the largest share of a services budget)? What caregiver (or teacher) training will be required? How can parents be assured of qualified staff in a high-quality early childhood setting?

Earlier in this profile, we noted the very low salaries for most categories of early childhood staff and the accompanying high turnover rate among these workers. Higher salaries might decrease the turnover rate, justify the individual worker's investment in preservice education, and allow states to increase staff educational requirements without creating staff shortages. However, with only limited government support likely for the near future, the families using the services must bear most of the financial burdens related to those services. When we consider that many families in need of services are those in which all adults are working to maintain a desired standard of living and that the salary levels of parents when they have young children are often lower than later in their employment careers, it becomes clear that families will not be able to significantly increase their payments for services to allow for increased salaries for early childhood staff. *This issue of salaries for providers of early childhood services is a critical one for the United States and one with no easy solution.*

Related to salaries is the issue of educational qualifications for providers of early childhood services. With the currently low salaries, what types of training or experience can one reasonably expect a service provider to have? Earlier we presented information about the minimal educational requirements, in most states, for early childhood care and education staff. This information, though understandable in light of the low salaries, is surprising considering that the National Day Care Study found staff qualifications, "especially education/training relevant to young children," to be positively related to both classroom interactions and increases on children's test scores (Ruopp et al., 1979). Also, it is important to remember that even in states with staff requirements, the requirements apply only to licensed settings, which by no means constitute all settings. Thus, even in states that require certain staff qualifications, the requirements apply to only a sub-group of providers. Finally, from a national perspective, the differing requirements among states pose problems for service providers moving from one state to another, as well as for families moving between states. *The issue of qualifications for early childhood staff in the United States is closely linked with the issue of salaries, and it is unlikely that the two issues can be resolved separately.*

Quality of Services

The quality of early childhood services is clearly related to staffing issues (salaries, qualifications). However, there are additional issues related to quality that need to be addressed in the 1990s. Research on the dimensions of quality for different types of settings and different groups of children needs to continue. In addition, we need to determine the best public policies and systems for developing and maintaining high-quality early childhood services. Are the present state systems of regulating early childhood programs adequate? Would a set of national guidelines that states would be required to follow ensure a higher level of quality? In the United States, could a set of national guidelines apply to all early childhood settings—or only to those settings receiving public funding (for example, Head Start or Social Service Block Grant monies)?

The current licensing system used by states serves primarily to set minimum standards. However, in many cases these minimum standards are lower than the levels found to be related to positive child outcomes in research studies. In addition, many states do not regulate certain types of settings or do not regulate specific characteristics within settings (for example, 32 states do not regulate group size for 4-year-old children in centers). Raising minimum standards to levels recommended by research studies, increasing the number of setting characteristics addressed by the licensing system, and including *all* major types of early childhood settings in the licensing system would be steps toward improving the development of high-quality early childhood programs.

During the past several years, the National Association for the Education of Young Children has been working, through its National Academy of Early Childhood Programs, to improve the quality of early childhood services by the development of accreditation criteria and procedures (NAEYC, 1984). The NAEYC accreditation system covers several program components, including curriculum, physical environment, and staff qualifications and development, and specific criteria are established for each component. So far, only a very small portion of the total number of early childhood care and education settings in the U.S. have participated in the NAEYC accreditation procedures. It is a good beginning, but *much more needs to be done to improve the quality of early childhood services during the next decade.*

Parent Information

If government fails to provide substantial support for early childhood services in the near future, parents will continue to assume the major responsibility for supporting, locating, and evaluating early childhood services. *A major issue for the 1990s, therefore, will be the development and dissemination of information to parents to allow them to become more-informed consumers of early childhood services.*

In communities where parents have few early childhood service alternatives, locating services is not a complex process. However, in communities where a variety of types of settings are in operation, many parents spend vast amounts of time searching out information about appropriate, available settings and possible openings in those settings. The process is further complicated by the high turnover rate of providers, which can produce unpredictable fluctuation in the quality or availability of care.

Over the past 15 years "resource and referral" agencies funded by various sources (state, local community, employers) have provided information to parents, employers, and others about early childhood services within their communities. Some resource and referral agencies prepare a listing of community early childhood services, which they provide upon request. Others prepare information about the characteristics of various types of care and about making a care choice; they are often willing to discuss individual care situations with parents and to assist them in their search process.

During the 1980s resource and referral agencies operated in at least some areas of nearly every state, but the funding of such agencies has been a continual struggle, and many communities still do not have one. Also, since some agencies provide only a basic listing of services, there is a need for preparation and dissemination of other information to help parents better select and utilize existing early childhood services. For example, some parents may desire information about different types of programs and how to make decisions about the "best" setting for their child and family. Other parents may desire information about how to identify a high-quality program, that is, about questions to ask and things to look for when visiting a potential setting. And some parents may desire information about what to expect from a provider (the procedure followed by the provider if a child becomes ill, for example), what their own responsibilities are (whether parents must pay for days when their child is unable to attend, for example), and how to clarify these matters when initially making arrangement with the provider. Those resource and referral agencies that have had sufficient funding have been instrumental in assisting parents and others. However obtaining additional funding to allow for an increase in the number of agencies as well as an increase in the types of assistance provided by agencies is a major issue to be dealt with in the 1990s.

A TIME FOR ASSESSMENT

The U.S. has experienced great changes in the area of early childhood care and education since the time of Lydia Sigourney's book *Letters to Mothers*. In the last 25 years, particularly, vast numbers of various types of care and education settings have developed to meet the increasing demand for services. However, the service system has remained a decentralized one, and to a large degree, each family is responsible for locating and supporting the services for their own children.

Now is the time to step back to assess the current system of early childhood care and education services in the United States. We must assess it in terms of its ability to meet the needs of young children and their families, in terms of its viability as an employment system for adults, and in terms of its relationships with other societal systems, such as employment and education. Most important, we need to assess the impact of the system on the children it is serving, to insure that we have a system that will help children develop and grow into productive adult members of the American society.

REFERENCES

Administration for Children, Youth, and Families. (1992). *Project Head Start statistical fact sheet.* Washington, DC: Department of Health and Human Services.

Almy, M. (1982). Day care and early childhood education. In E. F. Zigler & E. W. Gordon (Eds.), *Day care: Scientific and social policy* (pp. 476–496). Boston: Auburn House.

Berrueta-Clement, J. R., Schweinhart, L. J., Barnett, W. S., Epstein, A. S., & Weikart, D. P. (1984). *Changed lives: The effects of the Perry Preschool program on youths through age 19* (Monographs of the High/Scope Educational Research Foundation, 8). Ypsilanti, MI: High/Scope Press.

Children's Defense Fund. (1987). *Child care: The time is now.* Washington, DC: Author.

Children's Defense Fund. (1988). *State child care fact book.* Washington, DC: Author.

Children's Defense Fund. (1990). *Children 1990: A report card, briefing book, and action primer.* Washington, DC: Author.

Clarke-Stewart, K. A. (1982). *Daycare.* Cambridge, MA: Harvard University Press.

Clarke-Stewart, K. A., & Fein, G. G. (1983). Early childhood programs. In P. H. Mussen (Ed.), *Handbook of child psychology* (4th ed., Vol. 2, pp. 917–1000). New York: Wiley.

Cochran, M. (1982). Profits and policy: Child care in America. In R. Rist (Ed.), *Policy studies annals* (Vol. 6, draft version of article).

Dervarics, C. (1992). *The new federal role in children's programs.* Silver Spring, MD: Business Publishers.

Gray, S. W., Ramsey, B. K., & Klaus, R. A. (1982). *From 3 to 20: The Early Training Project.* Baltimore: University Park Press.

Hofferth, S. L., & Phillips, D. A. (1987). Child care in the United States, 1970 to 1995. *Journal of Marriage and the Family, 49* 559–571.

Kahn, A. J., & Kamerman, S. B. (1987). *Child care: Facing the hard choices.* Dover, MA: Auburn House.

Levenstein, P., O'Hara, J., & Madden, J. (1983). The Mother-Child Home Program of the Verbal Interaction Project. In Consortium of Longitudinal Studies, *As the twig is bent . . . Lasting effects of preschool programs* (pp. 237–265). Hillsdale, NJ: Lawrence Erlbaum.

Miller, L. B. (1979) Development of curriculum models in Head Start. In E. Zigler & J. Valentine (Eds.), *Project Head Start: A Legacy of the war on poverty* (pp. 195–221). New York: Free Press.

Mitchell, A. (1988). *The public school early childhood study: The district survey.* New York: Bank Street College of Education.

Morgan, G. (1987). *The national state of child care regulation, 1986.* Watertown, MA: Work/Family Directions, Inc.

National Association for the Education of Young Children. (1984). *Accreditation criteria and procedures of the National Academy of Early Childhood Programs.* Washington, DC: Author.

National Center for Education Statistics (1990). *The condition of education.* Washington, DC: Author.

Nixon, R. M. (1971). *Veto message—Economic Opportunity Amendments of 1971.* (S. 2007), 92nd Cong., 1st sess., Senate Doc. 92–48.

Ruopp, R., Travers, J., Glantz, F., & Coelen, C. (1979). *Children at the center: Summary findings and their implications* (Final report of the National Day Care Study, Vol. 1). Cambridge, MA: Abt Associates.

Scarr, S., & Weinberg, R. A. (1986). The early childhood enterprise: Care and education of the young. *American Psychologist, 41,* 1140–1146.

Schweinhart, L. J., & Mazur, E. (1987). *Prekindergarten programs in urban schools* (High/Scope Early Childhood Policy Paper No. 6). Ypsilanti, MI: High/Scope Press.

Seefeldt, C. (1988). Teacher certification and program accreditation in early childhood education. *The Elementary School Journal, 89,* 241–252.

Sigourney, L. H. (1838). *Letters to mothers.* Hartford, CT: Hudson & Skinner.

Spodek, B. (1973). *Early childhood education.* Englewood Cliffs, NJ: Prentice-Hall.

Spodek, B. (Ed.). (1982). *Handbook of research in early childhood education.* New York: Free Press.

Steinfels, M. O. (1973). *Who's minding the children?* New York: Simon & Schuster.

Thompson, W. R., & Grusec, J. (1970). Studies of early experience. In P. H. Mussen (Ed.), *Manual of child psychology* (3rd ed., Vol. 1, pp. 565–657). New York: Wiley.

Whitebook, M., Howes, C., & Phillips, D. (1989). *Who cares? Child care teachers and the quality of care in America* (Final Report, National Child Care Staffing Study). Oakland, CA: Child Care Employee Project.

Willer, B., Hofferth, S., Kisker, E., Divine-Hawkins, P., Farquhar, E., & Glantz, F. (1991). *The demand and supply of child care in 1990* (Joint Findings from the National Child Care Survey 1990 and A Profile of Child Care Settings). Washington, DC: National Association for the Education of Young Children.

Zigler, E. F., & Goodman, J. (1982). The battle for day care in America: A view from the trenches. In E. F. Zigler & E. W. Gordon (Eds.), *Day care: Scientific and social policy* (pp. 338–351). Boston: Auburn House.

Preventing Early School Failure: What Works?

Robert E. Slavin
Nancy L. Karweit
Barbara A. Wasik

Robert E. Slavin, **Nancy L. Karweit**, and **Barbara A. Wasik** can be reached at the Center for Research on Effective Schooling for Disadvantaged Students, Johns Hopkins University, 3505 N. Charles St., Baltimore, MD 21218.

From early childhood interventions to nongraded primary programs and one-to-one tutoring, research clearly shows that we know how to provide students the skills and knowledge they need to succeed.

Once upon a time, a town was having a serious health problem. Approximately 30 percent of its children were coming down with typhoid and other diseases because of contaminated drinking water. The town council allocated millions to medical care for the victims, yet some of them died or were permanently disabled. One day, an engineer proposed to the town council that they install a water treatment plant, which would prevent virtually all cases of the disease. "Ridiculous?" fumed the mayor. "We can't afford it!"

The engineer pointed out that they were already paying millions for treatment of a preventable disease.

"But if we bought a water treatment plant," the mayor responded, "how could we afford to treat the children who already have the disease?"

"Besides," added a councilman, "most of our children don't get the disease. The money we spend now is targeted to exactly the children who

need it!" After a brief debate, the town council rejected the engineer's suggestion.

The town council's decision in this parable is, of course, a foolish one. From a purely economic point of view, the costs of providing medical services to large numbers of children over a long time were greater than the cost of the water treatment plant. More important, children were being permanently damaged by a preventable disease.

In education, we have policies that are all too much like those of the foolish town council. A substantial number of children fail to learn to read adequately in the early grades. Many are retained, assigned to special education,

or maintained for many years in remedial programs. The financial costs of providing long-term remedial services after a student has already failed are staggering, but even more tragic are the consequences for individual children who fail so early.

Despite some improvements and a growing acceptance of the idea that prevention and early intervention are preferable to remediation, programs (and funding) for at-risk students overwhelmingly emphasize remediation. The unspoken assumption behind such policies is that substantial numbers of students—due to low IQs, impoverished family backgrounds, or other factors—are unlikely to be able to keep up with their classmates and will therefore need long-term support services to keep them from falling further behind.

If early school failure were, in fact, unavoidable, we might have a rationale for continuing with the policies we have now. But a growing body of evidence refutes the proposition that school failure is inevitable for any but the most retarded children. Further, the programs and practices that, either alone or in combination, have the strongest evidence of effectiveness for preventing school failure for virtually all students are currently available and replicable. None of them is exotic or radical.

By Robert E. Slavin, Nancy L. Karweit, and Barbara A. Wasik, "Preventing Early School Failure: What Works?" *Educational Leadership,* Vol. 50, No. 4, December 1992/January 1993, pp. 10-18. Reprinted with permission of the Association for Supervision and Curriculum Development. © 1992 by ASCD. All rights reserved.

In the following pages, we summarize the conclusions of our major, federally funded review (Slavin et al., in press) on the effects of programs intended to prevent early school failure. Our review focused on a variety of indicators of success and failure. Most early intervention programs involving students from birth to age 4 have used IQ, language proficiency, and other measures that predict school success and their outcomes. We reported these outcomes, but placed greater emphasis on measures of actual school success or failure: reading performance, retention, and placement in special education. Whenever possible, we emphasized long-term effects of early interventions.

We reviewed several types of early schooling programs. One important common feature of these programs is that they are expensive, and most are of similar orders of magnitude of cost. For example, reducing class size by half (from 30 to 15, for instance) involves hiring an additional certified teacher for each class. Yet this same teacher could teach a preschool class, could be added to the kindergarten staff to enable a school to have full-day kindergarten, or could tutor about 15 low-achieving 1st graders 20 minutes per day. Retention or provision of extra-year programs for kindergartners or 1st graders adds about $4,000, or one year's per-pupil cost per child. The costs of Writing to Read and other integrated computer-assisted-instruction programs require at least one additional aide per school plus initial and continuing costs roughly comparable to the cost of additional certified teachers. The popularity of all these programs indicates that we are willing to spend money to prevent early school failure, but which investments pay off?

The Reading Link

The consequences of failing to learn to read in the early grades are severe. Longitudinal studies find that disadvantaged 3rd graders who have failed one or more grades and are reading below grade level are extremely unlikely to complete high school (Lloyd 1978, Kelly et al. 1964). Remedial programs such as Chapter 1 have few if any effects on students above the 3rd grade level (see Kennedy et al 1986). Many children are referred to special education programs largely on the basis of reading failure, and then remain in special education for many years, often for their entire school careers.

Almost all children, regardless of social class or other factors, enter 1st grade full of enthusiasm, motivation, and self-confidence, fully expecting to succeed in school. By the end of 1st grade, many of these students have already discovered that their initial high expectations are not coming true, and they have begun to see school as punishing and demeaning. Trying to remediate reading failure later on is very difficult because students who have failed are likely to be unmotivated, with poor self-concepts as learners. They are anxious about reading, and they hate it. Reform is needed at all levels of education, but no goal of reform is as important as seeing that all children start off their school careers with success, confidence, and a firm foundation in reading.

Success in the early grades does not guarantee success throughout the school years and beyond, but failure in the early grades does virtually guarantee failure in later schooling. If there is a chance to prevent the negative spiral that begins with early reading failure from the start, then it seems necessary to do so. Even very expensive early interventions can be justified on cost-effectiveness grounds alone if they reduce the need for later and continuing remedial and special education services, retentions, and other costs (Barnett and Escobar 1987). While the cost-effectiveness estimates associated with the Perry Preschool Model (Berrueta-Clement et al. 1984) have been criticized as unrealistic by many researchers (see Holden 1990), they have contributed to a widespread acceptance of the idea that early intervention, even if expensive, ultimately pays back its costs. Given, then, that there is growing agreement on the proposition that investments in early intervention are worthwhile, we must turn again to the question of which forms of early intervention are likely to have the greatest impact.

Birth to Age 3 Interventions

Both child-centered and family-centered interventions with at-risk children can make a substantial and, in many cases, lasting difference in their IQ scores (Wasik and Karweit, in press). In child-based interventions, infants and toddlers are placed in stimulating, developmentally appropriate settings for some portion of the day. Family-centered interventions provide parents with training and materials to help them stimulate their children's cognitive development, to help them with discipline and health problems, and to help them with their own vocational and home management skills.

The IQ effects of the birth-to-3 programs were mostly seen immediately after the interventions were implemented, but longer-lasting effects were found in a few cases. The extremely intensive Milwaukee Project (Garber 1988) found the largest long-lasting effects. It provided 35 hours per week of infant stimulation, including one-on-one interaction with trained caregivers followed by high-quality preschool. Parent training and vocational skills training were also included. At age 10, the children (of mildly retarded mothers) had IQs like those of low-risk children, and their IQs were substantially higher than those of a randomly selected control group of at-risk children. As the children reached the 4th grade, they were reading a half year ahead of the control group, and special education referrals were also reduced.

A study of the Gordon Parent Education Program (Jester and Guinagh 1983), which provided impoverished parents with intensive training in child stimulation, found that at age 10, children who had been in the program at least two years still had higher IQs than did a randomly selected control group. Also, they had fewer than half as many special education placements (23 percent vs. 53 percent).

The Carolina Abecedarian Project provided at-risk children with intensive infant stimulation and preschool programs seven hours a day for at least five years, along with services to families. A longitudinal study (Ramey and Campbell 1984) found that K-2 children in the program had higher IQs and fewer retentions than similar control students.

The studies of birth-to-3 interventions demonstrate that IQ is not a fixed attribute. It can be modified by changing a child's environment at home and/or in special center-based programs. Birth-to-3 interventions can also influence special education referrals and retention. It apparently takes intensive intervention over a period of several years to produce *lasting* effects on measures of cognitive functioning, but even the least intensive models, which often produced strong immediate effects, may be valuable starting points for an integrated combination of age-appropriate preventative approaches over the child's early years.

Impact of Preschool

When compared to similar children who do not attend preschool, those who did attend have been found to have higher IQ and language proficiency scores immediately following the preschool experience, although follow-up assessments typically find that these gains do not last beyond the early elementary years at most (see Karweit, in press a; McKey et al. 1985). In addition, little evidence indicates that preschool experience has any effect on elementary reading performance.

Several studies do show that the most important lasting benefits of preschool are on other outcomes such as retention and placement in special education. Preschool has also been found to have a very long-term impact on dropouts, delinquency, and other behaviors (Berrueta-Clement et al. 1984). It may be that the effects of preschool on outcomes for teenagers are due to the shorter-term effects on retention and special education placements in the elementary grade. Retention and special education placement in elementary school have been found

> # The key issue for at-risk students is not *whether* additional costs will be necessary, but *when* they should be provided.

to be strongly related to dropping out of high school (Lloyd 1978).

Clearly, attendance at a high-quality preschool program has long-term benefits for children, but it is equally clear that preschool experience is not enough to prevent early school failure, particularly because we find little evidence to support preschool effects on student reading performance. Preschool experiences for 4-year-olds should be part of a comprehensive approach to prevention and early intervention, but a one-year program, whatever its quality, cannot be expected to solve all the problems of at-risk children.

The Kindergarten Question

Since the great majority of children now attend kindergarten or other structured programs for 5-year-olds, the main questions about kindergarten in recent years have focused on full-day vs. half-day programs and on effects of particular instructional models. Research comparing full- and half-day programs generally finds positive effects of full-day programs on end-of-year measures of reading readiness, language, and other objectives. However, the few studies that have examined maintenance of full-day kindergarten effects have failed to find evidence of maintenance even at the end of 1st grade (see Karweit, in press b).

Several specific kindergarten models were found to be effective on end-of-kindergarten assessments. Among these were Alphaphonics, Early Prevention of School Failure, and TALK. These are all structured, sequenced approaches to building pre-reading and language skills, which are thought to be important predictors of success in 1st grade. However, only Alphaphonics presented evidence of long-term effects on student reading performance (Karweit, in press b). IBM's Writing to Read computer program has had small positive effects on end-of-kindergarten measures, but longitudinal studies have failed to show any carryover to 1st or 2nd grade reading (Freyd and Lytle 1990, Slavin 1991).

Retention, Developmental Kindergarten, and Transitional 1st Grade

Many schools attempt in one form or another to identify young children who are at risk for school failure and give them an additional year before 2nd grade to catch up with grade-level expectations. Students who perform poorly in kindergarten or 1st grade may simply be retained and recycled through the same grade. Alternatively, students who appear to be developmentally immature may be assigned to a two-year "developmental kindergarten" or "junior kindergarten" sequence before entering 1st grade. Many schools have a "transitional 1st grade" or "pre-1st" program to provide a year between kindergarten and 1st grade for children who appear to be at risk.

Interpreting studies of retention and early extra-year programs is difficult. Among other problems, it is unclear what the appropriate comparison group should be. Should a student who attended 1st grade twice be compared to 2nd graders (his or her original classmates) or 1st graders (his or her new classmates)?

Studies comparing students who experienced an extra year of school before 2nd grade have generally found that these students appear to gain on achievement tests in comparison to their same-grade classmates but not in comparison to their agemates. Further, any positive effects of extra-year programs seen in the year following the retention or program participation consistently wash out in later years (Karweit and Wasik, in press; Shepard and Smith 1989). Clearly, the experience of spending another year in school before 2nd grade has no long-term benefits. In contrast, studies of students who have been retained before 3rd grade find that controlling for their achievement, such students are far more likely than similar nonretained students to drop out of school (Lloyd 1978).

Class Size and Instructional Aides

A popular policy in recent years has been to markedly reduce class size in the early elementary grades. Because it is so politically popular and straightforward (albeit expensive) to implement, class size reduction should in a sense be the standard against which all similarly expensive innovations should be judged.

Decades of research on class size have established that small reductions in class size (for example, from 25 to 20) have few if any effects on student achievement. However, research has held out the possibility that larger reductions (for example, from 25 to 15) may have a meaningful impact (see Slavin, in press).

The largest and best-controlled study ever done on this question was a recent statewide evaluation in Tennessee (Word et al. 1990). Kindergartners were randomly assigned to classes of 15, 25 with an aide, or 25 with no aide, and they maintained the same configurations through the 3rd grade. This study found moderate effects in favor of the small classes as of the 3rd grade. A year after the study, this difference was still positive but very small (Nye et al. 1991). Other statewide studies of class size reduction in the 1st grade in South Carolina (Johnson and Garcia-Quintana 1978) and Indiana (Farr et al. 1987) found even smaller effects of substantial reductions in class size.

The Tennessee class size study

> By every standard of evidence, logic, and compassion, dollars used preventively make more sense than the same dollars used remedially.

also evaluated the effects of providing instructional aides to classes of 25 in grades K-3. The effects of the aides were near zero in all years (Folger and Breda 1990). This is consistent with the conclusions of an earlier review by Schuetz (1980). However, there is evidence, cited below, that aides can be effective in providing one-to-one tutoring to at-risk 1st graders. Reducing class size may be part of an overall strategy for getting students off to a good start in school, but it is clearly not an adequate intervention in itself.

Nongraded Primary Programs

The nongraded primary is a form of school organization in which students are flexibly regrouped according to skill levels across grade lines and proceed through a hierarchy of skills at their own pace (Goodlad and Anderson 1963). This was an innovation of the 1950s and '60s that is making a comeback in the 1990s.

Research from the first wave of implementation of nongraded primary schools supports the use of simple forms of this strategy but not complex ones. In simple forms, students are regrouped across grade lines for

instruction (especially in reading and mathematics) and are taught in groups. Such programs primarily allow teachers to accommodate individual needs without requiring students to do a great deal of seatwork (as is necessary in traditional reading groups, for example). In contrast, complex forms of the nongraded primary—which make extensive use of individualized instruction, learning stations, and open space—are generally ineffective in increasing student achievement (Gutiérrez and Slavin 1992).

One-to-One Tutoring

Of all the strategies reviewed in this article, the most effective by far for preventing early reading failure are approaches incorporating one-to-one tutoring of at-risk 1st graders. Wasik and Slavin (1990) reviewed research on five specific tutoring models. One of these, the model used in Success for All, is discussed below. In addition, Reading Recovery (Pinnell et al. 1988) and Prevention of Learning Disabilities (Silver and Hagin 1990) use certified teachers as tutors. The Wallach tutoring program (Wallach and Wallach 1976) and Programmed Tutorial Reading (Ellison et al. 1968) use paraprofessionals and are correspondingly much more prescribed and scripted.

The immediate reading outcomes for all forms of tutoring are very positive, but the largest and longest-lasting effects have been found for the three programs that use teachers as tutors. Reading Recovery is a highly structured model requiring a year of training and feedback. It emphasizes direct teaching of metacognitive strategies, "learning to read by reading," teaching of phonics in the context of students' reading, and integration of reading and writing. Two follow-up studies of this program have found that strong positive effects seen at the end of 1st grade are maintained into 2nd and 3rd grade. Effects on reducing retentions were found in 2nd grade in one study, but these effects had mostly washed out by 3rd grade.

Prevention of Learning Disabilities

focuses on remediating specific perceptual deficits as well as improving reading skill. It usually operates for two school years (whereas Reading Recovery rarely goes beyond 1st grade). Reading effects of this program were substantial in two of three studies at the end of the program and remained very large as of the end of 3rd grade in one follow-up study.

Improving Curriculum and Instruction

One strategy for enhancing early reading performance is, of course, improving curriculum and instruction in the early grades. All of the tutoring programs cited above used a particular curriculum and set of instructional methods, and it is therefore impossible to separate the unique effects of tutoring from those of the materials and procedures used. Further, any comprehensive approach to prevention and early intervention must include an effective approach to curriculum and instruction in beginning reading.

We do not intend in this article to take on the current controversy about appropriate instruction in beginning reading. We generally agree with the conclusions reached by Adams (1990, p. 416) in a comprehensive, federally mandated review on the topic:

> In summary, deep and thorough knowledge of letters, spelling patterns, and words, and of the phonological translations of all three, are of inescapable importance to both skillful reading and its acquisition. By extension, instruction designed to develop children's sensitivity to spellings and their relations to pronunciations should be of paramount importance in the development of reading skills. This is, of course, precisely what is intended of good phonic instruction.

Adams goes on to define "good phonic instruction" as instruction that teaches word attack skills in the context of meaning, not in isolation from real reading.

The practice and theory of beginning reading are changing so rapidly at present that this is a poor time to make recommendations about appropriate practice. At the moment, very little evidence supports any of the new "whole language" approaches

Success in the early grades does not guarantee success throughout the school years and beyond, but failure in the early grades does virtually guarantee failure in later schooling.

in 1st grade beginning reading (see, for example, Stahl and Miller 1989), but such evidence may develop as these programs gain in sophistication and use.

Success for All

Each of the strategies presented above has focused on one slice of the at-risk child's life. While the birth to age 3 and preschool programs have often integrated services to children with services to parents, the programs for older youngsters often focus only on academics and, in most cases, only one aspect of the academic program such as class size, length of day, grouping, or tutoring in reading.

How much could school failure be prevented if at-risk children were provided with a coordinated set of interventions over the years designed to prevent learning problems from developing in the first place and intervening intensively and effectively when they do occur? This is the question posed in research on Success for All (Madden et al. 1991), which is designed to provide children with whatever programs and resources they

need to succeed throughout their elementary years.

Success for All emphasizes prevention and early intervention. Prevention includes the provision of high-quality preschool and/or full-day kindergarten programs; research-based curriculum and instructional methods in all grades, preschool to grade 5; reduced class size and nongraded organization in reading; activities to build positive relationships and involvement with parents; and other elements. Early intervention includes one-to-one tutoring in reading from certified teachers for students who are beginning to fall behind in 1st grade and family support programs to solve truancy, behavior problems, emotional difficulties, or health or social service challenges. In essence, Success for All combines the most effective interventions identified in this article and adds to them extensive staff development in curriculum and instruction and a school organizational plan to flexibly use resources to see that students read, stay out of special education, and are promoted each year.

Research on Success for All has found substantial positive effects on the reading performance of all students in grades 1-3, and on reductions in retentions and special education placements (Slavin et al. 1992). The lasting effects of Success for All into 3rd grade are the largest of any of the strategies reviewed in this article, but they cannot be interpreted as maintenance assessments, as the program continues through the elementary grades. However, with few exceptions, the program beyond the 1st grade consists of improved curriculum, instruction, and family support services, not continued tutoring.

Consistent Patterns

We see a consistent pattern in most of the programs and practices in our review. Whatever their nature, preventative programs tend to have their greatest impacts on outcomes closely aligned with the intervention and in the years immediately following the intervention period. The long-term research on effects of preschool on dropout and related variables is one exception to this, but on measures of IQ, reading, special education placements, and retention, preschool effects were like those of other time-limited interventions. The positive effects seen on these variables were strongest immediately after the program and then faded over time.

Some might take the observation that effects of early interventions often fade in later years as an indication that early intervention is ultimately futile. Such a conclusion would be too broad. What research on early intervention suggests is that there is no magic bullet, no program that, administered for one or two years, will ensure the success of at-risk children throughout their school careers and beyond. However, it is equally clear that children must successfully negotiate key developmental hurdles in their first decade of life, and that *we know how to ensure that virtually all of them do so.*

The first hurdle, for children from birth to age 5, is development of the cognitive, linguistic, social, and psychological bases on which later success depends. Second, by the end of 1st grade, students should be well on the way to reading. Each year afterward, students need to make adequate progress in basic and advanced skills. Their progress should enable them to avoid any need for remedial or special education and to be promoted each year.

Research on birth-to-3, preschool, and kindergarten programs shows that we know how to ensure that children enter 1st grade with good language skills, cognitive skills, and self-concepts, no matter what their family backgrounds or personal characteristics. Research on tutoring and on instruction, curriculum, and organization of early grades education shows that we know how to ensure that children enter 4th grade reading, regardless of their family and personal backgrounds. We have focused on early interventions, but it is important to note that many programs and practices show strong evidence of effectiveness

Clearly, attendance at a high-quality preschool program has long-term benefits for children, but it is equally clear that preschool experience is not enough to prevent early school failure.

for at-risk students throughout the grades (see Slavin et al. 1989). Rather than expecting short-term interventions to have long-term effects, we need to provide at-risk children with the services they need at a particular age or developmental stage.

Does this mean that we need to provide intensive (and therefore expensive) "preventative" services to at-risk students forever? Perhaps we do need this for a very small portion of students now served in special education. But for the great majority of students, including nearly all of those currently served in compensatory education programs and most of those now called "learning disabled," we believe that *intensive* intervention will only be needed for a brief period, primarily one-to-one tutoring in 1st grade. After these students are well launched in reading, they still need high-quality instruction and other services in the later elementary grades to continue to build on their strong base. Improving instruction is relatively inexpensive.

If a cook puts a high flame under a stew, brings it to a boil, and then turns

it off, the stew will not cook. If the cook puts a stew on simmer without first bringing it to a boil, the stew will not cook. Only by bringing the stew to a boil and then simmering will the stew cook. By the same token, intensive early intervention for at-risk children with no follow-up in improved instruction is unlikely to produce lasting gains, and mild interventions over extended periods may also fail to bring low achievers into the educational mainstream. Yet intensive early intervention followed by long-term (inexpensive) improvements in instruction and other services can produce substantial and lasting gains.

The best evidence for this perspective comes from research on Success for All. This program usually begins with 4-year-olds, giving them high-quality preschool and kindergarten experiences. These are enough for most children, but the program provides one-to-one tutoring, primarily in 1st grade, for those who have serious reading problems. After that, improvements in curriculum and instruction, plus long-term family support services, are intended to maintain and build on the substantial gains students make in tutoring. The program's findings have shown the effectiveness of this approach; not only do at-risk students perform far better than matched control students at the end of 1st grade, but their advantage continues to grow in 2nd, 3rd, and 4th grades. This is not to say that the particular elements implemented in Success for All are all optimal or essential. Other preschool or kindergarten models, reading models, or tutoring models could be more effective, and outcomes for the most at-risk children could probably be enhanced by intervening before age 4. What is important here is the idea that linking prevention, early intervention, and continuing instructional improvement can prevent school failure for nearly all students.

How Many Students Can Succeed At What Cost?

Our research summary shows that virtually every child can succeed in the early grades *in principle*. The number who will succeed *in fact* depends on the resources we are willing to devote to ensuring success for all and to our willingness to reconfigure the resources we already devote to remedial and special education and related services.

We have evidence (particularly from the Success for All research) to suggest that we can ensure the school success of the majority of disadvantaged, at-risk students using the local and Chapter 1 funds already allocated to these schools in different ways (primarily to improve curriculum, instruction, and classroom management in the regular classroom). However, to ensure the success of *all* at-risk students takes a greater investment. There is a large category of students who would fail to learn to read without intervention but would succeed with good preschool and kindergarten experiences; improved reading curriculum and instruction; and perhaps brief tutoring at a critical juncture, eyeglasses, family support, or other relatively inexpensive assistance. A much smaller group of students might require extended tutoring, more intensive family services, and so on. A still smaller group would need intensive intervention before preschool as well as improved early childhood education, tutoring, and other services to make it in school. One could imagine that any child who is not seriously retarded could succeed in school if he or she had some combination of the intensive birth-to-3 services used in the Milwaukee project; the high-quality preschool programs used in the High/Scope model; the tutoring provided by Reading Recovery or other models; and the improvements in curriculum, instruction, family support, and other services (along with tutoring) provided throughout the elementary grades by Success for All.

The cost of ensuring the success of these extremely at-risk children would, of course, be enormous. Yet a multi-risk child (such as a child from an impoverished and disorganized home with low IQ and poor behavior) will, without effective intervention, cost schools and society an equally enormous amount. Even in the mid-term, excess costs for special or remedial education over the elementary years are themselves staggering. This leaves aside the likely long-term costs of dropping out, delin-

> It is clear that children must successfully negotiate key developmental hurdles in their first decade of life, and we know how to ensure that virtually all of them do so.

quency, early pregnancy, and so on (see Barnett and Escobar 1987). The key issue for at-risk students is not *if* additional costs will be necessary, but *when* they should be provided. By every standard of evidence, logic, and compassion, dollars used preventively make more sense than the same dollars used remedially.

The good news in research on prevention and early intervention is that early school failure is fundamentally preventable. The implications of this should be revolutionary. At the policy level, it means we can choose to eradicate school failure, or we can allow it to continue. What we cannot do is pretend that we do not have a choice.

References

Adams, M.J. (1990). *Beginning to Read: Thinking and Learning about Print.* Cambridge, Mass.: MIT Press.

Barnett, W. S., and C. M. Escobar (1987). The Economics of Early Educational Intervention: A Review. *Review of Educational Research* 57: 387-414.

Berrueta-Clement, J. R., L. J. Schweinhart, W. S. Barnett, A. S. Epstein, and D. P. Weikart. (1984). *Changed Lives.* Ypsilanti, Mich.: High/Scope.

Ellison, D. G., P. Harris, and L. Barber. (1968). "A Field Test of Programmed and Directed Tutoring." *Reading Research Quarterly* 3: 307-367.

Farr, B., M. Quilling, R. Bessel, and W. Johnson. (1987). *Evaluation of PRIME-TIME: 1986-1987 Final Report.* Indianapolis: Advanced Technology.

Folger, J., and C. Breda. (April 1990). "Do Teacher-Aides Improve Student Performance? Lessons from Project STAR." Paper presented at the annual convention of the American Educational Research Association, Boston.

Freyd, P., and J. Lytle. (1990). "Corporate Approach to the 2 R's: A Critique of IBM's Writing to Read Program." *Educational Leadership* 47, 6: 83-89.

Garber, H. L. (1988). *The Milwaukee Project: Preventing Mental Retardation in Children At Risk.* Washington, D.C.: American Association on Mental Retardation.

Goodlad, J. I., and R. H. Anderson. (1963). *The Nongraded Elementary School.* Rev. Ed. New York: Harcourt, Brace, and World.

Gutiérrez, R., and R. E. Slavin. (April 1992). "Achievement Effects of the Nongraded Elementary School: A Retrospective and Prospective Review." Paper presented at the annual meeting of the American Educational Research Association, San Francisco.

Holden, C. (1990). "Head Start Enters Adulthood." *Science* 247: 1400-1402.

Jester, E. R., and B. J. Guinagh. (1983). "The Gordon Parent Education Infant and Toddler Program." In *As the Twig is Bent ... Lasting Effects of Preschool Programs,* edited by the Consortium for Longitudinal Studies. Hillsdale, N.J.: Erlbaum.

Johnson, L. M., and R. A. Garcia-Quintana. (1978). *South Carolina First Grade Pilot Project 1976-1977: The Effects of Class Size on Reading and Mathematics Achievement.* Columbia, S.C.: South Carolina Department of Education.

Karweit, N. L. (In press a). "Can Preschools Alone Prevent Early Learning Failure?" In *Preventing Early School Failure: Research on Effective Strategies,* edited by R. E. Slavin, N. L. Karweit, and B. A. Wasik. Boston: Allyn and Bacon.

Karweit, N. L. (In press b). "Issues in Kindergarten Organization and Curriculum." In *Preventing Early School Failure: Research on Effective Strategies*, edited by R. E. Slavin, N. L. Karweit, and B. A. Wasik. Boston: Allyn and Bacon.

Karweit, N. L., and B. A. Wasik. (In press). "Extra-Year Kindergarten Programs and Transitional First Grades." In *Preventing Early School Failure: Research on Effective Strategies*, edited by R. E. Slavin, N. L. Karweit, and B. A. Wasik. Boston: Allyn and Bacon.

Kelly, F. J., D. J. Veldman, and C. McGuire. (1964). "Multiple Discriminant Prediction of Delinquency and School Dropouts." *Educational and Psychological Measurement* 24: 535-544.

Kennedy, M. M., B. F. Birman, and R. E. Demaline. (1986). *The Effectiveness of Chapter 1 Services*. Washington, D.C.: Office of Educational Research and Improvement, U.S. Department of Education.

Lloyd, D. N. (1978). "Prediction of School Failure from Third-Grade Data." *Educational and Psychological Measurement* 38: 1193-1200.

Madden, N. A., R. E. Slavin, N. L. Karweit, L. Dolan, and B. A. Wasik. (1991). "Success for All." *Phi Delta Kappan* 72: 593-599.

McKey, R., L. Condelli, H. Ganson, B. Barrett, C. McConkey, and M. Plantz. (1985). *The Impact of Head Start on Children, Families, and Communities*. Washington, D.C.: CSR, Inc.

Nye, B. A., J. B. Zaharias, B. D. Fulton, C. M. Achilles, and R. Hooper. (1991). *The Lasting Benefits Study: A Continuing Analysis of the Effect of Small Class Size in Kindergarten through Third Grade on Student Achievement Test Scores in Subsequent Grade Levels*. Nashville: Tennessee State University.

Pinnell, G. S., D. E. DeFord, and C. A. Lyons. (1988). *Reading Recovery: Early Intervention for At-Risk First Graders*. Arlington, Va.: Educational Research Service.

Ramey, C. T., and F. A. Campbell. (1984). "Preventive Education for High-Risk Children: Cognitive Consequences of the Carolina Abecedarian Project." *American Journal of Mental Deficiency* 88: 515-523.

Schuetz, P. (1980). *The Instructional Effectiveness of Classroom Aides*. Pittsburgh, Penn.: University of Pittsburgh, Learning Research and Development Center.

Shepard, L. A., and M. L. Smith, eds. (1989). *Flunking Grades: Research and Policies on Retention*. New York: Falmer Press.

Silver, A. A., and R. A. Hagin. (1990). *Disorders of Learning in Childhood*. New York: Wiley.

Slavin, R. E. (1991). "Reading Effects of IBM's 'Writing to Read' Program: A Review of Evaluations." *Educational Evaluation and Policy Analysis* 13: 1-12.

Slavin, R. E. (In press). "School and Classroom Organization in Beginning Reading: Class Size, Aides, and Instructional Grouping." In *Preventing Early School Failure: Research on Effective Strategies*, edited by R. E. Slavin, N. L. Karweit, and B. A. Wasik. Boston: Allyn and Bacon.

Slavin, R. E., N. L. Karweit, and B. A. Wasik. (In press). *Preventing Early School Failure: Research on Effective Strategies*. Boston: Allyn and Bacon.

Slavin, R. E., N. A. Madden, N. L. Karweit, L. Dolan, and B. A. Wasik. (1992). *Success for All: A Relentless Approach to Prevention and Early Intervention in Elementary Schools*. Arlington, Va.: Educational Research Search.

Slavin, R. E., N. A. Madden, N. L. Karweit, L. J. Dolan, and B. A. Wasik. (1991). "Success for All: Ending Reading Failure from the Beginning." *Language Arts* 68: 47-52.

Slavin, R. E., N. L. Karweit, and N. A. Madden, eds. (1989) *Effective Programs for Students At Risk*. Boston: Allyn and Bacon.

Stahl, S. A., and P. D. Miller. (1989). "Whole Language and Language Experience Approaches for Beginning Reading: A Quantitative Research Synthesis." *Review of Educational Research* 9: 87-116.

Wallach, M. A., and L. Wallach. (1976). *Teaching All Children to Read*. Chicago: University of Chicago Press.

Wasik, B. A., and N. L. Karweit. (In press). "Off to a Good Start: Effects of Birth to Three Interventions on Early School Success." In *Preventing Early School Failure: Research on Effective Strategies*, edited by R. E. Slavin, N. L. Karweit, and B. A. Wasik. Boston: Allyn and Bacon.

Wasik, B. A., and R. E. Slavin. (April 1990). *Preventing Early Reading Failure with One-to-One Tutoring: A Best-Evidence Synthesis*. Paper presented at the annual convention of the American Educational Research Association, Boston.

Word, E., J. Johnston, H. P. Bain, B. D. Fulton, J. B. Zaharias, M. N. Lintz, C. M. Achilles, J. Folger, and C. Breda. (1990). *Student/Teacher Achievement Ratio (STaR): Tennessee's K-3 Class Size Study, Final Report*. Nashville: Tennessee State Department of Education.

Authors' note: This paper was written under a grant from the Office of Educational Research and Improvement, U. S. Department of Education (No. OERI-R-117-R90002). Any opinions expressed are our own, and do not necessarily represent OERI positions or policies.

Television, Kids, and the Real Danny Kaye

David Schatzky with Leanna Verrucci

David Schatzky, the executive director of the Children's Broadcast Institute in Toronto, is a teacher, communications consultant, psychotherapist, and veteran broadcaster. Leanna Verrucci is a researcher in children's psychological development and media.

Forty years ago in England, I saw my first television program, the coronation of Queen Elizabeth II. I viewed it as through a glass darkly—fuzzy, gray, and very small. But the very fact that a six-year-old boy could be transported into Westminster Abbey, hundreds of miles away, seemed to me a miracle. Since then, similar television snapshots of reality, shared by the rest of humanity, have formed for me and for all of us a catalog of life's highs and lows.

But great moments are not all that television brings into our lives. Nothing is alien to it; everything is grist for the mill. How much of this we expose our children to says a lot about our values and our society's commitment to children.

What should our children watch on television? Do we say to our kids, Don't watch what is there or what you enjoy, just watch what we say is good? I wish these were simple questions. And, as a parent, I am profoundly aware that there are no simple answers and that, if television is as important in the shaping of character and values as many claim, the answer could have a significant impact on the state and nature of society.

What the majority of North Americans watch is commercial television, which sells audiences to advertisers. If a market can be identified, a television format can be developed to cater to it. If beer drinkers want violence, a violent show can be made to satisfy beer drinkers and beer makers. If greed entertains, a show based on greed is easy to devise and sell to sponsors. If intolerance, pettiness, crassness, and personal putdowns have mass appeal, you can be sure programs will emerge to feed the sponsors' needs to reach those viewers. And all the while, children will be there, in great numbers, to soak it all up.

As much as we like to think that parents are there to mediate their children's viewing and to share family values with their offspring, the truth is that the pervasive nature of television is very powerful and that almost every North American, child or adult, is a captive of the television culture of the twentieth century. This shared experience includes Ninja Turtles, *Wheel of Fortune, CNN Headline News*, and, WWF wrestling. It is frightening to think of how television shapes our children's view of the world.

By the time my son Daniel, named after my idealized childhood image of Danny Kaye, turned five, he had already seen more programs and movies on television and on videotape than I had by the age of sixteen. In fact, in postwar England, where I lived until I was seven, people didn't have television and went to movies very rarely. Videotape had not been invented.

It was a big thrill for me in the year of the coronation to receive the royal commemorative edition of the Gideon Society New Testament from my school, even though I was Jewish. Every child in England got one. The message was clear. Rule Britannia. And each of us was expected to be devoted to Jesus and the queen. We did as we were told; we believed, we trusted, and we did not question or stray. That is not the message ingested by a child exposed to America's *Funniest* Home Videos.

Around the time all England watched the coronation on television, I was also taken to the cinema to see my first movie. I fell in love with Danny Kaye in *Hans Christian Andersen*. I thought Kaye was the most entertaining person on earth and as important as the queen.

I met Danny Kaye in person when I was ten and found out that, unlike the queen, he was not a nice person. "Can I have your autograph?" I asked. "Not now, kid," said UNICEF's ambassador to the children of the world. There was a big difference between the image and the reality.

When I grew up and became a broadcaster, I interviewed some people who had worked with Kaye. The producer of *The Court Jester* told me that working with him was no fun. Kaye had been impossible and kept walking off the lot in fits of temper. A theater publicist

From *The World & I*, June 1992, pp. 499-517. *The World & I*, a publication of The Washington Times Corporation. © 1992.

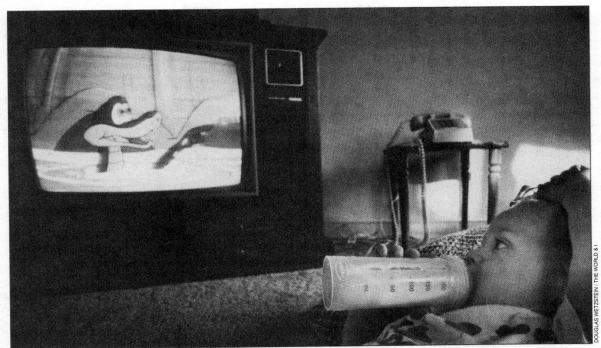

■ **Baby watching TV.**

told me that, of all the stars she had ever worked with, the one she would never want to see again was Danny Kaye, who had been demanding and nasty.

When my son was four years old, he asked me, after watching a video tape of *The Court Jester* at home, on our bedroom television set, "Is that the real Danny Kaye?" At first, I didn't know what he meant. He explained: "Daddy, is Danny Kaye in that movie the real Danny Kaye?" I tried to answer him. "Danny Kaye was a man who was an actor and a singer and a dancer. And as an actor he pretended to be other people. In *The Court Jester,* he pretended to be a man who disguised himself as a court jester, in order to save the king. But the real Danny Kaye is not the court jester, nor is he the man who disguised himself as the jester. And the real Danny Kaye is dead. He made that movie a long time ago. What you are seeing when we play the tape of *The Court Jester* is a movie Danny Kaye made a long time ago. It's like photographs. So yes, Danny Kaye was a real person. And that is what he looked like. But he isn't alive anymore. And when we play the tape on TV he's not really there."

And then Daniel surprised me: "Danny Kaye used to be alive. Now he's dead. When he was alive he made a movie called *The Court Jester.* He acted the part of the court jester. They filmed him doing this and made a copy of the film on tape. We play that tape and see Danny Kaye acting as the jester on our TV."

He appeared to understand. But he still didn't know the real Danny Kaye the way I did. And I haven't the heart to tell him yet.

Now the world has changed. Forever. Parents have never been so challenged to deal with the symbolic, psychological, technological, emotional, perceptual, and other implications of video entertainment on children. And children have been plunged into a world so complex that it is remarkable that they adapt so relatively well. It never occurred to me when I was four years old to question the reality of what I saw on the screen. It was an illusion, which I, like all children, accepted as reallty.

TELEVISION AND LITERACY

Research shows that preschool and young primary-age children are not developmentally sophisticated enough to make distinctions between reality and illusion. And that puts them at quite a disadvantage. R. D. Laing put it this way: "They are stone age children born into a nuclear world." And they are vulnerable. Child psychiatrist Arlette Lefebvre, of the Hospital for Sick Children in Toronto and a member of the board of the Children's Broadcast Institute, explains it this way, "Children believe what they see on TV, want to be what they see on TV, and become what they see on TV."

When one looks at how many television sets exist, how much time children spend watching, and the content of TV shows, that statement has frightening implications. In 1950, only 9 percent of homes in the United States possessed a television set. By 1975, 98 percent of U.S. homes were equipped. The television explosion that took place between 1950 and 1960 increased the number of household sets from 4 to 53 million, a rise of 1,200 percent. By 1980, this figure reached 144 million.

Now a typical kindergarten child watches thirty hours of TV a week. That is more than three eight-hour workdays, more time than he spends with friends, parents, at school, or reading books. In an average year, a child views over twenty thousand commercials. By the time children graduate from high school, they will have been exposed to twelve thousand hours of school and eighteen thousand hours of television.[1]

When taken on the whole, such statistics appear startling. How is it that a child of age two is "watching" over four hours of TV a day? How much does he absorb? How well does he understand? What are the effects, if any, of habitual viewing?

The effects of television on the developing child are numerous. Although television can give children much that is positive and enriching, most of the research literature focuses on its negative influences. Habitual viewing has been shown to impair children's imagination, undermine their perception of reality, reduce their physical well-being, and skew their perception of others.

Although television can give children much that is positive and enriching, most of the research literature focuses on its negative influences.

One of the most studied areas is students' reading ability and attentiveness: The decrease in both has been linked with the increased television viewing of young children. Investigators interviewed teachers who consistently pointed to many students' inability to focus on a specific task for any length of time, be it during solitary unidirectional play or listening to and enjoying a story told to them by an adult. And it appears to be getting worse. Although conclusive scientific research has not been conducted to date, experts in the area believe that the quick, slick, snappy format of television may be partially to blame for children's inattentiveness.

It is ironic that a program like *Sesame Street*, originally designed to help ghetto kids value and master basic literacy and numeracy, has had the additional effect of training kids to appreciate above all the quick-cut pacing of commercials and to expect ever-changing images rather than to enjoy the sustained contact of real relationships at home and at school.

As children get older and are exposed to music videos, game shows, sitcoms, and action dramas, they demonstrate even less tolerance for connection with real people and demanding academic content.

From television, a child learns to expect new images, sounds, and pictures every one to thirty seconds. When this does not take place in the classroom, the child becomes restless and seeks out new, faster paced stimuli or jolts. Even in secondary schools, teachers complain that television production standards have created in many students a desire for "pace and no content," a condition that militates against learning and is quite counterproductive to thoughtfulness, analysis, and self-discipline. Educators yearn for students who pay attention, work through problems, appreciate challenge, and master both content and themselves.

Sesame Street and other similar programs have helped form children who can pick out detail from a static picture in a way that previous generations could not.

In addition, research into the effects of television has focused on what teachers report as an overall decrease in their students' reading ability. Whereas teacher interviews supply anecdotal information of their general experiences and observations, scientific study into this area has focused on the relationship between eye movement and literacy levels. An accepted estimate is that 80 percent of what we learn is gained through the eyes.[2] Consistently, studies have found that a decrease in eye movement can be linked with a decrease in literacy.

The association between television viewing and decreased literacy has been shown to be connected with the small screen of the television, which requires little or no eye movement to watch. In addition, the "pull" of the television focuses the eyes in one direction, further decreasing the necessity for eye movement. Television does not strengthen the child's ability to focus when reading. Yet, at the same time, many primary-grade teachers report the opposite: that *Sesame Street* and other similar programs have helped form children who can pick out detail from a static picture in a way that previous generations could not. Go figure!

Other studies reach the common-sense conclusion that when children are watching television they are not reading books. In fact, Americans read shockingly little. On average, Americans watch approximately twelve thousand hours of television a year, in comparison to the pathetically infinitesimal five hours a year they spend reading books![3] In households where care givers read, children read: where care givers are couch potatoes, children watch TV. And in households where Mom reads and Dad watches TV, children generally copy Dad.

1. Kate Moody, *Growing Up on Television* (New York: Times Books, 1980).

2. Moody, *Television.*

3. Judith Van Evra, *Television and Child Development* (Hillsdale, N.J.: Laurence Erlbaum Associates, 1990).

PLAY AND IMAGINATION

A clearly negative effect television is presumed to have on a child's development is its association with a decrease in play. Although only one of several important features of play, the use of hands, eyes, and body is believed to develop numerous skills, ranging from a development of a sense of self to the development of sensitivity to others. The hand-eye-brain function is seen as so important that anthropologists believe that the growth of the human brain began when man started to use his hands to form tools. Thus, increased physical work was thought to increase brain work.

It is well documented that pretelevision children played more than post-television children. When they came home from school, pretelevision children played outside. Saturday mornings were spent with friends, participating in sports, reading, or just "hanging out," not glued to the television set watching six hours of back-to-back cartoons and commercials.

This inactivity has been noted by the American Pediatric Association and the Ontario Medical Association's Child Welfare Committee, who view with concern the effect of too much television on inactive youth. Increased childhood obesity, a decline in small muscle movement, and a generally overall low activity rate have all been noted to be on the upswing. Where children were once provided with the opportunity for physical activity within the school curriculum, this, too, appears to be falling by the wayside. Unfortunately, during the time of life when physical education programs would benefit youths, one of the first classes to go during budget cuts is the gym class.

Another developmentally sensitive area television is thought to affect is that of imagination. Imaginary play is an important prerequisite for the development of children's perceptual and emotional maturity, as well as their creative development. As early as eighteen months, the world of make-believe opens up for the child. It is at its peak all through the child's preschool years, although it will remain a part of the child's world until he reaches seven or eight years, when it has been shown to be replaced by daydreaming and more structured play.

Although the development of imagination surfaces early on in life, the benefits remain long into adulthood. It is the primary tool humans use to give meaning to life, to forge alternatives and to cope with difficulties and frustration. Ironically, the stage at which children are most primed to develop their imagination—between four and seven—is also the time they appear to be the most fascinated with television.

Researchers and laymen alike believe that, for the most part, television serves only to stifle the creation and development of a growing child's imagination, perhaps not dampening it fully, but hindering it considerably. Due to the noninteractive nature of television, a child can sit and watch for hours, without doing anything else at all. A child no longer needs to be bored, a state that may induce daydreaming, thinking, or creation. Ah yes, boredom has its uses!

On the other hand, there are many children who interact with television in a decidedly active way. Some color, draw, or write stories while watching television. Others dress up in costume and act out parallel stories. Some dance and sing or play musical instruments to accompany or augment the television experience. And for others, something on TV inspires them to ask questions or even find a book that deals with the same theme.

TELEVISION AND THE PERCEPTION OF REALITY

The single most criticized and worrisome aspect of television is the vision of reality that it conveys to children. A person in touch with reality views the television world and the real world as two different entities. Television presents reality from a distorted perspective on a number of issues and exposes children to a fictitious social system, omitting certain groups of people while portraying others as stereotypes.

Statistics bear out the fact that television underrepresents specific groups. Although children under eighteen are said to make up as much as 30 percent of the actual population, they constitute approximately 8 percent of the television population. With the exclusion of soap operas, males have been found to be two and a half times more likely to be present on television than women. It has been shown that half of all U.S. programming does not include any visible minorities, with Hispanics being the least represented, followed by blacks and Europeans.

Perhaps worse for growing children is the manner in which people are portrayed. Women are often painted as passive, dependent, and limited, with most commercials utilizing women in the housewife role to promote kitchen and bathroom products. And what kind of housewife? Well, a casting director for a very successful television dramatic series reports that she repeatedly tried to hire superb actresses, whose personalities matched the scriptwriter's description of the characters. Invariably her casting decisions were overruled by the producer, who would say: "I only want a longlegged blonde in that role."

Blacks and minorities are more often portrayed as unemployed than their white counterparts, and the majority of older men and women are depicted as silly or eccentric. Conversely, men are overrepresented in television programming and advertising. The majority of men are Caucasian, strong, knowledgeable, charming, and moneyed.

Do children watching television have a chance to develop healthy attitudes toward people if that kind of selectivity is the norm? Children as young as five use gender as an important defining characteristic and by the age of six think only in terms of sex role stereotypes. The overweening presence of stereotypes on television creates in children a false view of people, especially if the child has very little first-hand experience of the real world.

TELEVISION AND THE FAMILY

Historically, families provided the basis for a child's socialization, but increasingly television is becoming the child's socializer. Television has been shown to dominate family life. It is often the first thing turned on in the morning, the last thing shut off at night. More often than not, a child's schedule revolves around the evening's TV programs.

Initially, watching television was a social event that drew families together. More recently, however, with the increase of dual or triple or quadruple TV households, plus the epidemic of single-parent and double-income families, with absentee parents, or workers on shift, children are often left to watch their shows separate from their parents or siblings. In addition to feeling isolated, children whose parents cannot or will not be there to watch TV with them miss out on physical cuddling, emotional nurturing, clarifying explanations, and mind-expanding discussion.

Many children depend on the TV family as a basis for gathering information and guiding their conclusions about family relationships.

More damaging perhaps than the increased role that television has come to play in family life is the way in which it often portrays parents and families in general. Although life on television can be said to be far from realistic, the sad fact is that many children depend on the TV family as a basis for gathering information and guiding their conclusions about family relationships. Children watching television today see families that exude little love, respect, or dignity. They see parents whose behavior is dictated by the presence or absence of their children. Television has exposed parents' fears, along with their manipulation techniques, all for the child viewer to watch and absorb. Imagine basing your concept of what a family ought to be on *Married . . . with Children* or *The Simpsons*, two extremely popular programs among children in grades two to eight.

Conversely, the child may also be exposed to a falsely idealized family like the Huxtables on the Cosby show, where communication and respect are high, disputes are few, and problems which do exist are all solved, magically, within a half hour—all of which creates artificial and unachievable expectations.

In addition, parents must contend with a deluge of requests for advertised products they may not believe in,

pressure for permission to watch shows they may not approve of, and family scheduling disputes. Ironically, the medium that initially claimed to "bring families together" may drive them apart.

ATTENTION, COMPREHENSION, AND RETENTION

Only a small proportion of programming is designed specifically for children. Although children's programs exist, and children may even cite them on their list of favorite programs, they prefer to watch programs designed for adult audiences. Just like adults, children use television as a source of entertainment rather than intellectual stimulation. Preference is shown for programs, like sitcoms, that provide familiar routine. Due to the formulaic plot changes, with little character change, a "safe" form of entertainment is established, one that the child can learn to rely on, just like previous generations relied on the Bible. Is it a coincidence that the set of character descriptions and plot guidelines given to writers of episodes of television sitcoms is called "the bible"?

As much as many of us would like children to be exposed to "life as it really is," young children are shown to be quite unreceptive to news or documentary programs. They find them uneventful, too wordy and the mood too somber. In addition, the words-instead-of-images format requires a level of attention that children are unwilling or unable to provide.

Although a child may watch many of the same programs adults do, what the child sees and absorbs may be very different from what an adult does. Levels of attention, retention, and overall comprehension are dependent on the child's level of development, differences that result in the same program being viewed differently at varying ages and stages.

As children grow older, they pick up television cues with less effort and do not need to pay as close attention to every detail to understand the content and thrust of a program or commercial.

Visual attention appears to increase in the preschool years, level off during the school years, and decline in adulthood. If television producers want to capture the attention of young children, some of the following stimuli would increase their chances: lots of sound, lively and distinctive music, dramatic special effects, animation, alliteration, and humor. In addition, the presence of

■ **A child plays with toys advertised on the TV show he is watching.**

women, children, puppets, and repetition have all been shown to elevate attentiveness. Conversely, static drawings, adult men, and inactivity in general have all been associated with children tuning out and turning off.[4]

As children grow older, they pick up television cues with less effort and do not need to pay as close attention to every detail to understand the content and thrust of a program or commercial. And that may be why parents are always at their children not to do homework and listen to music and watch TV at the same time. In fact, these children are absorbing quite a bit of the television fare, if not the homework!

Additional studies have illustrated the positive correlation between a child's increased age and his diminished attention to television. Thus, as children grow older, it appears that they pay less attention to what they are watching. Opposing views exist on the reason for this finding, with some researchers suggesting that this is due to the child's increased efficiency in viewing behavior, while others believe that children learn that television requires little attention, and thus have become lazy. Although discrepancies exist within the literature on the subject of attention, studies that examine children's comprehension levels are unanimous in their findings. Consistently, research points to the conclusion that, as children mature, they show a reduced attention to TV.

It is evident that young children have difficulty comprehending and integrating a large portion of what they view on television. Studies have concluded that as late as

seven or eight years, children have difficulties in the perception, organization, and comprehension of presented material. They have difficulty separating the real from the imaginary, due largely to their inability to disregard certain perceptual stimuli and information.

Older children, on the other hand, possess the ability to organize visual cues, separate incidental information, integrate abstract stimuli, and make inference beyond what has been presented. As a result, they are less likely to misinterpret information.

Differences based on age or stage also become apparent when one examines a child's retention levels. Although children as young as five appear to possess the ability to cite the titles and scheduling of their favorite television shows and to recognize a program less than a second of its appearance; these abilities sharply contrast with their inability to remember specific details of a viewed program.

The tendency exists for children to remember a series by the most salient features of its heroes: Teenage Mutant Ninja Turtles' love of pizza and the colors of the individual mutants' headbands, for example. Few can recall what took place during the program, and even fewer are able to state the central issue of the show. Also the amount a child is able to remember about a specific program is inversely proportional to the number of shows that the child has watched. Thus, the less television a child watches, the more the child can remember of each show. It appears that the heaviest viewers do not burden themselves with the concept of recall but watch simply for the entertainment value. A couch potato is empty-headed, indeed!

---

4. Van Evra, *Child Development*.

CHILDREN AND ADVERTISING: THAT'S ENTERTAINMENT!

Anyone with a television set and young children can vouch for the veracity of the following. If the news or documentary format is the least liked by children, commercial advertising is the most. Providing all the prerequisites for entertainment—short, snappy, and repetitious—television advertising is often viewed by children as the ultimate form of entertainment. Frequently I have been scolded by my children for talking through a commercial. Or if I want to tape a program and ask if I should skip the advertisements, I am told in no uncertain terms that one or another of the commercials is their favorite. And if I preach against commercials, even though both my children (five and seven years old) are highly suspicious of the content, they make it clear that commercials are a beloved part of the television scene.

Television advertising is often viewed by children as the ultimate form of entertainment.

It is no surprise that commercials are so successful in capturing the child audience. The production values, as opposed to the content, are the best money can buy. A thirty-second commercial can cost hundreds of thousands of dollars to produce, more than the entire budget of a season of educational television programs produced by noncommercial networks for preschool children!

Children's advertising translates into megabucks, both for businesses that advertise on television and for the television industry. Well aware of the statistics citing that the average child will view four hundred ads per week, advertisers spend close to $700 million a year promoting their products to this age group. And in a recent Decima poll in Canada, over half the parents surveyed reported that they had bought at least one product in the previous month because of "something the children had seen on TV."

Although the advertising gimmicks of music, slogans, animation, and visual effects work to capture the attention of viewers of all ages, they work even better with the younger age group, due to the child's focus on perceptually salient features. The presence of these features is shown to work independently of the advertised product. In most of the favorite ads chosen by young children, the style of presentation was the primary reason cited for liking the ad, not the product itself. Consistently, children chose ads where the product was not specifically designed for them, but was more adult oriented. Examples of these were for soup, cars, televisions, and medication.

If an advertiser wants to be guaranteed a child's attention, the primary method to use would be humor. A commercial's ability to incite laughter was rated as the No. 1 attention-getting device. Conversely, hard-line, serious, point-driven messages are the best way to lose a child's attention.

As with television programming in general, the level of comprehension of advertising increases as the child grows older. Children as young as five or six possess a limited knowledge of commercials and their persuasive intent. They are still unable to fully distinguish fantasy from reality, and ads are often confused with programs. However, as many parents who have made an effort to teach their children how commercials work have shown, even preschool children can understand the process and become protected consumers.

As children reach approximately eight years of age, they are able to separate fantasy from reality and begin to grasp this reality: that the end result of advertising is to get us to buy the product.

By nine years of age, children have bought many products advertised on television, and they have subsequently been disappointed by them. This leads to the stage, at around ten years of age, where the child believes that all advertising is based on lies.

Finally, as children enter their early teens, they develop a more balanced opinion of advertising, begin to understand the fine line between product promotion and truth stretching, becoming more tolerant of the latter. By this age, children have developed a sophisticated appreciation of commercials as entertainment and have been shown to possess far more awareness of advertisers' intent than was once believed.

The ability of children to recall the content of commercials is staggering and also increases with age. Unlike the low retention levels for programs, children of all ages possess high retention levels for television advertising. In addition to possessing extensive knowledge of brand names, they are able to recite, often verbatim, endless commercials. My seven-year-old daughter announced to us recently that she had made a mess on the floor. "I can use Mr. Clean, Vim, or Comet to clean it up," she said.

Television as a marketing medium exploits children and makes life for parents very difficult. Although Peggy Charren, the founder of the now-extinct Action for Children's Television has successfully spearheaded legislation to limit advertising on U.S. children's television programming, standards in the United States are not at the same levels as elsewhere. For example, in Canada, only eight minutes per hour of advertising is allowed, four minutes less than in America. In Quebec, no television advertising aimed at children is permitted at all. (There is an unfortunate and unforeseen side effect to the ban on advertising: a drop in the production of children's programs.)

The Canadian Radio, Television and Telecommunications Commission insists that broadcasters adhere to the Broadcast Code for Advertising to Children. But even that is inadequate to the task. That code makes the following statement, and then ignores it: "Children, especially the very young, live in a world that is part imaginary, part real and sometimes do not distinguish clearly between the two." One would imagine that from that base, fantasy would be forbidden in commercials aimed at children. But no: "The foregoing does not imply a call for the elimination of fantasy in advertising. *Many childhood possessions become particularly meaningful as they are incorporated into the child's fantasy world and it is natural and appropriate to communicate with this audience in their own terms."* (My emphasis.)

I can only conclude that advertisers will do anything to create customers for life. They don't mind hijacking the inner life of children for the purpose of profit. They appear to have no scruples about using any trick in the book to separate children from their money, under the guise of making a child's purchases more "meaningful," by usurping fantasy and turning it into a sales tool. *Meaning* derives from experiences and relationships, not manipulative devices in commercials. A toy has value because Grandma gave it or because it is a child's first, or because it has real play value.

Should advertisers have the right to make their pitches directly to infants, toddlers, preschoolers, and even older children? Surely it falls to parents to expose their children to the marketplace and to introduce the concepts of taste, need, and value. Is it any wonder that so many North American parents allow their children to watch only PBS or other noncommercial educational networks?

THE BENEFITS OF TELEVISION

Although most research focuses on television's negatives, if utilized correctly, television does provide children with many good things. As long as it is not the child's *only* source for imaginative activity, it possesses the ability to stimulate the imagination; it can provide children with positive role models; it can expose them to the grandeur of nature, the magic of theater, the delights of music, dance, and film; and it can provide children with a window to the world, making them witness to different cultures, races, and beliefs. With the right programs, it can decrease stereotypical thinking by portraying individuals in a nonjudgmental manner, celebrating uniqueness. Through television, world events become accessible to children, and they may participate in world-changing events. Television can be a powerful teacher, if it is used well.

USING TELEVISION WELL

Parents should implement a few simple rules to achieve the maximum benefit from television: Treat it as only one of a number of activities; limit a child's viewing until they possess good reading skills; establish specific ground rules pertaining both to which shows they may watch, and the number of hours they may watch in total; watch television with their children, use it as a catalyst for discussion. Finally, allow television to be used sparingly as a source of entertainment.

The work done on the stages in a child's developmental growth and the immense body of research into the impact of television on children is only partially helpful to those of us trying to mediate children's television use. As a reader of this magazine, it's a safe bet that you value the printed word highly, that you try to take a thoughtful informed approach to life and that you are concerned that what children are exposed to on TV will affect who they become and the kind of relationships they have with friends, family, the community, society-at-large, and even the cosmos.

No matter what your expectations, there is one conclusion that is inescapable: Children need parents to mediate their television experience, especially since there are so many violent, lamebrained cartoons on the air; a plethora of silly and offensive sitcoms; and so much mindless titillation, trivialization, rudeness, vulgarity, materialism, and intolerance.

Childhood is a very special time of life, a time when the personality is being formed and a time of vulnerability. Young children are very impressionable, and do not have the ability to discriminate between good and bad messages and images. They respond viscerally to what they see and hear. Despite the remarkable efforts of some talented and dedicated producers and writers of first-rate quality children's television programs, their contributions are no substitute for a strong parental role in the lives of children, for whom the electronic media should be just one small part of a balanced diet of life.

The storyteller Robert Munsch says, "In a *literate* family, where parents read to children, television can be an interesting spice, but its use has to be limited—otherwise it's a drug." *Spice* is a good word. When we cook a meal, we add just a touch of spice. It's not the whole meal, but, if properly used, it makes the meal taste better. Spice is a carefully controlled, very small part of a much greater whole.

It would help if everyone would demand better television for children. Superb educational preschool programs will help ease preschoolers' transition into the world and introduce them to a wide range of healthy relationships. And as they get older, they require programs that are stimulating, challenging, and value-laden. They need good drama, like *The Chronicles of Narnia*, built around real heroes of the mythic mode, not mere celebrities. (According to Joseph Campbell, it is not television, but big-screen film that, like fine literature, tends to create the heroes and the character-building myths that children of all ages need to become truly human.)

THE FUTURE OF TELEVISION

People make frequent reference to the *postliterate age*, tying that phrase to what they see as the liberating power of technology. Experts sing the praises of *digital engineer-*

ing and *virtual reality*. What the postliterate age invokes for me is a frightening *Clockwork Orange*-style robotoid wasteland, with an illiterate, valueless, sociopathic, jolt-seeking youth underclass, injected against violent self-destruction or the overt annihilation of communities by being plugged into high-tech, ultrafast electronic games where the challenge is to make on-screen killers stalk on-screen victims and laser them into oblivion.

Postliterate could mean something different than that if the media moguls and the computer-game makers would put the interests of children and society first, instead of exploiting both for the sake of megaprofits. Postliterate could mean a happy marriage of print, television, and computer technology, and, in fact, those days are nearly here. According to the latest forecasts, children of the near future will be able to use a computer keyboard to access an incredible range of transmissions and data, including over-the-air broadcasts, satellite services, computer games, databases, interactive live television shows, and videotape libraries.

With digital technology, children will be able to mix and match, perhaps marrying parts of Disney's *Beauty and the Beast* with a Nintendo version of the Dungeons and Dragons game. If they wished, they could incorporate the theme music from I *Love Lucy* and a rock track from a music video channel while adding text from unlimited fonts. They could write and animate their own stories, creating original characters or lifting them from the comic strips of an electronic newspaper. They could convert a textbook on science into a sound composition, or edit a televised political debate or hockey game so that the loser wins. The possibilities are limitless, but they will be severely limited if children can't read, write, plan, and think. They will not be able to function in the postliterate world unless they are literate to begin with. Literacy must be a part of the postliterate culture, or there won't be any culture to be part of.

The future of North American society is indisputably tied in with the way television is used and abused. On one hand, television is not an issue like the ozone layer or world hunger. It is not, immediately, a matter of life and death. But, at the same time, it is absolutely necessary to put the interests of children first. If society does that, then it follows that television itself will change for the betterment of children. At home, we must pay attention to them, nurture them, stimulate them. The business world needs to be more sensitive to the needs of parents with young children at home so that moms and dads can be there when their children need them.

One or ten violent television programs will not create a psychopath. But parental neglect will. One or a hundred commercials will not turn a child into a materialistic, selfish creep. But parental neglect will. One hundred silly sitcoms will not turn a child into a delinquent. But parental neglect will. And if a child is put down at school, subject to racial attacks, deprived financially, and then

exposed to overdoses of television garbage, the prognosis is not good.

We need to encourage the best possible television programming for our children. Buried among the muck, there must be more enriching, ennobling, and enabling high-quality programs for children.

In Canada, the Children's Broadcast Institute has a quality statement that describes the kinds of programs that are needed. It says that they should be based on the needs and expectations of children, not adults. They should provide entertainment, stimulate intelligence and creativity, reflect the real world in which children develop, respect the dignity of children, provide a learning experience, and deal with reality from the point of view of children. Moreover, quality programs for children should allow children to be important participants or actors, if not main characters, and to play an active role, rather than being mere onlookers. Also, they should be designed to promote the intellect, emotions, and creativity of children in a systematic fashion in order to help them make strides in their personal development. They should respect the intelligence and critical judgment of children and their ability to reflect by avoiding over-simplification, stereotypes, propaganda, or intellectual laziness.

Programs should pay special attention to reality and yet still inspire the imagination—the two major environments in which children develop—and open up the world that exists outside the sphere of children: family, friends, school, street, city society, world, universe. With that definition as a measure, there is not much in the present television landscape to give us comfort.

There are other approaches, too, that could help us deal with television's impact on our children. One is media literacy, the teaching of critical viewing skills. This spring the Annenberg School of Communications launched a major initiative to promote critical viewing among grade-school children. Using classrooms, the media, and community organizations, the intention is to put the impact of television on the public agenda and to educate as many people as possible in the analytic techniques that would help children avoid the brainwashing and manipulation television is capable of. In Ontario, Canada, media literacy is on the official Ministry of Education curriculum, with well-worked-out guidelines and a body of teachers well informed in the ways and means of television techniques and analysis.

A media-literate society may be the best defense against the undermining excesses of television, a medium that, as Marshall McLuhan predicted, is already obsolete and has been incorporated into and subsumed by new developments.

As "old-fashioned" television is forgotten and the hundred-channel digitally engineered interactive universe takes over, real human contact and real-life experience are still our best hopes for a sane and survivable world.

The crisis of the
absent father

A quarter of U.S. children have little or no contact with their dads, and the social and emotional consequences are devastating.

RICHARD LOUV

Richard Louv, Connecting columnist for Parents Magazine, *is the author of* Father Love (Pocket), *from which this article has been excerpted.*

In a counselor's office at a Wisconsin high school, boys and girls discuss their largely absent fathers. One girl says that her father has barely said a word to her for two years. Another says that after her parents' divorce, her father "had the right to see me every weekend and stopped it, without explaining why." She has not seen her father in ten years.

"My dad's nobody to me," says one boy. "I've never once sat down and eaten dinner with him. But we've got pictures of me and my dad; we were real close when I was young."

According to the school counselor, the students' stories are typical not just of troubled kids but also of overachievers, the brittle students so eager to please. Asked to describe their vision of a "good" father, the teens are blunt:

"You can't stay out partying till five in the morning. If you're a father, you've got to be there to tuck your kid in and tell him bedtime stories at eight-thirty at night."

"The father of my kids is going to do stuff with them. He's not going to run away."

"If things don't work out between us, I don't care if he leaves me, as long as he doesn't leave the kids."

Is the United States in danger of becoming a fatherless society, shorn of its male parents not by war or disease but by choice? A look at the statistics of family life suggests that the answer may be yes.

How often fathers see— or don't see—their kids.

Increasingly, fatherhood has become a volunteer commitment. In 1990 more than one in four of all births was to an unmarried woman, a fivefold increase in 30 years, according to the Census Bureau. Today nearly a quarter of children born in this country live in female-headed households. More than half of all children in the United States can expect to live in such households before they turn 18.

Being raised by a single mother does not automatically deprive a child of a father, but 40 percent of kids who live in female-headed households haven't seen their fathers in at least a year. Of the remaining 60 percent, only a fifth sleep even one night a month in their father's home. Even fewer see their father at least once a week, according to a study by Frank F. Furstenberg Jr. and Kathleen Mullan Harris, both of the University of Pennsylvania.

Men between the ages of 20 and 49 spend an average of only seven years living in a house with young children, a decline of nearly 50 percent in three decades. What accounts for the high drop-out rate from fatherhood among U.S. men?

In many of my interviews around the country, fathers spoke in vague terms about their impact on their kids. They understood that fathering was important, but they often had a difficult time pinning down just what is important about it; they often struggled for words.

Our culture isn't much help. It suffers a kind of paternal amnesia, a masculine stumble. It seems to have forgotten the importance of fathering and to have divorced manhood from fatherhood. Too many men—and women—view fatherhood as a confusion, a burden, a list of chores and vague expectations. Fatherlessness itself is not the main problem; there are plenty of fathers. The problem is the loss of father love.

In its deeper dimensions, father love is nurturing, community building, and spiritually powerful. But at its most fundamental level, father love is expressed through a man's daily involvement with his family.

As mothers have moved into the work force, the logistics of raising children have become increasingly difficult. Clearly, fathers who share the work, pain, and love equally are needed more than ever.

Why does research focus on the mother-child bond?

The media, social scientists, psychologists, and pediatricians, however, have given little attention to the necessary role that fathers must play in their children's lives. For instance, most past research on child care and development has focused on infant-mother attachment. Among psychologists, the generally accepted theory is that children with a secure attachment to their mothers, especially during infancy, are more likely to feel confident and have good relationships with teachers and peers. But until very recently, the father's role as a nurturer was viewed by many researchers as secondary to the mother's.

Similarly, most research on infant health has focused on the behavior of the expectant mother. But what is the impact of the expectant father? The father's support of the mother may play a larger role in an infant's health than factors such as maternal income and educational attainment. For example, the mortality rate of infants born to college-educated but unmarried women is higher than for infants born to married high school dropouts.

Most single mothers work full-time, earn no more than

Fatherlessness is not the problem; loss of father love is.

$18,000 a year, and receive little child support. Half of children being raised by single mothers live in poverty, compared with 8 percent of those from two-parent families. But the cost of raising children without fathers is more than economic.

A rise in academic and behavior problems.
Children from divorced families (who usually live with their mothers), on average, score lower on reading and math tests. Children living with a single mother are twice as likely as children living with two parents to drop out of high school. Other long-range studies have shown that elementary school children from divorced families are absent more; are more anxious, hostile, and withdrawn; and are less popular with their peers than their classmates from intact families are. Almost twice as many high-achievers come from two-parent homes as come from one-parent homes, according to a study conducted by the National Association of Elementary School Principals.

Children from single-parent homes are more than twice as likely as children from two-parent families to suffer emotional and behavioral problems, according to a National Center for Health Statistics study. Moreover, the most reliable predictor of juvenile crime is not in-

come or race but family structure. Seventy percent of imprisoned U.S. minors have spent at least part of their lives without fathers.

It is true that many of these outcomes would be different if society offered more financial and emotional support to single mothers. But an equally important goal, one that is more important in the long run, is the improvement of the quality of fathering.

The vast majority of current fatherhood programs are directed toward poor parents, a reflection of society's prejudice that fathering is problematic mainly for the poor. This, of course, is not true. Some of the most interesting fatherhood programs, however, are now serving primarily poor teenage fathers.

babies, 14 hands went up.

"They just don't think like fathers," Ballard says. "They don't connect pregnancy with marriage or husbanding or fatherhood." At least 65 percent of his clients never had meaningful relationships with their fathers. Ballard is currently organizing similar programs in 17 other U.S. cities.

Many young fathers, however, *are* eager to help their children. The institute has offered vocational services, counseling, and prenatal and parenthood classes to nearly 2,000 teenage fathers and prospective fathers. In the 11 years since the program was started, more than eight in ten participants have reported daily contact with their children; 74 percent say that they have contributed

7 MOTHER'S USUAL RESIDENCE		7c. City, town,
a. State	b County	
N. Y.	Queens	Corona
la FATHER'S FULL NAME		
UNKNOWN		
la. NAME OF ATTENDANT AT DELIVERY		
	A. Rheeo	

Fifteen percent of kids don't even know who their fathers are.

Charles Augustus Ballard—president of the National Institute for Responsible Fatherhood and Family Development, a Cleveland group that works with teenage fathers—once asked a group of 15 boys how many

Married, single, or divorced, a man is enriched by fatherhood.

were fathers. Only two raised their hands. When he asked how many had

to their children's financial support. Progress is possible.

What is needed across the country is an ongoing effort to support and nurture good fatherhood, not only for low-income and teen parents but for fathers at all economic and age levels. Schools, churches, YMCAs, and businesses should offer more fatherhood courses. Some hospitals, for example, now offer classes to promote the bond between father and infant. Paul Lewis, creator of a fatherhood curriculum known as Dads University, says, "I tell men, 'Do it for your kids.' Most men, including noncustodial fathers, want to do what's right for their

kids but need help learning what the right thing is."

Needed: tougher laws on responsibility.
Beyond education programs, however, other policy changes are needed. Marriage must be encouraged; divorce laws must be reformed; and mediation to help divorcing parents resolve their child-rearing differences should be widely available. Today, dissolving a business contract is much more difficult to do in the United States than dissolving a marriage. No other contract may be breached as easily. Our laws should discourage separation by creating a braking mechanism, a waiting period of

---

Why children need fathers

Despite the paucity of studies on fatherhood, considerable evidence does exist attesting to the influence of nurturing fathers on their children.

● Children with involved fathers are more nurturing themselves and are much more likely to raise pets than other kids are, according to Yale Child Study Center psychiatrist Kyle Pruett, M.D. "I believe that these kids will find it easier to nurture their own children," notes Pruett.

● A 26-year study shows that paternal involvement was the single strongest parent-related factor in the development of empathy. "The father's influence was quite astonishing," says psychologist Richard Koestner, Ph.D., of Montreal's McGill University. Fathers who spend time alone with their children more than twice a week—giving baths, meals, and basic care—reared the most compassionate adults.

● Boys with strong, warm, nurturing fathers are more socially competent, more persistent at solving problems, and more self-directed, according to Norma Radin, M.S.W., Ph.D., a social-work professor at the University of Michigan, in Ann Arbor.   —R.L.

nine months before a divorce becomes final.

The Progressive Policy Institute, an offshoot of the Democratic Leadership Council, proposes that a "children first" principle should govern all divorces involving children. The judge's main task would be to piece together the best possible agreement to meet the needs of the children and their physical guardian.

Another theory gaining currency espouses eliminating Aid to Families With Dependent Children (AFDC), the nation's largest welfare program (created 58 years ago to support widowed women and their children), and replacing it with a system to support families that include fathers. Current AFDC rules prevent a woman from receiving full benefits if the father is at home and has an employment record or works more than 100 hours a month.

Child-support laws and collection techniques must be radically reformed. To help assure that fathers pay their child support, the Social Security number of both parents should appear on a child's birth certificate.

A canceled date with Dad is heartbreaking to a child.

From the time of each child's birth, absent parents should be expected to contribute a portion of their income to that child's support. Payments should be

The Murphy Brown problem

Ten days before Dan Quayle gave his speech declaring that the TV sitcom *Murphy Brown* mocked the importance of fathers, there was an op-ed piece in *The Washington Post* titled, "What Is Murphy Brown Saying?" The author was Barbara Dafoe Whitehead, a Democrat and research associate with the Institute for American Values. Here's what she had to say:

● "Childbirth is a time-tested way to boost ratings...but *Murphy Brown* will break new ground." The show, she wrote, reflects the dangerous but increasingly popular notion that fathers are expendable.

● Murphy Brown bears almost no resemblance to most real-life unmarried mothers, who are usually teenagers, desperately poor, and poorly educated. Despite the low odds that a single mother's child will receive enough positive parental contact, Whitehead wrote, "this idea [of not needing men] plays into powerful male fantasies of sexual freedom and escape from responsibility. . . ."

● A TV-dominated culture that encourages these fantasies is in for big trouble. Fathers should not be thrown out with the bathwater. (Indeed, the National Commission on Children had worked for two years to hammer out a 1991 bipartisan report emphasizing the need for government to encourage two-parent households.)

Clearly Whitehead had some useful criticism of the *Murphy Brown* scenario. Unfortunately Dan Quayle polarized the debate, reclaiming the family-values political turf for the Republicans.

"This was a step backward," says Whitehead. "In recent years we were finally creating some common ground between liberals and conservatives." The issue of family values was politicized and trivialized by politicians and by the media. —R.L.

collected by employers (just as Social Security taxes are today) and sent to the federal government, which would then send the money directly to the custodial parent. Failure to pay would be comparable to tax evasion.

Society tends to view change as something that happens either at a personal level or through national legislation. But James Levine, director of The Families and Work Institute's Fatherhood Project, a research and consulting group on fatherhood, sees a vast area for change between these two extremes. Levine maintains that unless the institutions that have a direct impact on families' lives—businesses, hospitals, churches, synagogues, social-service agencies, and schools—are transformed, neither personal change nor national legislation will accomplish much.

Levine points out a cultural resistance to fatherhood within business institutions as an example. "No matter how many hours he puts in at work, a father who is worried about his children is unlikely to be fully productive," he says. We do not tend to think of fathers as worried working parents. Before such assumptions can be challenged, they

must be the topic of open, and probably organized, conversation within company walls.

Even those institutions whose mission it is to care for and help children must examine their own attitudes toward fathers. Levine, for example, has found some of the strongest resistance to paternal involvement among women who work with and for children. "When we discussed their resistance to fathers, they would say, 'Yes, we know we should get fathers more involved,' but they were making little effort to do that," Levine says.

Most men want to do what's right for their children.

"Their ambivalence is emblematic of the attitude among many helping institutions—hospitals, mental-health organizations, schools," he continues. "My point is not to blame women. We must give voice to these feelings as the first

step toward making men and women equal partners in caring for their children."

Each family also must identify and challenge its own cultural prejudices about fatherhood. For example, when a man does take family leave or decides to be a part- or full-time dad, he may encounter subtle or not so subtle messages from relatives, such as, "Aren't you working? Don't you have a job yet?" The father may also send out mixed messages. He may say that he wants to do more at home but may also find the pressure to be the breadwinner a useful excuse to dodge his own responsibilities.

The truth, however politically untidy, is that men will not move back into the family until our culture reconnects masculinity and fatherhood, until men come to see fathering—not just paternity—as the fullest expression of manhood. Married, single, or divorced, a man is enriched by fatherhood, and a child's life is better for it. The good news, the great good news, is that an enormous payoff awaits society—and individual men and their families—as men move deeper into the dimensions of fatherhood. That movement has already begun.

The Day-Care Delusion

When Parents Accept the Unacceptable

Michael Hoyt and
Mary Ellen Schoonmaker

*Michael Hoyt is associate editor of
"Columbia Journalism Review" in
New York City. Mary Ellen Schoonmaker is an editor at "The Record"
in Hackensack, New Jersey.*

When the police arrived at her neat
brick house in Oxon Hill, Maryland—a middle-class suburb of Washington, D.C.—Nannie Marie Pressley
was not at home. The operator of a
family day-care business, she was out
with six of the children in her care,
unaware that a parent had called in a
complaint. The police found 22 children, ages 2 to 11, sitting quietly on
rows of benches in the basement, and
12 others, 3- to 7-year-olds, lying on
a sheet in another room, where an
infant was propped on a sofa. Up-
stairs, in a dark room that reeked of
urine, the officers discovered eight
infants strapped into car seats, and
one lying face down on the floor. In
another room were two infants sharing a crib. Pressley had left her teenage stepdaughter in charge of the
children—all 46 of them.

• On a recent hot day in a wealthy
suburb in New Jersey, police found
an 18-month-old boy locked in a car.
He was sweating and screaming by

the time a passerby noticed. According to the baby's father, a New York-
area writer, the child's sitter had
developed a serious toothache and
driven to her dentist's. Not knowing
what to do with the baby, she left him
locked in the car.

• Last year, at Wil-lo Haven Day
Care Center, a city-run facility that
serves working parents in the Crown
Heights section of Brooklyn, New
York, a tile from the ceiling fell and
hit the center's director on the shoulder, leaving a bad bruise. Given the
center's condition—broken windows,
no heat, dirty plastic sheeting for
window shades—the accident was not
a surprise. The director was just
thankful that the tile hadn't hit her
head. Or a child's.

Child-care conditions like these
could easily lead to tragedy. But what
is more troubling is the reaction of
many of the parents involved. For
example, at Pressley's family day-
care home, some mothers and fathers, even after learning of the overcrowded conditions there, did not object. "I'd take my kids back today
except that she was shut down," one
father told a reporter for *The Washington Post.* "I saw children there,
but I never took the time to count
them. She was a very good baby
sitter, and that's all I cared about,"
said the mother of a 7-year-old.

"Fire her? Are you kidding?" said
the New York writer of the sitter who
left his infant son in a hot locked car.
Although he told her never to do such
a thing again, he still believes, "She's
great with the kids."

> "If we just provide
> vouchers for every
> crummy day-care sit-
> uation, we're accom-
> plishing nothing."
> Rep. George Miller
> (D.-California)

The Brooklyn parents, afraid budget cuts would cause Wil-lo Haven to
close defended even that crumbling
facility. "I depend on it to help me
keep working and stay off welfare,"
the mother of a 3-year-old explained.

Often, parents do not see what is
right in front of their eyes. They tell
themselves that the day-care situation
they have found is good, even when
down deep they may know better. If
you criticize it, they get defensive.

Call it the Day-Care Delusion: The
mind rationalizes so that the body can
go to work. "Some parents have a

Day-Care Checklist | Name of Program _____

Use this list of questions as a scorecard. Make several copies and fill one out for each program you are considering. Answer each question using a scale of 1 through 5 (5 is the highest rating; 1, the lowest). Total each sheet so that you have a score for each facility you visit. (Questions are not listed in order of importance.)

How Do You Feel About:

1. The cleanliness and safety of the day-care environment? _____
2. The safety of the neighborhood? _____
3. The quality of the toys? _____
4. The amount of space available per child? _____
5. The meals and snacks served? _____
6. The procedures at mealtime and the diapering routines? _____
7. The time spent on physical activities? The amount of quiet time? _____
8. The gender and racial balance (both staff and children)? _____
9. The way rules are enforced? _____
10. The opportunities for family involvement? _____
11. The degree to which staff members are prepared to teach children? _____
12. The amount of one-to-one attention children get from the staff? _____
13. The amount of affection children get from staff? _____
14. The ratio of staff to children? _____
15. The availability of the program to parents—can you make unannounced visits? _____

16. The distance of the site from your home? Your workplace? _____
17. The hours of operation? _____
18. The cost of enrollment? _____
19. The overall philosophy? _____
20. The overall quality of the program? _____

Total score for this program _____

Other considerations:
Many other matters are important when choosing day care. Among them:
☐ In addition to low adult/child ratios, look for small group sizes.
☐ Sit in for a morning or drop in unexpectedly and watch how the children relate to the care provider and how she relates to them.
☐ Check the program for current license and liability insurance.
☐ Inquire about the history of the facility— how long has it been in operation, how much turnover has there been among children and staff?
☐ If the program rents or leases space, what is the duration of the rental agreement or lease?

—Angela Browne Miller

need not to see because they feel so desperate," says Mary Babula, executive director of the Wisconsin Early Childhood Association. "They have to choose what they can afford. Or maybe there's only one center that's open at 7:30 A.M., when they need child care."

Are these parents—the same people who fire off letters of complaint if a box of cereal doesn't have enough raisins—just lousy consumers of child care?

"Some of us go to more trouble in buying a car than in choosing child care," says Angela Browne Miller, who holds master's degrees in social welfare and public health and a Ph.D. in both social welfare and education. For her book, *The Day Care Dilemma,* Dr. Miller recently studied hundreds of different day-care settings and found that parents did not know how to evaluate the quality of the programs; nor did they take the time to find out. Whether from desperation or a lack of knowledge or money, parents are accepting the unacceptable.

To many, child care is still consid-

ered to be a woman's issue. But it's not. If all the working mothers in the United States suddenly quit their jobs to care for their children full time, the economy would crumble. Deprived of that income, hundreds of thousands of families would fall right out of the middle class, some to the poverty level.

With more than 10 million children in day care today, someone must take responsibility for lowering the risk to their well-being and raising the standards of care. Some say it should be the parents; others say it should be the Government. And the battle lines are drawn. Many people—including some mothers who choose to stay home with their children, senior citizens and childless couples—don't want their tax dollars spent on raising other people's kids. But with the growing number of single parents and women who work outside the home, it's clear that day care is here to stay.

Although the Federal Government sets standards for everything from food labels to nursing homes, it plays a minor role in child care, leaving regulation up to the states. As a re-

sult, there is a tremendous variety in the laws and enforcement of rules governing child care.

One of the leading proponents of Federal involvement, Congressman George Mill (D.-Calif.), points out that children are our most valuable asset, our future: "Government must take an active role, to make sure children's needs are met and their safety protected while in child care. There's no evidence that the marketplace will perform that function."

While there is a need for financial assistance, like tax credits and the new child-care vouchers the states are now offering, Miller says money is not enough: "If we just provide vouchers for every crummy day-care situation, we're accomplishing nothing. We have to go to the issue of quality. We have to have skilled, trained people who are properly paid, so we don't get massive turnover rates."

Congresswoman Patricia Schroeder (D.-Colo.) also calls for Federal action. If Government would see to it that child-care workers were better paid, she says, many of the problems concerning quality would clear up: "A lot of good people want to go into child care, but they also like to eat."

Miller and Schroeder would like to see the Federal Government establish national child-care standards that would address such issues as safety, child-developmental needs and training of care providers.

But quality child care is expensive, leaving some parents with little choice but to conclude that the kind of care they're able to buy is all right because it has to be.

After Jessica McClure fell into a backyard well and was trapped for 58 hours in Midland, Texas, in October 1987, it was clear there had been a safety hazard at the family day-care center run by Jessica's aunt and mother. If the Government had set minimum safety standards, that accident might have been prevented. (Other regulations are needed to insure that wastebaskets, cleaning supplies and medicines are covered and out of children's reach, and that all day-care providers frequently wash their hands, particularly after changing diapers or wiping runny noses, to prevent the spread of infection.)

Yet the dangers of inadequate care are usually not so obvious as open wells, falling tiles or one teenager left in charge of scores of children. The dangers may be more subtle, more psychological than physical. But they are real.

"The average quality of child care in this country is poor," says Edward Zigler, Ph.D., Sterling Professor of Psychology at Yale University and co-author, with Mary E. Lang, of *Child Care Choices* (The Free Press, 1991). Dr. Zigler has been visiting day-care centers and studying children for 35 years, and his findings are alarming: "My feeling is that at least one-third of the children in America are having child-care experiences that will compromise their development, by inhibiting their ability to trust, to relate to other children and adults, and to learn." If a child has had five years of inadequate child care, Dr. Zigler believes—ignored for long periods of time, lost in the crowd of other infants and toddlers, or left in a crib or playpen for hours on end—that child may not be ready to learn when it comes time to start school.

"We can tell by 9 months of age which kids are on a failure line or on the success line," says T. Berry Brazelton, M.D., FAMILY CIRCLE contributing editor and professor emeritus of pediatrics at Harvard Medical School. "So what we have to do is get to children early—get them feeling good about themselves, feeling self-confident—then they'll be ready to learn."

"Children learn for the same reasons birds fly—they are learning machines," Dr. Zigler says. One way we turn off that machine is by failing to provide early nurturing. Yet evidence is mounting that many American parents are settling for care that is just not good enough and fooling themselves into believing everything is O.K.

> One father found his family day-care provider's teenage son watching *Dawn of the Dead* on TV as toddlers ambled by the screen.

In her research, Dr. Miller focused on six day-care centers in California. She found programs that ranged from poor to mediocre; only one was rated "good." What is remarkable about Dr. Miller's study, however, is that the 241 parents she interviewed uniformly judged their programs as "excellent," despite Miller's much poorer ratings. Her findings exemplify the Day-Care Delusion.

In his book *Working and Caring* (Addison Wesley, 1985), Dr. Brazelton explains that a parent who shares a small child with another caregiver may grieve, feel guilty, inadequate, hopeless, helpless and even angry at having to give up the child. The parent pulls out emotionally—not because he or she doesn't care, but because it hurts so much to care. As a New Jersey mother of two laments, "Nothing is harder than leaving a baby. Even if you know you have to, and even if you know she's in good hands."

Day-care providers often report

that parents at all income levels rush out the door when they drop their kids off in the morning, and rush out again after picking them up in the afternoon. They ask few questions beyond "Did everything go O.K.?" They don't want to know any more, to be reminded that the child spent all day without them.

And in fact, not many parents will admit to having doubts about the place where they leave their child. One Brooklyn couple remembers leaving their 2-year-old daughter with a neighborhood woman who ran a family day-care home, despite having doubts from the beginning. "But we figured if other people like us liked her, she must be O.K.," the father remembers. Yet when he dropped his daughter off one morning and found the woman's teenage son watching the graphic horror movie *Dawn of the Dead* as the toddlers ambled past the TV screen, that was the end of the line. Other neighborhood parents, however, continued to rave about the woman.

Parents need to learn how to find all the child-care options available to them in their communities, and how to choose among them. This means knowing how to evaluate a child-care situation instead of relying on word-of-mouth references from other parents in the neighborhood, what questions to ask and what to look for, and their own rights and responsibilities. (*See "Day-Care Checklist."*)

One stumbling block for parents is that even in the worst situations, they find it hard to be critical of people to whom they have entrusted their children. Meryl Frank, who analyzed and spoke on child-care issues for five years while doing graduate work at Yale, came to know this dilemma well, but only after she had children of her own. "You rationalize," she says. "Parents are busy, harassed. They don't want to know what's wrong. It's a defense mechanism. You say, 'My children are not going to become mass murderers just because they go to this day-care center.'"

"The problem is that it's a provider's market," says Marilyn Ward, executive director of Everywoman's Resource Center, which handles child-care referrals in Topeka, Kansas. For many parents, the simple dearth of quality day care is the problem. "Parents have to work so hard to find something, they want to believe what they've found is a good program," Ward continues. "They don't want to start all over again."

Consider the situation faced last year by families on Orcas Island, a small community near Seattle, Washington, where instances of alleged sexual abuse of toddlers were reported at two local child-care facilities, one a day-care center and the other a family day-care home. When the day-care center in question was closed as a result, six parents wrote a letter to state officials asking that it be relicensed and reopened. Its closing left more than a dozen parents with nowhere to leave their children. They said the state had overreacted in shutting the center down.

In "Variations in Early Child Care: Do They Predict Subsequent Social, Emotional and Cognitive Differences?" Deborah Lowe Vandell of the University of Wisconsin and Mary Anne Corasaniti of the University of Texas at Dallas studied 236 Texas 8-year-olds, all white and mostly from middle-class families. The idea was to trace their early child-care histories and determine the effects of day care on them. The disturbing result was that children with more extensive day care were rated by teachers and parents as harder to discipline. They had poorer work habits, poorer peer relationships, and poorer emotional health than other children.

Vandell points to a similar study of 8-year-olds recently completed in Sweden, a study that came up with nearly opposite findings. In the Swedish study, children with extensive day-care histories were found to be less anxious, more independent and persistent; they also had better verbal skills than home-reared children.

Vandell suspects the difference in the two studies can be found in the quality of care. Sweden has some of the highest standards for child care in the world, with specialized training for caregivers and low child-to-adult ratios. Texas, on the other hand, has no educational requirements for family day-care providers and minimal requirements for caregivers at centers. In Texas, a single family day-care provider may be responsible for up to 12 children; in center-based care, one caregiver may have to watch as many as six infants, or up to 18 toddlers (4-year-olds).

Experts agree that the most important factor for all children is having a stable relationship with warm and skilled caregivers who have enough time to give them the attention they crave.

"If children don't have a relationship

BY THE NUMBERS

More than 10 million children under the age of 6 have mothers in the work force, according to the U.S. Department of Labor. Latest figures from the Census Bureau show that 29.9 percent are cared for in their own homes by a relative or sitter; 35.6 percent are in family day care or are cared for in a relative's or sitter's home; 24.3 percent are in organized child-care programs.*

The Children's Defense Fund reports:

● *Of the more than 6 million children who spend part or all of their day in child care outside their own home, nearly half—2.6 million—are not protected by any state regulations at all.* For example, 22 states do not require even minimal standards in family day care if fewer than five children are involved. Fourteen states do not regulate, or only partially regulate, child-care centers run by religious institutions, even though one-third of all child-care centers are run by religious groups.

● *When child care is regulated by the state, the standards are often inadequate to insure the safety and health of small children.* Nineteen states, for example, allow child-care centers to have a ratio of five or more infants to one adult. In Idaho, it's legal to have one adult for every 12 infants. Louisiana does not regulate family day-care homes serving fewer than eight children. Amazingly, 22 states have no group size limits whatsoever. As for basic health requirements: 13 states do not even require children in licensed or registered family day-care homes to be immunized against such preventable diseases as measles, polio, rubella, or mumps.

● *Regardless of regulations a state may have on its books, many fail to enforce them or to monitor child-care facilities.* Licensing officials in 18 states admit they lack the enforcement staff to see that their laws are being followed. Thus, a license on the wall can give parents a false sense of security. Sometimes complaints are not acted upon. Eight states report that they are unable to respond to all complaints. Do you think you have the unqualified right to visit your child's family day-care facility unannounced? Better check. Parents in 29 states currently do not have that right spelled out in law; yet it is crucial to insuring a child's safety and well-being. (Experts agree that more states are now beginning to pay attention to this issue.)

*The remaining 10.2 percent of children are either in kindergarten or in other forms of child care.

FAMILY CIRCLE evaluated each state based on statistics from "Who Knows How Safe?"—a report by the Children's Defense Fund on state policies as of April 1990. The five categories reviewed were regulation and inspection standards, child-to-staff ratio, group size, parental access, and staff training requirements. We also spoke with Gina Adams of the Children's Defense Fund, Gwen Morgan of Work Family Directions and Barbara Reisman of the Child Care Action Campaign—all experts on the states' role in child care. Their comments plus the results of our evaluation indicate that most states mandate mediocre child care at best.

The following ratings tell which states are doing well and which should be doing better. It should be noted that our rating system is based on an evaluation of laws currently on the books; it does not take into consideration the degree to which they are enforced, the amount of money the states are putting toward child care, or how recent budget cutbacks may have affected states' ability to insure quality programs.

GOOD
Calif., Colo., Conn., Del., Hawaii, Ill., Kan., Md., Mass., Maine, Minn., Mo., Utah, Vermont, Wash., Wis.

FAIR
Ala., Ark., Alaska, Ariz., Wash. D.C., Ind., Iowa, Ky., Mich., Miss., Mont., Neb., Nev., N.H., N.J., N.M., N.D., N.Y., Ohio, Okla., Oreg., Pa., R.I., S.Dak., Tenn., Tex., Va., Wyo.

POOR
Fla., Ga., Ind., La., N.C., S.C., W.Va.

Some states listed as fair or poor are doing well in other categories not addressed in these ratings.

FOR MORE INFORMATION . . .

To help you in choosing the best day care for your child, send for: "How to Choose a Good Early Childhood Program" or "Finding the Best Care for Your Infant or Toddler"—two free booklets from the National Association for the Education of Young Children, 1834 Connecticut Ave. N.W., Dept. HC/FB, Washington, DC 20009 (include a self-addressed stamped envelope with your request). ● The National Association of Child Care Resource and Referral Agencies will refer you to local resource and referral programs. Write: 2116 Campus Dr. S.E., Rochester, MN 55904; 507-287-2220.

[with a caregiver], they feel very insecure. They feel abandoned by their own parents," says Dr. Albert J. Solnit, Sterling Professor Emeritus in pediatrics and psychiatry at Yale and senior research scientist at the university's Child Study Center.

The number of children per caregiver is another important factor. The younger the children, the lower the ratio ought to be. (The National Association for the Education of Young Children recommends the following child-to-staff ratios: ● From 0 to 24 months, 3 to 1; maximum group size, 6. ● From 25 to 30 months, 4 to 1; maximum group size, 8. ● From 31 to 35 months, 5 to 1; maximum group size, 10. ● For 3-year-olds, 7 to 1; maximum group size, 14. ● For 4-year-olds, 8 to 1; maximum group size, 16.) Also, the smaller the size of the group the better, since children tend to feel lost in groups that make them compete for attention.

The results of too-high ratios and too-large group sizes are predictable. The National Child Care Staffing Study, a major study published by the Child Care Employee Project in 1990, observed a typical day-care situation in Atlanta, Georgia, a state that allows very high ratios and group sizes. The researchers found that preschoolers spent close to one-fourth of their time in aimless wandering and were ignored by caregivers for more than three-quarters of the observation period. Less than one in 10 of the preschoolers observed could engage in the complex pretending games that children of that age should be able to play.

"It all fits together," Dr. Solnit says. "Good care produces something attractive. With poor care, the child functions as if everything is an effort—eating, relating to adults or to playmates. They are like little ghosts."

If child-care conditions are to improve, parents must realize that no government agency or state licensing inspector can be as vigilant as they themselves can be. Maryland's child-care regulations are better than many others. Yet despite the fact that Nannie Marie Pressley flouted state rules in caring for 52 children by herself in an unlicensed day-care home, her only punishment was a $175 fine. Her facility was closed, but no charges were filed against her.

Parents need to ask specific questions when checking out child care: How many children are cared for? What activities are provided? How much weight is given to parents' wishes and their requests for time to talk about how the child is doing? Is the caregiver genuinely interested in both child and parents, and forthcoming with information?

"Look for a place where the care provider wants to know more about you," says Dr. Brazelton, "and where you can stop in at unexpected times. Be sure the provider will sit down with you—at least once a week, but even every day—to talk about your child."

Dr. Edward Zigler believes he has a solution to the Day-Care Delusion, a plan to insure that parents no longer have to accept the unacceptable. He envisions what he calls the "School of the 21st Century," built around the local public school (programs are currently under way in Missouri, Colorado, Wyoming, Kansas and Connecticut; sites in the works include Kentucky, Arkansas, Iowa and Oklahoma). It includes all-day, year-round, on-site child care for all preschoolers from age 3 to prekindergarten, as well as before- and after-school and summer care for children from kindergarten through at least sixth grade. The school offers a network of family day-care providers, training and support, gives referrals to parents, and helps find substitutes when an individual caregiver is sick or on vacation. Dr. Zigler's program would benefit children of stay-at-home mothers too, because he calls for the Federal government to provide cash allowances for new parents so they can either stay home or use the money to pay for quality day care.

Right now, parents in many parts of the country can only dream about such a program. "Finding [any kind of] child care is a struggle," says a mother with two boys in day care since infancy. "You feel you have to reinvent the wheel." And so parents continue to grapple with real problems, hoping to be able to convince themselves that they're doing their best for their children. *(See preceding page for day-care statistics and for additional sources of information.)*

Homeless Children: A Special Challenge

Linda McCormick and Rita Holden

Linda Perkins McCormick, Ph.D., is professor of special education at the University of Hawaii. She has had a variety of jobs with children who have special needs.

Rita Holden earned her master's degree in special education at the University of Hawaii and is now working for the Hawaii State Planning Council on Developmental Disabilities.

Kimo Kealoha is obviously very excited at the prospect of starting his first day of preschool. When asked what he wants to do at school, the tiny boy with large dark eyes says he wants to swing and to play in the sand. He shyly shows us a sheet of paper with a crooked "K" on it. "See, I can almost do my name."

Like other children across Hawaii, Kimo is eagerly looking forward to his first day of school. There is one difference where Kimo is concerned, however: Kimo is homeless. He lives with his mother and older sister in a

The authors acknowledge the Governor's Office of Children and Youth, State of Hawaii, and Homeless Aloha for their support for the survey and preparation of the report that generated the information for this article.

"tent city" in a city park. For six months, before the family was able to find space in the tent city, they lived in a car parked near one of the beaches. His mother feels lucky that they now at least have a canvas roof over their heads, but she doesn't know from one day to the next how long her family will be able to stay in the tent city or whether Kimo will be able to continue attending preschool. Sometimes Kimo goes to sleep hungry and arrives at preschool hungry and dirty, but it isn't because his mother doesn't care. She cares fiercely about giving her children what they need; however, she has little time to search for a job. Her priorities at this time are ensuring that her children are safe and trying to make sure that they have food and access to someplace to sleep and wash.

Every day in America, hundreds of thousands of children wake up homeless, through no fault of their own. There is no single cause of homelessness; there are many contributors. The decreasing supply of low-income housing is most often cited as an important contributor (Children's Defense Fund, 1988; Eddows & Hranitz, 1989).

The McKinney Act* defines a homeless person as "an individual who lacks a fixed, regular, and adequate nighttime residence; or has a primary nighttime residence that is a publicly operated shelter, an institution providing temporary shelter, or a public or private place not designed for the accommodation of human beings." The definition provided by La Gory, Ritchey, and Mullis (1987) is more succinct. They describe a homeless person as "anyone whose night residence is in a shelter, on the street, or in another public place." It can be argued that this definition should be broadened to include persons who are "precariously housed" (e.g., living in doubled-up families).

It is unfortunate that opinions concerning the homeless seem to be based more on prejudice and misinformation than on fact. The notion that the problem has roots in bungled deinstitutionalization policies is an example of questionable information. In reality, the problem is much broader than lack of community services for the mentally ill. Mentally ill adults are only 1 of 10 subgroups that Marin (1988) has identified within the homeless population.

While Marin's list is not inclusive, it shows the diversity of the homeless population. (Keep in

---

* The McKinney Act, passed in 1987 (amendments passed 1988), provides states with funds to assist the homeless, including assistance to schools to assure that each child of a homeless family has access to free public education.

From *Young Children*, Vol. 47, No. 6, September 1992, pp. 61-67. Reprinted by permission of the publisher, the National Association for the Education of Young Children.

57

Homeless parents say they need preschools that provide transportation or assistance with transportation, acceptance of their children without lots of red tape, "more than babysitting"—e.g., a developmental and educational program, and respite care (evenings and weekends).

mind that the subgroups are not mutually exclusive.) The subgroups are (1) veterans (primarily from Vietnam); (2) persons with mental retardation or mental illness; (3) persons who are physically disabled or chronically ill; (4) elderly persons on fixed incomes; (5) skilled persons (singles and families) without a source of income because of a recent loss of job; (6) unskilled single parents (often women who have been abused); (7) runaway children (many of whom have been abused); (8) alcoholics and drug-dependent persons; (9) immigrants (legal *and* illegal); and (10) traditional tramps, hobos, and other transients.

Researchers disagree on the actual number of homeless families in the United States; however, there is universal agreement that the number is growing everywhere (Bassuk & Rubin, 1987; Rossi, 1990). In Hawaii, where the interviews in this survey took place, the count was 1238 homeless families in 1989 (SMS Research and Marketing Services, Inc., 1990). This may not seem like a large number until you consider that Hawaii has a population of only slightly over one million people.

This article considers three issues: (1) developmental and behavioral characteristics of homeless young children and their parents, (2) how states and communities are attempting to meet the early education and care needs of young children in homeless families, and (3) the needs or problems that early education and care programs should address. Sources of information for this article included a literature review, a survey of programs across the country that are attempting to meet the

early education and care needs of children in homeless families, and interviews with major stakeholders concerned with services for young children in homeless families. These stakeholders were parents who are homeless, teachers in preschools serving children in families who are homeless, and directors of shelters for the homeless in Hawaii. Finally, the article presents recommendations that were generated from interviews with homeless families, shelter directors, and preschool personnel. These recommendations include establishing early childhood services for children and families who are homeless and modifying staff development to prepare early childhood personnel to better meet the needs of this population.

Characteristics of the population

Most of the growing body of literature on the homeless deals with health concerns. Relatively few studies consider the educational needs and characteristics of homeless children, and fewer still specifically address the needs of infants and preschoolers. We decided not to review studies dealing with battered women and their children or low-income families. Certainly these groups are not mutually exclusive; however, there are not sufficient data at this time to risk generalizing across the three populations. That common issues exist across the groups seems likely, but it is equally likely that the condition of homelessness may create distinct characteristics and problems that need specific attention apart from the problems of either poverty or family violence.

While most of the available data describe school-age children, there *are* data dealing with preschoolers (particularly preschoolers who are living with their parents in shelters). Data collection methods and sample sizes varied widely in the studies that generated these descriptive data. The information presented in this article summarizes the many studies that were reviewed. A proportion of the young children in homeless families have been observed to have the following characteristics:

• higher levels of problem behavior than children their age who are not homeless *and* higher levels than older children in the same shelters (Hughes, 1986);

• one or more developmental delays serious enough to warrant referral and further evaluation (Bassuk & Rubin, 1987);

• severe depression, anxiety, and learning difficulties (Bassuk & Rubin, 1987);

• more sleep problems, shyness, withdrawal, and aggression compared to same-age peers who are not homeless *and* diagnosed emotional disturbance (Bassuk & Rubin, 1987);

• severe separation problems, characterized by panic states, hysterical crying, vomiting, and severe anxiety interfering with the ability to participate in routine activities (Grant, 1990);

• poor-quality (superficial) relationships, sleep disturbances (many children engaged in oppositional and disruptive behavior in an effort to avoid napping), and short attention span (Grant, 1990);

• signs of emotional disturbance, including severe tantrums, dangerously aggressive and destructive behavior, extreme withdrawal, elective mutism, violent mood swings, and oppositional and manipulative behavior serious enough to interfere with peer relationships and readiness to learn (Grant, 1990); and

• significant delays in gross-motor development (particularly problems in movement through space and spatial relationships), speech and language development (particularly restrictions in expressive language and vocabulary development), and cognitive development (particularly with tasks requiring sequencing and organization) (Grant, 1990).

Bassuk and Rubin (1987) reported that almost 90% of the families in their sample were headed by a single mother. The median age for the mothers was 27 years of age. Others' studies (e.g., Wood, Valdez, Hayashi, & Shen, 1990) report that one-half or more of their sample of homeless families is composed of two-parent families. The reason that some studies underestimate the proportion of two-parent families may be related to the tendency to question only shelter directors or other "key" informants rather than the homeless family members. Two-parent families may falsely report themselves as single-parent families in order to qualify for services, including emergency shelter.

Among the characteristics associated with parents in homeless families are the following:

• maternal drug and alcohol abuse and psychiatric problems much greater than are found among mothers living in public or private subsidized housing (Bassuk & Rosenberg, 1988);

• a history of abuse as children and battering as adults (Bassuk & Rosenberg, 1988);

• fragmented support networks (Bassuk & Rosenberg, 1988); and

• a greater likelihood of having no health insurance coverage, having no preventive health care, and be-

Shelter directors say many parents are afraid that their children will be taken away from them, that homeless children are especially in need of help with social skills, and that many parents may not seem to be nurturing because, as children, they weren't nurtured themselves.

ing smokers than is found among nonhomeless poor (Winkleby, 1990).

What states are doing

A request for information about programs and services for preschoolers in homeless families was posted on SpecialNet (an electronic bulletin board) on three separate dates in the fall of 1990. Most of the responses to the SpecialNet message were referrals to other sources; all of these were followed up with requests for program information. The fact that these efforts were not very productive may be an indication that not many programs exist that identify themselves as specifically for preschoolers in homeless families. Despite many queries over a four-month period, we were able to collect information on only seven programs: three in Massachusetts, two in Georgia, one in Washington, and one in Missouri.

The information accumulated from these programs indicates wide variability in funding sources, community location, and programming. Some programs are on-site at the shelters, while others are located elsewhere. The major commonality across programs is the focus on the family as a whole, as evidenced by the availability of a range of services for parents and the opportunities for parent involvement in the programs. Services for families are directed to helping them meet broad family needs (either by providing these services directly or by providing information and referral services). Several of the contacts

yielded information with helpful programming suggestions, which influenced formulation of the recommendations presented below.

What stakeholders want

Three groups of persons were interviewed to determine the needs or problems that early education and care programs should address: homeless families, shelter directors, and staff members in programs presently serving young children from homeless families. Parents residing in four shelters were interviewed individually and in small groups at shelter sites. Also, a significant number of nonsheltered homeless parents were identified and interviewed. Contact with these parents was made through an organization serving nonsheltered homeless persons. (In Hawaii, most of these families are living on one of the beaches.) Directors of most of the state shelters were also interviewed.

The interview format was altered somewhat depending on the interviewees, but the issues were the same. Stakeholders were asked

• What is needed/wanted in the way of preschool education and care for children whose families are homeless?

• What do preschool personnel need to know or be able to do to best serve children whose families are homeless?

Parents' responses. There was consensus among the parents when asked what they need (or what they want) in the way of preschool education and care. They want/need the following:

• **Assistance with transportation.** Problems associated with arranging transportation came up repeatedly. One suggestion was monthly bus passes or bus tokens.

• **Day care with a developmental child care orientation.** Parents emphasized that their children need "more than babysitting."

• **Respite care.** Parents would like respite available in the evenings, during the day, and after school. They would like immediate respite help when they need it, and they felt that they should not have to always explain why it is needed.

• **Preschools that take children without "red tape."** Parents noted the need for "streamlining" the program intake process (doing away with complicated forms). Services should be available as soon as assessment requirements have been satisfied.

• **On-site schools.** This was the only issue on which there was some difference of opinion among parents (and some difference of opinion between parents and teachers, as discussed below).

• **Opportunities to share with one another.** Parents expressed a desire for meetings and other opportunities to share feelings and generally "talk story" with other parents.

• **Flexibility related to involvement/participation.** Parents want the opportunity to be involved, and they also want the freedom *not* to be involved with whatever program is provided for their preschoolers. They would like the flexibility to sometimes use the time when their children are in an early childhood program to do other things, such as take classes, do grocery shopping, go on job interviews, and so forth.

• **Mental health services.** Parents emphasized the need for mental health services for their children and for themselves. One parent mentioned the need for "self-esteem groups."

• **Information about available services.** Parents said they have a difficult time finding out what is available for their children. They want information about available preschool, day care, and respite services (e.g., costs, how to qualify, and so forth), particularly about funding options and transportation arrangements.

• **Classes.** Parents asked for classes on parenting, CPR, birth control, first aid, and nutrition.

As noted above, the only difference of opinion had to do with on-site versus off-site early childhood programs. Interviewees typically gave a reason or reasons for their preference. Parents' reasons for preferring early childhood programming at the same location as the shelter tended to center around their concerns about transportation. Some teachers who stated a preference for early childhood services to be provided in a location away from the shelter seemed particularly concerned about maintaining health and safety standards. Other teachers were concerned with providing opportunities for children to learn to separate from their parents. Another concern about setting up on-site programs related to the drawbacks of homogeneous grouping. There was concern that young children (*and* parents) classified as homeless not be segregated in such a manner that they could be stigmatized and denied opportunities for interactions with peers who are not homeless.

The "tone" of responses related to the issue of on-site versus off-site programs was perhaps more important than the words. The general impression was that location

---

Parents were very specific when asked what preschool personnel need to know or be able to do in order to provide quality services. Parents want preschool staff to know that

• children are embarrassed about being homeless;
• parents are dealing with many problems in addition to homelessness and their child's care (e.g., spouse abuse, depression, no money);
• even parents who may seem distracted really care about their children (just as much as do parents who have permanent housing);
• it is very stressful, difficult, and time consuming to have to organize transportation every day;
• most questions seem unnecessarily intrusive, and they make parents feel uncomfortable (because the reasons for the questions are usually not clear);
• children (and parents) should not be asked about absences or length of stay in a program (because they do not want to discuss these things, and they may not know when relocation will be necessary);
• parents would prefer—for whatever special educational and developmental services children need—to "just be provided" without blaming anyone or making a big issue of the problem;
• requests for children to bring baked goods or other goodies and school supplies often constitute a great hardship for families; and
• being homeless does not necessarily mean that a family is dysfunctional.

Shelter directors were asked what they would like to share with early childhood program personnel. They want early childhood professionals to know that

• many parents are afraid that their child(ren) will be taken away from them;

• homeless children are especially in need of help with social skills; and

• the reason many parents may not seem to be nurturing is that they do not know how to nurture (because they were not nurtured themselves as children).

Preschool personnel who have dealt with homeless children made some important points. They wanted to share this information with early childhood colleagues:

• Homeless children are more similar to their peers than they are different. The same basic good teaching practices and activities are generally effective with these youngsters.

• Peer friendships have to be actively encouraged. Do not assume that they will occur naturally.

• Play is particularly important. These children typically have no time or place for play when they are not at the center.

• Homeless children (like their peers) need a feeling of being competent and in control. Provide appropriate choices *and* challenges in a maximally supportive atmosphere.

• Stress is unavoidable when you are homeless. Some children may seem to be coping, but none are impervious to the stresses that being homeless places on the family.

• Even the most basic health and safety concerns may seem overwhelming to already overstressed parents. Be patient and sensitive or they will withdraw.

---

is not as much an issue as ensuring a high-quality program that serves families from diverse socioeconomic backgrounds and does not segregate the homeless.

Recommendations

The following recommendations for early education and care programs reflect input from all three stakeholder groups.

Persons working with homeless children and families need a mechanism for networking and sharing. One possibility would be task forces at the state level and at the district or community level in which people concerned with early childhood services for homeless children could build partnerships with one another and with parents.

Programs must be maximally flexible about scheduling. They need to open earlier and perhaps remain open later so as to meet the needs of parents with nontraditional work schedules. In addition to early education and care programs, there should be a range of available respite care options.

Funds must be made available to help with transportation expenses (if transportation cannot be provided). It will be necessary to seek more creative solutions to transportation problems (e.g., "taxi-pooling" and vans).

Programs must provide (or arrange for) social and case management services. Families need help to work out arrangements for resolving family problems, securing permanent housing, and preventing future homeless episodes. If programs cannot provide these services, they need to advocate for them and give full cooperation to whatever initiatives other agencies have in place for the family.

The following were recommendations for individuals and agencies concerned with providing preservice or in-service training for early childhood personnel who will serve children of homeless families. The stakeholders felt that staff development should

• **Emphasize the nature of the problems faced by homeless persons and their children.** Training should include viewing a tape that depicts life in a shelter or visiting sites where there are homeless families. Most important is understanding what life is like for these children when they are not in the early childhood center.

• **Emphasize that homeless children are similar in most ways to their peers who are not homeless.** Homeless children should not be singled out because of their homelessness. Support each child's individuality and help the child to feel that she is a part of the group. A major goal is to learn how to provide a secure and predictable environment where homeless children feel as psychologically safe and appreciated as do their peers. Quality early childhood services enhance the lives of all young children. These services are absolutely imperative for children when there are multiple risk factors in the family's environment.

• **Emphasize that homeless children may need special attention for specific developmental delays and emotional problems.** Teachers must be alert to signs of poor self-esteem, feelings of helplessness, anxiety, depression, and problems related to making friends. Teachers should be encouraged to make the effort to establish a special relationship with the homeless child—help the child feel important and worthwhile. Self-esteem-building activities are especially important for these children, who tend to have fragile self-concepts. Provide safe outlets for the child to express his feelings through art, music, puppets, clay, and other creative modes.

• **Emphasize that parents may need a great deal of support and encouragement to participate in the program or in self-help classes.** Early childhood personnel have a critical role in the lives of homeless children and their families because they can provide a buffering social support. The quality and stability of the support they provide can go a long way to mediate family stress.

• **Emphasize that children and parents especially need the support of center staff when the family moves to more permanent housing arrangements.** Change is stressful. Once the family has made the transition to permanent housing, the person who is coordinating social services will assist the family to form a support network in the new community and will help to get the children enrolled in appropriate early childhood and/or school programs. Early childhood personnel can smooth this transition by preparing the child for the new program and remaining available as friends for the child and the family.

• **Emphasize skills for collaboration and communication among professionals as well as parent-professional partnerships.** Unlike most housed families, homeless families typically have a number of past and present service providers who may not necessarily be apprised of one another's activities. The only solution to fragmented services and service overlap is communication.

• **Emphasize the importance of sensitivity and vigilance so as not to embarrass children or their families.** All training in early childhood education stresses the importance of sensitivity; it must continue to be a primary focus in staff development. Help these children by (1) using every opportunity to model self-control and coping skills; (2) helping children (and their parents) to see that they are not alone in having uncomfortable feelings; (3) letting children know that it is okay to feel angry, scared, lonely, or sad; (4) giving children the words to express their feelings; and (5) enhancing each child's (and parent's) self-esteem.

Conclusion

We enter the twenty-first century with a heightened sensitivity to family issues, including the plight of homeless families. Early childhood personnel have a critical role in the lives of young children and their families. Because of this we have an opportunity (and an obligation) to begin a program of action for young children and their families who are homeless. Homeless children have special needs, as do all children at one time or another in their lives.

> # Teachers who have had experience with homeless children say that of course they are more like other children than different from them, but that they have some special needs that must be met, particularly emotional needs.

References

Bassuk, E.L., & Rubin, L. (1987). Homeless children: A neglected population. *American Journal of Orthopsychiatry, 57*(2), 279–286.

Bassuk, E.L., & Rosenberg, L. (1988). Why does family homelessness occur? A case-control study. *American Journal of Public Health, 78*(7), 783–788.

Children's Defense Fund. (1988). A children's defense budget (FY 1989). Washington, DC: Author.

Eddowes, A.E., & Hranitz, J.R. (1989, Summer). Educating children of the homeless. *Childhood Education,* 197–200.

Grant, R. (1990). The special needs of homeless children: Early intervention at a welfare hotel. *Topics in Early Childhood Special Education, 10*(4), 76–91.

Hughes, H.M. (1986, March–April). Research with children in shelters: Implications for clinical services. *Children Today,* 21–25.

La Gory, M., Ritchey, F., & Mullis, J. (1987). *The homeless of Alabama* (Final Report of the Homeless Enumeration and Survey Project). Birmingham, AL: University of Alabama at Birmingham, Department of Sociology.

Marin, P. (1988). Helping and hating the homeless. *Harper's Magazine, 1*(87), 40.

Rossi, P.H. (1990). The old homeless and the new homelessness in historical perspective. *American Psychologist, 45*(8), 954–959.

SMS Research and Marketing Services, Inc. (1990). *Hawaii's homeless.* (Report prepared for Hawaii Housing Authority).

Stewart B. McKinney Homeless Assistance Amendments Act. Public Law 100–628. (1988).

Winkleby, M.A. (1990). Comparison of risk factors for ill health in a sample of homeless and non homeless poor. *American Journal of Public Health, 80*(9), 1049–1052.

Wood, D., Valdez, R.B., Hayashi, T., & Shen, A. (1990). Homeless and housed families in Los Angeles: A case study comparing demographic, economic, and family function characteristics. *Public Health Reports, 105*(4), 404–410.

Helping Crack-Affected Children Succeed

Mary Bellis Waller

Mary Bellis Waller is the Clinical Program Coordinator at the University of Wisconsin-Parkside. Her address is Wood Rd., Box 2000, Kenosha, WI 53141-2000.

A classroom for young children affected by crack does not look like other early childhood settings with their mobiles, bright bulletin boards, and a constant stimulation of the senses. The classroom for crack-affected students is austere. There are no bulletin boards and no examples of children's art until, perhaps, late in the year, when the children can handle such stimulation. Only a few toys and books are in view, and other materials are hidden on shelves behind a simple fabric curtain. The lights are low, and there is little to distract the child. Learning and teaching areas are set up so that each child can be alone while learning. Play equipment usually used outdoors, like basketballs and climbing bars, is available inside the classroom so children can learn how to handle it appropriately and hone their gross motor skills with simple exercise. Tumbling mats are also available for the same purpose.

The classroom I'm describing isn't necessarily lacking in funds, nor is it a place where the teacher has failed to provide the kind of rich environment students need. On the contrary, this teacher has made the important modi-

> **Children impaired by this cheap form of cocaine are as intelligent as other children; their affect and social skills are damaged. Adaptations in teaching methods and the classroom environment can help them achieve academic success.**

fications needed to meet the special needs of children exposed to crack and cocaine. As former Wisconsin governor Lee Sherman Dreyfus observed, "There are only two kinds of school districts: those that have crack-affected children, and those that will have."

Who Are Crack-Affected Children?

Chasnoff and associates (1990) report that about 14 percent of pregnant women use drugs or alcohol that can cause permanent physical damage to a child during pregnancy. Approximately 400,000 children are born

annually to mothers who used crack or cocaine during pregnancy. These drugs are chemically similar and have the same effects on fetuses.

A recent study by Yazigi and associates (1991) shows that cocaine molecules bond to human sperm in lab tests. The ramifications of this are not clear, but it is possible that some children are affected by paternal use of these drugs immediately prior to conception. Extensive medical research documents actual changes in the fetal central nervous system in response to crack and cocaine (Chasnoff et al. 1985, 1986, 1989, 1991; Lewis et al. 1989; MacGregor 1987; Rodning 1989; Ryan 1987). This has enormous implications for early care providers and schools.

How They're Different

Children affected by crack and cocaine look like other children: they show the full range of size, vigor, and intelligence. However, many of them also show a number of problems that do not simply resolve themselves. Unless those crack-affected children receive specially designed interventions, they will continue to experience the problems during each developmental stage.

Infancy. Crack-affected infants are susceptible to Sudden Infant Death Syndrome (SIDS), apnea, and other sleeping disorders. Many have tremors and convulsions. They are easily overwhelmed by stimuli, responding with a hyper-startle or, in the extreme, by losing consciousness. These infants have difficulty paying attention, and they cannot track visually (Ryan 1987; Schneider 1990; Weston et al. 1989; Van Baar et al. 1989a, 1989b).

More important, crack-affected infants are often averse to being touched and to being looked at, as these strong stimuli threaten to overload them. Consequently, they do not cuddle and often fail to bond with a caregiver. This failure to bond is an important indicator that the child may have great difficulty forming relationships in the future.

In a series of interviews with teachers who had worked with crack- and cocaine-affected children, I found that the problems identified in infants by medical researchers continue in different form through elementary school and into the teens (Waller, unpublished). As a teacher educator working with hundreds of these children and their instructors, I also found that teachers have discovered effective methods for working with such children.

Preschool. As toddlers, crack-affected children are often hyperactive, late in developing language, and late in walking. They are self-absorbed, impulsive, unaware of others, and unable to focus attention for any length of time. By age 3, they are often isolated because other children do not trust their unpredictable mood swings and sometimes violent outbursts.

These toddlers do not understand cause and effect relationships, either in classroom discipline that prescribes a timeout for certain behaviors or in play where jumping off a table causes pain. They do not feel remorse for hurting others, and they do not seem to develop conscience.

Crack-affected toddlers can do what they are told and shown, but they cannot plan their own time or activities. In general, they seem to have trouble organizing their experiences and making sense out of them. Their play is random, disorganized, and pointless. They often do not understand games, and they are unable to focus attention long enough to learn them.

School age. The oldest crack-

Crack-affected children are overwhelmed by ordinary experiences, and they need stability, routine, and sameness in the classroom to feel secure enough to learn.

affected children today are only 8 years old, but older children whose mothers took cocaine during pregnancy offer us a window on how crack-affected children will act when they reach high school. Teachers report that cocaine-affected school-age children are still impulsive and sometimes violent. Also, they are distractible, hyperactive, and disruptive, and school discipline does not seem effective. These children show learning and memory problems, and they are slow to develop friendships. They often remain isolated, even into high school, and their social skills are hampered by their inability to set limits or recognize appropriate limits for speech and behavior. As they grow older, they embarrass peers because of their inappropriate social behaviors and blurted comments. Cocaine-affected children are unable to catch nonverbal cues. Their efforts to make friends are hampered by this, because they do not understand what another's smile or frown means in terms of their own behaviors. This makes classroom motivation and discipline especially difficult because a teacher's expressions have no meaning.

Their learning is affected by a

continuing problem with cause and effect. Middle school teachers report that the cumulative and sequential nature of mathematics has posed a substantial problem to cocaine-affected teens, while language-based subjects are more accessible for them. They are still unable to structure or plan their own activities, and they are easily influenced by others because they are lonely and lack friends.

How Can Schools Respond?

Teachers report that crack-affected children who experience early intervention tailored to their problems can be mainstreamed successfully into regular classes. They estimate that if children are identified by age 2, a two-year intervention will teach a child enough to be mainstreamed. If the schools do not see a student until age 5, as often happens, a longer intervention may be necessary. Few believe that the crack-affected child will need to be in special education classes all through school, unless no appropriate intervention is ever provided.

Schools must acknowledge that cocaine and crack are easily available in any area of the country and that affluence does not protect against recreational drug use. Schools must also acknowledge that many exposed children will never officially be identified. There is tremendous denial on the part of drug-using parents, and only a fraction of them will admit to behaviors which harmed their children.

On the basis of identification of a cluster of behaviors often associated with crack use, children need to be placed into an intervention environment where special teaching techniques will be used. Placement must be understood as only temporary, for a period of 1 to 3 years. The child will return to regular classes as soon as basic academic and social skills have been mastered.

Inside the Intervention Classroom

Teachers in intervention classrooms need to emphasize long-term expectations for their students. It can be frustrating to teach and reteach the same thing daily for weeks and find that students still don't understand it, but this is what often happens with crack-affected children. Their intellect works, and can be reached, but a longer timeline may be necessary.

Teachers need to forget all they know about their repertoire of exciting teaching styles. Crack-affected children can be overwhelmed by ordinary experiences, and they need stability, routine, and sameness in the intervention classroom to feel secure enough to learn.

Since their affect appears to be flawed, teachers must work with the intellect, which is undamaged. Words are the way to the intellect, so early therapy with speech is vital to reach the crack-affected child at all. Facial expressions have no meaning (or inappropriate meaning) to crack-affected children, so they must be taught *in words* in home and school. Encouragement and praise must be done verbally, not simply with a smile or a friendly look.

It's important to use one teaching modality. Because of their inability to order their experiences, crack-affected children cannot recognize one lesson taught five different ways. Crack-affected children will believe they're learning five different things! Teachers must teach, tell, reteach, retell, model, demonstrate, and have the child demonstrate the lesson.

Teachers of crack-affected children report idiosyncratic learning and memory problems. Students are taking in all the information, but the "filing system" required to recall information is flawed. Teacher after teacher tell stories like this: A 5-year-old child learns to tie her shoelaces one morning and demonstrates she knows how to do it. That afternoon, she again demonstrates her skill. But day after day, the child cannot remember how to tie her shoes, and must be retaught.

The parents finally buy her shoes that are fastened with Velcro. Two weeks later, the teacher sees the child tying another child's shoes. This same disrupted rhythm is exhibited in academic areas. All the 6- and 7-year-olds I have seen so far have been able

Crack-affected children who experience early intervention can be mainstreamed into regular classes.

to read, but their comprehension lags far behind decoding. Teachers may respond to such memory problems by allowing more wait time for students to respond, but they also must be prepared to reteach and reteach.

Teaching Social Skills

Social skills also must be taught in words and modeling. Since the children are unable to pick up on nonverbal cues on their own, words are again the vehicle. Hints and facial expressions are meaningless to a crack-affected child; direct instruction in sharing, greeting, and thanking is necessary. Role playing is appropriate for school-age children, because it allows actual practice in face-to-face interactions with other children, providing a structured social occasion with specific tasks to achieve.

Play must also be taught in words and modeling. Play has no intrinsic value to crack-affected children; they are disorganized and make no sense out of their experience. Their physical activities are random and without point. Play and games must be taught by direct instruction, then by guided play, then by play under supervision. The instruction must be specific so children do not see play and games as a time they need to arrange for themselves.

Routine and familiarity are vital in maintaining attention and facilitating learning. Transitions are particularly hard for crack-affected children, and the teacher must prepare students for transitions from active to quiet activi-

ties, from class to lunch or dismissal, from school to field trips, and from one subject to another. Preparation is done by talking about and reviewing all the things that will happen with the change, perhaps by questioning the children about the transition or sometimes by role playing (as in preparing for a field trip).

Effective Restraint

Teachers of crack-affected children must also know how to safely restrain children when they become hyperactive or threaten to hurt others. This restraint serves as a safety mechanism for the child, who cannot regain self-control when hyperactive. Teachers report that children who have been restrained become conditioned to eventually calm themselves when merely hugged for a moment by the teacher. The child struggles momentarily, then sighs and relaxes, achieving balance again.

Teachers cannot assign blame for disruptive behaviors. The most successful teachers with crack- and cocaine-affected children are those who recognize that the child has no self-control and the behavior needs to be changed. Time-outs are often effective, but physical restraint may be necessary. For children with good language skills, it can be effective to take away privileges and give a full explanation of why and under what circumstances privileges are lost. This needs to be explained over and over.

Avoiding Overload

Small groups are effective for presenting one idea or set of materials at a time and ensuring that children have achieved mastery. Teachers need to check on task completion frequently, because lack of perseverance is often a problem.

Teachers should focus students' attention on the paper, book, or toy in the lesson. For example, the teacher may place the child's hand on the page and move it down to focus attention. A good teacher knows that touching a child, speaking to her, and looking into her eyes at the same time can be overwhelming. There is a better chance of success if the teacher touches the child's hand while speaking in a low voice and avoiding eye contact.

Art and music must be carefully introduced in a highly structured manner. Without structure, these subjects are too stimulating because they reach several senses simultaneously. Teachers suggest working with one color crayon at a time, or teaching simple songs without accompaniment. Several teachers have reported success with humming or singing without words, so students aren't overloaded.

The Future

Interviews with teachers, parents, and foster parents of older cocaine-affected children, some of them teenagers, indicate that the behaviors seen in younger children can persist until adulthood. Without intervention, the impulsivity and inability to internalize rules of appropriate behavior will result in early sexual activity and drug and alcohol use. This probably means drug-impaired children born to drug-impaired children who are unable to care for them.

Without intervention, we are looking at millions of healthy, vigorous, intelligent sociopaths in the schools and in society. A long-term research study on the moral development of crack-affected children is now under way in Wisconsin (Waller, in press), and it will provide information on whether interventions can help in the development of conscience and internalization of social rules.

With intervention, children can learn and complete school. With intervention, children can learn appropriate social behaviors and interactions.

Schools have a choice.

> # Without intervention, we are looking at millions of healthy, vigorous, intelligent sociopaths in the schools and in society.

References

Chasnoff, I.J., K. A. Burns, W. J. Burns, and S. H. Schnoll. (1986). "Prenatal Drug Exposure: Effects on Neonatal and Infant Growth and Development." *Neurobehavioral Toxicology and Teratology* 8: 357-362.

Chasnoff, I. J. (1991). ""Cocaine Use in Pregnancy: Mother and Child." Keynote address to the Illinois Special Education Leadership Institute Third Annual Initiative Conference.

Chasnoff, I.J., D. R. Griffith, S. MacGregor, K. Dirkes, and K. A. Burns. (1989). "Temporal Patterns of Cocaine Use in Pregnancy: Perinatal Outcome." *Journal of the American Medical Association* 261, 12: 1741-1744.

Chasnoff, I.J., H. J. Landress, and M. E. Barrett. (1990). "The Prevalence of Illicit-Drug or Alcohol Use During Pregnancy and Discrepancies in Mandatory Reporting in Pinellas County, Florida." *The New England Journal of Medicine* 322, 17: 1202-1206.

Chasnoff, I.J., W. J. Burns, S. H. Schnoll, and K. A. Burns. (1985). "Cocaine Use in Pregnancy." *The New England Journal of Medicine* 313, 11: 666-669.

Lewis, K.D., B. Bennett, and N. H. Schmeder. (1989). "The Care of Infants Menaced by Cocaine Abuse." *American Journal of Maternal Child Nursing* 14: 324-329.

MacGregor, S.N., L. G. Keith, I. J. Chasnoff, M. A. Rosner, G. M. Chisum, P. Shaw, and J. P. Minogue. (1987). "Cocaine Use During Pregnancy: Adverse Perinatal Outcome." *American Journal of Obstetrics and Gynecology* 157: 686-690.

Rodning, C., L. Beckwith, and J. Howard. (1989). "Prenatal Exposure to Drugs: Behavioral Distortions Reflecting CNS Impairment?" *NeuroToxicology* 10: 629-634.

Ryan, L., S. Ehrlich, and L. Finnegan. (1987). "Cocaine Abuse in Pregnancy: Effects on the Fetus and Newborn." *Neurotoxicology and Teratology* 9: 296-299.

Schneider, J.W. (1990). "Infants Exposed to Cocaine In Utero: Role of the Pediatric Physical Therapist." *Topics in Pediatrics*. Lesson 6.

Van Baar, A.L., P. Fleury, and C. A. Ultee. (1989a). "Behavior in First Year After Drug Dependent Pregnancy." *Archives of Disease in Childhood* 64: 241-245.

Van Baar, A. L., P. Fleury, S. Soepatmi, C. A. Ultee, and P. J. M. Wesselman. (1989b). "Neonatal Behaviours after Drug Dependent Pregnancy." *Archives of Disease in Childhood* 64: 235-240.

Waller, M. B. (In press). *Crack-Affected Children: A Teacher's Guide*. Newbury Park, Calif.: Corwin Press.

Waller, M. B. (Unpublished). Survey of Teachers of Crack-Affected Children.

Weston, D.R., B. Ivins, B. Zuckerman, C. Jones, and R. Lopez. (June 1989). "Drug Exposed Babies: Research and Clinical Issues." *Bulletin of National Center for Clinical Infant Programs* IX.

Yazigi, R. A., R. R. Odem, and K. L. Polakoski. (1991). "Demonstration of Specific Binding of Cocaine to Human Spermatozoa." *Journal of the American Medical Association* 266, 14: 1956-1959.

Questions about Serving Children with HIV/AIDS

The human immunodeficiency virus (HIV), which causes acquired immune-deficiency syndrome (AIDS), has been described in the literature for at least a decade. In the past five years, much concern has been raised about the numbers of children who are HIV-positive. As the second decade of HIV/AIDS is well under way, the number of pediatric cases is expected to rise significantly. In the early years of the epidemic, the life expectancy of children with HIV/AIDS was limited. However, with advances in treatment, more children are living longer and thus entering school.

Sherri Savage,
Phyllis Mayfield,
and Martha Cook

Sherri Savage is a doctoral candidate, Phyllis Mayfield is Assistant Professor, Early Childhood Special Education, and Martha Cook is Assistant Professor, Early Childhood Special Education, at the University of Alabama, Tuscaloosa, AL.

Public awareness of HIV /AIDS has created a new set of concerns for day care providers, schools, and parents. Many of these concerns are based on fears of the risk of the potential transmission of HIV/AIDS to others. However, legal attempts to exclude children with HIV/AIDS from group care and educational settings have largely been unsuccessful (Blackman & Appel, 1987).

Day care centers, Head Start programs, and public and private schools have served or should anticipate serving children with HIV. A recommendation by the American Academy of Pediatrics Task Force on Pediatric AIDS (1989) states that children with HIV/AIDS who are well enough to participate should be accepted into existing programs. Additionally, legislation mandates that children with HIV/AIDS cannot be excluded from participation in programs in which normal children typically participate

(Americans with Disabilities Act, 1990).

The purpose of this article is to address commonly asked questions related to HIV/AIDS in child care settings. A second goal is to provide accurate knowledge to child care providers and parents in an attempt to alleviate fears surrounding HIV/AIDS.

The most frequently asked questions about HIV/AIDS in child care settings are:

1. Can the Virus be Transmitted by Biting?

There is no documented evidence to support that HIV/AIDS may be transmitted by biting (Centers for Disease Control, 1989; Lifson, 1988; Rogers, White, Sanders, Schable, Ksell, Wasserman, Bellanti, Peters, & Wray, 1990). The three modes of transmission cited by the Centers for Disease Control (CDC) are (1) sexual transmission; (2) blood-to-blood; and (3) mother to child. Even if a child with HIV/AIDS did bite another child, the depth of the bite and the limited amount of virus transmitted in saliva is considered of no consequence in acquiring HIV/AIDS. The virus itself is blood-borne, therefore, it is easily destroyed once outside the human body. According to the American Academy of Pediatrics Task Force on Pediatric AIDS (1992), most recommendations

state that the majority of children with HIV infection should be allowed to attend schools and day care centers.

2. Who Has the Right to Know the HIV/AIDS Status of all the Children in the Center or School?

The stigma attached to HIV/AIDS has underlined the need for policies and procedures appropriate for dealing with the issues of confidentiality and public access to information. The American Bar Association (ABA) Commission on the Mentally Disabled and the ABA's Center on Children and the Law have published a report to assist public and private agencies in developing and implementing their own confidentiality policies. The right to privacy is the basis for confidentiality. All HIV-related information is confidential, including clinical or laboratory analysis, an individual's identity, and unique identifiers such as driver's license numbers, hospital identification numbers, or social security numbers. Confidentiality is further extended to the relatives and partners who may be identified through the primary individual.

Disclosure of HIV-related information must be through informed consent, which is specific in nature and must be in written form. Informed consent requires that the individual, or his or her legal representative, understand what information is requested and must understand the implications of his or her actions.

According to the ABA (1992), the perceived need to protect staff members or others from casual contact with individuals infected with HIV is not a sufficient basis to provide access to or disclosure of HIV-related information, without the individual's consent. Furthermore, the "need-to-know" standard must serve the individual's needs, not the needs of the staff. In general, employees in the school classroom or daycare setting would have no need to know whether one of their students is HIV-infected. Unless the child's HIV status is related to special-education services, automatic disclosure to a principal, a counselor, or a teacher will not serve the child's educational needs. If the child requires "reasonable accommodations" under Section 504 of the Rehabilitation Act of 1973, disclosure of the disability (HIV infection) must be made on a "need-to-know" basis, which is determined by the parents.

3. Should Day Care Workers and Teachers Exercise Precautions During Daily Routines?

Universal precautions should be a part of any program for children. The following guidelines should be in place in day care centers and schools:
Guidelines for Handling Blood and Other Body Fluids in Schools
Gloves: Wear disposable, waterproof gloves; dispose of the gloves in a plastic bag or lined trash can, secured and disposed of daily; wash hands for ten seconds with soap and warm running water after disposing of used gloves.
Handwashing: Use soap and warm water with vigorous washing under a stream of running water for approximately ten seconds. Rinse hands under running water and dry thoroughly with paper towels or a dryer.
Disinfecting: A solution of 9 parts water to 1 part household bleach (mixed daily) or EPA-registered germicide will destroy HIV, and can be used to clean all body-fluid spills. *Responding to HIV and AIDS*, 1989.

4. Can the Center or School Deny a Child Admission Based on the Child's HIV status?

Children cannot be denied admission to a center or school and cannot be denied special services and accommodations because of their HIV status. These children are protected by the Americans with Disabilities Act of 1990, which bars discrimination in employment, transportation, public accommodations, and telecommunications. These children may qualify for special-education services, or they may be protected by Section 504 of the Rehabilitation Act. Numerous research has determined that HIV transmission by casual contact in day care, school settings, or families is absent. Therefore, the American Academy of Pediatrics, the Surgeon General's Workshop on Children with HIV Infection and Their Families, and the National Association of State Boards of Education have recommended, on a case-by-case basis, the placement of children with known HIV infection in regular schools and day care settings appropriate for their age and developmental level (Meyers & Weitzman, 1991).

5. Can a Day Care Worker or Teacher Refuse to Teach a Child Who is HIV Positive?

No. Children with HIV/AIDS have their rights protected by federal law, which assures them that they may attend school. As an individual, if you are not comfortable in teaching a child with HIV/AIDS, it would be prudent to be honest with your supervisor. Consider the detrimental effects imposed on Ryan White when school officials denied him access. After a court battle, he won his case, but the damage to his self-esteem and privacy could not be recaptured in that setting.

6. What Should the Day Care Worker or Teacher Do if the Other Children Shun the Child with HIV/AIDS?

Teachers can use several strategies to prevent discrimination against a child with HIV/AIDS. Teach the children, in simple terms, what HIV/AIDS is, how children get it (transmission), and how children do not get it (prevention). This can be accomplished through reading children's books, such as: *Children and the AIDS Virus* (1989) by Rosemarie Hauscher and *Come Sit by Me* (1990) by Margaret Merrifield.

Examples to use with children from Merrifield (1990) are:

"What's AIDS?" Karen asked one night at supper. "AIDS is a sickness. Why do you ask?" asked Father.

"Because Sebastian said he can't play with Nicholas anymore because Nicholas has AIDS."

"Do you play with Nicholas?" Michael asked.

"Yes, he's my friend," she answered.

"Does he look sick?" her brother asked.

"I don't know." Karen shrugged her answer and continued to eat her spaghetti.

Mother sat down close to Karen and told her this . . .

"When you get sick with a fever, a cough or a runny nose, thousands of healthy fighter cells in your blood help make you get better. But if Nicholas has AIDS, some of the most important fighter cells in his blood can't fight anymore. They can't help him get better from his fever, cough or runny nose like yours do."

Karen asked, "If I play with him, will I get AIDS?"

"No," answered Mother. "You can play with Nicholas, eat with him, sleep by him, hug him, and do the things you normally do with all the other children." (pp. 13-14)

Second, role-play with the children how it feels to be left out of games and playtime by their friends. Help the children to understand that being left out and being made fun of really hurts. Then the children can model appropriate accepting behaviors. A children's video by the American Red Cross, *Camp Itsamongus*, helps children get a grasp on understanding HIV/AIDS.

For more information, contact the National AIDS Hotline, 1-800-342-AIDS; the National AIDS Clearinghouse, 1-800-458-5231; or the American Red Cross, 1-800-26 BLOOD. For local information, check with the local Department of public health or your local PTA.

7. How Do Day Care Workers or Teachers Answer Parents' Questions About HIV/AIDS in the Classroom?

Your role as a teacher is to educate parents about HIV/AIDS. Assure them that there is no danger that their child will acquire HIV/AIDS through casual contact in the classroom or anywhere. Provide them with materials to read which explains the disease. Show the parents a videotape about HIV/AIDS. Emphasize that education is the best prevention. Provide awareness of the prejudices that accompany HIV/AIDS. For more information and materials, contact the American Red Cross, HIV/AIDS Education Office, 1709 New York Avenue, N.W., Suite 208, Washington, D.C. 20006 (phone: 1-202-434-4077) or call the American National Red Cross Hotline, 1-800-26-BLOOD.

8. Wouldn't it Be Better for the Child with HIV/AIDS to Receive Care in the Home?

It is medically appropriate for the child with HIV/AIDS to attend school as long as his or her immune system is strong. Children with HIV/AIDS may be more susceptible to germs and infections than the other children in school. A risk assessment of the child may be determined by a physician. Common sense practices of removing the child from school during epidemics of infections, such as measles or chicken pox may be recommended. Each child's school status should be determined on a case-by-case basis with input from the parents, doctors, and school personnel.

9. Won't These Children Be Better Served by Special Education?

Just because the children have HIV/AIDS does not mean that they require special education. Most children with HIV/AIDS function well in a regular classroom. Children with HIV/AIDS would not be eligible for special-education services unless they are evaluated and meet the given criteria, which are based on the degree that the impairment adversely affects their educational performance. Sometimes, children with HIV/AIDS qualify for services under the Other Health Impaired category, which means "limited strength, vitality, or alertness due to chronic or acute health problems which adversely affect educational performance."

It is apparent that HIV/AIDS will not disappear in the near future. Further, it is predicted that the numbers of children with HIV/AIDS will continue to increase. The education of parents, day care providers, and teachers about HIV/AIDS will determine the degree of acceptance of children with HIV/AIDS in the future. Education is the best prevention for HIV/AIDS, but a caring, accepting, safe environment must be a part of the daily experience of children living with HIV/AIDS. Informed school personnel and day care providers will play a crucial role in educating the community about HIV/AIDS.

References

American Academy of Pediatrics Task Force on Pediatric AIDS. "Infants and Children with Acquired Immunodeficiency Syndrome: Placement in Adoption and Foster Care." *Pediatrics*, 1989, 83, pp. 609-612

American Academy of Pediatrics Task Force on Pediatric AIDS. "American Academy of Pediatrics: Guidelines for Human Immunodeficiency Virus (HIV)-Infected Children and Their Foster Families." *Pediatrics*, 1992, 89(4), pp. 681-683.

American Red Cross HIV/AIDS Instructor's Manual, 1992.

Blackman, J., & Appel, B. "Epidemiologic and Legal Considerations in the Exclusion of Children with Acquired Immunodeficiency Syndrome, Cytomegalovirus or Herpes Simplex Virus Infection from Group Care." *Journal of Pediatric Infectious Disease*, 1987, 6(11), pp. 1011-1015.

Centers for Disease Control. "AIDS Patients with No Identified Risk: Lack of Evidence for New Modes of Transmission." Poster presented by L. Conley, T. Bush, and M. Chamberland at the Fifth International Conference on AIDS, Montreal, Canada, June 4-9, 1989.

Ginzburg, H. "The Legal Perspective: A Summary of the American Bar Association's AIDS/HIV and Confidentiality Model Policy and Procedures." *Pediatric AIDS and HIV Infection: Fetus to Adolescent*, 1992, 3(2), pp. 76-80.

Hauscher, R. *Children with the AIDS Virus.* New York: Clarion Books, 1989.

Lifson, A. "Do Alternative Modes of Transmission of Human Immunodeficiency Virus Exist? A Review." *The Journal of the American Medical Association*, 1988, 259(12), pp. 1353-1355.

Merrifield, M. *Come Sit with Me.* Toronto, Canada: Women's Press, 1990.

Meyers, A., & Weitzman, M. "Pediatric HIV Disease: The Newest Chronic Illness of Childhood." *Pediatric Clinics of North America*, 1991, 38(1), pp. 169-194.

Responding to HIV and AIDS. Morrow, GA: National Education Association on Health Information Network, 1989.

Rogers, M., White, C., Sanders, R., Schable, C., Ksell, T., Wasserman, R., Bellanti, J., Peters, S., & Wray, B. "Lack of Transmission of Human Immunodeficiency Virus from Infected Children to Their Household Contacts." *Pediatrics*, 1990, 85, pp. 210-214.

U.S. Congress. Americans with Disabilities Act of 1990. Public Law 101-336.

Child Development and Families

We cannot separate the child from his or her family or home environment. Therefore, for professionals in early childhood education, much of what is done involves the child's family. Teachers and caregivers know families come in many different arrangements, and the more familiar they are with the people the child sees on a regular basis, the easier communication with those individuals will be.

Families and their childrearing beliefs and strategies have changed greatly in the last few decades, and so must parent education and the ways in which teachers communicate with families. More than one-half of all American children can be expected to spend part of their childhood in some type of nontraditional family. By the year 2000, it is estimated that 60 percent of children will spend some time before the age of 18 in a single-parent family. These families need to be supported; moreover, they have special needs that require early childhood educators to be especially vigilant to potential complications and problems that may affect the children's learning processes.

"How Boys and Girls Learn Differently" will appeal to teachers, parents, and any other professionals who interact with children on a regular basis. Susan Chira examines the effects of nature and nurture on development. Much has been written concerning the ways in which teachers relate to girls and boys in the classroom. Researchers have identified a portion of the brain that affects the ways adult males and females approach a situation (i.e., what to do when you are out driving and get lost). Learning styles in children are being examined to determine the best approaches for classroom instruction.

The changes taking place in American families have been one reason the field of early childhood education has grown so rapidly in the past decade. Along with more dual-income families and single-parent families in our communities comes the need for quality early childhood programs. Caregivers and teachers who are trained to work with the special problems and situations that families face will enable the school setting to be a consistent force in the lives of young children and will provide them with a safe, exciting, and nurturing environment. The nuclear family can no longer depend on an extended family network to provide care, assistance, or daily support. Families relocate often and do not have direct access to family resources. It is increasingly necessary for educators to assist children and their parents as they strive to work and learn together.

Parents who doted and swooned over their babies of the eighties are finding these often spoiled and catered-to children extremely difficult to parent in the nineties. "Little Big People" looks at the mixed message being sent to many young children by their parents. No demand for material goods was denied, yet no respect for authority

was ever expected. Learning how to parent is a lifelong process involving all ages and income levels of parents.

Professionals who are aware of the enormously varied life circumstances that children and parents experience today are mindful not to offer magic formulas, quick remedies, or simplistic solutions to complicated, long-standing problems of living and growing together. What many parents do seem to appreciate is a sense that they are respected and given up-to-date objective information about their child. Parents who understand that the education process involves a partnership between them, the teachers and school staff, and community groups will be more willing to share relevant information with those involved. Barry Frieman's "Separation and Divorce: Children Want Their Teachers to Know" has already been shared with many parents by professionals who have established a reciprocal, open relationship with the families of children in their classes. Often teachers and caregivers are amazed when parents ask if the major changes that have occurred in their child's life in the past few months—i.e., parents separate, family income decreases, custodial parent increases work schedule, family moves to smaller, less expensive housing—will affect the child's behavior. Teachers must reassure parents that as professionals, they will use the information parents share in a confidential manner to better assist their child to play, learn, and develop.

Looking Ahead: Challenge Questions

What behaviors of infants are present at birth? How do infants respond to the stimulation in their world?

Do parents really treat girls and boys differently? What can parents do to ensure equal treatment for all their children?

How is learning affected because of the sex of the child?

What makes the separation process so difficult for infants and toddlers? Are there specific steps teachers can take to assist parents and children in this process? Give three examples.

What strategies should be used by teachers working with children who have little respect for authority?

Why is it important for teachers and caregivers to know of major changes affecting young children and their families? How can this information be obtained?

The Amazing Minds of Infants

Looking here, looking there, babies are like little scientists, constantly exploring the world around them, with innate abilities we're just beginning to understand.

Text by **Lisa Grunwald**
Reporting by **Jeff Goldberg**

Additional reporting: **Stacey Bernstein, Anne Hollister**

A light comes on. Shapes and colors appear. Some of the colors and shapes start moving. Some of the colors and shapes make noise. Some of the noises are voices. One is a mother's. Sometimes she sings. Sometimes she says things. Sometimes she leaves. What can an infant make of the world? In the blur of perception and chaos of feeling, what does a baby know?

Most parents, observing infancy, are like travelers searching for famous sites: first tooth, first step, first word, first illness, first shoes, first full night of sleep. Most subtle, and most profound of all, is the first time the clouds of infancy part to reveal the little light of a human intelligence.

For many parents, that revelation may be the moment when they see

their baby's first smile. For others, it may be the moment when they watch their child show an actual

---

At three months, babies can learn—and remember for weeks—visual sequences and simple mechanical tasks.

---

preference—for a lullaby, perhaps, or a stuffed animal. But new evidence is emerging to show that even before those moments, babies already have wonderfully active minds.

Of course, they're not exactly chatty in their first year of life, so what—and how—babies truly think may always remain a mystery. But using a variety of ingenious techniques that interpret how infants watch and move, students of child development are discovering a host of unsuspected skills. From a rudimentary understanding of math to a

sense of the past and the future, from precocious language ability to an innate understanding of physical laws, children one year and younger know a lot more than they're saying.

MEMORY

Does an infant remember anything? Penelope Leach, that slightly scolding doyenne of the child development field, warns in *Babyhood* that a six- to eight-month-old "cannot hold in his mind a picture of his mother, nor of where she is." And traditionally psychologists have assumed that infants cannot store memories until, like adults, they have the language skills needed to form and retrieve them. But new research suggests that babies as young as three months may be taking quite accurate mental notes.

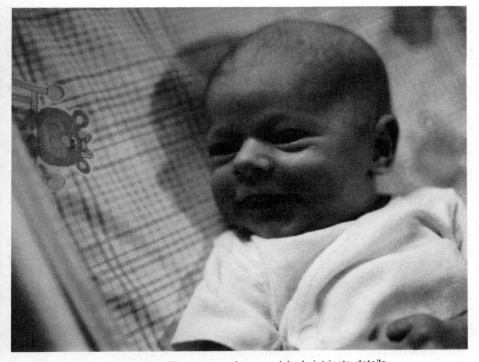

Babies show an unexpected ability to remember surprisingly intricate details.

skills. Three years ago she placed 16 six-month-olds in a pitch-dark room with objects that made different sounds. Using infrared cameras like Haith's, she observed how and when the infants reached for the objects. Later, realizing she had created a unique situation that couldn't have been duplicated in real life, she wondered if the babies would remember their experience. Two years after the original experiment, collaborating with psychologist Nancy Myers, she brought the same 16 children back to the lab, along with a control group of 16 other two-and-a-half-year-olds. Amazingly, the experimental group showed the behavior they had at six months, reaching for objects and showing no fear. Fewer control-group toddlers reached for the objects, and many of them cried.

Says Myers: "For so long, we didn't think that infants could rep-

At five months, babies have the raw ability to add.

resent in their memories the events that were going on around them, but put them back in a similar situation, as we did, and you can make the memory accessible."

MATH

At least a few parental eyebrows—and undoubtedly some expectations—were raised by this recent headline in *The New York Times:* "Study Finds Babies at 5 Months Grasp Simple Mathematics." The story, which re-

In his lab at the University of Denver, psychologist Marshall Haith has spent much of the past four years putting infants into large black boxes where they lie and look up at TV screens. The program they see is a Haith invention: a sequence of colorful objects appearing on different sides of the monitor. Using an infrared camera linked to a computer, Haith follows the babies' eye movements and has found that after only five tries the babies can anticipate where the next object will appear. With a little more practice, they can foresee a four-step sequence. And up to two weeks later, most can still predict it. Says Haith: "The babies are not just looking. They're analyzing, creating little hypotheses."

Similar findings by Carolyn Rovee-Collier, a psychologist at Rutgers University, suggest that infants can remember surprisingly intricate details. In a typical experiment, she places a baby in a crib beneath an elaborate mobile, ties one of the baby's ankles to it with a satin ribbon, then observes as the baby kicks and—often gleefully—makes it move. When, weeks later, the baby's feet are left untied and the mobile is returned to the crib, the baby will try to kick again, presumably recalling the palmy days of kicking the last time. But if the mobile's elements are changed even slightly, the baby will remain unmoved—and unmoving. "When we change things," explains Rovee-Collier, "it wipes out the memory. But as soon as we bring back what had become familiar and expected, the memory comes right back. What we've learned from this is that even at two and a half months, an infant's memory is very developed, very specific and incredibly detailed."

Rachel Clifton, a psychologist at the University of Massachusetts, says that an infant's experience at six months can be remembered a full two years later. Clifton stumbled upon her findings while researching motor and hearing

ported on the findings of Karen Wynn, a psychologist at the University of Arizona, explained that infants as young as five months had been found to exhibit "a rudimentary ability to add and subtract."

Wynn, who published her research in the renowned scientific journal *Nature,* had based her experiments on a widely observed phenomenon: Infants look longer at things that are unexpected to them, thereby revealing what they do expect, or know. Wynn enacted addition and subtraction equations for babies using Mickey Mouse dolls. In a typical example, she had the babies watch as she placed a doll on a puppet stage, hid it behind a screen, then placed a second doll behind the screen (to represent one plus one). When she removed the screen to reveal three, not two, Mickey Mouse dolls, the infants stared longer at such incorrect outcomes than they had at correct ones. Wynn believes that babies' numerical understanding is "an innate mechanism, somehow built into the biological structure."

Her findings have been met with enthusiasm in the field—not least from Mark Strauss at the University of Pittsburgh, who a decade ago found that somewhat older babies could distinguish at a glance the difference between one, two, three and four balls—nearly as many objects as adults can decipher without counting. Says Strauss: "Five-month-olds are clearly thinking about quantities and applying numerical concepts to their world."

Wynn's conclusions have also inspired skepticism among some researchers who believe her results may reflect infants' ability to perceive things but not necessarily an ability to know what they're perceiving. Wynn herself warns parents not to leap to any conclu-

sions, and certainly not to start tossing algebra texts into their children's cribs. Still, she insists: "A lot more is happening in infants' minds than we've tended to give them credit for."

LANGUAGE

In an old stand-up routine, Robin Williams used to describe his son's dawning ability as a mimic of words—particularly those of the deeply embarrassing four-letter variety. Most parents decide they can no longer speak with complete freedom when their children start talking. Yet current research on language might prompt some to start censoring themselves even earlier.

At six months, babies recognize their native tongue.

At Seattle's University of Washington, psychologist Patricia Kuhl has shown that long before infants actually begin to learn words, they can sort through a jumble of spoken sounds in search of the ones that have meaning. From birth to four months, according to Kuhl, babies are "universal linguists" capable of distinguishing each of the 150 sounds that make up all human speech. But by just six months, they have begun the metamorphosis into specialists who recognize the speech sounds of their native tongue.

In Kuhl's experiment babies listened as a tape-recorded voice repeated vowel and consonant combinations. Each time the sounds changed—from "ah" to "oooh," for example—a toy bear in a box

was lit up and danced. The babies quickly learned to look at the bear when they heard sounds that were new to them. Studying Swedish and American six-month-olds, Kuhl found they ignored subtle variations in pronunciation of their own language's sounds—for instance, the different ways two people might pronounce "ee"—but they heard similar variations in a foreign language as separate sounds. The implication? Six-month-olds can already discern the sounds they will later need for speech. Says Kuhl: "There's nothing external in these six-month-olds that would provide you with a clue that something like this is going on."

By eight to nine months, comprehension is more visible, with babies looking at a ball when their mothers say "ball," for example. According to psychologist Donna Thal at the University of California, San Diego, it is still impossible to gauge just how many words babies understand at this point, but her recent studies of slightly older children indicate that comprehension may exceed expression by a factor as high as a hundred to one. Thal's studies show that although some babies are slow in starting to talk, comprehension appears to be equal between the late talkers and early ones.

PHYSICS

No, no one is claiming that an eight-month-old can compute the trajectory of a moon around a planet. But at Cornell University, psychologist Elizabeth Spelke is finding that babies as young as four months have a rudimentary knowledge of the way the world works—or should work.

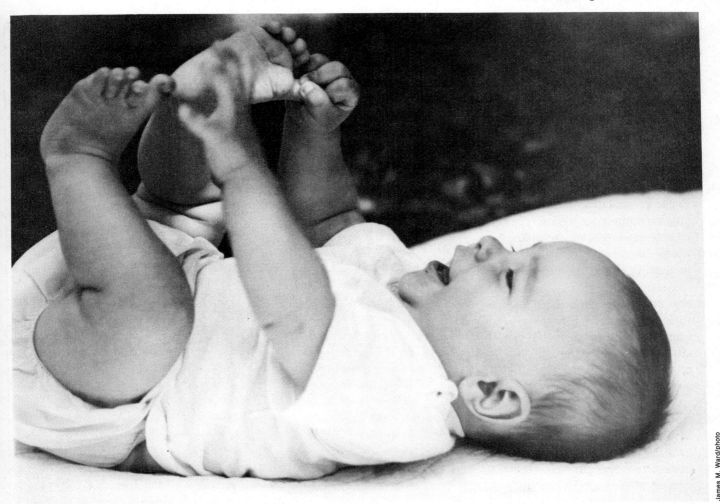

Babies learn how physical objects behave by moving their body parts.

*Babies have a built-in
sense of how objects
behave.*

Spelke sets her young subjects up before a puppet stage, where she shows them a series of unexpected actions: a ball seems to roll through a solid barrier, another seems to leap between two platforms, a third seems to hang in midair. Like Karen Wynn with her math experiments, Spelke measures the babies' looking time and has recorded longer intervals for unexpected actions than for expected ones. Again like Wynn, Spelke be-

lieves that babies must have some "core" knowledge—in this case, about the way physical objects behave. Says Spelke: "At an age when infants are not able to talk about objects, move around objects, reach for and manipulate objects, or even see objects with high resolution, they appear to recognize where a moving object is when it has left their view and make inferences about where it should be when it comes into sight again."

The notion of an infant's possessing any innate mechanism—other than reflexes like sucking that fade with time—would have shocked the shoes off the pioneers of child development research, who believed, as some still do, that

what we know can be learned only through experience. But the belief in biologically programmed core knowledge lies at the heart of the current research—not only with math and physics but with other cognitive skills as well. Indeed, Carnegie Mellon's Mark Johnson believes that the ability of infants to recognize the human face is not learned, as previously thought, but is present at birth. Studying infants, some only 10 minutes old, Johnson has observed a marked preference for pictures of faces to pictures of blank ovals or faces with scrambled features. He believes that we are born with a "template" of the human face that aids our survival by helping us recognize our meal ticket.

EMOTIONS: THE SHY AND THE LIVELY

A growing number of researchers believe early temperament may indicate later troubles.

One thing that infants are *not* good at is hiding what they feel. Fear, glee, rage, affection: Long before babies start talking, emotions tumble out of them in gestures, tears and belly laughs. But measuring infant temperament—finding a way to quantify its traits—has always been harder than measuring skills.

Around the country, researchers are now combining questionnaires filled in by parents, home visits by trained observers, and newly devised lab tests to explore the mystery of temperamenat. Concentrating on babies older than eight months (the age at which the full range of infant emotions has emerged), investigators have designed more than 50 experimental situations to provoke emotions from fear to sadness, from interest to pleasure. Most children's reactions fall within an average range on such tests. But there are babies on either extreme, and psychologist Nathan Fox at the University of Maryland has begun to explore their responses. Putting his babies in electroencephalogram (EEG) helmets, he has found that particularly inhibited babies show a distinctive brain-wave pattern, which others believe may predict later emotional problems, including depression. Although some scientists agree that early behavior can predict later temperament, other researchers argue that enduring character traits are the exception, not the rule. For psychiatrist Stanley Greenspan of Bethesda, Md., the ability of infants to change is an article of faith. Specializing in babies as young as three months, Greenspan says he can treat what he calls the garden-variety problems of sleep disorders, tan-

Long before babies begin talking, emotions are graphically expressed in their gestures and facial expressions.

WHO/photo

trums and anger in a few sessions. (Don't imagine tiny couches for infant patients; although the babies are closely observed, it's the parents who often get treatment.) For more severe problems, such as suspected learning disorders, he recommends more intensive early intervention—often involving a team of therapists—and has found that this can make a huge difference: "Babies who were very scared, shy and inhibited can completely change and become very assertive, outgoing and confident over a number of months."

The University of Washington's Mary Rothbart has compared infants in Japan, the Netherlands and the U.S. and notes that northern European mothers are most prone to ignore their babies' fussiness with a stiff-upper-lip approach. When tested at one year by having their mothers leave a room, the Dutch babies are the most distressed and ignore their mothers upon their return. Psychologists call this response an "insecure attachment relationship," and some regard it as an early warning of later anxiety disorders. Says Rothbart: "In the process of soothing a baby, you're helping to teach it to shift its attention away from negative sensations. Adults with anxiety disorders may never have learned to do this." Tellingly, when Dutch mothers were instructed to soothe and play with their fussy babies, the follow-up sessions showed positive results. "With intervention," concludes Rothbart, "you can turn things around."

TAKING INFANTS SERIOUSLY

The ultimate question becomes, should education begin at three months?

One question that might leap to the minds of parents newly informed of their infants' skills is a simple one: So what? What does it mean if children really have these unexpected abilities?

Pointing to the findings on memory that she has published with partner Rachel Clifton, Nancy Myers suggests that if memories of the babies' experience allowed them to be unafraid in the pitch-black room, then exposing children to a wide variety of events and places may make them more accepting of similar situations later on. "I don't want to say that mothers should make an extreme effort to stimulate their babies," Myers says, "but taking a baby to different places, allowing him to see and smell different things, is an important means of establishing familiarity. It will allow the baby to feel freer in the future."

But what about other kinds of skills: Should infants' innate abilities with language or math be consciously nurtured and pushed along?

In Philadelphia, instructors at the Institutes for the Achievement of Human Potential have been coaching parents since 1963 to teach their babies to read from birth. Touting "genetic potential," their program recommends that parents write out on cards everything from "nose" to "kiss" to "Mommy." The new findings about infants' skills have hardly gone unnoticed at the Institutes, where director Janet Doman says: "For the past thirty years, we've been saying that children can learn at very early ages. It's nice to know that science is finally validating what we've known all along."

Yet many of the scientists performing the experiments question the value of such intensive efforts. Says Rutgers's Carolyn Rovee-Collier: "Most of us agree that an infant could be taught to recognize letters and numbers. But the problem is that parents who do these kinds of programs start investing a lot in their infants and become very bound up in their success. It puts great strain on the infants and the parents."

University of Denver psychologist Marshall Haith agrees: "Babies are born prepared to take on the world. We've got to get away from the feeling that we've got this wonderful brain sitting there and we've got to keep pumping information into it. Nature wouldn't have done anything so stupid."

To most researchers, the moral of the story seems to be: Respect your baby, but don't go nuts. "Don't waste your child's fun months," says Karen Wynn, who says her findings about math "should be viewed as no more than a new insight for parents who have young children." Says the University of Pittsburgh's Mark Strauss: "Ideally, we can tell parents a lot more about subtle things they can watch happening in their infants, and that will make watching and getting involved more fun."

how boys and girls learn differently

And what you need to know to make sure your child has an equal chance to succeed in school

Susan Chira

Susan Chira reports on education for The New York Times.

The first day of school—a new teacher, new friends, new lessons. And for boys and girls, very different learning experiences to come.

Gender has become the latest buzzword in education, as recent headline-making reports have pointed to a great disparity in the ways each sex is taught and each might best succeed. What should parents be watching for to ensure that their child, whether boy or girl, gets the best from school?

HOW EACH SEX MAKES THE GRADE

No matter what parents thought before they had children, most soon become convinced that boys and girls are distinct creatures. Whether the traits are inborn, the result of hormones or different brain structure—as some experts claim—or the result of being treated differently—as others believe—is hotly debated.

But for whatever reason, from the moment they enter the classroom, boys and girls *do* tend to behave differently. In experiments at a variety of preschools, psychology professor Aletha Houston, Ph.D., of the University of Kansas in Lawrence, showed that girls were more likely to choose activities overseen by adults, while boys were more likely to wander off and play independently. Young boys are generally the more active sex; girls tend to have more self-control and to be more compliant and sociable.

As they grow, boys tend to have stronger large motor skills—those that help them run, climb, throw balls. These physical abilities often translate into more developed spatial skills (having good mental pictures of how shapes fit together, being adept at puzzles or Lego building blocks), which lead to an easier time with math.

Girls, on the other hand, tend to have stronger verbal skills and so, in the beginning, are better readers. They're also generally more attentive listeners and have more advanced fine motor skills—the ones that help them hold a pencil.

In many ways, therefore, boys often start school behind girls. But by junior high, there's a flip: On standardized tests, boys just about match girls in verbal skills, and they start pulling way ahead in science and math.

The most dramatic change, though, and perhaps one that affects all future learning, is how each sex views its own abilities. During the teen years, boys' self-esteem rises, whereas girls' plummets. Harvard psychologist Carol Gilligan, Ph.D., studied preadolescent girls at two private schools, one in Ohio, the other in New York State. Most, she found, had been spunky as young girls. But by adolescence, they suffered a dramatic loss of confidence. Asked their opinions on any number of even personal issues, these formerly outspoken girls would answer hesitantly—"I don't know," or "I'm not sure what I think."

And a survey of 3,000 teens commissioned by the American Association of University Women (AAUW) confirmed Dr. Gilligan's findings on a national scale. This 1991 report showed that girls emerge from adolescence with far less self-confidence than boys. These teenage girls were more likely than boys to say they wanted to look like someone else or—of even more concern—to *be* someone else.

AT THE STARTING GATE

The first time parents may directly encounter the "gender question" is at kindergarten enrollment. For the most part, girls' strengths help them adjust to school more quickly. "Being able to sit still and listen will get you further in kindergarten classrooms than running, jumping, and good spatial skills," says Barbara Willer of the National Association for the Education of Young Children.

As a result, parents of boys are increasingly being advised to hold their sons out of school for a year, a practice known as redshirting (from the school-athletics tradition of holding promising young players—in red shirts—on the bench for a year). Not only are five-year-old boys often less mature than their female classmates, the argument goes, but today's kindergarten classroom gives them less opportunity to develop the necessary maturity. These days most kindergartens are more like first grade used to be, with children often expected to be able to recognize the alphabet and to spell and print their names.

Some experts applaud the move to start school later, reasoning that if a child's first experience at school is unhappy, his later years will be, too. But a growing number believe that holding a child back has no impact at best—and can actually be harmful. A recent study of more than 2,500 children by the Gundersen Medical Foundation in La Crosse, Wisconsin, found that children who start kindergarten at age six rather than five do not necessarily fare better. And other researchers argue that boys who start kindergarten at six are often *too* far ahead of their classmates, intellectually and emotionally. They'll get bored, and they can easily turn off school altogether.

If you're not sure what to do, talk to your son's nursery school teacher and to a kindergarten teacher in the school he'll be attending. Think, too, about your son's experience in preschool, play groups, or other classes—has he liked playing with other children? Does he seem to be keeping up with them? Some parents have even been advised to consider their son's height; tall boys might be "pushed" ahead a bit, but shorter ones could feel more comfortable having another year to mature. In the end, your intuition about your own child is the best guide.

BAD NEWS FOR GOOD GIRLS
Because teachers often work so hard to help boys in the skills they lack, the girls get ignored. A recent report by the AAUW reviewed virtually all major studies on girls and education and concluded that girls are being short-changed. Teachers call on boys more than girls, reports Myra Sadker, Ed.D.,

---

what's hot in sex ed

Seventeen states now require public schools to teach sex education; another thirty encourage it. In 1970, it was required in only one state. That's good news for the nine out of ten parents who say they want sex ed for their kids. But what kind of sex ed schools should provide is still controversial.

Fifteen of the seventeen states call for abstinence to be emphasized, and that has fueled the popularity of Sex Respect, a ten-session program in which middle school students attend "abstinence assemblies," chant chastity pledges ("Do the right thing! Wait for the ring!"), and ponder the pitfalls of premarital sex: pregnancy, disease, and loss of self-esteem. Over the past three years, nearly 1,700 school districts have adopted Sex Respect—and more have chosen one of 15 programs modeled on it.

But parents in several states have fought abstinence-only classes, stating that they teach fear, guilt, shame, sexism, and ignorance. They prefer programs that face up to the reality of teen sexuality—a recent Centers for Disease Control survey reports that 54 percent of youngsters have had sex by the time they graduate from high school. In these classes, students are taught it pays to say no but also learn how to protect themselves if they choose to say yes.

Last October, in an effort to set standards and stem the tide of teen pregnancy and AIDS (now the sixth leading cause of death for 15- to 24-year-olds), the Sex Information and Education Council of the U.S.—with input from the American Medical Association, the National Education Association, and 14 other groups—issued guidelines calling for comprehensive sex ed from kindergarten through twelfth grade. The proposed curriculum covers the basics, such as abstinence and contraception, but also breaks daring new ground: teaching early in elementary school exactly how intercourse takes place and, for older students, explaining that homosexuals have relationships that can be as fulfilling as those of heterosexuals. —LINDA CHION-KENNEY

---

professor of secondary education at American University in Washington, D.C., and offer them more detailed, constructive criticism. Even the praise is more specific and useful. With girls, more attention is paid to the *appearance* of the work—"This looks okay." But boys are more likely to hear: "Good ideas in the first paragraph, but you need to look more closely at development." Girls seem hesitant to use school computers—and get less encouragement from teachers to try.

It's not that teachers intentionally overlook girls' needs—it's the squeaky-wheel syndrome: Boys speak up when they don't understand, but girls stay silent. When teachers videotape their classes to check for differences in the way they treat boys and girls—as researchers have suggested they do—they're often surprised by what they find. "I realized that a number of the

girls were having some of the same learning difficulties as the boys, but I recognized it more in the boys," says Trini Johannesen, a teacher in Stockbridge, Michigan, on leave to serve as vice president of the Michigan Education Association. "The girls were simply less overt."

A NEW EDUCATION FOR TEACHERS
Taping classes is just one way teachers and researchers are learning to recognize and correct differences in the way they treat boys and girls. Luvenia Jackson, an assistant principal at the Riverdale Middle School in Riverdale, Georgia, who helps train other teachers, also checks seating plans. If boys are placed in front—as they frequently are so teachers can keep an eye on them—girls often receive less attention, she finds. She also suggests that

teachers keep a tally of the number of times they call on boys and girls.

Johannesen has observed that girls take more time to think through their answers, while boys will shout them out, less worried if they're right. She advises teachers to wait longer before calling on *anyone* and to encourage more independence and problem solving on the part of girls. "If a girl is looking into a microscope and she says it's fuzzy," Johannesen says, "the teacher's tendency will be to fine-tune the instrument, rather than asking, 'What part of the microscope do you think could solve that problem?'"

When it comes to math and science, researchers are looking into a number of strategies they hope will close the gender gap. "Cooperative learning"—a hot new teaching method that divides the class into groups, with students working together on math problems or jointly editing each others' writing—has been especially helpful. Teachers find that students thrive in such groups. But girls do particularly well in math with this method, possibly because they feel more comfortable in a supportive environment.

Additionally, researchers suggest that when teaching math and science, teachers avoid using typically male metaphors—such as examples that involve sports. Girls may also respond better if teachers make it clear that math and science are tools for solving everyday problems that affect real people. Teachers should talk about famous women scientists and invite dynamic women scientists and engineers into class.

PARENTS AS COACHES

When it comes to ensuring equal opportunities, both boys *and* girls can benefit from at-home efforts. Since reading to kids is the single best way to prepare them for learning to read, boys especially may benefit from lots of time looking at books.

what kids *won't* be reading this year

Book banning in public schools, which hit an all-time high last year, is expected to increase again this fall, according to People for the American Way, an anticensorship organization in Washington, D.C.

Books believed to contain profanity or sexual material have long been favorite targets, but today censors are even more sensitive. *Laugh Lines,* **a collection of riddles by Joan Blank, was pulled from a California elementary school for its "demeaning manner" toward the reader who can't solve the puzzles. Censors in an Iowa district claim** *Rolling Harvey Down the Hill,* **by Jack Prelutsky, is insulting to chubby people, and Dr. Seuss's** *The Lorax* **was challenged in a Laytonville, California, school district because it made fun of loggers.**

—ROBBIN MCCLAIN

For girls, choosing toys that encourage spatial reasoning—blocks, construction toys, gyroscopes, puzzles—will put them on more equal footing. Making sure that daughters get plenty of running-around and climbing play will also help.

Educators advise that parents exert themselves to bring nature and mini-science lessons into children's lives. Both sexes will profit, but it's especially important to show girls that these subjects can be fun. At the beach, talk about shells, fish, and the ocean, or if your own knowledge is shaky, bring along a children's book that introduces marine biology. A drive over a bridge can spark a conversation about how bridges are built—the beginnings of engineering.

If your daughter complains that the teacher never calls on her or that "the boys get all the attention," try to help her to find ways to change the situation. And bring up the subject at a parent-teacher conference. Even if your daughter doesn't complain, you might be suspicious if her report card shows that she always "listens carefully" or if the teacher is effusive in praising the child's cooperation. You don't want to encourage unruliness, obviously, but it's important to make sure your daughter isn't afraid to speak up or that the teacher isn't neglecting her because she is so quiet and compliant.

The AAUW offers guidelines for parents and teachers to determine if schools are treating girls fairly. It advises that you check statistical results—find out what percentage of boys and of girls take higher-level math and science classes. Are there enough funds for girls' sports? Also, ask teachers and administrators whether they have the same expectations of boys and girls in all subjects; whether both boys and girls are encouraged to play sports; whether guidance counselors and others are sensitive to gender issues, or encourage the girls to take traditionally female classes like home economics and typing, while they push the boys toward computer study.

With the right information, parents and teachers can work together to make sure that boys and girls not only get through school but thrive there.

Little Big People

*A generation of affluent parents have raised the precocious,
worldly children they wanted to be—and are now confronted with
the results of their experiment.*

Lucinda Franks

*Lucinda Franks, a Pulitzer Prize-winning journalist, is
the author of the novel "Wild Apples."*

One day last may, my son's third-grade classroom
was left in the care of a substitute teacher. For
reasons still undetermined, a small riot broke
out, with children fighting, shrieking and shoving
chairs. Nine-year-olds going berserk in springtime is
not unprecedented, but consider what happened next:
The new principal lectured them with a sternness they
were unaccustomed to. Then she made them write
letters of apology and then they fell apart all over
again. Those who claimed they had not participated in
the brawl came down at dismissal time tearful and
incensed at the burden of collective guilt imposed upon
them. "Isn't it illegal for her to punish those of us who
did nothing?" one boy asked his mother. "Should we
sue her?" asked another. When told they should show
more respect for authority, one girl said, "Why should
we respect her when she showed no respect for us?"

In the office of a child therapist recently, a 10-year-
old girl leaned back and gazed at her mother with half-
lidded contempt. The child was there because her
divorced parents couldn't do anything with her. Her
father was bitter because he had brought her along to
buy his girlfriend an engagement gift and she had
sulked the whole time. Her mother complained that
she refused to make friends with the mother's boy-
friend. "How do you expect me to have a relationship
with him," the girl said with the ennui of a 40-year-old,
"when he's always in your bedroom?"

The therapist shook her head when she recounted
the visit: "Sometimes I think I'm too old-fashioned to
practice in today's world. Half the time the children act
like adults and the adults behave like children."

For decades now, children have been growing up
faster and faster, each new generation emerging
more precocious than the last. But today's crop
of under-12's, particularly in middle- and upper-middle-
income families and particularly in urban America,
seems to have reinvented—or even bypassed—childhood as we knew it. They are proud, independent and
strong-willed; they are worldly-wise and morally serious. They are a generation that has been raised to
challenge and doubt authority, to take little at face
value—in short, to enter the world of maturity long
before they are mature.

This was no accident. The parents of many of these
children—those of us who began our families later in
life—came of age in the Vietnam War years. Our ideas
of child rearing were like our ideas about everything
else: radically different from our parents, who thought
a child was just a child, even when the child got old
enough to march against wars and otherwise protest-
the way the elder generation ran the world. Those of us
who were veterans of the 60's and 70's swore that we
would treat our children with respect. We vowed that
we would fold our own offspring into our daily lives,
treating them like "little people," empowering them
with the rights, the importance and the truth telling
we had been denied. We wanted to create the children
we always yearned to be. And now, many years later,
we are confronted with the results. Did it turn out the
way we meant it to? Will our independent children
thank us for making them the center of the universe,
or have we robbed them of a childhood they can never
regain?

The explosion in communications—with television
and movies thrusting sophisticated material on grade-
schoolers—as well as increasing competition for college
placement has intensified childhood burnout. The kids

of yesterday, who wandered into meadows of fantasy, whose tears were reserved for skinned knees and broken toys, has given way to the kid who is strapped to the competitive fast track before he is out of diapers. The urban, affluent child is crammed with gymnastics and tennis and French lessons and then is crowded with even more activities by working parents who try to make the most of the time they have with their children. The child who could once be seen playing cops and robbers in the park is no longer even in the park but at home simulating the same thing on his Nintendo screen. He is a computer whiz, a little philosopher, a tiny lawyer, bursting with opinions on the President, on the best museums, the best vacation spots and the college he thinks he will attend.

For childish comfort, he is taken into the capricious arms of television: the great cuddly dinosaur Barney leads him in singing "we're a happy family" and then the child switches the channel to see that the man who taught him tennis is a pedophile who has put a bullet through his brain. Language more appropriate to teenagers can be heard in elementary-school halls. One mother of a 7-year-old confided that a boy had told her daughter, "You're so yucky you must have sex with Nazis."

Economic hardship has long stolen childhood from the poor. The severity and the causes of their problems, which have only intensified, are far different from those of affluent children. Yet for the first time, these more privileged children are thrust unshielded into the middle of family crisis that would paralyze an adult: a parent is dying of AIDS or the child is a mediator in violent dramas of drug addiction or divorce.

Even in stable families, small children with two working parents learn to shift for themselves, cooking and caring for siblings and picking up the attitudes of their elders. Our generation—reared in an era in which sex was not discussed, conflict was suppressed and emotional distance was maintained—opened the gates for our children. But each day, the bleak river of honesty that runs through their lives grows dangerously higher.

"I was determined that there was going to be no more scary secrets, no more J. Edgar Hoover, when I got to be a parent; everything was going to be up front," says Marcia Roesch, a school admissions coordinator. "I talked and talked, but I wasn't listening and I wasn't keeping a sense of balance and appropriateness with my children. I hear parents all the time asking their kids 'Is that O.K.?' as though they need their kids to approve every decision."

Says Candace Stern, a New Jersey mother of an 8-year-old: "I used to express my insecurities and everything else to my daughter. One day, we were watching a takeoff of Little Red Riding Hood on Sesame Street and I thought it was hilarious. Then I looked at Caitlin and she was terrified. It was then that I realized that I didn't really know what was in her mind and that what she heard, what she held onto, was much different than what I, an adult, retained."

Contrary to our assumptions, we have found that children are much more than little people. They are the possessors of rather eccentric states of mind that some experts fear are being altered by the early use of computers and other technology.

"There is a period of childhood, until about age 9, when children should exist in a dreamlike state," says Kay J. Hoffman, an educator at a progressive school in Rockland County in New York. "Instead, they are being hardened too early, jarred into an awake adult consciousness that is preventing the natural development of their imaginations. The trend to intellectualize early education is a dangerous one. I see more children with high anxiety levels and learning problems caused by the enormous pressure that is being put on them to think and speak like adults before they are ready."

Highly verbal children will use words, without really understanding them, as coin of the adult realm. "They use them for protection, to push away their own experience as children," says one doctor who asked not to be identified to protect his patients. "One 4-year-old that I tested kept running out of the room saying he had to go get his 'concentration.' He couldn't just be a child and say, 'I don't want to do this test!' He had to parrot an adult concept that he hardly understood because he was afraid to disappoint me."

I think sometimes we cannot know how profound that fear runs in our children, especially since we have burdened them with such a sense of their own importance. At times, their officiousness seems to be bluff; they simply cannot afford to be wrong. In making them feel so trusted and believed, we have not only bridged the generation gap, we might have overlapped it. As we hover over their development as though we were tending orchids in a greenhouse, are we not also guilty of a kind of neglect? In integrating them into our daily lives, have we taken away their freedom to do childish things? Parents or nannies of old stayed at home and babbled and played games; we take them to department stores, to work, to lunch, to movies and plays. Parents push for intimacy so much that one child was overheard telling her mother, "If you say I can have my feelings one more time, I'm going to throw up."

Says Miriam Siffert, a grandmother in Manhattan: "We sent our children to the most progressive schools, but they knew their place. They knew their time. We didn't take them to dinner parties or on trips to Europe. But I see my grandchildren taking over the house, taking over adult conversation."

Peggy Rosenblatt, a mother of two, concurs: "There is so much familiarity and so little distance. We tell them where we are going, what we are doing. We ask their opinion as though they were our best buddies, and then we are surprised when we tell a 10-year-old to do something he doesn't want to do and he says, 'You can't make me.'"

So uncomfortable are we with being in authority that we have made a crusade of elevating our children at the expense of ourselves. Consider the way we portray ourselves in children's movies; no Mary Poppins or Clark Kent these days; instead, enter Hook, so realistically evil that he breaks the bounds of old-time fantasy, or an all-too-believable Mom and Dad who keep leaving their son home alone.

"Sometimes it seems like there is no bottom line anymore," says Sara Adler, a grade-school teacher for 20 years. "I have some kids who yell 'child abuse' if you discipline them. They know tag lines, but they don't know the lines they cannot and should not cross. The parents think, 'What are the teachers doing!' And the teachers wonder what is going on inside the homes."

We have abrogated the moral authority our parents wore as easily as gloves. In Westchester County in New York, for instance, where kids in their early teens come into the city to party until the early hours of the morning, some parents are afraid to give their children curfews for fear they will move out and live with a friend.

Even children themselves think that things sometimes go too far. "Trust me, I know some kids who are guilty of parent abuse," Jonathan Stein, 10, says. "They feel like they own their parents and that they could just take all their parents' money out of their bank account and run away if they wanted."

Michelle Denburg, a high-school senior, adds: "Some of my teachers were afraid to be authority figures. They couldn't control their class and partly it was the fault of the parents because they would say negative stuff about a teacher and then expect their kids to respect those teachers."

In spite of the confusion these children experience, few would disagree that they are, in many ways, a splendid generation. My son, Joshua, 9, and his friends are amazing in their generosity, sensitivity, ability to stretch across an intellectual canyon and meet adults on their own terms. They have highly developed senses of justice and fairness, rejecting stereotypes and embracing oddities in their peers, whether a hair style or a disability. They are disdainful of smoking and drug use, can sniff out hypocrisy and have social consciences that are poignant. They are so worried about the few trees on their block that last year they formed an earth club to keep them free of litter. At times, the child in our children pokes endearingly through the veneer of sophistication. "Mom, please don't buy Ivory soap anymore" as his most recent environmental request. "Why?" I asked. "Be-

cause they shoot elephants to get the ivory, don't they?" he replied.

Paul Shechtman, a New York lawyer, reports that when he argued with his daughter, 6, about going to school with a rip in the knee of her jeans, she asked him for one good reason why she shouldn't wear them. "Because my father never would have let me," he said, exasperated. "Just because your father made a mistake," she replied, "why should you?"

"At that moment," Shechtman said, "I knew that I had succeeded as a parent. Now, of course, I do have to live with my success."

Helene Stein, mother of three children 14 and under, including Jonathan, says she gets "a kind of wicked pleasure when I compare my children's childhood with my own." She and her sister had to be bathed, with hair brushed and bathrobes on, before they came to the table. "My parents were the ones who spoke," she says. "We listened. With my kids, I drop everything if they seem to want to talk."

Since the end of the Victorian era, when children emerged as entities that would be heard as well as occasionally seen, childhood has been considered increasingly precious. Members of my generation, however, gave new definition to the cult of child worship. When I was pregnant, one friend teased me for turning my apartment upside down and buying a king-size bed (big enough for three): "You'd think you were preparing for the arrival of Caesar." After Josh was born, I filled notebooks recording his every wiggle. And my husband insisted on carrying him in a sling on his hip virtually everywhere, including to cocktail parties, where, to everyone's horror, he let him sip beer. Not being able to recall one of my pictures ever gracing my mother's refrigerator door, I later hung his drawings of little people manning complicated machines up and down the hallway. One day, when 4, he smiled indulgently and said, "Mom, you'd think our house was the Metropolitan Museum of Joshua!"

Some parents applaud both the acceleration and involvement of today's children in the real world. A librarian expressed disbelief when a third-grader asked for books on the Holocaust. "We read those books together," his mother, Carol Saper, explains, "and we talk about them. I think it has made my son a more sensitive, caring person."

Nearly all parents, however, feel their best efforts are continually subverted by television. Much of the time, exhausted, overextended parents are caught unawares. "I'm a working mother and I move mountains to organize everything just right—we even manage to eat dinner together, but there's always some crack for the kids to fall through," says Susan Mascitelli, a hospital administrator who has a son, 9, and a daughter, 3. "The kids leave the table early and my husband

and I finally have 10 minutes of peace and then suddenly I hear the kids howling with laughter at "Married with Children," about a couple that hates each other and a child who acts like a hooker. The fact that they even understand this disgusting program stuns me."

Last year, one school on the Upper West Side of Manhattan held parent meetings to discuss a fourth grade whose girls were so sexually precocious that they were hotly pursuing certain boys and refusing to speak to others. "The last straw was when one child invited kids to his home for a dating party when his parents were out," says Ann Beaton, who has children aged 10, 7 and 1. "The kids' parents just delivered them with no questions asked. The girls wore halter tops and tiny bicycle shorts. It's hard to know whether they just wanted to look like Julia Roberts in "Pretty Woman" or whether they knew what they were up to."

Some parents complain that the culture has sexualized children long before they desired it. One third-grader, asked to list questions she had during a sex education course, replied, "Why do we have to know about stuff like this?"

Dr Richard A. Gardner, a child psychiatrist and author who has recently been outspoken in his defense of adults he thinks have been falsely accused of sex abuse, believes that although these crimes do exist, the country is undergoing a wave of sex abuse hysteria: "When I was a child, I had a book about having a fun day with Uncle Ralph. Now, Uncle Ralph is depicted as the kind of guy who, as soon as Mom goes into the kitchen, has his hand in your pants." Gardner says that data show the proliferation of early childhood sex abuse prevention programs are creating confusion and anxiety in youngsters and he predicts those programs will also result in sexual inhibition, mistrust and even long-term sexual dysfunction.

Schools and parents alike have begun taking steps to address these problems. Stephen M. Clement, the headmaster of a boys school in Manhattan, for instance, imposes strict order on the older boys who set standards of behavior for the younger ones: "One of our boys walked in bleeding—he had been mugged for his baseball cap. A school must try to provide a safe haven and some better models."

At Kay Hoffman's school in Rockland, teachers make unilateral decisions for young children so that they will have a good inventory of adult choices on which to base their own decisions later on. "We try to slow children down," Hoffman says. "We don't barrage them all at once. Learning evolves out of their own experience." The school also advises parents to ban television and not to talk about current events. "As soon as I did that, my child began to relax and act like a little girl again," says Candace Stern, whose daughter attends the school. "Her uncle was in Desert Storm and we didn't even tell her he had gone to Jidda until after it was all over. When we finally told her that he had been in a war, she asked, 'What side was he on?'"

Some worry about the repercussions of this generation's having lost its fleeting chance to be a child. "A person who does not have the opportunity to move through the stages of childhood at his own pace ends up with something missing," Jill Comins, a family therapist, says. "As an adult, he will search endlessly for it. He will experience powerful and regressive tugs backward."

Others, however, predict success. "I've been watching these kids grow up, grade by grade," says Gardner P. Dunnan, headmaster of a co-educational school on the Upper East Side. "They have had so much openness, so many opportunities, such a great arena to learn and grow, by the time they are adults they will be wonderful individuals and citizens."

Perhaps our children are simply rebelling against their parents much earlier than we did. And perhaps that means that they won't have to do it later. Perhaps our children will grow up to be the kind of people who wouldn't dream of inventing the motto "Never Trust Anybody Over 30."

"I feel they are in transition," says Sara Lebar, who lives in Greenwich Village. "We changed the rules and we have to expect them to react. I think that the next stage will be that our kids will be our friends, in a way we never were to our parents. Allison may not give me the respect I gave my mother, but I never aspired to be like my parents. And already Allison wants to be an environmentalist just like me.

For those of us who love our wonderful strong-willed children just the way they are—or almost just the way they are—there is a move afoot to readjust certain things ever so slightly. One day not long ago, having asked my own son several times to straighten out his room—which could not be penetrated because of a string that crisscrossed from wall to wall in some obscure scientific experiment—and having received no reply to this apparently trivial request, my voice became significantly louder. He finally looked up. "I'm not comfortable with cleaning out my room right now," he said.

"Get comfortable," I replied.

"Why?" he gazed at me.

"Because," I said, startled, as out of my mouth tumbled words that could have been taken out of a balloon in a comic strip of the 60's, "you are a child and I am the mother. You do not have the right to tell me what to do. On the other hand, I have the right to tell you what to do as long as you live under my roof."

First he gave me a withering look. Then he thought about it for a minute. And then he said "O.K." and headed for his room.

Separation and Divorce: Children Want Their Teachers To Know—

Meeting the Emotional Needs of Preschool and Primary School Children

Barry B. Frieman

Barry B. Frieman, Ed.D., is an associate professor of early childhood education and a teacher trainer at Towson State University in Baltimore. Barry is a licensed clinical social worker in Maryland, helping children and families, and he has worked with children individually and in groups at the Children of Separation and Divorce Center in Columbia, Maryland.

Incidence of divorce

The extent to which divorce touches the lives of preschool and school-age children is pointed out by Strangeland, Pellegreno, and Lundholm's (1989) projections indicating that "in 1990 close to one third of the children in the United States can expect that before their eighteenth birthdays, their parents will be divorced." The sting of divorce affects children whose parents are just separating, as well as those whose parents have been divorced for four or five years. Many couples separate or divorce during their children's first eight years. Often children who were young when their parents divorced only begin to deal with the divorce when they are older and become more skilled in language—when they are in preschool or the primary grades. Children whose

parents have remarried and who end up with stepparents and stepsiblings face another set of issues that merit a discussion of their own in a different article.

The effect of divorce on children

Separation and divorce have a powerful emotional effect on children (Keith & Finlay, 1988; Hetherington, Stanley-Hagan, & Anderson, 1989). Young children often are confused about the state of their parents being separated— the acute process of divorcing— and being legally divorced. For young children both of these states create the same emotional issues because one parent is gone from the home.

Preschool and young elementary school children often bring the extreme feelings that they experience over these major changes in their lives into the classroom or other child care setting—how could they do otherwise? Teachers and other caregivers need to deal with children's feelings of anger, sadness, anxiety, abandonment, loneliness, being out of control, or being overburdened with the prospect of possibly having to take on some of the responsibilities of an absent parent.

Children may act out their feelings concerning separation and divorce in disruptive ways or, alternatively, may become extremely passive and withdrawn. Adults who have an awareness of the kinds of changes that these children are going through can provide a level of support to the children and also prepare themselves to deal with some of the disruptions that could impede the normal flow of group or classroom activity.

Children give clues about what teachers can do

Teachers, child care staff for school-age children, family day care providers, and other significant adults in children's daily lives can get clues about how to help children by listening to the children. During the past few years, I have been working with elementary school children whose families are in the process of separation and divorce. The discussions that occur with these families provide important insights into the children's feelings about their teachers' role in helping them through a trying period in their lives. Although most of the following discussion applies to all adults involved regularly with young chil-

From *Young Children*, Vol. 48, No. 6, September 1993, pp. 58-63. Reprinted by permission of the publisher, the National Association for the Education of Young Children. © 1993 by NAEYC.

Meeting the emotional needs of young children is an integral part of the early childhood educator's job

We teach the whole child and are charged with meeting not only children's cognitive needs but also their emotional, physical, social, and peer needs (Bredekamp, 1987).

Young children's emotional needs are best met through the use of a developmentally appropriate program that provides the teacher with many tools to facilitate emotional growth. Children are given lots of opportunities to express their feelings through

- dramatic play;
- expressive art materials, such as paint and clay;
- music and movement;
- relevant literature; and
- language (pertinent conversation).

Creative teachers can incorporate many of these components, commonly found in kindergarten programs and always recommended in primary-grade curricular materials, into the early grades to help maximize the emotional well-being of children as well as to best meet their cognitive needs (Kostelnik, 1992; Wassermann, 1992).

The early childhood teacher is in the perfect position to help children struggling with divorce and other family problems. Adjustment to a stepfamily, the death of a parent, violent or sexual abuse, or frequent violence in the child's neighborhood present unique problems. Although this article specifically focuses on divorce, the excellent early childhood teacher will recognize many of the techniques noted below as those she or he uses to help all children coping with the problems of life.

Although teachers may learn about a pending separation or divorce from children or parents, often they are only aware of an abrupt change in a child's classroom behavior.

dren, I focus on primary school children and their teachers.

One of the most consistent points that these young school-age children make is that they want their teachers to know about their family's situation. The children believe that they will do better work in school if their teachers understand what is going on in their lives. Children hope that teachers, knowing about the pressures the children are experiencing, will be more tolerant of occasional lapses in their school performance.

Karen, a first grader, illustrates the point when she says, "I'm thinking about the divorce sometimes in school and not doing my work. I don't want my teacher to think that I don't care about my work." Karen is a good student

who wants her teacher to see her distraction as a reflection of her concern about her family's problem rather than as a lack of interest in school. Scott, another first grader, expresses a similar concern, "I want her to know so that when I'm feeling sad, she will know the reason and not yell at me."

Children hope that their teachers will be able to provide them with extra emotional support. Effective teachers have already established a warm, trusting relationship with the children they teach. A child will look toward a trusted teacher in time of need, as six-year-old Anton does when he says, "If I have a problem, I can go to her and she will know what I'm talking about." Likewise, five-year-old Tim says, "I want my teacher

to know because if I get sad, and my teacher knew about the separation, I could talk to her."

Francesca, a first grader, demonstrates the confidence that she has in her teacher when she says, "If I say something weird about the divorce, she would make me talk about it." Francesca trusts that her teacher will hear and help her deal with any fears she has about her parents' divorce.

Finding out about the separation or divorce

Although teachers *may* learn about a pending separation or divorce from children or parents, often they are only aware of an abrupt change in a child's classroom behavior. This sudden change should serve as a red flag to the teacher, suggesting that an inquiry might be in order.

Mike, for example, is a kindergartner who normally separated easily from his parents when he was dropped off in the morning. Suddenly Mr. Bernstein, his teacher, noticed that Mike began to cry when his parent left him at school. Mr. Bernstein took the initiative and called Mike's mother to share his perception of a change in Mike's classroom behavior. This was an important first step for the teacher toward helping the parent identify that her child could be reacting to a home situation in school.

Mr. Bernstein asked Mike's

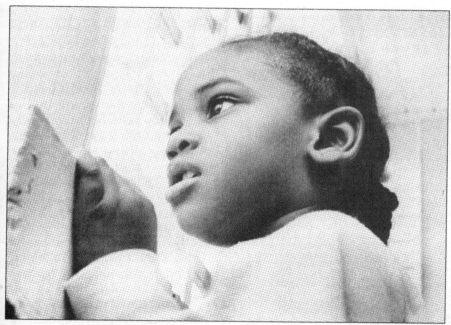

Separation and divorce have a powerful effect on children. Teachers need to acknowledge and deal with children's feelings of anger, sadness, anxiety, abandonment, loneliness, being out of control, or being overburdened with the prospect of possibly having to take on some of the responsibilities of an absent parent.

Teachers also need to be sensitive to the ways in which the child's normal schedule may become disrupted by parental separation or divorce. Home projects, previously carefully done and turned in on time, might suddenly start appearing late because the child stayed with the noncustodial parent in another house, and that parent didn't know about the project. In addition, participating in a home learning project may not be a priority of the noncustodial parent, who is trying to catch up with six days of missed parenting. In these situations the teacher needs to be understanding about why the home project was not done and provide a special time before or after school when she can help the child complete the assignment.

A teacher who is aware of the child's stressful home situation will also be better prepared to monitor and control potentially disruptive behavior in the classroom. Some classroom behavior is unacceptable under any circumstances. Even if a child is experiencing problems related to parental separation or divorce, he or she may not hit or in any way hurt another classmate. The teacher still needs to set appropriate limits and offer a socially acceptable outlet for the child's feelings; for example, a teacher might tell a kindergarten child who just started a fight with another child, "I understand that you are angry about the separation of your parents. It's OK to be angry, but you may not hit

mother, "Is there anything going on in your family that I should be aware of in order to help your son?" The woman was guarded in her response. Parents are often reluctant to discuss family problems with a teacher. In such a situation the teacher needs to reassure parents that the reason he or she wants to know personal family information is in order to better help their child, not to pry into the family's private life.

Why the teacher needs to know

A teacher who is aware of a separation or divorce situation will be able to more accurately assess the involved child's academic performance. Children in these situations will lack concentration at times and will occasionally appear sad. The child who may sometimes seem to be "spaced out" in class might be preoccupied with his family problems (Bisnaire, Firestone, & Rynard, 1990).

Knowing that a child is in the middle of a parental separation or divorce, a teacher can be more accepting of the child's unusual behaviors. The teacher might also be able to regain the child's academic focus by modifying an assignment to concern the issues with which the child is preoccupied. A teacher who notices a child drifting during free-reading time, for instance, can go over to him and say, "Chris I know it's difficult to concentrate when you are concerned about your parents' separation. Instead of reading, why don't you write about how you're feeling in your journal?"

Children believe that they will do better work in school if their teachers understand what is going on in their lives. Children hope that teachers, knowing about the pressures the children are experiencing, will be more tolerant of occasional lapses in their school performance.

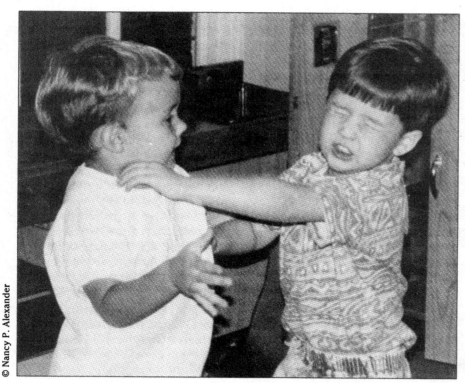

Children may act out their feelings concerning separation and divorce in disruptive ways or, alternatively, may become extremely passive and withdrawn. Adults who have an awareness of the kinds of changes that these children are going through can provide a level of support to the children and also prepare themselves to deal with some of the disruptions that could impede the normal flow of classroom activity.

"What did that make you think about?"

These comments will encourage the child to talk about his or her feelings. Let's say, for example, that a child comes up to the teacher and tells her, "I'm really tired this morning. I couldn't sleep because of all the noise." In this situation the teacher might respond, "Tell me about all the noise, Sally." The teacher's open-ended reply invites Sally to talk about her parents' fighting and how the fighting frightened her.

Once a child begins to open up about her bad feelings, the teacher should not agonize about saying the "right" thing to make it all better. Unfortunately, nothing a teacher can do will delete the child's pain and not one thing she can say will magically alleviate it. The teacher can be most supportive by offering comments, such as

"It's hard isn't it?

"That must have made you feel bad (sad, scared)."

"Could I give you a hug now?"

These comments demonstrate to the child that the teacher cares about her feelings.

Isolated children

Some children have a difficult time expressing their feelings directly, particularly those young children who have isolated them-

another person. If you feel angry, go over and punch the clay or the bag in the corner, or draw an angry picture, or sit by yourself for a few minutes to think and get control; and when you are ready to talk about how you feel, let me know and I will be happy to listen." In this instance the teacher instituted kind, respectful—but firm—limits.

Listening to the child

Children often share important personal information with their teachers, sometimes in an indirect manner. One of the teacher's most valuable tools in being supportive is letting the young child know that his teacher is willing to listen. Conversational techniques can be helpful in getting a child to share what is on his mind. Once the child provides an opening, the teacher needs to reply in a way

that shows the child that the teacher cares and is willing to listen. The teacher can make comments, such as

"Tell me about how you are feeling right now."

"Tell me about it."

"That must have been difficult for you."

"How did that make you feel?"

Young children's emotional needs are best met through the use of a developmentally appropriate program that provides the teacher with tools to facilitate emotional growth. Among these tools are empathetic listening, expressive art materials, unit blocks, music and movement activities, relevant books and connected conversation, time to play, and time for friendships.

selves from their friends. These children can be reached through developmentally appropriate materials for young children, such as clay, water, paint, crayons, puppets, books, and housekeeping props.

Teachers can encourage children at the easel to paint a picture about their family. Angry children can be given clay to pound and shape, and water to manipulate.

Rhonda was an angry, isolated four-year-old who seemed to be having problems coping. Her teacher, Ms. Mindel, was having a difficult time reaching her through art or housekeeping play materials. Noticing Rhonda sitting alone during playtime, Ms. Mindel picked up a tiger puppet and approached her.

Although Rhonda would not talk to her teachers or any of the other children in the class, she was quick to talk to the tiger puppet on Ms. Mindel's hand. The tiger learned that Rhonda was extremely angry at her mother for leaving the house. Through the puppet Ms. Mindel was able to

help Rhonda understand that she was not bad if she was angry at her mother. Ms. Mindel used the tiger to help Rhonda practice talking to her mother about how she felt.

Classroom activities

By providing activities in which children can play out their concerns, the teacher can help them express their feelings. Unfortunately many children in the early grades are not given the chance to play; this is all too true in many preschools, too. Dress-up materials, readily accessible art supplies, music experiences, and movement activities are often not included, as they should be, as an integral part of a developmentally appropriate program.

Teachers in the primary grades, working in developmentally *in*appropriate systems, can strive to weave more creative art, music, and movement experiences into their classroom day. If this is not possible, primary teachers can

borrow materials from kindergarten teachers and provide them for use during breaks in the day or during recess and lunch.

Teachers' limits

Teachers cannot solve the problems of children experiencing parental divorce, but they *can* help children cope. Many children whose families are involved in the divorce process are concerned about abandonment. As caring teachers, we may want to reassure children that no matter what happens, we will always be there for them, but unfortunately this is a promise that we often cannot keep. One of the consequences of divorce is that parents frequently sell the family home or move into different living quarters, which sometimes necessitates a shift to another school for the child. The teacher can, however, work to make sure that the current school situation is stable and predictable.

During divorce, children sometimes experience a feeling of loss of control. Their world is turned upside-down and is often changing quite rapidly. The teacher can be helpful in this regard by being consistent, particularly in setting limits, and by offering many choices of worthwhile activities so that the child *does* have opportunities to be in control.

Children of divorce are often dragged into the struggle between their parents. Tommy, an eight-year-old, was concerned because his father was depressed. He didn't want to leave his father because, "Dad will become lonely and get sad again and cry." Therapeutic intervention outside the school was aimed at helping Tommy's parents keep him out of the conflict, but the teacher also was able to help. The teacher gave Tommy the time he needed to be an eight-year-old and to play unencumbered by his parents' problems. A daily playtime, even

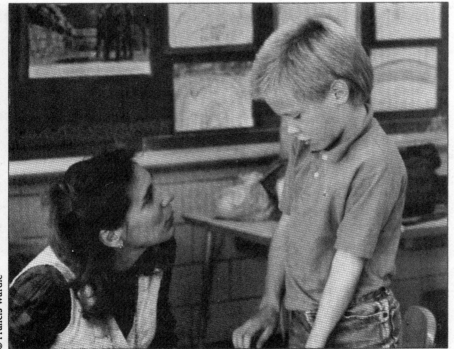

One of the teacher's most valuable tools in being supportive is letting the young child know that his teacher is willing to listen.

in the primary grades, is an essential part of a developmentally appropriate curriculum for this and many other reasons.

Helping parents

Relating to parents who are not on good terms with each other can be difficult. To be effective in supporting a child in a separation or divorce situation, the teacher must make an effort to communicate with both parents, not just the custodial parent.

Both parents are important people in the child's life, and, as such, both play an important role in shaping the child's behavior. If a teacher requires that a parent set limits for the child at home, she should send a note to each parent, not just one.

The teacher must also avoid getting herself involved in the parents' dispute. If a parent tries to include the teacher in the ongoing conflict, the teacher should refer the parent to the appropriate community social service or mental health agency that specializes in counseling services. The teacher can tell the parents that for her to be of help to their child, she needs to stay out of the parental dispute. She can assure both parents that she will work to be their child's advocate, report individually to both of them, and stay neutral.

Summary

Through understanding and the use of selected communication skills, teachers can learn to im-prove the academic performance and facilitate the emotional well-being of the children in their classes. In this way teachers help children cope with the powerful emotions experienced during the separation or divorce process.

References

Bisnaire, L.M.C., Firestone, P., & Rynard, D. (1990). Factors associated with academic achievement in children following parental separation. *American Journal of Orthopsychiatry, 60*(1), 67–76.

Bredekamp, S. (Ed.). (1987). *Developmentally appropriate practice in early childhood programs serving children from birth through age 8* (exp. ed.). Washington, DC: NAEYC.

Hetherington, E.M., Stanley-Hagan, M., & Anderson, E.R. (1989). Marital transitions: A child's perspective. *American Psychologist, 44*(4), 303–312.

Keith, V.M., & Finlay, B. (1988). The impact of parental divorce on children's educational attainment, marital timing, and likelihood of divorce. *Journal of Marriage and the Family, 50*(4), 798–809.

Kostelnik, M.J. (1992). Myths associated with developmentally appropriate programs. *Young Children, 47*(4), 17–23.

Strangeland, C.S., Pellegreno, D.C., & Lundholm, J. (1989). Children of divorced parents: A perceptual comparison. *Elementary School Guidance & Counseling, 23*(2), 167–174.

Wassermann, S. (1992). Serious plan in the classroom. *Childhood Education, 68*(3), 133–139.

Helpful books for parents

Children of Separation and Divorce Center. (1987). *Talking to children about separation and divorce: A handbook for parents.* Columbia, MD: Author.

Gardner, R. (1970). *The boys and girls book about divorce.* New York: Bantam.

Gardner, R. (1977). *The parents book about divorce.* New York: Bantam.

Grollman, E. (1969). *Explaining divorce to children.* Boston: Beacon Press.

Books for young children

Brown, M. (1986). *Dinosaur's divorce.* New York: Little, Brown.

Caines, J. (1977). *Daddy.* New York: HarperCollins.

Clifton, L. (1974). *Everett Anderson's year.* New York: Holt, Rinehart & Winston.

Hazen, B.S. (1978). *Two homes to live in: A child's eye view of divorce.* New York: Human Sciences Press.

Helmering, D.W. (1981). *I have two families.* Nashville, TN: Abington.

LeShan, E. (1978). *What's going to happen to me?* New York: Four Winds Press.

Mayle, P. (1988). *Divorce can happen to the nicest people.* New York: Harmony.

Mayle, P. (1988). *Why are we getting a divorce?* New York: Harmony.

Sharmat, M. (1980). *Sometimes mama and papa fight.* New York: HarperCollins.

Zolotow, C. (1971). *A father like that.* New York: HarperCollins.

For further reading

Caughey, C. (1991). Becoming the child's ally—Observations in a classroom for children who have been abused. *Young Children, 46*(4), 22–28.

Feeney, S. (1988). Ethics case studies: The divorced parents. *Young Children, 43*(3), 48–51.

Greenberg, P. (1988). Ideas that work with young children. Discipline: Are tantrums normal? *Young Children, 43*(6), 35–40.

Honig, A.S. (1986). Research in review. Stress and coping in children (Part 1). *Young Children, 41*(4), 50–63.

Honig, A.S. (1986). Research in review. Stress and coping in children (Part 2)—Interpersonal family relationships. *Young Children, 41*(5), 47–59.

McCracken, J.B. (Ed.). (1986). *Reducing stress in young children's lives.* Washington, DC: NAEYC.

Morgan, E.L. (1989). Talking with parents when concerns come up. *Young Children, 44*(2), 52–56.

Wallach, L.B. (1993). Helping children cope with violence. *Young Children, 48*(4), 4–11.

"Don't Leave Me":

Separation Distress in Infants, Toddlers, and Parents

Susan is ten months old. Her mother carries her into the child care center and sits her on the floor while she unpacks the diaper bag. Susan plays happily while her mother is in the room. When her mother tells her good-bye, Susan screams and crawls to the door after her.

Lisa J. Godwin
Melissa M. Groves
Diane M. Horm-Wingerd

Lisa J. Godwin lives in Charlotte, NC. Melissa M. Groves is Assistant Professor, Child Development/Family Relations Program, Indiana University of Pennsylvania. Diane M. Horm-Wingerd is Assistant Professor, Department of Human Development, University of Rhode Island.

Julio has been enrolled in family day care since he was six weeks old. At seventeen months of age, he has never shown any sign of separation distress. His parents separated, and Julio began to cling and cry every morning when dropped off.

Priya is seven weeks old. Her father calls the child care center five or six times each day to check on her.

These scenes, witnessed by the authors during a single week at one child care center, are familiar to child care providers. Although they are common, separations are confusing and painful to watch (Jervis, 1989). Separation and the distress that often accompanies it have most commonly been studied as characteristics of a child's attachment to his or her mother

(McBride & DiCero, 1991). The emphasis has typically been placed on the child's experiences and reactions during the separation process (McBride & DiCero, 1991). However, as astute caregivers know, parents (maybe more than children) have anxiety about separating (Jervis, 1989). This anxiety is logical and even desirable, as it shows concern about the child's welfare and interest in the child care experience. Yet little attention has focused on separation from the parents' perspective (McBride & DiCero, 1991). The separation distress experienced by infants, toddlers, and parents and the ways of alleviating the distress in both parents and children are the focus of this article.

What Is Separation Distress?

An understanding of the theory and pattern of separation reactions can assist caregivers in their work with parents and children. The first important step is recognizing that the anxiety or distress is real (Gellens, undated), and that it is part of normal parent-child relationships.

As stated previously, separation distress or anxiety has most often been studied in terms of a child's attachment to his or her mother. *Attachment* is the term used by Bowlby (1969/1982, 1973, 1980) and other theorists (e.g., Ainsworth, 1973) to describe the special emotional bond or relationship that develops between parents and their children. It is basic to human nature to form such attachments and to respond with anxiety, sadness, or anger to a separation from an attachment figure; this is termed *separation distress* or *anxiety* (Jervis, 1989). We may intuitively adopt a "deficit model," which implies that something is wrong with the parent or child who clings or cries (Jervis, 1989). However, separation reactions are clear indicators of the attachment relationship (Moore, 1987). Since separation reactions are a part of normal, healthy attachment relationships, the absence of a reaction in a parent or a child may be cause for concern in that it may signal an unhealthy or insecure parent-child relationship. Research has documented that early healthy attachment relationships are related to higher levels of later mastery motivation, cognitive development, problem solving, positive affect, and positive social relations (Bretherton, 1985). Thus, it is important for caregivers to understand and facilitate all aspects of healthy parent-child attachments.

How Do Children Display Distress?

Bowlby thought of attachment, like any relationship, as a gradual process that occurs over the first year of life, blossoming near the end of the first year and intensifying up to about eighteen months (Moore, 1987). Research has documented a predictable developmental progression of separation responses which are related to a child's level of cognitive development (McBride & DiCero, 1991).

Infants under seven months of age rarely show any signs of separation distress. Young infants (under three months) do not distinguish between themselves and the parents and therefore do not feel any anxiety at separating, as long as their needs are met by the child care providers (McBride & DiCero, 1991). Between three and seven months of age, the child may begin to show some wariness of strangers, based on the comparison he or she is making between the faces of familiar and strange individuals. However, the recognition of strangers is not always translated into distress at separation, particularly when the caregiver is familiar (Kagan, 1984; McBride & DiCero, 1991). The absence of overt displays of separation distress does not mean that the optimal time to place infants in a child care setting is before seven months of age. These early months are important for both child and parent in developing secure attachments.

Starting around seven months of age, obvious distress is often seen in infants at separation. As the child is developing person permanence, he or she is unhappy with the knowledge that the parent is leaving or is not present. Wariness of strangers, or stranger anxiety, also becomes more intense at eight or nine months of age.

These developments may lead to intense separation experiences for many seven- to twelve-month-old infants and their parents. After twelve months of age, the distress may not be experienced as strongly, as the child becomes more adept at holding the image of the parent in memory and in using this mental image to sooth and comfort himself or herself (Kagan, 1984). However, the ability to hold and use these mental images varies, and the lack of overt protest does not mean that distress is absent. In fact, prolonged separation may be associated with the continuation of overt distress behaviors in children twelve months or older (Maher, Pine, & Bergman, 1975).

Distress and protests may reappear in toddlers eighteen to twenty-four months old. Earlier wariness reemerges for some children during this age span as they become more aware of the nature of the relationship with the parents, and as they increasingly separate from the parents and gain independence (Malhler et al., 1975). These older infants are dealing with both the cognitive and the emotional demands of separation from the attachment figure, and they often respond with distress during periods of separation (Balaban, 1985).

Although separation has been found to occur cross-culturally and to be age-related, it is important to note that not all children openly exhibit signs of distress (McBride & DiCero, 1991). Additionally, those children who demonstrate separation distress display a range of reactions (McBride & DiCero, 1991). Some children cry and cling; others withdraw. Other signs are the appearance of repetitive habits ("tics") and physical symptoms such as diarrhea, disturbances in sleep patterns, disruptions in eating habits, and listlessness or inactivity (Staff, 1989). Some children display regressive behavior or misbehavior at home or school (Staff, 1989). Other children display their anxiety in more subtle ways, such as through symbolic play, conversations with peers or caregivers, or the use of transitional objects (i.e., a blanket) (Gottschall,

1989). At every age, illness, fatigue, hunger, strange situations, and other stressors intensify the child's reactions (Bretherton, 1985). While loud protests typically prompt immediate responses, caregivers must be attentive and sensitive to the subtle ways children communicate that they are uncomfortable or unhappy. It is important for caregivers to recognize and appropriately respond to this vast array of reactions in children.

What Are Parents' Reactions?

Parents also experience separation anxiety, which has been defined as the unpleasant emotional state which accompanies separation from the child (Hock, 1984). Research supports the notion that mothers experience separation distress. Although it has not been documented in the literature, discussions with and observations of fathers indicate that they, too, experience separation anxiety or distress (McBride & DiCero, 1991). The experience includes feelings of worry, sadness, and guilt (Hock, McBride, & Gnezda, 1989). Parental separation anxiety may be exhibited at departure by attempts to delay leaving and through extensive questioning about the caregiver's competence. At reunion, anxiety may be expressed by picking up and soothing a child who is obviously content or by verbal expressions of worry made to the child (Hock et al., 1989). Other behaviors include repeated calling or visiting during the day, expressing feelings of inadequacy or jealousy, and feeling competition with the caregiver for the child's love and affection. Some parents may appear unconcerned about leaving their child in care. It is important to recognize that all these parental behaviors are common reactions to the separation experience.

How Can We Help Children?

There are many strategies that caregivers can use to ease the stress of separation for children. These strategies include implementing helpful school policies, adopting specific behaviors during separation episodes, and meeting children's developmental needs.

Policies concerning initial entrance into the child care setting can do much to alleviate a child's distress at separation. Experts agree that children should be allowed gradual entrance into a new setting. Children need time to become comfortable with new people and routines before being left for long periods of time. These suggestions have proved helpful:

Home visits by the new caregiver can serve as the beginning of the child's gradual entrance into the child care setting. Home visits present the caregiver to the child in a familiar and safe setting and additionally provide the caregiver with valuable insights into the child's home life (Gestwicki, 1987).

Visits of the child and the parent to the child care setting in advance of the actual enrollment also increase feelings of comfort and familiarity for the child as well as for the parent (Jervis, 1987).

On the first day of actual enrollment, parents should stay until the child becomes comfortable in the setting. Even parents of very young children should stay for some time so that they can get a feel of what the child's day will be like. No guidelines exist regarding the minimal or optimal amount of time that parents of newly enrolled children should spend to help with adjustment to the setting. For some, less than a day is sufficient; for others, longer periods of time may be needed. While the insistence that a parent stay with the child during an adjustment period may be difficult for the parent because of employer or other demands, it is critical in order to establish a good beginning for the child (Staff, 1989).

A final policy concerns how children are left at child care. Preparation for separations is essential for fostering trust in the child. Even infants should be informed in very simple terms about when and why the parent is leaving, and about when he or she will return (Gonzalez-Mena & Eyer,

Subjects & Predicates

1989). Parents should never be allowed to "sneak away" in an attempt to avoid distress, as this will decrease trust and increase anxiety for the child (Balaban, 1985). Parents should always walk into the setting, help the child put away his or her things, see that the child is settled, and then say good-bye. It is essential in establishing trust in the caregiver that parents accompany their child into the room, not just to the front door (Gestwicki, 1987). A goodbye ritual generally proves helpful (e.g., read one story, then wave goodbye at the door). After the initial adjustment to the child care setting, parents should depart immediately after saying good-bye; lingering too long may contribute to distress.

Specific caregiver behaviors have been shown to help alleviate separation distress:

First and foremost, caregivers can assist during the separation experience by providing a consistent, secure environment. Consistency in caregivers, routines, and environments are critical if the child is to come to trust that the parent will return (McBride & DiCero, 1991).

Arrival times are crucial times. Greet each child individually and acknowledge that child personally.

Acknowledge and accept children's feelings, which may range from mild anxiety to severe sadness or anger (Gonzalez-Mena & Eyer, 1989). Caregivers need to let children know that it is acceptable for them to miss someone they love. By being honest, stating the facts, and verbalizing emotions, caregivers can help to reassure the child and extend the child's understanding (Gonzalez-Mena & Eyer, 1989).

If the child becomes upset during the day and misses his or her parent, reassure him or her that the parent will be back. Specify the time in language that the child can understand (e.g., "Your dad will pick you up after snack").

Deal with each situation with an appropriate degree of seriousness. Remember, the distress is real, and it should not be denied or used as a basis of ridicule. In responses to children, balance concern with confidence that the parent will return (Gonzalez-Mena & Eyer, 1989).

Allow children different ways of being and feeling comforted (Gonzalez-Mena & Eyer, 1989). Some may want to bring an object or wear an item from home in order to have a visual link with home and/or parents. Other children find comfort in an attachment object, such as a security blanket or a stuffed animal (Jalongo, 1987). It is appropriate to allow the child to use such objects to help alleviate distress (Bredekamp, 1987).

Other key issues and strategies for alleviating children's distress are specifically based on age:

For the child under seven months, the most crucial issue is helping the parents feel comfortable. The more comfortable the parent feels about the caregiver and the setting, the less likely he or she is to feel greatly distressed over leaving the child. Even young children sense parents' distress and anxiety and respond accordingly.

For the child who is seven to eighteen months of age, it may be helpful to take a cautious method of approach. These older infants may be experiencing stranger or separation anxiety, and they may be wary of new people and situations. Caregivers should greet the child warmly, but from a distance if necessary. Caregivers should be sensitive to the children's cues; some prefer not to be picked up, while others need to be held (McBride & DiCero, 1991). Transitional objects from home and the establishment of good-bye routines become useful at this stage.

Symbolic play, such as hide-and-seek and books that deal with the separation experience, such as *The Runaway Bunny* by M. W. Brown (1942), *You Go Away* by D. Corey (1976), or *Are You My Mother?* by P. D. Eastman (1960), can be helpful with toddlers between eighteen and twenty-four months of age. Establishing more concrete links with home, such as photographs displayed at the child care setting, can also be used effectively with toddlers.

How Can We Help Parents?

For both parents who are showing signs of distress or uneasiness at separation from their child and those parents who are not, caregivers need to step in and assist them in feeling more comfortable. The following strategies may help:

Parents must feel comfortable about the setting. Just because they have chosen a setting does not mean that they will feel totally at ease in leaving their child. Like the child, the parent needs time to get to know the policies, routines, caregivers, and other aspects of the setting. The gradual entrance policy suggested earlier will be as helpful to the parents as to the child.

Parents must feel welcomed. They must feel that their presence in the setting is not an intrusion, and that their child is welcomed and valued. Warm greetings, invitations to come in and participate, and genuine interest in the family's overall welfare should be directed to both parent and child.

Effective communication is essential. Parents should be informed about all events, activities, and concerns affecting their child. Frequent phone calls, letters, and face-to-face communication should be initiated by the caregiver. At child care centers, hav-

ing extra staff on hand during arrival and departure times allows teachers the opportunity to communicate with parents. Parents should also be encouraged to contact the caregivers with concerns as well as positive news and comments (Gestwicki, 1987).

Parents need reassurance that the feelings, both their's and their child's, are normal. They may feel somewhat foolish about feeling guilty or sad about leaving their child, or they may feel that their child is unusual in exhibiting (or *not* exhibiting) signs of distress. Providing information about developmental milestones may prove helpful, as may encouraging interactions between parents who are experiencing distress and those who have previously faced similar concerns.

A strong sense of trust between parent and caregiver must be built. Being honest with parents, providing open communication, showing empathy to parent and child, meeting the needs of the child, and demonstrating genuine interest in the child and the family will all lead to a trusting relationship. Caregivers should avoid making judgmental or negative statements about parents to other caregivers or parents; comments are easily overheard and will quickly destroy any trust.

Help the parents know what to expect from their child during separations. Discuss the developmental changes occurring in the child, and help the parents to understand the implications of these changes in their child's behavior. Explain the importance of consistency and the effects of inconsistency (i.e, increased anxiety and confusion).

Reduce feelings of jealousy and competition between parents and caregivers (McBride & DiCero, 1991). Reinforce the notion that children have a primary attachment to their parents, and that this attachment allows the child to become attached to others. Reassure the parents of the child's feelings and need for them. Seek the parents' advice regarding the behaviors and care of the child. Avoid sending messages that you know the

---

Phrases that Reassure Parents

"She doesn't cry when you leave because she's too little to remember that people exist when she can't see them. I can tell that you're special to her, though, by the way she responds to your voice and the way she smiles when she sees you."

"I know it's hard on you now that she has started to cry when you leave. Does it help to know that she has started doing this because she is achieving new concepts nd starting to remember more?"

"He's adjusting well because he trusts you, and he can tell that you feel good about leaving him here with us."

"The reason she has been able to become attached to us is that she has such a secure attachment to you. You've taught her to trust others to take good care of her."

"He doesn't cry when you leave because he feels secure that you will come back for him."

"She cries when she sees you because you are so comforting. She can be herself and 'let go' with you."

"He is crying because he knows he'll miss you. He usually calms down very quickly, because he knows that you'll come back for him."

"She may not want to tell you good-bye because it's hard for her to let you leave. Some children handle their sad feelings by clinging or crying; other show their emotions very differently."

"Some children don't cry when they first start a new program because it is still new, different, and challenging for them. It may be difficult in a few days or weeks when the novelty wears off."

"I know it's difficult for you to leave on mornings like this when he is having a hard time separating. Toddlers [or two-year-olds] aren't very consistent. That's one of the reasons it is so important for us to be consistent with them."

child better than the parent does. Do not allow situations that force the child to choose between the caregiver and the parent, and do not compete with the parent for the child's attention or affection.

Reassure parents who may be feeling unloved, overly missed, or guilty. The inset lists several phrases which serve to reassure parents.

Help the parents to help their child adjust. Remind them that the child is perceptive of their feelings and behaviors. Facilitate leave-taking and reunion routines by being sensitive to parents' spoken and unspoken requests for help.

Helping Susan, Julio, and Priya

Susan is at a difficult age. She is at the point where she is most likely to exhibit signs of distress to strangers and at separation. Susan's mother may need some help in understanding Susan's developmental needs. This is a good time to start implementing departure routines such as reading one book and waving good-bye at the window. The caregiver can help by encouraging Susan to become involved in the activities in the room and should be careful to respond to Susan's preference for being held or having interaction occur from a distance.

Julio has been experiencing many changes in his life and is probably feeling stressed, as are his parents. Because there have been so many changes, consistency in routines is even more important now. If no good-bye routine exists, one should be developed. Providing pictures of both Mom and Dad may help reassure him. In addition to the changes in his life, Julio is experiencing some developmental changes. Mom and Dad may feel reassured that not all of the changes in Julio's behavior can be attributed to the marital separation.

Priya's dad is obviously feeling some anxiety about leaving his newborn. Though Priya is not likely to exhibit any signs of distress, her dad needs some reassurance. Providing ample information about Priya's daily routine, frequent contact with the caregiver, and reassurance that the parents are still the primary figures in Priya's life may alleviate some of the anxiety. Also, patience with the phone calls is needed until the father develops a sense of trust in the caregivers.

In every case, it is important to view separation as a process rather than a problem (Leipzig, 1989). Because they are an important developmental process, we want to support and facilitate separations and the associated experiences of parents and children rather than squelch the distress. Separation distress is never completely overcome, nor should it be. With special attention, however, it can be less stressful for children, parents, and caregivers.

This manuscript is based on material presented by the authors at the 1991 Annual Conference, Southern Association on Children Under Six, in Atlanta, GA.

References

Ainsworth, M. D. S. "The Development of Infant-Mother Attachment." In B. M. Caldwell & H. N. Ricciuti (Eds.), *Review of Child Development Research*, Vol. 3, pp. 1-94. Chicago: University of Chicago Press, 1973.

Balaban, N. *Starting School: From Separation to Independence (A Guide for Early Childhood Teachers)*. New York: Teachers College Press, 1985.

Bowlby, J. *Attachment and Loss: Vol. 1. Attachment*. New York: Basic, 1969/1982.

Bowlby, J. *Attachment and Loss: Vol. 2. Separation*. New York: Basic, 1973.

Bowlby, J. *Attachment and Loss: Vol. 3. Loss, Sadness and Depression*. New York: Basic, 1980.

Bredekamp, S. (Ed.) *Developmentally Appropriate Practice in Early Childhood Programs Serving Children from Birth through Age 8*. Washington, DC: NAEYC, 1987.

Bretherton, I. "Attachment Theory: Retrospect and Prospect." In I. Bretherton & E. Waters (Eds.), "Growing Points of Attachment Theory and Research" (pp. 3-35). *Monographs of the Society for Research in Child Development*, 1985, 50 (1-2, Serial No. 209).

Brown, M. W. *The Runaway Bunny*. New York: Harper & Row, 1942.

Corey, D. *You Go Away*. Chicago: Whitman, 1976.

Eastman, P. D. *Are You My Mother?* New York: Random House, 1960.

Gellens, S. *Considering Separation Problems*. (Information from the Southern Association on Children under Six). Little Rock, AR: SACUS, undated.

Gestwicki, C. *Home, School, and Community Relations: A Guide to Working with Parents*. Albany, NY: Delmar, 1987.

Gonzalez-Mena, J., & Eyer, D. W. *Infants, Toddlers, and Caregivers*. Mountain View, CA: Mayfield, 1989.

Gottschall, S. "Understanding and Accepting Separation Feelings." *Young Children*, 1989, 44 (6), pp. 11-16.

Hock, E. "The Transition to Day Care: Effects of Maternal Separation Anxiety on Infant Adjustment." In R. C. Ainslie (Ed.), *The Child in the Day Care Setting*. New York: Praeger, 1984.

Hock, E., McBride, S., & Gnezda, T. "Maternal Separation Anxiety: Mother-Infant Separation from the Maternal Perspective." *Child Development*, 60, 1989, pp. 793-802.

Jalongo, M. R. Do security blankets belong in preschool? *Young Children*, 1987, 42 (3), pp. 3-8.

Jervis, K. *Separation*. Washington, DC: NAEYC, 1989.

Kagan, J. *The nature of the child*. New York: Basic, 1984.

Leipzig, J. "Making Sense of Separation." *Day Care and Early Education*, 1989, 17 (2), pp. 39-40.

Mahler, M., Pine, R., & Bergman, A. *The Psychological Birth of the Human Infant*. New York: Basic, 1975.

McBride, S. L., & DiCero, K. "Separation: Maternal and Child Perspectives." In N. Lauter-Klatell (Ed.), *Readings in Child Development*, pp. 62-66. Mountain View, CA: Mayfield, 1991.

Moore, S. G. *Social Development of the Young Child: Two Theories, Two Stories*. ERIC Document Reproduction Services No. ED 297 875, 1987.

Staff. "Early Separation: Working with Parents as a Team" (Interview with Alice Honig). *Scholastic Pre-K Today*, August-September, 1989, pp. 46-49, 63.

Beyond Parents: Family, Community, and School Involvement

Teachers and administrators are not adequately prepared to address the range of children's social and psychological needs. They know what ought to be done, but not how to do it. Fortunately, as the authors point out, there are others who can help.

Patricia A. Edwards and Lauren S. Jones Young

Patricia A. Edwards and Lauren S. Jones Young are associate professors of education at Michigan State University, East Lansing.

A child lives in many worlds. Home, family, school, neighborhood, and society shape the contours of childhood and adolescence. Action in one sphere ripples through the others. In the best of circumstances, these realms are complementary and reinforcing—guiding children's positive development into informed citizens and economically independent adults. The best of circumstances, however, elude large numbers of children, especially poor children of color who live in the inner city.

Recent hopes for successfully launching U.S. children into the 21st century have been pinned on reclaiming a part of our past—the involvement of parents as partners in the education of their children. The importance of parent involvement in children's schooling has been a persistent theme in the research and school reform efforts of the last three decades.[1] Studies point to higher student achievement when parents participate in school activities, monitor children's homework, and otherwise support the extension into the home of the work and values of the school.[2]

Family/school involvement is a two-way street. Children are more likely to make smooth transitions between home and school when they see aspects of themselves and their experiences reflected in the adults who teach them. Parent voices can strengthen the school program

and mediate tensions between school and community; open exchanges hold the possibility of aligning the expectations of schools and families. Many of us who grew up in stable, close-knit neighborhoods knew that many eyes—including those of our teachers—watched us and would tell our mamas when we misbehaved.

In the past, neighbors, teachers, and parents spoke in a common voice. James Comer, a professor of child psychiatry at Yale University, likes to tell a childhood story about how his mother and his teacher would meet at the local A & P. They would talk about his progress and behavior in school, sharing and reinforcing family and school values. He comments: "When schools were an integral part of stable communities, teachers quite naturally reinforced parental and community values. At school, children easily formed bonds with adults and experienced a sense of continuity and stability, conditions that were highly conducive to learning."[3] For many children today, those kinds of communities and the ready support of nearby relatives and friends have vanished.

That parents no longer run into their children's teachers at the local grocery store says much about the changes that have taken place in poor urban neighborhoods and in growing numbers of poor rural communities. Teachers—black or white—rarely live in the same economically depressed neighborhoods as the children they teach. Many middle-income and working-class African-American families have also moved out, assisted in large part by eased racial restrictions in housing.[4] Gone too are many of the businesses and social institutions—the foundation and vitality of community life—that these families supported.

At the same time, transformations in the urban economy have limited the kinds of jobs available to high

From *Phi Delta Kappan*, May 1992, pp. 72, 74, 76, 78, 80. Reprinted by permission of the authors and *Phi Delta Kappan*.

school graduates and dropouts. While it was once possible to find good-paying jobs in automobile, steel, and other kinds of heavy manufacturing, the kinds of jobs available in the inner city today pay wages that fail to keep pace with the costs of raising a family. In the inner cities, those with little economic security are concentrated in the same areas, living with the daily stresses that accompany economic hardship and desolate neighborhoods.

Once the norm, the married-couple household, with father employed and mother at home caring for the children, is a disappearing pattern. Economic concerns drive mothers to work long hours outside the home. The number of children affected by unwed parents, divorce, and separation continues to rise. From 1970 to 1989 the proportion of children living with one parent jumped from 12% to 24%, and many of them were living with mothers struggling to make ends meet.[5] At any given time, one-fourth of American children live with one parent, usually a divorced or never-married mother; among African-American and Latino children, that figure skyrockets to 55% and 30% respectively.[6]

Adults other than a child's parents are taking on significant child-rearing roles. While the extended family's involvement in child rearing is not new among African-Americans, for example, the scope of that involvement is growing. Parents who thought that their child-rearing days were over are increasingly raising their grandchildren. In the last 20 years, the percentage of black children being raised by a grandparent has risen from 3.2% to 12.5% (or one in eight).[7] Households with children under 18 years of age now commonly include foster parents, extended families, children living with other relatives, adoptive parents, or reconstituted and blended families.

One of every five children in the U.S. lives in a family whose income is below—often far below—the poverty level; that rate doubles among blacks and Latinos.[8] While poverty levels rise and fall, children remain the most impoverished age group, and obstacles to their well-being continue to mount. The realities of impoverishment should horrify a wealthy nation, but we shut our eyes to the social context of childhood in the inner city. Poverty brings a host of risk factors in addition to empty pockets. Lack of immunizations and health care, poor nutrition, inadequate housing, homelessness, acquired immunodeficiency syndrome (AIDS), substance abuse, and violence become regular features of poor children's lives. The crack-cocaine epidemic is touching every corner of low-income urban African-American communities, manifesting itself in babies exposed prenatally to drugs, mothers too strung-out to see to the needs of their children, and neighborhoods under siege. The problems are complex and interrelated, but together they undermine the strength and frustrate the efforts of poor families and their communities.

The resilience of families is impressive. Contrary to popular images—and irrespective of family structure—most families today are not in disarray and are not failing to meet their child-rearing responsibilities.[9] It is necessary to sort out the group called "parents," noting the range in their experiences, in their relationships with their children, and in their feelings about school. Some have a high regard for education; for others, their children's schooling is a relived struggle amid more pressing concerns. The goals and values of individual families will vary and may differ from those of the teacher and the school. It is this individuality that parents bring to parent involvement efforts. Yet too often parent involvement strategies are developed as if these important variations did not exist, and the results are disappointing. Until schools acknowledge the range in dispositions, backgrounds, experiences, and strengths among families, efforts to establish sound home/school communication and partnerships will continue to falter.

JUSTIFYING FAILURE

Students' home lives are both blamed for children's low achievement in school and seen as children's salvation.[10] In growing numbers of communities the significant adults and institutions in children's lives pull in opposite directions.

As the two major institutions that socialize children, families and schools share a long history—often one of tension and mistrust.[11] While most schoolpeople stress the importance of parents as their children's first and primary teachers, in reality large numbers of parents are excluded from routine exchanges with schools. Meetings scheduled during working hours, few communications to parents from school, few opportunities to observe in classes, and a variety of other factors make parents feel unwelcome and uncomfortable in their relations with schools.

Just as most schools have not yet figured out how to facilitate strong parent involvement, neither have they adjusted well to new family and community realities. Teachers are among the first to witness the human costs of society's wider failures, but, while cognizant of those changes in their classrooms, they and other educators have been slow to question the "one style fits all" pattern of home/school practices.[12] Family/school practices are steeped in assumptions about childhood, family, community, and school roles. When conceptions of what should be don't mesh with what is, educators often attribute that failure to parents' irresponsibility, lack of interest in their children, and lack of skills.[13] Tensions rise, and blame is volleyed back and forth between school and home. An example from a rural southern school illustrates this point.

Donaldsonville Elementary School had been recognized for its "good curriculum," even though teachers were disappointed with the progress of their students. Eighty percent of the student population were African-American children, and 20% were white children; most were members of low-income families. Teachers felt that they were doing all they could to help these children at school. Without parental assistance at home, the children at Donaldsonville were going to fail. The teachers' solution was to expect and demand that parents be involved in their children's education by reading to them at home.

To the teachers this was not an unreasonable request. There is good evidence of positive gains made by "disadvantaged" elementary students when parents and children work together at home on homework and learning packets.[14] What the teachers did not take into account was that 40% of the school's parents were illiterate or semi-literate. When the parents didn't seem willing to do as the teachers asked, teachers mistook parents' unfamiliarity with the task being asked of them, coupled with low literacy skills, for lack of interest in their children's education. The continued demand that parents read to their children at home, which had a particular meaning in teachers' minds, sparked hostility and racial tensions between teachers and parents. Each group blamed the other for the children's failures; each felt victimized by the interaction. Children were caught between their two most important teachers—their classroom teacher and their parent.

The principal and the teachers recognized that they had to mend the serious rift between them and the parents. The principal stated that she wanted to "unite the home, school, and community." Creating a process for parents to become integral and confident partners in their children's schooling was the first step. But how to begin? Should the process be expected to emerge from traditional—and failed—interactions between home and school? Five other cases will allow us to explore this matter further.

Case #1: The drug bust. A first-grade student was absent for 16 consecutive days. The student's concerned teacher did what most teachers would do: she attempted to contact the child's parent. She sent several letters home and telephoned the parent, but the number was no longer a working one. The teacher even called one of the parent's neighbors to inquire if the neighbor would inform the parent of the need to arrange a conference. None of these efforts to reach the parent proved successful.

Sharing her concerns with the principal, the teacher learned that the mother had previously been arrested for drug use and that a baby had been removed from her home during her last incident with the police. The principal's fear that the mother might have resumed her involvement with drugs was borne out when the mother was arrested a few days later. The children were placed in foster homes; the mother faces a 20-year prison sentence.

Case #2: My sister's children. A teacher's attempt to contact a third-grader's parent led to the discovery that the parent was missing. The child's 17-year-old aunt stated that she had not heard from her 22-year-old sister and did not know where she was.

Case #3: Caught in the middle. A mother who had custody of her 5-year-old son suspected that her former husband had been sexually abusing the boy. Consequently, the mother did not want the school to contact her former husband about their son's performance in school. The father, however, demanded that he be kept informed by receiving the same communications from the school that were sent to his former wife. He further charged that the mother was an alcoholic and that he was in a better situation to respond to the child's needs.

Schools must do more than merely refer students to social services and health departments. They must become multiple-service brokers for children.

Case #4: The school as a battleground. The faculty in a large urban school felt that it was under siege. Drug paraphernalia littered the school grounds. Gang fights were common occurrences. Tensions between teachers and parents had reached the point that teachers felt their lives were in jeopardy.

Case #5: Bewildered in kindergarten. A kindergarten teacher with more than 20 years of experience was at a loss as to how to develop a workable instructional program for a young child who was acting, according to the teacher, "strange." The child's learning style did not fit any pattern that the teacher had observed in all her years of teaching. She arranged a conference with the parent to better understand how best to work with this child. During the course of that conversation, the parent revealed that her daughter had tested positive for the virus that causes AIDS. The mother added, "I want the best for my child, but I just don't know what is going to happen to her schoolwise." While the teacher did not verbalize her feelings at the time, she later confided to a colleague that she did not know the best way to develop the child's learning potential.

A DIFFERENT FRAMEWORK

Like the situation in Donaldsonville, each of these cases raises significant questions about the appropriate role of schoolpeople in the lives of children and their families and communities. How far into the home and neighborhood should the school's responsibility extend? What forms should home/school partnerships take? How are teachers to be helped with designing instructional programs for children with neurological disabilities stemming from viruses, addiction, and environmental pollutants?

Schoolpeople are going to have to think differently about what they want for children and what they expect from families and communities. In Donaldsonville the missing link was forged by a program created by a local university professor who never accepted the assumption of parents' lack of interest in their children's success. She solicited community support to attract parents to a reading program, where they would be assisted in learning how to read and how to read with their children. She called on community leaders to recruit parents they knew in contexts outside the school. Church leaders black and white, agreed to preach from their pulpits about the importance of helping children learn to read. They regularly urged parents to attend the weekly reading sessions to learn to help their children in school, noting the importance of literacy as a tool of faith.

A local bar owner emerged as a strong supporter of the reading program, informing mothers who patronized his establishment that they would no longer be welcome unless they put as much time into learning how to read to their children as they spent enjoying themselves at his bar. He provided transportation to school and back home for participating mothers and secured funds from the city social services department for child care for parents who otherwise could not attend. A grandmother organized a campaign to telephone program participants each week. In sum, the bridge that connected home and school was found in the broader community.

In poor rural communities like Donaldsonville and in inner-city neighborhoods, the social context calls for rethinking the definitions and processes of home/school interactions. Boundaries separating the responsibilities of home, school, and community are blurring, calling into question traditional conceptions of parent involvement as a one-to-one relationship between parent and teacher. Despite the research on the benefits of parent involvement, traditional practices will continue to fall short for a wide band of children in poverty. John Blendinger and Linda Jones, among others, advise us to reach out to parents in new ways, to help parents connect to resources, to create environments where parents feel welcome, and to organize various avenues for participation.[15] Each of these steps is important, but they are insufficient for many poor communities. What these strategies typically lack is an ecological approach to strengthening all aspects of the child's development—a perspective underscored by Shirley Brice Heath and Milbrey McLaughlin, who question the adequacy of schools as social institutions, "because they are built on outmoded assumptions about family and community."[16]

Where should schools draw the line? Are schools the new place to accommodate the interwoven needs that children bring with them to the classroom? If we believe that schools have an obligation to assist students with aspects of their social and personal lives that interfere with their cognitive and social development, then we must rethink our structures, practices, and purposes.

Schools must do more than encourage parent involvement isolated from the broader social context; they must do more than merely refer students to social services and health departments. They must become multiple-service brokers for children.

Social, emotional, physical, and academic growth and development are inextricably linked. As the social supports for children weaken, teachers have to devote much more time and energy to non-instructional demands. Teachers' and administrators' primary responsibility is instruction, but, as a practical and moral matter, they cannot ignore the social and psychological dimensions of their students' lives. Changing social contexts demand changing practices. This view not only stretches the boundaries of parent/school involvement but redefines its purpose: not just higher academic achievement, but the well-being of children in its fullest sense.

Several efforts currently under way are redefining the relationships of school, family, and community. Schoolpeople are forging alliances with an array of community organizations and agencies.[17] They are extending notions of the "family," making room for single parents, working parents, foster parents, grandparents, and others having significant responsibility for children. They are challenging the separateness of systems designed to support children and their families. And they are devising strategies to meet a fuller range of children's needs, using family and community resources.

This work is a lot to ask of educators whose professional education did little to prepare them for it. Yet many individual teachers and administrators today are up to their elbows in such tasks, trying to respond to children's physical and social needs as they are pulled away from other responsibilities. Addressing the deepening needs of urban poor children today will tax all available resources both in and outside of schools. One thing is clear: teachers and schools cannot do it alone. An ecological approach and shared responsibility through multiple partnerships could free educators to better focus on learning needs. Donaldsonville is an example of how one school mobilized resources within families and the community to build positive learning experiences for children.

Schoolpeople will need to develop repertoires of styles and strategies that acknowledge the interrelationships of the social and the individual, they will need to reconceptualize the networks of community organizations and public services that might assist, and they will need to draw on those community resources. Developing an integrated, accessible system of support for children and their families requires adopting different philosophies of service provision and removing the boundaries separating services—a prospect made more difficult as agencies compete for scarce public dollars. Yet, until such partnerships are formed, schools will not be able to sponsor the kinds of home/school/community relationships considered so important to children's inschool growth and development.

Moving to broader notions of community alliances means moving beyond incremental tinkering or simply assessing deficiencies of parents, teachers, schools, and communities. The framework that we propose calls for a coordinated network of multiple resources that builds on family and community strengths. Experience shows that teachers and administrators desperately want to be successful, but, because they are not adequately prepared to address the range of children's social and psychological developmental needs, they are left frustrated. They know what needs to be done, but not how to do it.[18] There are others who can help.

This discussion leads us to offer five recommendations:

1. Home/school strategies should be founded on the strengths of families and their understandings of their children.

2. Efforts should be organized around preventive strategies. Thus school personnel must understand the children and families that they serve—including the wide range of social, personal, economic, and psychological stresses that families may be encountering. They will need to assess how this information will facilitate closer relationships with families to support children's in-school and out of school development.

3. Schools should explore multiple models for reaching out to families and to agencies involved with the families that they serve.

4. Drawing on community resources should become part of the school's daily routine, enabling speedy responses to children's immediate needs.

5. Prospective educators should encounter these issues in their professional preparation programs.

These proposals call for greater inclusion of adults who are important in children's lives and in vastly different ways from our traditional conception. Illustrating some of those different kinds of involvement—the convergence of school, family, and community in full support of children—has been the aim of this article. The time has come to reframe home/school relations diligently and seriously in light of the old African saying: "The whole village educates the child."

NOTES

1. Urie Bronfenbrenner, *The Ecology of Human Development: Experiments by Nature and Design* (Cambridge, Mass.: Harvard University Press, 1979); and Anne T. Henderson, ed., *The Evidence Continues to Grow: Parent Involvement Improves Student Achievement* (Columbia, Md.: National Committee for Citizens in Education, 1987).

2. Joyce L. Epstein, "Toward a Theory of Family-School Connections: Teacher Practices and Parent Involvement," in Klaus Hurrelmann, Franz-Xaver Kaufmann, and Friedrich Losel, eds., *Social Intervention: Potential and Constraints* (New York: Walter de Gruyter, 1987); and Shirley Brice Heath and Milbrey Wallin McLaughlin, "A Child Resource Policy: Moving Beyond Dependence on School and Family," *Phi Delta Kappan*, April 1987, pp. 576-80.

3. James P. Comer, "Home, School, and Academic Learning," in John I. Goodlad and Pamela Keating, eds., *Access to Knowledge: An Agenda for Our Nation's Schools* (New York: College Entrance Examination Board, 1990), p. 23

4. William Julius Wilson, *The Truly Disadvantaged: the Inner City, the Underclass, and Public Policy* (Chicago: University of Chicago Press, 1987).

5. U.S. Bureau of the Census, *Martial Status and Living Arrangements: March 1989* (Washington, D.C.: U.S. Government Printing Office, Current Population Reports, Series P-20, No. 445, 1990).

6. Ibid., p. 3.

7. Ibid., p. 4.

8. Children's Defense Fund, *The State of America's Children, 1991,* (Washington, D.C.: CDF, 1991), p. 24.

9. *Speaking of Kids: A National Survey of Children and Parents* (Washington, D.C.: National Commission on Children, 1991), p. 41.

10. Virginia Richardson and Patricia Colfer, "Being At-Risk in School," in Goodlad and Keating, pp. 107-24.

11. Sara Lawrence Lightfoot, *World's Apart: Relationships Between Families and Schools* (New York: Basic Books, 1978).

12. Joyce L. Epstein, "How Do We Improve Programs for Parent Involvement?" *Educational Horizons*, January 1988, pp. 58-59; and Barbara Lindner, *Family Diversity and School Policy* (Denver: Education Commission of the States, 1987).

13. Anne C. Walde and Keith Baker, "How Teachers View the Parents' Role in Education," *Phi Delta Kappan*, December 1990, pp. 319-22.

14. Jim Cummins, "Empowering Minority Students: A Framework for Intervention," *Harvard Educational Review*, February 1986, pp. 18-36.

15. John Blendinger and Linda Jones, "Parent Involvement in Schools," unpublished manuscript prepared for Boulder (Colo.) Public Schools, 1989.

16. Shirley Brice Heath and Milbrey Wallin McLaughlin, "Community Organizations as Family: Endeavors That Engage and Support Adolescents," *Phi Delta Kappan*, April 1991, pp. 623-27.

17. Lisbeth Schorr, *Within Our Reach: Breaking the Cycle of Disadvantage* (New York: Anchor Press, 1988).

18. Lauren S. Jones Young, "Restructuring Institutional Arrangements: Toward a Comprehensive Child Policy," in Gary A. Griffin and Anna Lowe, eds., *Creating an Agenda for Urban Educational Research and Development: Proceedings of a Wing-spread Conference* (Chicago: College of Education, University of Illinois, 1989), pp. 25-35.

How Schools Perpetuate Illiteracy

To break the cycle of illiteracy—how "the poor get poorer"—schools must help parents understand how to help their children at home.

LA VERGNE ROSOW

La Vergne Rosow is a literacy volunteer, a community college literacy and ESL instructor, and a literacy consultant. Her address is P.O. Box 85, Huntington Beach, CA 92648.

"What's this word?" 9-year-old Mitzi asked her mother.

"What word?"

"This one," she said as she crashed her finger down on the first of 10 words she had to do for homework.

"Uh, well, you know you're supposed to sound it out. Now sound it out."

"I did! *Do or. Do or. Do or!*" She'd learned her lessons well. "D-o" spells *do* and "o-r" spells *or*. Both child and mother knew how to sound out a word they couldn't read, and Mitzi was skillful at finding the little words in the big words, too. "How do I make a sentence with 'do or'?" she asked as she turned over the packet of papers.

"Um, well, I can think of it, but when I try to tell you it, it don't come out right. Just do the best you can. I'm not supposed to tell you *everything*," the young mother said, trying to maintain some semblance of dignity before her child.[1]

The little girl turned the packet over again to try the next word. She was supposed to write a sentence with each of the 10 words on the mimeographed list. By Friday, having done each of 4 activities with the words, she was expected to be able to spell all 10 words on a test. This was only day 2 of a 4-day homework assignment. (Later Mitzi's mom explained that just figuring out what the words on the list were was only part of the problem. Then they had to construct sentences that had only words they could already spell. The proposed sentences always grew shorter and shorter as the struggle progressed.) Ten minutes had passed, and Mitzi still hadn't written the first sentence.

Suddenly she said, "Is it *door?*" and then turned the packet over to start writing.

"Um, no, I don't think so. I think that's spelled another way," her mother answered thoughtfully.

"Well, then, how do you spell *door?*"

"I think it's dore, you know, *dore.*"

A True Life Drama

The little girl seemed to be trying to take in the logic of her mother's phonetic performance. I leaned forward, hoping to be invited into the dialogue, but heard instead the echo of a literacy and language lecture by Steve Krashen on how the rich get richer. Those who are rich in literacy fortify their children with good stories and beautiful books long before they enter school; the poor readers don't even understand that process and so per-petuate illiteracy from generation to generation.[2] Now, having no invitation to intervene, I was forced to witness this true life drama of what Krashen calls how "the poor get poorer."

Having already repeated the 1st grade, Mitzi was facing the dreaded prospect of failing the 2nd, due to poor performance in language arts. Her mother was an adult nonreader. "I can read the words," she had explained, "but when it comes to explaining it, it's just like a wall goes up, and I can't say what I mean." By a wall going up, I'd immediately figured she was talking about stress, the *Affective Filter*[3] that stops learning and performance. But Mitzi's mom meant instead that she couldn't comprehend text. I was there to help her learn to read when Mitzi had come home from school. Not knowing whether the child knew why I was visiting her mom, and having gotten no introduction, I was not free to move in on the mother/daughter ritual that served only to teach Mitzi that schoolwork is tough and she is never able to do it well.

Krashen had lectured about the ease with which students accustomed to print-rich environments breeze through schoolwork on words they had already learned through pleasure reading. "Those who are readers typically know what most of the words mean already. They have seen them before, in Judy Blume's novels or in Dungeons and

When children of the literate elite need help, their parents can fill in the blanks the school has missed. When children of the print poor need help, they have nowhere to turn.

Dragons. . . ."[4] Meanwhile, children from nonprint homes and classrooms are left to flesh out the loser's end of the bell-shaped curve. When children of the literate elite need help, their parents can fill in the blanks the school has missed. When children of the print poor need help, they have nowhere to turn. The girl who already knows 9 of the 10 assigned spelling words from pleasure reading will make a 100 percent if she studies the 1 unknown word and 90 percent if she does nothing. The girl who can't read will be faced with 10 new words, an almost overwhelming task of memorization. If she really struggles, she'll earn a C-. In school, that is how the rich get richer and the poor get poorer. They'll imagine that if they had just studied a little harder or worked a little longer they would have done better. "And like the victims of child abuse, they blame themselves."[5] I'd heard the lecture . . . more than once. School is a test . . . to see who already knows the most and to see whose parents can do the best job. Now I was witnessing the demonstration.

From One Generation to the Next

After 30 or 45 minutes of guesswork, Mitzi ran out to play, knowing that her faithful mother would be waiting to help her with another hour and a half of homework when she came in.[6] She couldn't know that the production of sentences is a test, a call for *output* that shows what the reader already knows; output is simply anything the learner can say or write. Sentence production

was not *input* designed to give the new or nonreader information.[7] Based on what is understandable and relevant to the learner, input becomes acquired without learner effort. Nor could Mitzi's mom know that this assignment was difficult because it employed a bot-

tom-up strategy. It required that the learner remember all sorts of meaningless little pieces of the language, like "do," and put them into bigger pieces: sentences. She had been told that if she did this enough, she would know how to spell, and that would then help her

---

Teachers Can Foster Family Literacy

Illiteracy does run in families, but we can end it in our classrooms. And, with funds for extra supplies, books, released time, and help from our schools, K-12 teachers can extend a hand to the parents of the "Mitzis" in our classrooms. We can:

• Make our classrooms examples of "print-rich environments" by providing plenty of books, magazines, posters, and notes.

• Invite parents to story times or other literacy events and help them to enjoy these occasions with their children. Help parents to understand that good questions are designed to stimulate thought, not extract correctness.

• Send books home that we have read to the children. Tell parents that talking about books will help their children learn to appreciate literature.

• Communicate with parents in clear language; find speakers of their languages when they are not proficient in English.

• Tell parents about adult literacy services such as Adult Basic Education and Literacy Volunteer programs. Encourage them to seek help, assuring them that it is never too late to learn to enjoy reading; but forewarn people of possible disappointments like the numbers of months on waiting lists, so that initial problems don't seem like personal affronts.

• Tell parents about local library story hours and services, and invite the librarian to meet them.

• Teach parents how to identify good book features such as: predictable text, Caldecott and Newberry Medalists, their own children's recognition and delight over books made familiar at school. Perhaps a very simple, large-type checklist can help.

• Teach parents not to fall for gro-

cery and drug store workbooks and other skill-level materials. Then point out where they can buy inexpensive books in the neighborhood, such as used book stores, flea markets, library sales, school purchase bargains (Scholastic Books), and chain stores.

• Visit children and parents in their homes to gain insights into their interests. In the process, you may find resources for the entire classroom, such as a parent who can sing folksongs.

For *homework*, teachers should assign enrichment tasks—not activities that ask students to finish incomplete classroom work, use materials that are not available, or obtain teaching at home when none may be available. Instead, the school-related homework should foster love of learning and build a bridge between classroom activities and life at home. For example, teachers can:

• Encourage children to read nursery rhymes or songbooks already made familiar at school.

• Suggest family projects such as handprint collections or pressed flowers, which will be used for school writing; in turn, the writing projects will then be returned to the home as reading materials.

• Give directions for making finger- and hand-puppets that match poems learned at school, and invite students to roleplay or dramatize stories from home for their classmates at school.

Making school/home connections with the parents of the Mitzis in your classrooms is a tough task—but a very good investment. Breaking the cycle of illiteracy continues to pay off generation after generation. □

—La Vergne Rosow

reading; in reality, only those students who are already readers can back into this kind of task successfully. She couldn't know that no struggle would have been involved in pulling a part (a word) out of a whole, such as a real story.

For Mitzi and her mom, there was never any storytelling or picture book enjoyment. But because Mitzi's mother was bent on not having her child do poorly in school the way she herself had, night after night, they labored over writing sentences for sounds like "door."

Finally, Mitzi had hit the word *floor,* and when she said it, her mother realized there was a pattern connection. "Yes, now, if that one's *floor,* what's this one?" she asked pointing back to word number one.

"But you said . . ." Mitzi, a very bright child, had already learned in one lesson the spelling "d-o-r-e."

I wondered what if, instead of *floor,* the familiar word had been *look* or *poor* or *boot.* What other reasonable and wrong connection might have been triggered? How many little transfers of poverty occur in the name of homework each night across this land as illiteracy passes from one generation to the next?

Keeping Secrets from the Have-Nots

Who is accountable when all the mothers of all the Mitzis just don't measure up? Without knowing the futility of their efforts and the waste of their scarce funds, how many take the cue from this kind of school assignment and buy grocery store workbooks to occupy what would be pleasure book times for the literate elite?

Why aren't mother and child seeing beautiful pictures in books brought home from school and sharing favorite stories that Mitzi has heard again and again in class instead of impoverished little mimeographs with lists of meaningless words? Who profits when the values of the literate haves are kept secret from the illiterate have-nots? Surely we know too much of the reading process to pretend this disparity is created in ignorance. The assignment to sound out "do or" and to produce a sentence from it robs Mitzi of real reading time, but Mitzi doesn't know that. And Mitzi's mother doesn't know that. Can this kind of "literacy lesson" pass as a naive accident in our bountiful domain where consistently "the poor get poorer"?

[1] A 1988 survey of adult nonreaders showed that the biggest reason adults seek literacy help is self-esteem. L. Rosow, (November 1988), "Adult Illiterates Offer Unexpected Cues into the Reading Process," *Journal of Reading*: 120-124.

[2] S. D. Krashen, (1988), USC lecture notes (unpublished).

[3] Krashen describes the *Affective Filter*, the metaphor for the stress barrier that prevents new information from coming into the brain and appropriate known information from being accessed. S. D. Krashen, (1985), *Inquiries and Insights: Second Language Teaching, Immersion and Bilingual Education, Literacy*, (Hayward, Calif.: Alemany Press, a division of Janus Book Publishers, Inc.), pp. 10-11.

[4] Ibid, p. 108.

[5] Ibid.

[6] Not every nonreading mother is so faithful. The mother of another 9-year-old child, Arthur, had a thousand important things to keep her from having to face working with her child on school assignments. L. Rosow, (November 1989), "Arthur: A Tale of Disempowerment," *Phi Delta Kappan* 71, 3: 194-199.

[7] For a comprehensive discussion of input vs. output, see S. D. Krashen, (1989), "We Acquire Vocabulary and Spelling by Reading: Additional Evidence for the Input Hypothesis," *Modern Language Journal* 73, IV: 440-464.

Author's note: I am pleased to report that through subsequent tutoring, Mitzi's mother has just finished reading the first book of her life.

I would like to thank Professors David Eskey and William Rideout, Jr., for help with the Mitzi case.

Appropriate Educational Practices

- **Preschool and Primary Programs (Articles 19–26)**
- **Assessment (Articles 27–29)**

Since the late 1960s, we have seen increased attention paid to appropriate educational practice. High interest in best practice comes from the expansion of our understanding of young children's physical, social-emotional, and intellectual development. We have learned that all development is interrelated and requires an integrated educational approach. Expanded information on how children grow and learn has led teachers to look more carefully at supportive ways of facilitating learning experiences.

In the last several years, professional associations have taken the responsibility of publishing excellent manuals and position papers that describe developmentally appropriate practice (e.g., Bredekamp, S., 1987. *Developmentally Appropriate Practice: From Birth to 8 Years*). Educational journals are filled with articles by practitioners and researchers who have continued the search for effective practice. Teacher groups are finding these materials useful for planning the learning environment. This concern for better practice is leading teachers to examine their entire program structure. Teachers' attention is drawn toward appropriate educational practice because it integrates what they know about children with ways to teach them.

Appropriate practice is children in action. Children are busy constructing with blocks, working puzzles, and creating with paint brushes. They ride, invent, cook, and compose throughout the day. *Appropriate practice is teachers in action.* After setting the stage, teachers are busy holding conversations, guiding activities, and questioning children. They observe, draw conclusions, plan, and vary the activities throughout the day. Appropriate practice goes beyond a list of do's and don'ts, because the learning environment of busy people is constantly in flux. That means practice should be based on broad developmental principles, but designed within the context of a particular program. This is the emphasis of Marjorie Kostelnik's article, "Recognizing the Essentials of Developmentally Appropriate Practice."

Appropriate practice accommodates for individual differences. Children's rates and styles of development require teachers to use a variety of strategies. Sensitivity to the differences of individual children means making adjustments in the classroom environment. It may mean making some changes in equipment or adapting learning materials so more children can use them. Often, it will require the teamwork of teachers and other professionals to communicate and decide the best environment and practice for special needs children. Several articles in this unit discuss ways to go beyond planning for an entire class or group to providing for individuals.

Appropriate practice involves all children, regardless of handicapping condition. Teachers can find assistance in providing for special needs children by partnering with special educators and families. Early intervention programs are making use of family service plans that link the partners in coordinating and delivering the services children need. This is maximum inclusion for children, rather than exclusion by handicapping condition. Teachers in programs that are designed to include all children will find themselves reexamining their roles and practices. They will be learning how to work alongside special educators and personnel from other agencies as well as with the whole family. Several articles in this unit focus on developmentally appropriate strategies necessary for all children.

One essential of appropriate practice is authentic assessment of children's progress. As Susan Andersen points out in "Trouble with Testing," reliance on testing as the only measure of achievement is too narrow when practice is developmentally appropriate. So, more inclusive techniques become necessary. Teachers find that it is useful to develop skill in a variety of observational formats that can be carried out within the context of the program. One technique currently being used by teachers is the assessment portfolio, which is a way to archive the work done by children. Keeping periodic records of children's development along with their work aligns well with appropriate practice. This variety of assessment methods provides a much broader picture of children's performance than is available in programs that are test-driven.

Authentic appropriate practice, based on children's development, has no short cuts and cannot be trivialized. Putting thought and planning and process behind the words involves using knowledge of child development to inform caregiving decisions and curricular choices. By working out specifics of routines and procedures, materials, and assessment suitable for young children, the early childhood professional strengthens skills in decision making. This is a crucial role for a teacher interested in developmentally appropriate practice.

Looking Ahead: Challenge Questions

What are the essentials of developmentally appropriate practice?

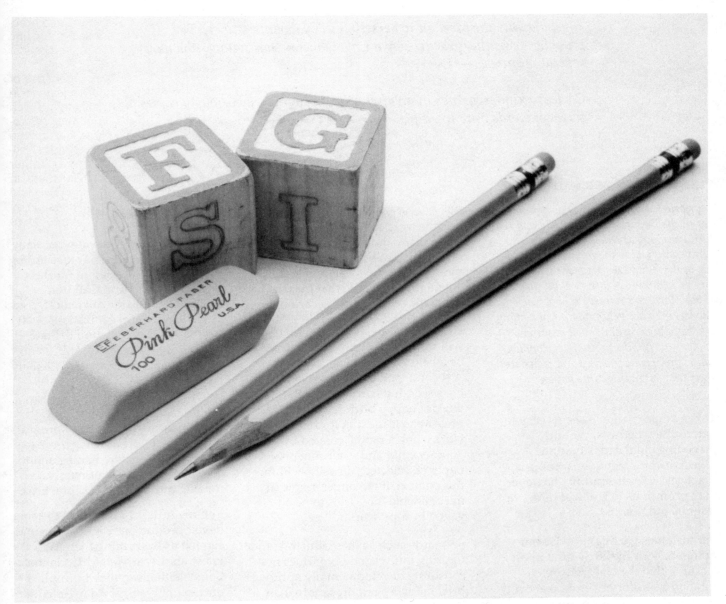

Before reading the article "What Good Prekindergarten Programs Look Like," identify five aspects of an effective, appropriate prekindergarten program.

What are the provisions of the most recent federal laws concerning special needs children? How can teachers provide developmentally appropriate settings for special needs children?

What does authentic assessment mean? Other than testing young children, how can teachers assess progress?

A look at DAP in the real world

Recognizing the Essentials of Developmentally Appropriate Practice

A group of four year olds have been in circle time for 40 minutes.
— not DAP

Aiysha wants the easel all to herself. LaToya wants a turn. The provider helps the girls develop a time table for sharing over the next several minutes. — DAP

Carlos, a kindergartner in an after school program, laboriously copies a series of words onto lined paper. — not DAP

Marjorie J. Kostelnik, PhD

Marjorie J. Kostelnik, PhD, is a professor in the Department of Family and Child Ecology at Michigan State University and is the program supervisor of the Child Development Laboratories on campus. A former child care, Head Start, and nursery school teacher, she has been actively involved in helping a variety of early childhood programs explore the implications of developmentally appropriate practice and translate their understandings into action.

Taken at face value, it seems easy to determine whether or not the preceding child care situations reflect developmentally appropriate practices. Closer scrutiny, however, may prompt us to reassess our original judgments.

For instance, we might revise our opinion about the circle time upon learning that the children are enthralled by a storyteller who actively involves them in the storytelling process and who has prolonged the group in response to the children's requests to "tell us another one." Likewise, helping children to share is usually a worthy endeavor. But, in this case, Aiysha only recently became a big sister and is having to share many things for the first time — attention at home, her room, and most of her things. Knowing this, we might determine that making her share the easel on this occasion is unnecessarily stressful. Helping LaToya find an alternate activity that will satisfy her desire to paint could be a better course of action for now. A second look at Carlos reveals that he is working hard to copy the words "happy birthday" for a present he is making for his mom. He is using a model created by another child and is writing on paper he selected himself. Within this context, it no longer seems so questionable for Carlos to be engaged in copy work.

Scenarios such as these illustrate that figuring out what does or does not constitute developmentally appropriate practice requires more than simply memorizing a particular set of do's and don'ts. It involves looking at every practice in context and making judgments about each child and the environment in which he or she is functioning.

Judgments Related to DAP

The guidelines for developmentally appropriate practice put forward by the National Association for the Education of Young Children (NAEYC) and later corroborated and embellished by organizations such as the National Association of State Boards of Education (NASBE) and the National Association of Elementary School Principals (NAESP) provide an excellent resource for thinking about, planning, and implementing high quality programs for young children. They serve to inform our decision making and to give us a basis for continually scrutinizing our professional practices.

Yet, regardless of how well they are developed, no one set of guidelines can tell us everything there is to know about early childhood education. Neither can they be applied unthinkingly. Every day practitioners find themselves in situations in which they must make judgments about what to value and what to do. Some of these situations demand on-the-spot decision making; others allow time for longer deliberation.

From *Child Care Information Exchange*, March/April 1993, pp. 73-77. © 1993 by Exchange Press, Inc. Reprinted with permission from Exchange Press, Inc., P.O. Box 2890, Redmond, WA 98073.

Some involve relatively minor incidents; others are much more serious. Some require making major changes in the environment or in one's teaching behavior; others necessitate only minimal changes or none at all. Yet, hurried or meticulously planned, small or large, involving more or less action, practitioners continually have to decide whether or not their actions and programs enhance or detract from the quality of children's lives.

Confusion Over DAP

Spokespersons for NAEYC, NASB, and NAESP have tried to underscore the evolving nature of developmentally appropriate practice and the contextual nature of its application. Unfortunately, some people eager for quick answers or a finite set of rules for working with young children have overgeneralized the guidelines. Suggested alternatives have become ironclad rules — issues of "more and less" have become "all or none." A number of erroneous assumptions have also arisen about DAP. Some of these include:

• There is only one right way to carry out a developmentally appropriate program.

• Developmentally appropriate programs are unstructured ones in which practitioners offer minimal guidance, if any at all, to the children in their care.

• In developmentally appropriate programs the expectations for children's behavior and learning are low.

• Developmentally appropriate practices cannot be adapted to meet the needs of particular culture groups or children of varying socio-economic backgrounds.

• Developmentally appropriate practice can be achieved simply by acquiring certain kinds of toys.

Assertions such as these have fueled a growing debate about the meaning, usefulness, and unitary nature of DAP. The resulting examination and exchange of views is healthy for the field, but it has also led some child care administrators to feel confused about what developmentally appropriate practice really is and how to achieve it. In addition, some directors are unsure which elements of developmentally appropriate practice are the most critical or where to begin in operationalizing the concept in their programs.

All of this uncertainty is compounded by the fact that every child care staff is comprised of people whose familiarity and experience with developmentally appropriate practices vary. Furthermore, some staff members may question whether certain of the practices espoused in written documents are sensitive to the unique needs of the population with whom they work. Others may feel overwhelmed at the thought of memorizing a long list of guidelines. Still others may not see an item on the list that addresses a particular situation with which they must cope. Many of these concerns arise from a preoccupation with the details of developmentally appropriate practice rather than with its essence. That essence lies in three principles common to every major interpretation of DAP suggested thus far.

The Essence of DAP

1. Developmentally appropriate means taking into account everything we know about how children develop and learn and matching that to the content and strategies planned for them in early childhood programs.

2. Developmentally appropriate means treating children as individuals, not as a cohort group.

3. Developmentally appropriate means treating children with respect — recognizing children's changing capabilities and having faith in their capacity to develop and learn.

In other words, we must first think about what children are like and then create activities, routines, and expectations that accommodate and complement those characteristics. In addition, we must know more than a few descriptive facts about a child, such as age and gender, to design appropriate programs. We have to look at children within the context of their family, culture, community, past experience, and current circumstances to create age-appropriate, as well as individually-appropriate, living and learning environments. Finally, we must recognize the unique ways in which children are children, not simply miniature adults. Experiences and expectations planned for children should reflect the notion that early childhood is a time of life qualitatively different from the later school years and adulthood.

Although each of us may interpret these basic tenets in slightly different ways, they provide a common foundation for defining high quality early childhood programs. Such programs are ones in which children of all abilities, ages, races, cultures, creeds, socio-economic, and family lifestyle backgrounds feel lovable, valuable, and competent.

The Need for Knowledge

Having specialized knowledge about child development and learning is the cornerstone of professionalism in early childhood education. Such knowledge encompasses recognizing common developmental threads among all children as well as understanding significant variations across cultures. Interviews with child care providers and observations of their work with children consistently find that those who have such knowledge are better equipped and more likely to engage in developmentally appropriate practices. Instead of treating their interactions with children as wholly intuitive, they bring factual information to bear on how they think about children and how they respond to them.

Understanding child development provides practitioners with insights into children's behavior and helps adults better grasp the context within which those actions occur. This expands providers' notions of what constitutes normal child behavior. As a result, they are more likely to accept typical variations among children as well as accurately recognize potential problems that may require specialized intervention. Familiarity with child development also offers clues to child care workers about the sequence in which activities might be presented to children and the degree of developmental readiness necessary for children to achieve particular goals.

Understanding how young children think and expand their concepts and skills is the key to creating appropriate physical environments for children, to determining appropriate adult/child interactions, and to developing activities and routines that support rather than undermine children's natural ways of learning.

Children As Individuals

Practitioners are called on daily to make decisions that require them to see each child as distinct from all others. The adult must weigh such variables as the child's age, what the child's current level of comprehension might be, and what experiences the child has had. Although *age* is not an absolute measure of a youngster's capabilities and understanding, it does serve as a guide for establishing appropriate expectations. For instance, knowing that

preschoolers do not yet have a mature grasp of games with rules, child care workers would not consider a four year old who spins twice or peeks at the cards in a memory game as cheating. Nor would they require preschoolers to adhere to the rules of the game in the same way they might expect grade-schoolers to do.

The kinds of *previous knowledge and skills* a child brings to a situation should also be taken into account. Obviously, children with little or no exposure to a particular situation or skill would not be expected to perform at the same level of competence as children whose backlog of experience is greater. For instance, standards for dressing independently would be different for a three year old than those for a six year old, not only because of differences in maturity, but because the older child has had more practice.

Contextual factors also contribute to determining the developmental appropriateness of certain decisions. For example, under normal circumstances, Ms. Sanchez's goal is to foster independence among the children in her family child care home. Ordinarily, children are given the time to make their own decisions, to repeat a task in order to gain competence, and to do as much as possible for themselves. However, these goals and strategies have to be modified during a tornado drill. Under such circumstances, children have no choice about taking shelter, nor can they take their time dressing themselves. As a result, slow dressers get more direct assistance than is customarily provided.

Physical resources and available time affect judgments as well. This explains why a huge mud puddle on the playground could be viewed as a

place to avoid or an area for exploration. Which judgment is made depends in part on what kind of clothing the children are wearing, whether soap and water is available for clean up, whether it is warm enough to go barefoot, and whether there is enough time for children to both play in the mud and get cleaned up before moving into the next part of the day.

The Function of Respect

Respect involves having faith in children's ability to eventually learn the information, behavior, and skills they will need to constructively function on their own. Thus, having respect for children implies believing that they are capable of changing their behavior and of making self-judgments. Caregivers manifest respect when they allow children to think for themselves, make decisions, work toward their own solutions, and communicate their ideas.

For instance, it is out of respect for children that child care workers allow them to make choices ranging from which activity to pursue to where to sit at the lunch table. For this reason, too, practitioners encourage toddlers to pour their own juice, preschoolers to become actively involved in clean up, and school-age children to help determine the activities for the day. Although any of these activities could be more efficiently and skillfully accomplished by adults, respect for children's increasing competence involves allowing them to experience the exhilaration of accomplishment. Similarly, adults who respect children know that self-control is an emerging skill that children achieve over time given adequate support and guidance. With this in mind, children's transgressions are handled as gaps in knowledge and skills, not as character flaws.

Applications

Each time child care workers are faced with having to determine to what extent their actions are congruent with developmentally appropriate practice, it is useful to ask the following questions:

• Is this practice in keeping with what I know about child development and learning?

• Does this practice take into account the children's individual needs?

• Does this practice demonstrate respect for children?

These queries can be used to address immediate concerns or to serve as the basis for long-term deliberations. They can stimulate individual thinking or consideration of program practices by an entire staff. Newcomers to the field use the preceding questions to hone their understanding of the fundamental nature of children. Seasoned veterans often go beyond the basics to consider the extent to which their practices take into account gender and cultural differences among children as well as differences related to socioeconomic status. In every circumstance, the answer to all three questions should be yes. If any answer is no, it is a strong sign that the practice should be reconsidered, revamped, or discarded. If there is uncertainty about a question in relation to a certain practice, that practice is worth examining further.

To illustrate the power of these essential principles as tools for meaningful reflection, take a moment to consider the first question above. In my own experience, I have started the reflective process by asking child care workers to describe the children with whom they work (focusing on how they believe those youngsters develop and learn). Often practitioners use adjectives such as active, curious, talkative, or playful. The procedure of generating descriptive words often leads to thought-provoking discussions to which both experienced and less experienced members contribute. If people decide they aren't sure about some items (e.g., What do children really learn from play? Do children from varied backgrounds develop and learn in the same way?), their questions serve as the impetus for staff research or the basis for additional in-service training. Next, we create a chart to examine what implications such characteristics have for program practice. This is accomplished by listing child development and learning traits in one column and corresponding practices that support or match those traits in a second column. A typical example is offered below.

A chart such as the one illustrated here serves two major functions. First, the people who create it become increasingly invested in the practices they identify. These are likely to be ones they take care to address in the future because they can see the logic of such strategies in

Child Traits	Child Care Practices
Children are active learners.	**The child care teacher:** gives children opportunities for gross motor activities each day. includes a daily free-choice period during which children can move freely. creates a schedule in which quiet, inactive times are followed by longer, more active periods. keeps inactive segments of the day short.
Children are curious.	**The child care teacher:** builds activities around children's interests. provides many chances for children to explore materials and concepts. encourages children to pose problems and investigate solutions.
Children are playful.	**The child care teacher:** integrates play throughout the day. provides children with a variety of props and other manipulative objects. encourages children to create and use their own ideas within their play. creates a classroom design and schedule that allows children to move about freely. monitors and enhances children's play as an observer or as a participant. evaluates the sound and activity level within the program in terms of the quality of children's play — recognizes that high quality play is often noisy and active.

relation to children they know and care about. Second, their ideas can be compared to those in published documents. As practitioners make such comparisons, they find many similarities between their ideas and those of experts in the field. This contributes to greater staff confidence and helps to make the NAEYC guidelines for developmentally appropriate practice more personally meaningful.

Summary

Ultimately, for DAP to have a major impact on the early childhood profession, people must see the principles which undergird it as extensions of their own values. These shared values will be what make DAP an integral part of our thoughts and actions rather than just a fad soon to be replaced by another.

In addition, fundamental values such as these are likely to remain constant, even as the strategies we use to address them differ from one circumstance to another or change over time. Supporting child care workers as they examine the essentials of developmentally appropriate practice is not only an important administrative responsibility, it is one that promises to yield lasting rewards for staff and for children.

Developmental Continuity:

From Preschool Through Primary Grades

Nita H. Barbour and Carol A. Seefeldt

Nita H. Barbour is Associate Professor, Department of Education, University of Maryland—Baltimore County. Carol A. Seefeldt is Professor, Department of Human Development, University of Maryland at College Park.

Claudia and Consuela, teachers at different schools in the same district, are having dinner together. Claudia exclaims: "What is this business of developmental continuity? Mr. B, my principal, came by and said that we're going to have someone from central office come and talk to us about it."

"That's really interesting," replies Consuela. "Our school is going to be used as a pilot school for this developmental continuity. We began the process really because of our parents. At a PTA meeting a couple of years ago, an irate father asked just what we were doing to his son. When his son was at the preschool program next door, he could choose his activities where he loved reading books, telling stories and writing messages. Kindergarten the following year wasn't too bad, it seems. The child could occasionally paint and make some choices after he had completed his alphabet pages. The father's real anger came after his son entered 1st grade. He began losing all interest and delight in a school where he had no choices and was being made to feel he couldn't read. The

father questioned whether 1st grade had to be so rigid. He was seeing his son go from loving books to developing a dislike of reading."

"How did you respond to that?" asks Claudia.

"Of course, there were many different reactions and lots of dialogue. Eventually, we began to realize that children really ought not to have to adjust to major changes as they move from home to child care experiences to kindergarten and primary grades. It was then that we started to reach out to the teachers in the preschool in our neighborhood. We are really trying to make smoother transitions for the kids as they move from preschool to the public schools. We are also reorganizing parts of our instruction within and across classrooms to provide continuity of curriculum for children from preschool through the primary grades. We are including the child care director and some of the teachers in this planning."

"Really," says Claudia. "Do you think it's working?"

"We're really enthusiastic about the changes we've made. All this

year we've spent a lot of time working with the teachers who had our kids last year and those who will have them next year. We are realizing how much more we can do with these kids now, since we know them so much better. For some of us at least, we want to try having them over a longer period of time so we can provide the best and most interesting instruction."

Claudia and Consuela's dinner conversation starts a dialogue that gives suggestions to classroom teachers for restructuring their classrooms and their instruction. In the upcoming ACEI book, *Developmental Continuity: From Preschool Through Primary Grades*, these same two teachers raise such questions as:

- What is developmental continuity?
- What kind of curriculum would emerge from its principles?
- How is a classroom organized to accommodate differences?
- What are the first steps toward effecting change in the classroom?

As they ask these questions, the

From *Childhood Education*, Annual Theme Issue 1992, pp. 302-304. Reprinted by permission of Nita H. Barbour, Carol A. Seefeldt, and the Association for Childhood Education International, 11501 Georgia Avenue, Suite 315, Wheaton, MD. © 1992 by the Association.

authors suggest solutions and comment on practices that are based on theory and research. In the remainder of this article the authors give brief vignettes of the process of facilitating developmental continuity from preschool through primary grades.

What Is Developmental Continuity?

Developmental continuity describes a way of providing instruction that permits children to progress according to their rate and style of learning. In the curriculum that emerges, learning experiences link children's prior knowledge and flow in a natural progression toward more sophisticated content. The classroom for this approach is organized so that as children acquire knowledge, learn skills and develop positive attitudes toward learning, they experience success. Their progress in academic achievement supports social, emotional and physical development as well as individual learning styles. Such classrooms allow teachers to build on children's natural motivation, while challenging them to pursue new interests and strive to attain more abstract and complex skills.

What Kind of Curriculum?

Consuela's curriculum did change from a subject-oriented curriculum. Her framework for instruction became an integrated curriculum that allowed children to acquire concepts and learn needed skills at their own level of development.

Consuela shares with Claudia some of her general procedures: "In my 2nd-grade class, we discuss at least one 'topic' each day. In the beginning, I usually choose the topic from the social studies and science units. Now, however, children sometimes express an interest in learning about things and that becomes the topic. Our topics may last one day or one month, depending upon the children's interest and the skills they are learning. Since a 'topic' is never completed, it can

be studied later in a more involved and extended way."

"But without the curriculum guides to follow, how do you know what to do?" queries Claudia.

"Well, it's a continual process of thinking and planning," Consuela responds. "Perhaps if I took you through the process that I am going through right now to extend my 2nd-graders' interest in leaves to a study about trees, it might help."

As Consuela shares her thinking and planning process she concludes, "Though we will add new concepts and probably new skills as our themes develop, here are some of the concepts, skills and activities that I've jotted down. As you'll see, I always note whether I think the activity is best suited for small group or total group."

Study of Trees

■ Use a small branch of the apple tree in the yard as a stimulus for connecting leaves to trees. (Total group)

■ Brainstorm with children why trees are important to us and what questions they might have about trees. (Total group)

■ Read Parnell's book *The Apple Tree* to the entire class for general discussion relating to the concepts that children can discover about trees. (Total group)

Some possible concepts from the book are that trees:
— provide food
— change during the seasons
— provide, joy, delight (aesthetics)
— provide shelter to insects and birds.

Other concepts include:
— Some of the creatures are threatened in the tree.
— Other creatures find protection.
— This tree grows in a meadow.

■ Children will select books on trees during reading workshop time. (Small groups or individuals)

In reading, children are studying the setting of the story. From reading *The Apple Tree* and other books about trees, they can examine the

setting (and thus the kind of environment that trees need). Concepts of setting are:
— Where and when does the story take place?
— Do time and place change throughout the story?
— Do people or things change with place or time?
— What in the book clues us to the time and place of the story?

■ In social studies, children are studying mapping skills. (Total group for developing or modeling the process of doing the activity and small groups for completing activities)

On global maps, children will locate the places where their stories take place and put identifying stickers with the title of their book on the maps.

Children will make topographical maps and place models of their trees appropriately. This project will require art activities for making three-dimensional tree models (clay, cardboard cutouts, pipe cleaners for trunks, small sticks for branches and colored paper for leaves) and for making a large map with various topographies represented.

Children will create time lines for months or for years using such coding as "In my time," "When Mother was young," "When Grandpa was young," etc. Children whose books reflect passage of time will illustrate on the time line differences in the trees over time.

■ For writing, children regularly keep journals. As they are reading about trees, they will be encouraged to reflect in their journals: (Individuals)
— What is the setting for my book?
— What things did I learn about how trees affect me?
— What would I like to read more about?

Interesting words from their books will be listed, so as children create stories they will have an easy access to new words. Those interested will create stories or reports about their trees.

"Wow!" Claudia interjects,

"You've done lots of thinking and putting ideas together."

"Yeah, that's how I plan," remarks Consuela. "I believe I have enough material and ideas to start this week's project. Now comes getting ready for the beginning event."

How Is the Classroom Organized?
When such an integrated curriculum responds to each group of children and to individuals within the group, there is no one formula for selecting and arranging equipment and materials within any space or room. Fundamental to Consuela's belief, however, is arrangement of the environment since that will communicate to children, their parents and others in the school the teacher's expectations for children's learning. The physical environment can tell children that they are expected to be socially, physically and intellectually active or that they are going to be passive recipients of someone else's knowledge. It can invite children to give free reign to their intellectual curiosity or inhibit their need to find out and learn.

Because children under 7 or 8 learn through activity, each classroom should challenge children to intellectual, physical, social and mental activity. Classrooms arranged with interest, learning or activity centers give children spaces to learn with groups or by themselves and provide the materials necessary for active learning. The arranged environment becomes another teacher, challenging children to think, motivating them to explore, enticing them to find out.

How To Get Started
Changing a classroom to support developmental continuity does not happen overnight. It takes time and experimenting. And it takes the support of many. The principal and area supervisors are key players and need to be informed about developmental continuity. Parents and influential community people need to support the classroom teacher's efforts and witness the benefits of children excited about learning math, science and social science concepts as they learn to read and write. Strong links with other professionals who work or have worked with the students enable teachers to provide the environments most enabling for each particular child. Children learn best when the adults in their lives collaborate to provide supportive environments.

The reader finds that Claudia became interested in the new process. She felt overwhelmed at trying to accomplish such a large task, but Consuela helped her understand that steps are taken one at a time. "It is an evolution we wish to achieve—not a revolution!"

What Good Prekindergarten Programs Look Like

Janice Molnar

Janice Molnar, PhD, is a researcher at the Bank Street College of Education in New York. Her article is based on material she contributed to *Early Childhood Programs and the Public Schools*, by Anne Mitchell (also of Bank Street) and Michelle Seligson and Fern Marx (of the Wellesley College Center for Research on Women) and published by Auburn House © 1989, part of Greenwood Publishing Group in Westport, Connecticut. Their book presents the results of a four-year study of early childhood programs carried out by Bank Street and Wellesley with funding from the Carnegie Corporation of New York and the Ford Foundation.

Reprinted with permission.

All parents want their children to get the best possible start in education. And an increasing number of parents want this to happen when their children are only three and four years old.

Parents and taxpayers look to the public schools to make this happen. But we have to ask if the nation's public schools are ready and able today to provide high-quality early childhood education for every child coming through their doors. More particularly, are the schools prepared to introduce children to the world of education with an effective, appropriate, high-quality prekindergarten program?

To answer that key question, the Public School Early Childhood Study carried out a mail and telephone survey of early childhood program directors at the state level and child advocates in all 50 states and the District of Columbia; we also did a pin-point mail survey of some 1,225 public school districts. We then visited 13 public school prekindergarten programs in 12 states to get a sense of what was happening "at ground level." Two people spent five days at each site observing staff and classroom practices and conducting face-to-face interviews.

Programs Are Remarkably Diverse

From all this data, we were able to get a fairly accurate picture of prekindergarten programs in public schools. We learned that, first of all, they are remarkably diverse. They reflect a range of implicit assumptions about young children and how they learn. Even within a given school with a particular approach to the education of young children, shades of difference could be seen between one classroom and another down the hall.

Thus, the one thing we can say without qualification about the classrooms we visited is that it is impossible to generalize. Even in sites which had a clearly articulated philosophy and set of guidelines, the way the program was translated by the teacher in the daily rhythm of classroom activities and social exchange varied considerably. In this respect, at least, they are like early childhood programs everywhere.

Environment and Materials

Across the 13 sites, most classrooms we visited had the kinds of materials traditionally found in any early childhood environment: child-sized tables and chairs, for example, and appropriate shelving and storage space. Large numbers of rooms had child-sized sinks (61 percent) and storage space for children's personal belongings (75 percent), indicating that many of the prekindergartens were housed in space designed specifically for young children.

The vast majority (80 percent or more) of the 76 classrooms on which we had the most complete information had creative play equipment: small toys, construction toys, puzzles, blocks, art and crafts materials, and housekeeping furniture and accessories. Record players and records were observed also in these classrooms (over 80 percent), and over half had additional audio equipment such as tape recorders.

Young children learn best through

From *Streamlined Seminar,* Vol. 9, No. 5, May 1991, pp. 1-7. Reprinted with permission of the National Association of Elementary School Principals.

active engagement with "open-ended" materials—painting easels, for example, or musical instruments—that allow them to explore at their own pace, in their own way, and to the extent of their own interest. Unfortunately, 30 percent of the observed classrooms did not have easels (in a couple of cases, they were present but used as small bulletin boards). Just over half had sand/water tables (though for health reasons state regulations forbade them in a few of the sites). Not even half the classrooms had pets or other nature/science materials (43 percent and 45 percent, respectively). Not quite one-third of the classrooms had musical instruments; only 10 percent had a piano.

Young children also require challenging materials that help them gain mastery over their environment by focusing on a particular concept or set of skills. In the observed classrooms 55 percent had math manipulatives (cuisinaire rods, unifix cubes, number puzzles); 38 percent had language games (picture lotto, story sequence cards, letter puzzles). These kinds of materials extend children's language, reasoning, and conceptual abilities in a focused way, when used in combination with open-ended materials. We know that closed-ended, paper-and-pencil activities are inappropriate for young children. Not only can they be a frustrating waste of children's time, but in many cases they may permanently blunt children's curiosity and desire to learn. Nevertheless, 22 percent of the observed classrooms had commercial textbooks and/or workbooks.

Appearances Can Deceive

Of course, what matters is neither the presence nor the absence of particular materials but rather how materials are used. For example, we visited one relatively new and attractively designed open-classroom environment that, at first glance, was quite impressive: the classroom space was colorful and well organized, materials were new and plentiful.

But a second glance revealed that this "materials catalogue come to life"

(to quote one of our observers) *lacked* life. There was little to suggest that this was a space used by children. Children's work was not displayed. Teachers did not interact freely with children. By the end of our visit, the newness had worn off to reveal a sterile, uncreative, and unattractive environment.

On the other hand, we visited a dark windowless classroom in a 60-year-old, worn-out building. This new prekindergarten was short of commercially produced toys, games, or other educational materials. But it had a highly skilled teacher with many years of Head Start experience, who filled the room with teacher- and parent-made materials and created a language-rich environment full of challenge and stimulation. It was a fertile, creative, and attractive environment.

Cultural Diversity—or Sterility?

The lack of attention to cultural diversity was particularly disturbing in classrooms in which the children and teaching staff were themselves of diverse backgrounds. A southern classroom of young black children was devoid of culturally relevant materials (with the exception of a single picture of an Asian family hung on the wall); its teacher explained, "We celebrate Black History Month and Martin Luther King, Jr.'s birthday. You should be here then."

A northern classroom of black, white, Hispanic, Asian, and Native American three-year-olds offered no clue—whether through materials, bulletin board displays, storybooks, snacks, or songs—of the rich cultural community within its four walls. In this particular classroom of predominantly non-English-speaking children, there were no language games, no communication arts materials, and no cultural or child art displays (the January bulletin board displayed penguins frolicking in a winter scene); and there were only white dolls in the dramatic play areas.

Particularly striking was the fact that across all classrooms, very little children's work was displayed. Nor were

many teacher-made materials present. In general, classroom displays were commercially produced and culturally neutral, using animals or cartoon personalities in place of people (a Thanksgiving display in one classroom featured Walt Disney characters dressed as Pilgrims and Indians).

What About Learning Centers?

Learning centers help organize classroom space to facilitate small-group instruction and independent learning. They allow for individualizing the classroom program through self-selected, child-centered activities.

Usually the "standard" centers—for housekeeping, blocks, library, and art—were present in the observed classrooms. Rarer were the centers for math, nature/science, and enriched dramatic play. Dramatic play areas encourage children to explore well beyond the traditional housekeeping roles, for example, with costumes, real-world objects (firefighters' helmets, suitcases, steering wheels) and other props that support a wide range of fantasy play.

In fact, given the materials we saw at hand, there were nevertheless fewer learning centers than one would expect. The situation regarding blocks is typical. Although almost every classroom (92 percent) had blocks, only 17 percent had areas set aside for blocks. In the remaining classrooms, there was insufficient space for blocks, so that the space more resembled a storage area (several shelves of blocks) than a center designed for concentrated creative activity. Further, although over half (58 percent) of the classrooms we visited had math manipulatives, not even a quarter (22 percent) had them arranged in a math center to facilitate their use.

This lack of organization of the classroom environment does not encourage a child's independent use of materials but instead pushes teachers to direct the way the child will use materials.

In busy and stimulating environments, it is also important for children to have private spaces where they "can get away from it all." Very few classrooms—even among the very best we saw—had planned quiet or cozy areas for children.

Given the importance of gross-motor play in the psychomotor development of young children, we were surprised at the lack of provision for gross-motor activity among the classrooms we visited. The majority of programs evidenced inadequate space, equipment, and time for appropriate attention to gross-motor development.

In many programs gross-motor play was a token part of the schedule or used solely when the children "needed to let off some steam." In one daily half-day program, only 40 minutes of gross-motor activity *per week* was scheduled. This particular program happened to be a very academically structured program. The rationale for the lack of emphasis on gross-motor activity was based on limited time: "We only have an hour of structured [academic] time and we don't want to take away from it."

"Gross-Motor Rooms"

This situation was in stark contrast to the half-day schedule of another site, which gave a very high priority to gross-motor activity. In this three-hour program, there were two daily periods of gross-motor play. The day opened with 30 minutes in one of the program's two "gross-motor rooms." These were open areas, around which several classrooms were clustered. The spaces were carpeted and equipped with climbing equipment, large blocks, and other materials supportive of indoor, large muscle activity. Later in the day, a 40-minute outdoor play period was scheduled.

In inclement weather, children had the use of an indoor gymnasium, which was equipped to allow for the kind of full-scale gross-motor activity that's usually possible only outdoors: tricycling, running, rope climbing, tumbling, swinging, jumping. We observed the teacher, aide, and children together playing number-based tag games; creating imaginary worlds comprised of block towers and tunnels and other stimulating activities. These periods of-

fered far more than just "letting off steam." In this program physical activity is viewed as a creative learning opportunity.

What About Curriculum?

The terms "developmental" and "developmentally appropriate" are widely used in the print and oral rhetoric surrounding the prekindergarten curriculum, but in practice they are not widely understood.

Four sites described their programs as "developmental." However, to borrow the words of a teacher trainer we interviewed, "There is far more talk about developmental philosophy than there is actual developmental education."

Perhaps our biggest shock came in a district whose written philosophy was a well-articulated treatise on developmentally appropriate education; it stressed the uniqueness of each individual child's trajectory of development and the importance of self-selected, experiential activities. We were, therefore, unprepared to see unit-based classroom instruction for four-year-olds. Each teacher followed approximately the same sequence of lessons. Pre- and post-tests were included with each unit, and criterion mastery tests were administered after each series of five units. Children were divided into ability groups based on their scores on the pretests. Lessons were presented according to difficulty "beginning with the lowest order of skills competencies and proceeding systematically to higher level tasks." In a six-and-a-quarter-hour day, only a half-hour was scheduled for independent activity in one of the classrooms we visited.

In another classroom in this site, the "Classroom Rules" were posted on the bulletin board. They read as follows: "Please obey all rules/Listen, teacher is talking/Pay attention/Follow directions/Be quiet when guests are present/Stay in line (hands behind)/Be quiet when resting and testing." This classroom was in direct opposition to the program's philosophy of a child-centered

environment, child-initiated activity, warm adult-child interactions, and expressive language and individuality.

Misunderstandings at Both Extremes

This complete misperception of the meaning of "developmentally appropriate" most commonly resulted in an excessive "academic" orientation. However, we observed one site in which a "play-based" curriculum almost completely excluded materials with an explicitly cognitive orientation. Overall, the classrooms in this site ranged from good to excellent in terms of materials, room arrangement, and activities observed. We would have been hard pressed to find fault, were it not for the virtual absence of math manipulatives, language games, and science materials.

Considered together, these two extremes of misunderstanding reflect a more serious misconception of early childhood curricula. Too often, the choices are conceived on an either-or dimension: either a "traditional" laissez-faire, play-based program, or a formal, academic one. This is a false choice. Lilian Katz' useful distinction between *academic* and *intellectual* rigor helps explain the mistake made by the latter district:[1]

Academic rigor refers to strong emphasis on completion of school-like tasks, exercises, grade level achievement, grades and test scores, following instructions and meeting requirements, conforming to procedures and conduct necessary to succeed in the academy and to fulfill its institutional requirements. *Academic* also suggests being out-of-touch and abstract. In contrast, *intellectual* rigor refers to characteristics of the life of the mind and its earnest quest for understanding, insight, knowledge, truth, solving intellectual puzzles, and the like.

Thus an early childhood program that is developmentally appropriate goes beyond "just" play to intellectually challenge children through the use of problem-solving materials.

Home-made Approaches That Work

Between these two points on the continuum, we saw a mix of challenging, age-appropriate, developmentally based curricula. An especially good example is "Changes," an integrated art and science curriculum jointly developed by two teachers in St. Louis. On the day of our observation, the teacher passed around a bowl of clay powder and encouraged the ten children to use their senses and talk about how it looked, felt, and smelled. Next, a wet squishy ball of clay and a dry ball were passed around. Children were asked to compare the two. Each child had a chance to hold the two pieces.

The next step was to compare a piece of clay fired in a "special oven" with a piece that had been air-dried. The teacher asked the children, "What would happen if you put these two pieces in water?" After discussing this for a few minutes, they tried it out, placing first the fired piece and then the air-dried piece into a dish of water. The teacher explained they could leave the pieces in the water and return to them later.

Then the group moved to another part of the room and worked with clay set up on tables. They busily kneaded it with their hands and used rolling pins, clay bricks with designs on them, and other tools. The teacher walked about, asking children what they were doing without disrupting or directing their activity.

Later, the children returned to the two pieces of clay in water to see what had happened to them. The teacher talked to each child, showing respect and encouraging his or her self-expression. The clay was taken out of the water and passed around and again the children were asked to see how they could change it.

In another site, a harvest theme was expressed throughout one classroom. Books and displays on gardening, farming, soil, and similar topics were featured prominently. In the middle of the room a large dirtbox (actually, a child's wading pool) was filled with large root vegetables—rutabagas, potatoes, yams, carrots—which the children re- peatedly dug up and reburied with great enthusiasm.

In the classroom down the hall, children strung clay beads, painted at the easel with crushed blueberries, made pottery out of salt dough, and played with log houses, tipis, and hogans in conjunction with a Native American theme.

In yet another site, a "storekeeper" rang up groceries on an adding machine in the dramatic play area, while in another part of the room a small group of children tried to predict what would happen to their "pigs-in-a-blanket" they were about to place in a toaster oven.

Teachers in these programs, however, said it was not easy to convince parents that their children were really learning and not "just playing." When teachers build on children's actual experiences, they often cannot "prove" that specific learning objectives are being reinforced—even though many are. Yet, because they don't get cut-and-dried explanations, some parents can't understand how experiential activities can be more valuable than structured, paper-and-pencil-based "pre-reading" and "pre-math" activities.

Other Curriculum Approaches

Several districts used locally developed or nationally standardized unit-based materials but did not hide behind the "developmental" label. They tended to be urban districts serving largely minority populations.

One district used the Distar program in its double session, half-day prekindergarten program. Distar is a structured, direct-instruction approach to teaching language. We observed an afternoon session that began when the children counted to 30, sang the ABC song, took attendance (the teacher called out each name, and each child responded, "I am here" or "I am present" and put his or her name card on the attendance chart), and discussed the colors and designs on each other's clothes.

The class then began a series of three unrelated 10-minute Distar lessons: one on vehicles, one on the days of the week, and one on the concepts "wet" and "dry." While the teacher worked with the first group of four boys (the children were grouped by ability) on vehicles, a second group of six children worked with the aide. The aide drew different shapes (circle, triangle, square, and rectangle); each child, in turn, copied the aide's drawings. The third group worked independently on puzzles. Every 10 minutes, each group stopped and rotated to the next activity.

Following this highly structured learning period, the class went to group music, followed by a group art activity. Fortunately, it was then time for the children to go home.

Another district used three National Diffusion Network programs: (1) Early Prevention of School Failure, (2) Project STAMM, and (3) Talents Unlimited.

The Early Prevention of School Failure Program follows a diagnostic and prescriptive approach to the following areas: gross motor and fine motor skills, auditory skills, visual skills, and language skills. From a screening done during the first three weeks of school, supplemented by data from parents, a profile of each new incoming child is constructed. On the basis of these profiles, the teachers place children in three ability groups in each classroom, then proceed to introduce new skills and reinforce others for a prescribed set of concepts. Student profiles are updated throughout the year (teachers use checklists for this) and then passed on to each child's next grade-level teacher.

Project STAMM (Systematic Teaching and Measuring Mathematics) is a sequential math program for grades K-2. It encourages the use of concrete materials in mathematical problem solving and is accompanied by a teacher management system for observing and recording each child's performance.

Talents Unlimited is a systematic program to enhance recognition and use of thinking skills. Children develop thinking skills through the "talent" areas of productive thinking, communication, forecasting, planning, and decision making.

The three programs were chosen by

a district-level steering committee as best meeting the learning objectives of the district.

Narrow Objectives

These and several other curriculum approaches we observed in the course of our site visits were characterized mainly by narrow, discrete skill objectives, ability groupings, limited autonomy for teachers, and limited opportunities for initiative, creativity, and spontaneity for the children.

Nonetheless, these standardized curricula were generally well received by parents. "We have statistics on parent satisfaction. They're more than 90 percent satisfied in all categories," said a district administrator. One parent liked the prekindergarten program "because it's pushing my child to learn more and be prepared for the academic rigor of kindergarten." "Children excelling. That's the bottom line," said another parent. Teachers were not surprised by positive parent response: parents like pencil-and-paper activity, they say, because it proves their children are "really learning."

Many teachers also liked the curriculum. However, it must be noted that the more enthusiastic opinions were voiced by teachers with little to no prior experience teaching preschool-aged children. Rather, they tended to be individuals who came to early childhood education with an elementary background and who appreciated a standardized curriculum because it "told them what to do." Moreover, it resembled their teaching styles before being assigned to prekindergarten.

Concern for Continuity

Curriculum is one element of the child's experience in an early childhood program. Continuity is another. If a child is in a stable group of children, with the same staff for most or all of the day in the same location, a high degree of continuity is demonstrated. If the child experiences smooth and understandable changes from year to year, continuity is high. But if changes are abrupt and disturbing, continuity is low.

There is, for example, the problem of *daily continuity*. In one program the child and parent arrive together at 7:00 a.m. and have breakfast. The child then greets his or her teacher and goes off to play with one of the 15 other children in the room. After the teacher and mother converse, the mother leaves for work.

When the child's father arrives at 4:30 p.m., the child is happily playing with the same children and the same teacher in the same room the mother saw that morning. The father is able to talk to the teacher about his child's day.

In another program the child is dropped off at 8:30 a.m. and stays with an aide in a group of 20 "early birds" until 9:00 a.m., when the teacher arrives. The child goes, with a few others, to another room to join the rest of the preschool class (24 children in all). They spend the next three hours there. Then some children go home, while the rest go to a large cafeteria to eat lunch with about 150 kindergartners and first graders. After lunch the prekindergarten children go to the child care room for a nap until 3:00 p.m. Then they wake up and move to another room with other children who have just arrived from all-day kindergarten. They all stay there until 5:00 p.m.: some are then picked up and the rest move to another room for later pick-up. A prekindergartner in this school is passed in and out of six different groups of children.

Being part of a relatively stable group of children and adults is a more beneficial educational experience for young children than being part of a changing and unstable group. Children who form secure relationships with teachers are not only better able to make a smooth transition between home and school but are also able to use the teacher as a source of security during the day. The essential elements of a secure relationship are the availability and predictability of the teacher.

There is also the concern for *long-term continuity*. One goal of a good early childhood program is to ensure a smooth transition from prekindergarten to kindergarten. This assumes a similarity of focus and intent between prekindergarten and kindergarten classroom environments and activities. But this is no longer certain because kindergarten is becoming "what first grade once was": *i.e.,* the real point of entry into the school system, when the child begins academic instruction. We saw that clearly in the kindergartens we visited.

Almost without exception, the kindergarten consisted of a highly structured, academically oriented experience. Time was rigidly scheduled and divided into non-integrated learning periods (reading time, math time, music time, large group time). The majority of the day's activities were teacher directed. Independent activity guided by child choice was generally limited to brief play times—as short as 15 minutes in half-day kindergartens. Learning materials, especially for language arts and math activities, were heavily reliant on workbooks and worksheets that supplemented standardized reading and math series. (We have already noted that 22 percent of the observed *pre*kindergarten classrooms used workbooks; in comparison, 78 percent of the *kindergartens* in those same sites used workbooks.) Even open-ended activities like art tended to emphasize total-group art "projects," in which each child is directed to make the same thing (identical turkeys for Thanksgiving or hearts for Valentine's Day).

Given the more rigid nature of the receiving kindergarten environment, continuity between prekindergarten and kindergarten is not necessarily a good thing. For example, the smoothest continuity occurred in those districts which pushed the structured kindergarten and early elementary curriculum downward into prekindergarten (in short, imposing a developmentally inappropriate program upon the children). Ironically, continuity was poorest in those sites in which the prekindergarten program was developmentally appropriate and the kindergarten program was not.

This pattern is not good. *Both prekindergarten and kindergarten should focus on an upward extension of earlier development* rather than a downward extension of schooling. The research shows that young children learn best through direct, concrete experience of the world rather than through the symbolic manipulations more often associated with formal instruction (particularly with reading instruction).

They're Flunking Kindergarten

There is no evidence that greater long-term gains result from kindergarten programs heavy with academic instruction.[2] In fact, the opposite may be true. Across the country parents are complaining that their children are in danger of flunking kindergarten, and many children are being made to repeat the kindergarten year.

There seem to be four solutions to this problem: three would change the child, the fourth would change kindergarten.

The first "solution" is to make the prekindergarten program more academic, with standardized curricula, teacher-directed academic activities, and play as the reward—not the medium—for learning. It is not a useful solution.

A second "solution" is the growing popularity of the "developmental kindergarten." This only adds a second, "transitional" year of kindergarten, either between prekindergarten and kindergarten (called "developmental" kindergarten or "readiness" kindergarten) or between kindergarten and first grade (called "pre-firsts" or "transitional firsts"). This is a well-intentioned—but generally ineffective—response to the fact that many children today who can't meet the demands of kindergarten and first grade are either held back or referred to special education.[3]

A third "solution" is to push up the entrance age to kindergarten. In the past 30 years, the average age of kindergartners has been creeping up: a child who might have been among the oldest in the class in 1958 would now be one of the youngest.[4] Yet, no matter what the cut-off date for kindergarten

entry, some children would be "older" (born in the first three months of the cut-off year) and some would be "younger" (born in the last three months) and would be grouped accordingly.

The fourth, and optimal, solution to the mismatch between prekindergarten and kindergarten is to re-think the kindergarten program as a developmental, age-appropriate program for meeting the needs of a diverse group of children.

We saw efforts in several districts to improve the kindergarten through upward diffusion of the prekindergarten program. In all cases, some degree of interaction between prekindergarten and kindergarten teachers was involved.

A districtwide, multiyear strategy is being used in one district we visited. Its director of elementary education and the early childhood supervisor want continuity from prekindergarten through first grade. Their long-range plan is to institute a developmentally appropriate curriculum for all children age three through age six.

This district's prekindergarten program is a model of appropriate activities for three- and four-year-olds. A wide variety of materials and equipment is available, teachers are well-trained, and children have many choices. The program philosophy is expressed in the motto, Learning through Play.

When full-day kindergarten was proposed, the planning committee included teachers from prekindergarten, kindergarten, and first grade. Their curriculum was so successful it was also proposed for part-day kindergartens.

Conclusion

Today, the debate over the role of public schools in early childhood education is ready to move beyond the question of *whether* to the question of *how.*

Good programs for children cannot be mandated, but the necessary condi-

tions can be specified. These would include the following:

- children in small groups
- caring and well-prepared teachers who have specific child-related training in their background, as well as experience with young children
- the leadership of principals who are knowledgeable about childhood development and early childhood education and supportive of ongoing staff development
- a clearly stated philosophy of early childhood education
- an underpinning of sound principles of child development and theories of education
- a clear, coherent curriculum, yet one with broad enough goals for teachers to work creatively within it
- and a partnership of teachers and parents.

Leadership is critical. In public school programs, the school and community leadership must be committed to appropriate practice throughout its prekindergartens, kindergartens, and early elementary grades. It must also be committed to providing the financial and human resources for staff development and the retraining of teachers and administrators so that a sound philosophy of early childhood education can be translated into practice.

Notes

1. Katz, L. G., J. D. Raths, and R. D. Torres (1987). *A place called kindergarten.* Urbana, Ill: Clearinghouse on Elementary and Early Childhood Education, p. 29.

2. Spodek, B. (1982). The kindergarten: A retrospective and contemporary view. In L. G. Katz (Ed.), *Current topics in early childhood education.* Norwood, N.J: Ablex Publishing Corporation.

3. Shepard, L.A. and Smith, M. L. (1986). Synthesis of research on school readiness and kindergarten retention. *Educational Leadership,* 44 (3), 7886. In fact, there is no evidence that an extra year of schooling solves the problems it was intended to solve. In what may be the only review of transitional classes, Lorrie Shepard and Mary Lee Smith conclude that "children in these programs show virtually no academic advantage over equally at-risk children who have not had the extra year. Furthermore, there is often an emotional cost associated with staying back." (p. 85).

4. Shepard and Smith (1986), p. 81.

Early childhood professionals need to work together to establish safe learning environments and promote growth, development, and appropriate behaviors in the children they serve.

Collaborative Training in the Education of Early Childhood Educators

Barbara Lowenthal

Barbara Lowenthal *(CEC Chapter #302) is an Associate Professor, Department of Special Education, Northeastern Illinois University, Chicago.*

Recent legislation and governmental policy have made it necessary to ensure collaboration in the training of early childhood and special educators. Both Public Law 99-457 (The Education of the Handicapped Amendments of 1986) and the regular education initiative proposed by the federal government have provided a rationale for this cooperation (Guralnick, 1981, 1982; Hanson & Hanline, 1989; Lilly, 1986; Strain & Kerr, 1981; Will, 1986). Early childhood special educators will need to be taught how to practice collaboration, which is defined by Weaver (1979) as "not mere cooperation or a matter of good will, but an agreed-upon distribution of power, status, and authority" (p. 24).

P.L. 99-457 mandates that preschoolers with special needs be placed in the least restrictive environment (Wang, 1989). For quite a few of these children, this mandate means that they will participate in typical preschool settings. One of the difficulties with this requirement is that, historically, many preschoolers with disabilities have been served by public and private agencies other than the schools. These agencies have a great deal of practical experience with and information about these children that schools may lack.

Another difficulty in fulfilling the mandates of P.L. 99-457 is that many public schools will need to establish additional preschool classes, which will require new teachers. Besides the school settings, integrated placement for these young children could be in other sites such as day care centers and day care homes. Therefore, early childhood personnel will need preparation in intervening in these settings as well.

Research clearly indicates that personnel who are well trained are more effective than those who are not (Tingey-Michaelis, 1985). The question then becomes how best to train early childhood personnel, both regular and special, to meet the challenges of teaching in integrated settings (Guralnick, 1981; Hanson & Hanline, 1989). The competencies expected of regular early childhood teachers and those required of special educators are discussed in this article, and possible commonalities and differences between the two roles are elucidated.

Early Childhood Teacher Competencies

Competencies expected of regular early childhood educators can be described in terms of the requirements for the Child Development Associate (CDA) credentials that were initiated in 1972 to alleviate staff shortages and provide training for Head Start and other child care staff (Trickett, 1979). The competencies are summarized in the following list (Jones & Hamby, 1981; Peters, 1981):

1. To establish a safe, healthy environment.
2. To advance physical and intellectual competence.
3. To ensure a well-run program responsive to participant needs.
4. To maintain a commitment to professionalism.

In reviewing these competencies, it is clear that the regular early childhood teacher must be able to accommodate a wide range of abilities, developmental levels, and social-emotional needs of children in the preschool classroom (Bredekamp, 1987; Moyer, Egertson, & Isenberg, 1987). The special educator also will need to do this, but will require extra training in alternative approaches

to intervention, methods and strategies, best practices in consultation and collaboration, available resources, and skills in the processes of referral and transition.

The competencies of the special educator will both overlap and differ somewhat from those required of the regular preschool teacher. These competencies can include knowledge of curricula, class management, professional consultation and communications, teacher-family relationships, child-child interactions, exceptional children, referral, assessment and individualized teaching, and professional values (Guralnick, 1982; Hanson & Hanline, 1989; Hurley, 1989; Zeitlin, du Verglas, & Windhover, 1982). A summary of each of these competencies follows.

Curricula

The term is used here to include the ability to identify curricular goals for teaching each child functional skills for daily living (Hanson, 1984). This ability will be helpful in the development of individualized education programs. Functional skills can be taught effectively through classroom routines and through the use of a curriculum built on a framework of play.

Class Management

This refers to the efficient management of schedules, instruction, materials, and child behaviors within the classroom ecology. Time schedules should be set but be sufficiently flexible to allow for differences in time requirements of individual children. Transitions can be smoothly structured so that children can move from one activity to another as their individual needs dictate. For effective behavior management, the special educator needs training in the following skills: identification of potential reinforcers for each child, positive behavior reinforcement through the use of these reinforcers, provision of sufficient materials to promote cooperation, use of class activities that require cooperation, and reinforcement of appropriate behavior through peer modeling (Cook, Tessier, & Armbruster, 1987).

Professional Consultation and Collaboration

Early childhood special educators need to be able to communicate with regular early childhood teachers to develop common goals for children, methods, materials, assessment, instruction, and evaluation. Personal characteristics that

Early childhood teachers need to work together to make transition for students a positive experience.

can assist in developing good communication include being empathic and open, being able to establish good rapport, respecting different points of view, and being positive and enthusiastic (West & Cannon, 1987).

Teacher-Family Relationships

As a result of P.L. 99-457, early childhood special educators need training in a broad-based, family-focused approach. Some components of this approach include (a) promoting positive child and family functioning through assistance based on the family's identified needs and goals; (b) using family strengths and informal support systems as a basis for empowering the family to make use of existing resources to meet their needs; and (c) allowing families to exercise control over the extent to which they want to be involved in the preschool program (Dunst, 1985; Dunst, Trivette, & Deal, 1988; Hanson, 1984; Hanson & Krentz, 1986; Turnbull, Summers, & Brotherson, 1984).

Child-Child Interactions

Special educators have a responsibility to assist the children in their classes to learn how to interact with one another in appropriate ways and to cooperate in working toward common goals.

Exceptional Children

Special educators need to have both a practical and a theoretical understanding of the characteristics of young exceptional children in all domains of development. This knowledge should be combined with information about how to further children's feelings of independence and task mastery. Preschool children with special needs should be allowed to assume as much control over their environment as possible. The gradual shift of balance of power from teachers to children will facilitate their task engagement and enhance motivation (Dunst, 1985).

Referral

An important skill for early childhood special educators is to know when and where to refer a child with disabilities and his or her family if they require related services such as speech, occupational, and physical therapy; child and family counseling; and health services.

Both special education teachers and regular education teachers need to be able to discuss time schedules of the children.

Assessment and Individualized Teaching

Early childhood special educators need to learn a variety of assessment techniques in order to best determine the strengths and weaknesses of every child. An ecological approach should be stressed that incorporates an understanding of both the child's unique characteristics and environmental influences affecting his or her development. Assessment information can be obtained through observation, case history, tests, and interviews. After assessment, individualized teaching should be stressed using a broad array of teaching methods. Both special educators and regular teachers need training in these techniques, which should emphasize the generalization of skills from one developmental area to another. Teaching techniques that use basic classroom routines as their framework can best develop this generalization of skills. Teaching methods should be as unintrusive as possible so that children are encouraged to explore, play, and experiment as ways of learning (Safford, 1989).

Professional Values

Preschool educators, both regular and special, must incorporate into their personal value systems a respect and consideration for the rights of every child and his or her family.

Special Educator as Resource

Special educators must also recognize another important aspect of their role: that of resource to the regular preschool teacher, especially with regard to mainstreaming needs. A special education teacher's positive and helpful approach toward integration of children with disabilities in the regular preschool class can affect the attitude of the classroom teacher not only about integrating a particular child but also toward the principle of mainstreaming itself (Salend & Johns, 1983).

A related aspect of this resource role is knowledge of successful transition practices when transferring the child with disabilities from a segregated to an integrated preschool setting. To accomplish this transition, the special education teacher must be familiar with the environment of the regular class, the curriculum and behavioral expectations for the children, class schedules, and routines. This will require the special educator to visit the regular class and observe its ecology so that he or she can teach the skills the exceptional child needs to function in the mainstream setting. Another essential transition practice is to be sensitive to the family regarding mainstreaming. This will promote the family's independence and feelings of control (Dunst, Trivette, & Deal, 1988).

Similarities

There are many similarities between the required competencies for regular and special early childhood educators. One of the most significant is that both types of teachers work with preschool children who are at different developmental levels and have varying cognitive and personal-social characteristics within a group program. What is good early childhood practice for typical children in most cases appears to be good for those who have special needs. The presence of children with disabilities does not require a different style of teaching from that which is appropriate for most other youngsters (Bailey, Clifford, & Harms, 1982).

Another significant competency that both kinds of educators should possess is the ability to establish positive and respectful relationships with families. Empathy, responsiveness to family needs, and promotion of family independence and empowerment are essential abilities for both special and mainstream early childhood personnel (Dunst, Trivette, & Deal, 1988; Turnbull, Summers, & Brotherson, 1984; Turnbull & Turnbull, 1986).

Early childhood professionals need to work together to establish safe learning environments and promote growth, development, and appropriate behaviors in the children they serve. Both special educators and regular preschool teachers must be committed to professionalism and ethical values and have a functional knowledge of child development, class management, and record-keeping. However, special educators

have a greater need for alternative approaches in intervention, curricula, and techniques of behavior management, and they need a deeper understanding of atypical development in children. Knowledge of referral sources; related services; best practices in consultation, collaboration, and transition; and family advocacy is useful as well.

A Proposal for Promoting Collaboration

Because of the regular education initiative and the mandates of P.L. 99-457, special and regular preschool teachers need to cooperate more with one another and in some cases even work together in the same classrooms. One way to ensure this collaboration and cooperation might be to train all future preschool teachers in both regular and special early childhood education. Since the required competencies are similar for both kinds of teachers, it might be best to issue a joint certification. Then all preschool teachers would take core courses in normal and atypical development of young children, child psychology, assessment, curriculum and teaching methods, evaluation, classroom management, teaming, and working with families. More detailed coursework could then be required in alternative methods for intervention, techniques for integration, technology for children with special needs, transition, referral and consultation, and knowledge of available resources.

The program could be field based, with practica in integrated settings. Some practicum hours could be credited for doing respite care for interested families, since this work could assist preservice teachers in gaining a better understanding of family needs, strengths, and support systems. Since the training would be intensive and take longer than the customary bachelor's degree requirements, it could lead to a master's degree in the areas of regular and early childhood education. This joint certification would then follow the guidelines of P.L. 99-457, help integration to succeed in mainstreamed settings, and ensure collaboration in the training of early childhood special and regular educators.

References

Hanson, M. J., & Hanline, M. F. (1989). Integration options for the very young child. In R. Gaylord-Ross (Ed.), *Integration strategies for persons with handicaps* (pp. 177-193). Baltimore: Paul H. Brookes.

Hanson, M. J., & Krentz, M. K. (1986). *Supporting parent-child interactions: A guide for early intervention program personnel.* San Francisco: Department of Special Education, San Francisco State University.

Hurley, O. (1989). Implications of P.L. 99-457 for preparation of preschool personnel. In J. Gallagher, P. Trohanis, & R. Clifford (Eds.), *Policy implementation and P.L. 99-457* (pp. 133-146). Baltimore: Paul H. Brookes.

Jones, L., & Hamby, T. M. (1981). Comments on "A review of the Child Development Associate Credential." *Child Care Quarterly, 10,* 74-83.

Lilly, S. (1986). The relationship between general and special education: A new face on an old issue. *Counterpoint, 6,* 10.

Moyer, J., Egertson, H., & Isenberg, J. (1987). The child-centered kindergarten. *Childhood Education, 63,* 235-242.

Peters, D. L. (1981). New methods for educating and credentialing professionals in child care. *Child Care Quarterly, 10,* 3-8.

Safford, P. L. (1989). *Integrated teaching in early childhood.* White Plains, NY: Longman.

Salend, S., & Johns, J. (1983). A tale of two teachers: Teacher commitment to mainstreaming. *TEACHING Exceptional Children, 15,* 82-85.

Strain, P. S., & Kerr, M. M. (1981). *Mainstreaming of children in schools: Research and programmatic issues.* New York: Academic Press.

Tingey-Michaelis, C. (1985). Early intervention: Is certification necessary? *Teacher Education and Special Education, 8,* 91-97.

Trickett, P. (1979). Career development in Head Start. In E. Zigler & J. Valentine (Eds.), *Project Head Start* (pp. 315-338). New York: Free Press.

Turnbull, A. P., Summers, J. A., & Brotherson, M. J. (1984). *Working with families with disabled members: A family systems approach.* Lawrence: University of Kansas, Kansas University Affiliated Facility.

Turnbull, A. P., & Turnbull, H. R. (1986). *Families, professionals, and exceptionality: A special partnership.* Columbus, OH: Merrill.

Wang, M. (1989). Implementing the state of the art and integration mandates of P.L. 94-142. In J. Gallagher, P. Trohanis, & R. Clifford (Eds.), *Policy implementation and P.L. 99-457* (pp. 33-58). Baltimore: Paul H. Brookes.

Weaver, J. F. (1979). Collaboration: Why is sharing the turf so difficult? *Journal of Teacher Education, 30,* 24-25.

West, J. F., & Cannon, G. (1987). Essential collaborative consultation competencies for regular and special educators. *Journal of Learning Disabilities, 21,* 56-63.

Will, M. (1986). Educating children with learning problems: A shared responsibility. *Exceptional Children, 52,* 411-416.

Zeitlin, S., du Verglas, G., & Windhover, R. (Eds.). (1982). *Basic competencies for personnel in early intervention programs.* Monmouth, OR: Western Technical Assistance Resources.

Bailey, D. B., Clifford, R. M., & Harms, T. (1982). Comparison of preschool environments for handicapped and nonhandicapped children. *Topics in Early Childhood Special Education, 2,* 9-20.

Bredekamp, S. (1987). *Developmentally appropriate practice in early childhood programs serving children from birth through age 8.* (expanded edition). Washington, DC: National Association for the Education of Young Children.

Cook, R., Tessier, A., & Armbruster, V. (1987). *Adapting early childhood curricula for children with special needs.* Columbus, OH: Merrill.

Dunst, C. J. (1985). Rethinking early intervention. *Analysis and Intervention in Developmental Disabilities, 5,* 165-201.

Dunst, C. J., Trivette, C. M., & Deal, A. G. (1988). *Enabling and empowering families.* Cambridge, MA: Brookline Books.

Guralnick, M. J. (1981). The efficacy of integrating handicapped children in early childhood settings: Research implications. *Topics in Early Childhood Special Education, 1,* 57-71.

Guralnick, M. J. (1982). Programmatic factors affecting child-child social interactions in mainstreamed preschool programs. In P. S. Strain (Ed.), *Social development of exceptional children* (pp. 71-92). Rockville, MD: Aspen.

Hanson, M. J. (1984). Early intervention: Models and practices. In M. J. Hanson (Ed.), *Atypical infant development* (pp. 361-384). Austin, TX: PRO-Ed.

Preschool Classroom Environments That Promote Communication

Michaelene M. Ostrosky

Ann P. Kaiser

Michaelene M. Ostrosky *(CEC Chapter #46) is a Doctoral Student and* **Ann P. Kaiser** *(CEC Chapter #69) is Professor, Department of Special Education, Peabody College of Vanderbilt University, Nashville, Tennessee.*

Children learn what language *is* by learning what language can *do* (Bates, 1976; Hart, 1985). The function of language depends upon it's effects on the environment. An environment that contains few reinforcers and few objects of interest or meets children's needs without requiring language is *not* a functional environment for learning or teaching language.

Recent research suggests that environmental arrangement is an important strategy for teachers who want to promote communication in classrooms (Alpert, Kaiser, Ostrosky, & Hemmeter, 1987; Haring, Neetz, Lovinger, Peck, & Semmell, 1987). To encourage use of language, classrooms should be arranged so that there are materials and activities of interest to the children. In addition, teachers must mediate the environment by presenting materials in response to children's requests and other uses of language (Hart & Rogers-Warren, 1978). Creating such opportunities and consequences for language use through environmental arrangement can play a critical role in a child's language acquisition (Hart, 1985).

Both social and physical aspects of the environment set the occasion for communication (Rogers-Warren, Warren, & Baer, 1983). The physical environment includes the selection and arrangement of materials, the arrangement of the setting to encourage children's engagement, and scheduling of activities to enhance children's participation and appropriate behavior. The social environment includes the presence of responsive adults and children and the verbal and nonverbal social interactions that occur among the people in the environment. In addition, contingencies for language use, the availability of a communication partner, the degree to which adults preempt children's communicative attempts, and the affective style of the listener have an impact on children's language acquisition and production (Hemmeter, 1988).

As shown in Figure 1, the social and physical aspects of the environment are linked to communication when an adult mediates the physical environment in response to children's use of language. The adult links the child's language to the environment by ensuring that the child's communication attempts are functional and reinforced. As a mediator, the adult can use an incidental teaching process to model and prompt elaborated language in order to expand the child's current skills (Hart, 1985).

Environmental arrangement can en-courage children to initiate language as a means of gaining access to materials and getting help. By providing the materials requested by a child, the adult serves the important function of specifically reinforcing that child's use of language. In addition, the environmental arrangement supports the adult in attending to the child's interest and communication attempts, thereby increasing the likelihood that the adult will respond to the child's interest and provide materials contingently (Haring et al., 1987).

Seven Strategies for Arranging the Environment

The basic goal of environmental arrangement is to increase children's interest in the environment as an occasion for communication. The environment is managed and arranged to promote requests and comments by children and to support language teaching efforts by adults. Using the environment to prompt language includes the following steps:

1. Focusing on making language a part of children's routines.
2. Providing access to interesting materials and activities.
3. Providing adult and peer models who will encourage children to use

language and respond to their attempts to do so.

4. Establishing a contingent relationship between access to materials or assistance and use of language.

The seven environmental strategies described here are designed to (a) increase the likelihood that children will show an interest in the environment and make communicative attempts and (b) increase the likelihood that the adult will prompt the use of language about things of interest to the children by providing clear and obvious *nonverbal* prompts for them to communicate. When the environment is arranged in this way, attractive materials and activities function as both discriminative stimuli and reinforcers for language use.

Interesting Materials

Materials and activities that children enjoy should be available in the environment. Young children are most likely to initiate communication about the things that interest them. Thus, increasing the likelihood of children's interest in the environment increases the opportunities for language use and teaching. Teachers usually know which toys and materials individual children prefer. However, a simple inventory of preferences can be taken at staff meetings or by systematically observing children's choices during free play. Parents often can provide information regarding their children's preferred toys and activities. Once toy preference has been determined, teachers can enhance interest in the environment by making such toys or materials available. For example, if a child enjoys bead stringing, various shaped and colored beads, noodles, and sewing spools could be made available. Identifying preferred activities and materials is especially important for a young child with severe disabilities. Variations in activities and materials must be carefully monitored to ensure that the child remains interested. For example, a child with severe disabilities who likes squeak toys may enjoy a variety of these toys but not like a Jack-in-the-box that makes a similar sound. Rotating the toys available at any given time is also a good way to make old toys more interesting; when they reappear they seem brand new!

Out of Reach

Placing *some* desirable materials within view but out of reach will prompt children to make requests in order to secure the materials. Materials may be placed on the shelves, in clear plastic bins, or simply across the table during a group activity to increase the likelihood that the children will request access to them either verbally or nonverbally. These requests create opportunities for language teaching, since when children request a specific material they are also specifying their reinforcers (Hart & Rogers-Warren, 1978). Thus, a teacher who prompts language and provides the requested material contingent on the child's response effectively reinforces that response. The effectiveness of this strategy can be enhanced by showing the children materials, naming the materials, and then waiting attentively for the children to make requests. During snack time or before a cooking activity, a teacher can prompt children to make requests by placing the cooking materials across the table from them. Children with severe disabilities might gain access to these materials by point-

Figure 1. Social and physical aspects of the environment set the occasion for communication as the adult serves as the mediator in response to children's use of language.

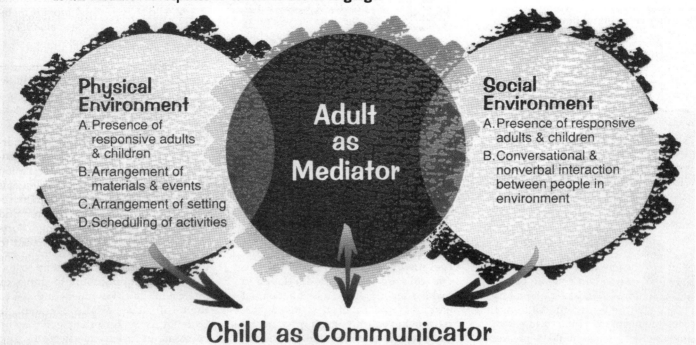

ing or eye gazing, whereas more skilled children might be encouraged to use signs, words, or even complete sentences. Teachers must be careful not to frustrate students by placing too many communicative demands on them. A balance of requesting materials and playing independently is important in every activity.

Inadequate Portions

Providing small or inadequate portions of preferred materials such as blocks, crayons, or crackers is another way to arrange the environment to promote communication. During an activity the children enjoy, an adult can control the amount of materials available so that the children have only some of the parts that are needed to complete the activity. When the children use the materials initially provided, they are likely to request more. Providing inadequate portions of an interesting and desirable material creates a situation in which children are encouraged by the arrangement of the physical environment to communicate their needs for additional materials. For example, during snack time, an adult can encourage requests by presenting small servings of juice or pieces of a cookie rather than a whole cookie. A child who enjoys watching the teacher blow bubbles can be encouraged to make requests if the teacher blows one or two bubbles and then waits for the child to request more.

When children initiate language with requests for more, the teacher has the opportunity to model and prompt more elaborate language as well as to provide functional consequences for the children's communicative attempts. For example:

Teacher: (Blows two bubbles and stops.)
Child: "More"
Teacher: "Blow more bubbles?"
Child: "Blow more."
Teacher: (Blows more bubbles)

Choice Making

There are many occasions when two or more options for activities or materials can be presented to children. In order to encourage children to initiate language, the choice should be presented nonverbally. Children may be most encouraged to make a choice when one of the items is preferred and the other is disliked. For example, the adult may hold two different toys (e.g., a big yellow dump truck and a small red block) and wait for the child to make a verbal or nonverbal request. If the child requests nonverbally, the adult has the option of prompting the child to verbalize ("Tell me what you want") or simply modeling a response for the child ("Yellow truck"). Children's verbal requests can be followed with expansions of their language ("You wanted the yellow truck") or models of alternative forms for requesting ("Yellow truck, please").

Assistance

Creating a situation in which children are likely to need assistance increases the likelihood that they will communicate about that need. The presence of attractive materials that require assistance to operate may encourage children to request help from adults or peers. A wind-up toy, a swing that a child needs help getting into, or an unopened bottle of bubbles are all examples of materials that can provide a nonverbal prompt to ask for help.

Sabotage

Setting up a "sabotage" by not providing all of the materials the children will need to complete a task (e.g., paints and water but no paintbrush following an instruction to paint), or by otherwise preventing them from carrying out an instruction, also will encourage them to make requests. This environmental strategy requires children to problem solve and indicate that something is wrong or missing. They must first determine what is needed, and this initial discovery may require prompts from an adult. The missing materials are cues for the children to communicate that something is not right or that additional materials are needed. Sabotage is an effective prompt for language when the cues are obvious and children's cognitive skills are sufficiently developed to make detection of the missing material easy and rapid. Sabotage should be carried out in a warm, engaging manner by the teacher; the episode should be brief and never frustrating to the child.

Silly Situations

The final environmental strategy is to create a need for children to communicate by setting up absurd or silly situations that violate their expectations. For example, an adult who playfully attempts to put a child's shoes on the adult's feet may encourage the child to comment on the absurd situation. During snack time, an adult can set up an absurd situation by placing a large piece of modeling clay or a colored block on a child's plate instead of a cracker, then waiting expectantly for the child to initiate a verbal or nonverbal request.

Children develop expectations for the ways things should be in everyday environments. They learn routines and expect that things will happen in a particular order. When something unexpected happens, they may be prompted to communicate. Of course, children must *have* expectations before the expectations can be violated. Thus, use of this strategy must be tailored to the individual skills of the children and to their familiar routines. For example, a child who always stores articles of clothing and materials in a specific "cubbie" will probably notice when an adult places a silly picture over it; a child who does not consistently use a specified "cubbie" would be unlikely to notice and respond to such a change in the environment.

Making the Strategies Effective

To make these seven environmental strategies work, the teacher must follow the student's lead. The teacher must notice what the child is interested in, establish joint attention on the topic of interest, and encourage the child to make communicative attempts. By monitoring the child's interest and identifying which materials and activities the child enjoys, an adult can select the ones that will best serve as reinforcers for language.

The nonverbal cues that accompany the environmental arrangement strategies should be faded over time so the child is responding more to things of interest in the environment and less to the adult's cues (Halle, Marshall, & Spradlin, 1979). For example, it may be necessary at first for teachers to shrug their shoulders, raise their eyebrows, and tilt their heads, while extending their hands containing different toys, in order to direct children's attention to the environment and to the opportunity for choice making. As children become more skilled at initiating requests, fewer and less obvious nonverbal prompts should be given.

The use of environmental strategies must be tailored to each child's cognitive level and responsiveness to the environment. For example, putting a coat on a child backward and waiting for the child to communicate that something is wrong may require additional prompts if the child is unable to problem solve at this level. For environmental strategies to be effective, they must be geared to each child's level and they must cue communicative responses that are emergent in the child's repertoire.

Conclusion

How adults respond to children's communication attempts when they are elicited by environmental arrangement is extremely important. Immediate feed-back and access to the desired material or requested assistance, as well as a positive affective response, are essential consequences for communication attempts. As in all applications of naturalistic teaching processes, these episodes should be brief, positive, successful for the children, and designed to reinforce the children's use of language and their social engagement with adults (Hart & Rogers-Warren, 1978).

References

Alpert, C. L., Kaiser, A. P., Ostrosky, M. M., & Hemmeter, M. L. (1987, November). *Using environmental arrangement and milieu language teaching as interventions for improving the communication skills of nonvocal preschool children.* Paper presented at the National Early Childhood Conference on Children with Special Needs, Denver, CO.

Bates, E. (1976). Pragmatics and sociolinguistics in child language. In O. M. Moorehead & A. E. Moorehead (Eds.), *Normal and deficient child language* (pp. 411–463). Baltimore: University Park Press.

Halle, J., Marshall, A., & Spradlin, J. (1979). Time delay: A technique to increase language use and facilitate generalization in retarded children. *Journal of Applied Behavior Analysis, 12,* 431–439.

Haring, T. G., Neetz, J. A., Lovinger, L., Peck, C., & Semmell, M. I. (1987). Effects of four modified incidental teaching procedures to create opportunities for communication. *The Journal of the Association for Persons with Severe Handicaps, 12,*(3), 218–226.

Hart, B. M. (1985). Naturalistic language training strategies. In S. F. Warren & A. Rogers-Warren (Eds.), *Teaching functional language.* Baltimore: University Park Press.

Hart, B. M., & Rogers-Warren, A. K. (1978). Milieu language training. In R. L. Schiefelbusch (Ed.), *Language intervention strategies* (Vol. 2, pp. 193–235). Baltimore: University Park Press.

Hemmeter, M. L. (1988). *The effect of environmental arrangement on parent-child language interactions.* Unpublished master's thesis, Vanderbilt University, Nashville, TN.

Rogers-Warren, A. K., Warren, S. F., & Baer, D. M. (1983). Interactional bases of language learning. In K. Kernan, M. Begab, & R. Edgarton (Eds.), *Environments and behavior: The adaptation of mentally retarded persons.* Baltimore: University Park Press.

The development and dissemination of this paper were partially supported by Grant No. G008400663 from the Office of Special Education and Grant No. G008720107 from the National Institute for Disability and Rehabilitation Research. The authors are grateful to Cathy Alpert and Mary Louise Hemmeter for their contributions in the development of these environmental arrangement strategies.

Preschool Mainstreaming: Attitude Barriers and Strategies for Addressing Them

"Imagine for a moment that you have a child who today is happy, healthy, attending his or her local school, and progressing normally. Reflect for a moment on where you would want the child to go to school should he or she be in a car accident and become unable to walk without assistance and unable to learn as quickly" (Forest, 1992).

Deborah F. Rose and Barbara J. Smith

Deborah F. Rose, M.S.W., is a research associate at Allegheny-Singer Research Institute, and Barbara J. Smith, Ph.D. is a research scientist at Allegheny-Singer and the executive director of the Division for Early Childhood of the Council for Exceptional Children.

This article is adapted from "Attitude Barriers and Strategies for Preschool Mainstreaming," a paper in the Policy and Practice in Early Childhood Special Education Series.

The regulations governing the Individuals with Disabilities Education Act (IDEA) require that children with disabilities be placed in the Least Restrictive Environment (LRE) in which the individual child will learn (1991, 34 CFR § 300.550). Placement decisions—made by public school placement teams consisting of school administrators, teachers, parents, related service personnel, or whoever is appropriate for an individual child—must determine (1) the "regular educational environment" where the child would be educated were she or he not identified and labeled as eligible for special education and related services, and (2) whether the special education and related services can be appropriately delivered in that setting. Additionally, decisions to educate children in settings other than the "regular educational environment" can occur only when "the nature and severity of the handicap is such that education in regular classes with the use of supplementary aides and services cannot be achieved satisfactorily" (1991, 34 CFR § 300.550).

School districts have exercised a variety of options in order to meet the LRE requirements of the IDEA. School districts that operate preschool programs for typically developing children have integrated children with disabilities into their public school classrooms. Districts that do not offer preschool services to typically developing children have collaborated with community-based preschool and child care programs to deliver special education and related services in natural preschool environments (Smith & Rose, 1991). Many districts, however, are encountering policy and attitudinal barriers to placing preschool children with disabilities in community programs. Each of the key players—members of the placement team, as well as teachers and administrators in community-based programs—holds a set of beliefs about where children with disabilities are best educated, the role of the family in the child's early education, and the quality of community-based programs.

Are attitudes a problem?

A recent national survey of special education program and policy officials; program directors of child care, Head Start, and special-education services; and parents collected information about the greatest barriers to preschool mainstreaming, including issues of education policy, attitudes, and curricula and methods.

Nearly 60% of the survey respondents cited attitudes as a barrier to preschool mainstreaming. Those identifying attitudinal barriers varied by position; for example, all responding parents, compared to fewer than one third of child care directors, believed that attitudes were a barrier to mainstreaming.

What are the attitude barriers and strategies?

The types of attitudes reported on the survey were categorized according to the following concerns: (a) turf, (b) teacher preparedness, (c) awareness, (d) "someone will lose," and (e) communication/collaboration/respect. Although numerous attitude barriers were cited, few solutions to those barriers were offered by the survey respondents. The strategies discussed here represent op-

From *Young Children*, Vol. 48, No. 4, May 1993, pp. 59-62. © 1993 by Deborah F. Rose and Barbara J. Smith, St. Peter's Child Development Center, Inc., 2500 Baldwick Road, Suite 15, Pittsburgh, PA 15205. Reprinted by permission.

tions suggested by survey respondents or case-study subjects and expert consultants to the project.

Turf issues

Barriers. History and tradition are the things of which turf issues are made. The pride that the special-education community feels in the provision of services to children with disabilities was evident in survey responses to the attitude question. Survey respondents reported that many special educators are "holding on to the segregated systems of educating children" because of these turf issues.

The location of the preschool program (school based versus community based) was another concern expressed by survey respondents. As more children with disabilities are placed in community-based preschools that are not under the direct purview of the public school system, special educators report concern about how "their" children are being educated. Special educators believe that they have been trained specifically to provide "the best" education experiences for children with disabilities. Survey respondents reported a loss of control over the very methods, techniques, and curricula that they were taught would be most effective when educating children with disabilities. Respondents also expressed concern about the receptivity of community-based programs to technical assistance from special educators. With the changing role of special education in some states, it is not surprising that turf issues are recognized as barriers to mainstreaming. Survey respondents also expressed concerns about job security.

Some respondents reported that they believe that more intensive services can be provided to children and families if the public and private education systems are kept separate.

Strategies. Placement teams should have representation from parents and community providers. Encouraging an airing of the values that are brought to the table by each team member affords the best opportunity to discuss turf barriers. Frequent, structured, ongoing discus-

sions will allow a sharing of team members' expertise and the opportunity for all team members to become familiar with one another. The school and the team should establish a vision statement about preschool mainstreaming. If the public school administrator does not consider facilitating group discussions to be one of her personal strengths, someone who has expertise could be solicited to this end. Perhaps a nearby university or human-service provider could supply such expertise.

Some of the strategies listed here in other categories will also help to address turf issues.

Teacher preparedness issues

Barriers. Often public school personnel must meet different teacher certification requirements than Head Start or community-based preschool teachers. This difference in personnel requirements has contributed to public school personnel harboring some doubts about the expertise of community-based and Head Start teachers. Survey respondents reported concern about having children with disabilities placed in community-based preschool settings due to a lack of available resources and support personnel. Some respondents reported that parents may be reluctant to have their child placed outside the public school system due to a lack of teacher training related to the needs of children with disabilities.

Community-based providers expressed concerns about their own ability to educate children with disabilities, particularly those with severe disabilities or medically fragile children. Child care teachers reported that special educators lack basic child development knowledge that child care teachers believe they have.

Survey respondents reported that the curricula of some pre-K and kindergarten programs have an academic focus. This academic orientation can appear to preclude the placement of children with disabilities in those classrooms.

Strategies. Improved communication and training between and among the various service systems may ef-

fect change. Historically, regular-education teachers have been prepared for the inclusion of children with disabilities by being provided information about the disability characteristics of such children and legal requirements (Ayers & Meyer, 1992). This type of preservice training does nothing to provide the teacher with the tools needed to effectively teach children who do not learn typically. Most regular-education teachers have been informally adapting curricula and methods to fit the individual learning needs of typical children. Community service providers need to be supplied with the best information and technologies related to the learning needs of children who do not learn typically. They also should have available to them ongoing consultation from special-education personnel.

Special education has excelled at individualizing education for children with diverse learning needs. Additionally, special education has long recognized the role of the child as a social being—a precursor to productive adult social interactions (Ayers & Meyer, 1992). Early childhood special education has a "family focus" that can be shared as well, whereas the "regular" early childhood field has a strong background in child development to share.

Joint training can be used as a means of sharing each program's expertise. If the attitude barriers truly lie with different preservice training requirements, then providing the community-based program with the expertise of special-education personnel should decrease the teacher-preparedness barriers. Providing special-education personnel with training conducted by community-based personnel allows community-based providers to feel more valued, as well as offering special-education personnel the opportunity to gain some of the community-based providers' child-development expertise.

Including parents who wish to participate in the training will afford them the opportunity to see the public and private systems work cooperatively and to share their expertise. Providing an opportunity for parents not only to participate in the training but to provide training to the team on their areas of expertise can increase the parents' stake in the process.

Awareness issues

Barriers. Survey respondents reported that more information sharing is needed at all levels with respect to children with disabilities. A lack of understanding was reported related to specific disabilities, medical needs, early childhood programming and services, curricula and methods, and integration efforts. All of the survey groups except parents reported these concerns. The parents of typically developing children were not surveyed, but respondents reported that parents, in general, appear to be uninformed about research findings related to the benefits of integration for all children.

Strategies. A number of systems are already in place for the information-sharing activities that appear to be needed. Some states have their own technical-assistance systems, while the federal government funds Regional Resource Centers and the National Early Childhood Technical Assistance System (see Sources for further information). These technical-assistance networks have access to current research findings related to integration. Part of the mission of each of these technical-assistance networks is to provide awareness materials.

Visiting model programs that are already integrating children with disabilities provide teachers and parents with the opportunity to talk with their counterparts. Seeing a high-quality integrated preschool program in action may dispel a great number of fears. Arrange a round-table discussion for all participants to discuss the successes and challenges of their program. Talk openly about the difficulties encountered when the program began and the ways that the host program handled the challenges; for example, recount

your training needs and fiscal concerns. The host program has the unique perspective of having lived through the challenges and successes of integration and should prove a useful resource.

Communication/collaboration/respect issues

Barriers. Parents reported that the people making decisions about their children do not really know the issues because the decision makers do not have children with disabilities themselves. Public school personnel believe that community providers are not receptive to technical assistance from the special-education community.

Attitude barriers to communication, collaboration, and respect all seem to stem from the same source—misinformation about other people and programs. This lack of information sharing has been reported to occur at all levels (local, state, and federal). It is difficult to have respect for a program about which little is known and where no relationship with the provider exists.

"Public school officials at the [sic] state and local level do not make information available about preschool mainstreaming," stated one survey respondent. Similarly, respondents reported that information about specific programs such as Head Start or child care programs was not being effectively communicated.

Strategies. In the words of one survey respondent, "Special educators who begin collaborating with 'regular' early childhood teachers often talk about unexpected learning they experience—learning about typical behavior and developmentally appropriate approaches. The unanticipated 'lesson' is that children with special needs are *children* first

and values begin to shift." Administrators must make a commitment to providing teachers and related service personnel with the necessary time away from their classrooms to collaborate effectively with their counterparts. Providing common planning time during the school day will allow personnel to talk with one another (Ayers & Meyer, 1992).

As the literature on transdisciplinary teaming suggests, to collaborate effectively requires an amount of "role release" or skill trading among participants (McCollom & Hughes, 1988). When collaboration is truly encouraged, the participants can freely share their knowledge with others, knowing that, in return, they will gain knowledge from the other participants.

Some state departments of education have demonstrated a commitment to collaboration by defining their statewide integration philosophy and encouraging each local school district to adopt the state's philosophy. The New Mexico State Department of Education has issued a "full inclusion" statement that outlines their rationale and expressed commitment to the advancement of inclusionary schools.

"Someone will lose" issues

Barriers. Respondents expressed concern for the early educational experiences of children with disabilities as well as typically developing children in integrated placements. Some respondents reported that parents of both typically developing children and children with disabilities were concerned that integration could have a negative effect on the services their children receive.

—*Attitudes related to typically developing children.* Respondents expressed the concern that typically developing children in integrated preschool placements would not receive a quality preschool experience because the children with disabilities would require an inordinate amount of time and attention from the classroom teacher. Respondents also expressed the fear that the child with a disability would be too disruptive to the classroom and would pull

---

Early childhood special education has a "family focus" that can be shared, whereas the "regular" early childhood field has a strong background in child development to share.

---

resources from the typically developing children.

—*Attitudes related to children with disabilities.* Many survey respondents reported that public school personnel are reluctant to take advantage of community-based preschool placements because they fear a loss of control over the child's education—a revisiting of the turf issues discussed earlier. Specifically, the public school special-education personnel are concerned that they will not be able to adequately supervise the child's individual education program (IEP). Survey respondents reported that parents and public school personnel are reluctant to have children placed in regular-education classrooms because they fear that their child will not receive the specialized instruction or intensity of services that may be provided in specialized settings. One respondent expressed resistance to community-based preschool programs as follows: "public school programs are 'better' with certified teachers and greater resources." One survey respondent reported that "it is still a common belief among parents and educators that students with disabilities will be 'happier' and get better 'special' services in traditional special-education settings."

Strategies. Integration can only be considered successful if it is done in a thoughtful way with careful consideration of all of the supports that will ensure success. Indeed, the law requires that the necessary services and supports be provided (34 CFR § 300.550). Community-based teachers who believe that they lack the expertise and training to effectively teach children with disabilities must be provided with the necessary training and afforded the opportunity for frequent meetings with team members, including special-education personnel. Both community-based teachers and special-education personnel could benefit from visiting model preschool mainstream sites where they could see that all children benefit from being together.

Parents of children with disabilities, as well as parents of typically developing children, who are reluctant to have their children participate in integrated programs must be respected. Perhaps they would feel differently if they were aware of the benefits associated with mainstreaming. They should be provided the wealth of current research findings that report positive outcomes related to mainstreaming preschoolers.

Conclusion

Public school placement team members hold opinions related to the children with whom they work, the parents of those children, and community-based service providers. Each of them also has her or his own definition of, and attitude about, the philosophy of inclusion or mainstreaming. Exploring these attitudes as a group that includes the community service provider and parents will likely result in more appropriate individualized placement decisions for the children and families being served.

Both regular- and special-education personnel need to be prepared through preservice and in-service training to become a part of a new school community, a community that recognizes that all children learn, all children contribute, and all children belong. Children with disabilities in mainstream settings must receive at least what they were receiving in specialized settings. Mainstreaming is meant to enhance the child's education through provision of a normalized social context for learning.

Staff-development activities can be employed in the hopes that changes will occur in teacher attitudes, classroom practices, and child outcomes (Guskey, 1986). Guskey believes that there is a temporal sequence to these events. Staff-development activities lead to changes in teachers' classroom practices through providing specific tools for the teachers' use. The teachers' new learning can lead to changes in child outcomes, and improved child outcomes should lead to changes in teachers' beliefs and attitudes.

Sources for further information

Council for Administrators in Special Education (CASE) of the Council for Exceptional Children, 615 16th Street, N.W., Albuquerque, NM 87104, 505–243–7622

The Division for Early Childhood (DEC) of the Council for Exceptional Children, 1920 Association Drive, Reston, VA 22091, 703–620–3660

National Association of State Directors of Special Education (NASDSE), 1800 Diagonal Road, Suite 320, King Street Station 1, Alexandria, VA 22314, 703–519–3800

National Early Childhood Technical Assistance System (NEC–TAS), Suite 500, NCNB Plaza, Chapel Hill, NC 27514, 919–962–2001

National Head Start Resource Access Program, Administration for Children, Youth and Families, Office of Human Development Services, U.S. Department of Health and Human Services, P.O. Box 1182, Washington, DC 20013, 202–245–0562

U.S. Office of Special Education Programs Early Childhood Branch, 400 Maryland Avenue, S.W., Washington, DC 20202, 202–732–1084

References

Ayers, B., & Meyer, L.H. (1992, February). Helping teachers manage the inclusive classroom: Staff development and teaming star among management strategies. *The School Administrator*, 30–37.

Forest, M. (1992). Full inclusion is possible. *The inclusion papers: Strategies to make inclusion work* (pp. 14–15). Toronto, Canada: Inclusion Press.

Guskey, T.R. (1986). Staff development and the process of teacher change. *Educational Researcher, 15*(5), 5–12.

Individuals with Disabilities Education Act. (1991, October). 34 CFR § 300.550, 20 U.S.C. (secs. 1411–1420).

McCullom, J.A., & Hughes, M. (1988). Staffing patterns and team models in infancy programs. In J.B. Jordan, J.J. Gallagher, P.L. Huntinger, & M.B. Karnes (Eds.), *Early childhood special education: Birth to three* (pp. 129–146). Reston, VA: Council for Exceptional Children/Division for Early Childhood.

Smith, B.J., & Rose, D.F. (1991). *Identifying policy options for preschool mainstreaming.* Monograph. Pittsburgh, PA: Research Institute on Preschool Mainstreaming, Allegheny-Singer Research Institute. (ERIC Document Reproduction Service No. ED 338 403)

A Place for Marie:
Guidelines for the Integration Process

Gail Solit

Gail Solit, MA, is the director of the Gallaudet University Child Development Center and is one of the co-authors of **Access for All: Integrating Deaf, Hard of Hearing and Hearing Preschoolers,** *a videotape and manual, available through the Gallaudet Bookstore, (202) 651-5380, for $17.95 plus $3 shipping and handling.*

Marie, who is four years old, is deaf. Her parents, who are also deaf, have used American Sign Language with Marie since her birth. Marie is bright, friendly, likes to converse, and is sometimes bossy — a pretty typical four year old. She attends a preschool for deaf children three days a week. Her parents and teachers feel she will benefit from attending a nearby child care center on the other two days of the week. Her working parents also need child care before and after school when the preschool for deaf children is not open.

Today more and more children with disabilities are entering child care settings. Though teachers may need a somewhat different orientation and new skills to work with children with a wider range of abilities, sound early childhood practices and teaching principles provide an effective foundation. To maximize the effectiveness of their work with these children and their families, teachers and directors need to work together to address the following topics.

Center Philosophy

Most high quality early childhood programs have developed a philosophy statement that speaks to the importance of providing a good program for all children and parents. Yet sometimes "all children" means all nondisabled children. It is a very important process for staff, parents, and other professionals to review and, where necessary, expand the center's philosophical statement to ensure that it is inclusive for all children.

It is important for everyone involved to examine their feelings about working with children and adults who have disabilities and to explore how they feel about working with other professionals to provide appropriate services for all children and their parents. A strong explicit written philosophy statement will serve as a guide for parents and staff.

Staff Training

Marie's new teacher needs to learn about deafness. She doesn't need to become an expert; but she needs to know enough to understand evaluation data, to explain deafness to other parents and children, and to plan an appropriate educational program for Marie.

This teacher's situation is similar to that of a teacher who is new to teaching two year olds and must now learn about them — or a teacher who will be working with a child from a culture that she knows little about. Most early childhood educators expect to continually learn about children and families. As a program begins to include children with differing abilities, all staff must make a commitment to learn about each child from a variety of sources.

• Listening to parents

Since Marie's parents are also deaf, they know what this disability means for Marie. They can provide her teacher with a wealth of clinical information and terminology, and they can explain what life is like for a child who is deaf.

Parents of children who have differing abilities have listened to many, many specialists talk about their child. They have received training on how to position or hold their child who has cerebral palsy; they know how to use an inhaler to help a child with asthma. Most parents are eager to pass on their knowledge so the teacher can do a better job caring for their child.

• Access to specialists

Teachers should have access to all the specialists who work with a child after that child is enrolled in their classroom. Specialists provide both theoretical and practical information about the child and about the ability.

• Focused in-service training

Directors can design training opportunities to provide teachers with the information they need. Important topics include: understanding federal laws about children with differing abilities, the benefits of early intervention and inclusion, working with families, encouraging positive social interactions between children, team building, and assessment procedures. Local colleges, universities, or early childhood training institutes can be accessed by staff to acquire information on these and other relevant topics. Many books and videotapes on these topics are available through early childhood and special education presses.

Photograph by Subjects and Predicates

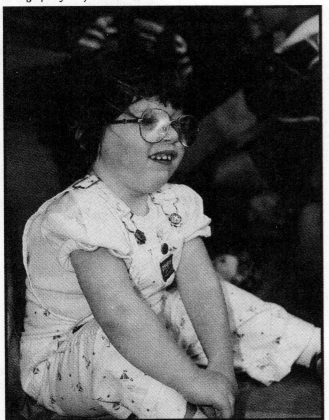

Now that the teacher knows basic information about Marie, she is ready to work with her. The teacher learns that Marie has a moderate hearing loss, with no developmental or cognitive delays. Marie wears hearing aids. The audiologist taught the teacher how to check the hearing aid to ensure it is working. The teacher learns that the hearing aid will make sounds louder, but it will not necessarily clarify speech. The parents explain that Marie uses American Sign Language to communicate. The director decides to find a volunteer who can sign to Marie, communicate with the teacher, and also be a role model for Marie. The teacher also receives release time to attend sign language classes.

The audiologist explains how to adapt the classroom environment so there are less auditory distractions for Marie. The teacher learns that many aspects of the program do not need to change because Marie will benefit from the high quality early childhood classroom that is already in place.

Federal Laws

An essential area of training for early childhood teachers is information about the federal laws mandated for children with disabilities and their parents. Teachers who work in early childhood programs need to know what is expected of them.

Public Law 101-476, the Individuals with Disabilities Education Act (IDEA) which passed Congress in 1990, shapes what educators and parents can expect and demand for their children who are differently abled. Part H (the Infants and Toddlers Program) of IDEA is a grant program to assist states in developing early intervention programs for infants and toddlers with disabilities in settings which are as similar as possible to programs that serve infants and toddlers without disabilities. Part B of IDEA states that to the extent possible children with disabilities should receive their special education services in regular education settings, often referred to as the least restrictive environment (LRE).

Information regarding federal legislation is available through the Office of Special Education and Rehabilitative Services (OSERS), United States Department of Education, 400 Maryland Avenue SW, Washington, DC 20202 — (202) 205-9084; the National Early Childhood Technical Assistance System (NEC*TAS), 500 Nations Bank Plaza, 137 East Franklin Street, Chapel Hill, North Carolina 27514 — (919) 962-2001; and the lead agencies which provide special education services for children in each state.

Team Development

Many early childhood educators already see themselves as part of a team: center team, classroom team, and teacher and parent team. In many high quality early childhood programs, teachers meet regularly to divide center tasks, to plan activities to meet curriculum goals, and to discuss progress and growth of children with each other and with parents.

Children with disabilities are guaranteed a service coordinator by law. The center providing care becomes one of the sites which the service coordinator manages for children and their families. All professionals, including child care teachers, who work with the child, together with the child's parents, become members of this multidisciplinary team. This team meets regularly to develop and implement the best Individual Educational Program (IEP) for the child and his/her family or an Individual Family Service Plan (IFSP).

Working within a multidisciplinary team may be a new skill for some teachers. Some teamwork training may be required to help teachers learn to communicate across abilities and to share responsibilities in regard to children and their families.

Marie's child care teacher attends all meetings about Marie's educational plans, together with Marie's parents, the audiologist, the sign language trainer, and the teachers from the preschool serving children who are deaf. During the meetings everyone adds their observations and assessments about Marie's progress. The plan for Marie states that an adult who signs needs to be in the child care class with Marie, that the audiologist visits the child care center monthly, and that the sign language trainer visits the classroom every two weeks. Through these meetings and other less formal conversations, everyone is working to create the best program possible for Marie.

Physical Environment and Staffing Patterns

Each classroom environment must be designed to meet the needs of the age of the children served, and it must reflect the cultures of these children. When a child who has a disability enters the classroom, the teacher needs to be ready to once again change the environment. Sometimes the changes required are physical (special chairs, standing tables) and sometimes they require staff adjustments. For a more thorough discussion about adapting environments, read the article by Diane Trister Dodge, "Places for ALL Children: Building Environments for Differing Needs."

Marie's teacher learns that for Marie's needs only a few physical environmental changes are required. Marie will function best in an environment which is visual and has many hands-on materials and activities; this classroom, already visual and highly interactive, meets the needs of all the children.

Marie's teacher learns if she wants to get everyone's attention, calling from one end of the classroom is no longer a fair or effective method because Marie will miss the message. Instead she needs to walk over to Marie, tap her on the shoulder, get her attention, and then make her announcement.

In most special education classes, the ratio of staff to children is small to allow for more individual attention. Adding staff to facilitate inclusion is often a financial issue which requires administrative attention. But there are several other methods of solving staff needs which do not require money.

One method, depending on the child's particular abilities and needs, is the utilization of volunteers, such as the Foster Grandparent Program or student interns. The director can contact local volunteer organizations or college or university programs to organize a group of assistants.

A second method to help with staffing is to bring other members of the child's interdisciplinary team into the classroom. Often, the other professional or parent can be present in the classroom during the intervention activity. Individual attention can be provided to one child with other children watching or participating — a benefit to all.

When the audiologist and the sign language trainer come to Marie's classroom they play two games with a small group of children. While they play Twister, all the children in the group, including Marie, learn the signs for red, yellow, blue, green, your turn, right, and left. During a role playing game the children have to express various feelings through body language, an important part of American Sign Language.

A third method to create more individual time between teacher and children is to redesign specific daily routines. During circle or meeting time, most early childhood programs read a story, discuss the day's events, or review the calendar and weather with a large group of children. A simple solution for providing more individual attention to a child with a disability within a large group is to have two concurrent meeting times instead of one.

Individual Needs

Most early childhood educators subscribe to the importance of a developmentally appropriate program for young children. Developmentally appropriate includes two concepts: age appropriateness and individual appropriateness.

All of the above adaptations and additions to Marie's class and program relate to making the program meet her individual needs. These individual needs include Marie's learning style (visual and interactive), accounting for Marie's family background (the wishes of Marie's parents), and individual personality (Marie is friendly, likes to converse, and is at times bossy).

Through her knowledge of typical development, her new knowledge about deafness, and her insights about Marie, Marie's teacher can now plan appropriate activities. For Marie, who is basically developing as a typical four year old, only a few changes are needed in the curriculum. As long as everything is presented to her in American Sign Language, all good early childhood activities should be appropriate for her. Her teacher will formulate ideas of how best to alter the curriculum through the discussions with the specialists and parents at the IEP or IFSP meeting.

Information and Support

One of the adjustments teachers may need to make is how they talk to children about children with differing abilities. Because of the work of educators like Louise Derman-Sparks and the ABC Task Force, many early childhood teachers are already skilled in appropriate ways to help children accept and respect each other. Teachers need to be ready to answer questions about the child with a disability — knowledgeably and honestly.

When children asked, "Why does Marie speak funny?" the teacher answered, "Marie's speech sounds different than yours because Marie has never heard speech. Her sounds are hers; each of us has a different sounding voice. Marie does not rely on her speech to communicate but instead uses her hands. She uses American Sign Language. All of us will be learning sign language so we can better communicate with Marie and she can communicate with us. There is nothing wrong with Marie because her speech sounds different, and you do not need to be afraid of her."

Another adjustment teachers may need to make is to actively encourage social interactions between disabled and nondisabled children. Teachers may want to design some carefully planned learning activities to encourage sharing, cooperation, and interaction until all the children are comfortable with each other. Activities which pair children to complete tasks or games which include small groups of children are good ways to develop trust and tolerance between children. Once children are comfortable with each other, they will begin to see that they have much in common.

The idea of inclusion is being implemented throughout our society. Through legislation like the Americans with Disabilities Act of 1990, and because of societal attitudinal changes, more and more people who are disabled are included in settings where they were not included before. Many parents want their children to be able to interact with all kinds of people, without fear and intolerance. They want to have their children in programs that are reflective of the larger community.

Some parents may need additional information about specific disabilities to help them feel comfortable with the idea of inclusion. They may worry that including a child with a particular need will mean that their child will receive less attention. Some parents will worry that their child will copy behaviors of the child with special needs. And some parents will worry that if a child who has a medical condition is included in their child's program, their child may not remain healthy.

All of these are serious concerns that need to be discussed. Teachers need to understand and share the commitment to the center's philosophy and policies regarding integration so that they can explain and share these beliefs. Teachers need to interact in a partnership with parents, listen empathetically, and develop a mutual investment with each parent and child.

In Marie's class some of the hearing four year olds went home and "turned off their voices." They tried to communicate with their parents by using the few signs that they knew and by inventing other signs. Some parents were concerned that having a deaf child in the class would slow down their child's verbal language development. Knowing that four year olds learn about concepts through play and role playing, Marie's teacher explained that the hearing children were trying out a role, just as they might try on the role of Mommy or a fire fighter. The teacher explained that the four year olds would not continue to keep their voices off for long because it would not be an effective method of getting what they wanted from the hearing adults, who did not sign in their home. The teacher also suggested that the parents capitalize on their child's interest in learning another language. The teacher recommended children's sign language books and video tapes that the parents could purchase or borrow from the

Preferred Words for Referring to Disabilities

Blind. Describes a condition in which a person has loss of vision for ordinary life purposes. *Visually impaired* is the generic term preferred by some individuals to refer to all degrees of vision loss. Use *boy who is blind, girl who is visually impaired.*

Congenital disability. Describes a disability that has existed since birth but is not necessarily hereditary. The term birth defect is inappropriate.

Deaf. Deafness refers to a profound degree of hearing loss that prevents understanding speech through the ear. *Hearing impaired* is the generic term preferred by some individuals to indicate any degree of hearing loss — from mild to profound. It includes both hard of hearing and deaf. *Hard of hearing* refers to a mild to moderate hearing loss that may or may not be corrected with amplification. Use *woman who is deaf, boy who is hard of hearing,* or *people who are hearing-impaired.*

Developmental disability. Any mental and/or physical disability that has an onset before age 22 and may continue indefinitely. It can limit major life activities. Term includes individuals with mental retardation, cerebral palsy, autism, epilepsy (and other seizure disorders), sensory impairments, congenital disabilities, traumatic accidents, or conditions caused by disease (polio, muscular dystrophy, etc.).

Disability. General term used for a functional limitation that interferes with a person's ability, for example, to walk, lift, hear, or learn. It may refer to a physical, sensory, or mental condition. Use as descriptive noun or adjective, such as *persons who are mentally and physically disabled* or *man with a disability. Impairment* refers to loss or abnormality of an organ or body mechanism, which may result in disability.

Down syndrome. Describes a form of mental retardation caused by improper chromosomal division during fetal development. Mongol or mongoloid are unacceptable.

Handicap. Not a synonym for disability. Describes a condition or barrier imposed by society, the environment, or by one's own self. Handicap can be used when citing laws and situations but should not be used to describe a disability. Say *The stairs are a handicap for her.*

Learning disability. Describes a permanent condition that affects the way individuals with average or above-average intelligence take in, retain, and express information. Some groups prefer *specific learning disability,* because it emphasizes that only certain learning processes are affected. Do not say slow learner, retarded, etc. Use *has a learning disability.*

Mental disability. The Federal Rehabilitation Act (Section 504) lists four categories under mental disability: psychiatric disability, retardation, learning disability, and (physical) head trauma. Use these four terms for specific instances; otherwise, *mental disability* or *cognitive impairment* is acceptable.

Nondisabled. Appropriate term for people without disabilities. Normal, able-bodied, healthy, or whole are inappropriate.

Seizure. Describes an involuntary muscular contraction, a brief impairment or loss of consciousness, etc. resulting from a neurological condition, such as epilepsy. Rather than epileptic, say *girl with epilepsy* or *boy with a seizure disorder.* The term convulsion should only be used for seizures involving contraction of the entire body.

Small/short stature. Do not refer to people under 4'10" as dwarfs or midgets. Use *person of small (or short) stature.* Dwarfism is an accepted medical term, but it should not be used as general terminology. Some groups prefer "little people." However, that terms implies a less than full, adult status in society.

Spastic. Describes a muscle with sudden abnormal and involuntary spasms. Not appropriate for describing someone with cerebral palsy. Muscles are spastic, not people.

Speech disorder. A condition in which a person has limited or difficult speech patterns. Use *child who has a speech disorder.* For a person with no verbal speech capability, use *woman without speech.* Do not use mute or dumb.

Spinal cord injury. Describes a condition in which there has been permanent damage to the spinal cord. *Quadriplegia* denotes substantial or total loss of function in all four extremities. *Paraplegia* refers to substantial or total loss of function in the lower part of the body only. Say *man with paraplegia* or *woman who is paralyzed.*

Excerpted with permission from Guidelines for Reporting and Writing About People With Disabilities, Third Edition, a copyrighted publication of the Research & Training Center on Independent Living (RTC/IL) at the University of Kansas. Permission to reproduce any portion of Guidelines must be obtained by advance written approval from the RTC/IL. To obtain a copy of the updated edition of Guidelines (the Fourth Edition is tentatively scheduled for release in September), or for more information, write or call: The Research and Training Center on Independent Living, University of Kansas, 4089 Dole Building, Lawrence, KS 66045, (913) 864-4095 (voice/TDD), FAX (913) 864-5063.

library so that they all could learn American Sign Language together.

Addressing these issues will help directors and staff work together and with parents to integrate children with differing abilities. Their center philosophy will reflect their commitment to working with all children. They will grow as educators as they see themselves as members of a larger team; and as they develop an adaptive environment, new staffing patterns, and a curricula which meets the individual needs of each child; and as they learn to communicate effectively and empathetically with all children and parents.

References

Bredekamp, S. (editor). **Developmentally Appropriate Practice in Programs Serving Children Birth Through Age 8, Expanded Edition.** Washington, DC: National Association for the Education of Young Children, 1987.

Bruder, M. B. **Early Childhood Community Integration: An Option for Preschool Special Education.** Washington, DC: Office of Special Education and Rehabilitative Services, Winter 1993.

Cook, R., A. Tessier, and V. Armbruster. **Adapting Early Childhood Curricula for Children with Special Needs.** Columbus, OH: Merrill Publishing Co., 1987.

Derman-Sparks, L., and the ABC Task Force. **Antibias Curriculum: Tools for Empowering Young Children.** Washington, DC: National Association for the Education of Young Children, 1989.

Dodge, D., and L. Colker. **The Creative Curriculum for Early Childhood, Third Edition.** Washington, DC: Teaching Strategies, Inc., 1992.

Solit, G., M. Taylor, and A. Bednarczyk. **Access for All: Integrating Deaf, Hard of Hearing and Hearing Preschoolers.** Washington, DC: Gallaudet University Pre-College Programs, 1992.

Infants and Toddlers with Special Needs and Their Families

A Position Paper of the Association for Childhood Education International by David Sexton, Patricia Snyder, William R. Sharpton and Sarintha Stricklin

David Sexton is Professor and Chair and William R. Sharpton is Associate Professor, Department of Special Education and Habilitative Services, University of New Orleans, Louisiana. Patricia Snyder is Assistant Professor, Department of Occupational Therapy, Louisiana State University Medical Center, New Orleans. Sarintha Stricklin is Instructor, Human Development Center, LSU Medical Center.

Several recent trends reflect increased interest in developing and providing services for infants and toddlers with special needs and their families. First, evidence is mounting that indicates early intervention is valuable for diverse groups of very young children who exhibit a variety of special needs and for their families (Guralnick, 1991). Second, legal safeguards were established for the rights of individuals with disabilities, which have important implications for service-providing agencies and individuals. Third, there is much discussion about lowering the age for entering public schools (Gallagher, 1989). Fourth, more people are becoming aware of the need to provide greater

support for child and family care (Kelley & Surbeck, 1990; Shuster, Finn-Stevenson & Ward, 1992).

Finally, a consensus is emerging that the functions of early intervention, child care and early childhood education (birth through age 8) are inextricably bound together; that "quality" or "best practices" cannot be achieved without systematically addressing the interrelationships among all three fields (Kagan, 1988, 1989; Mitchell, 1989; Salisbury, 1991; Sexton, 1990). In fact, Burton, Hains, Hanline, McLean and McCormick (1992) suggest that if quality early intervention, child care and early childhood education services are ever to become a reality, then it will be necessary to formally unify the three historically distinct fields.

Recognizing the widespread concern for infants and toddlers, including those with special needs and their families, the Association for Childhood Education International (ACEI) addresses three related issues in this position paper: 1) access to services, 2) quality assurance and 3) preparation of personnel. The final section offers some major conclusions and recommendations related to infants and toddlers with special needs and their families.

ACCESS TO SERVICES

ACEI reaffirms its belief that all young children and their families have a fundamental right to quality care, education and special intervention.

ACEI leads the way in advocating for the right of all children and their families to quality care and education. For example, ACEI/Gotts issued a position paper on this fundamental right in 1988. Although children with special needs and their families are not explicitly addressed, the paper clearly argues for complete, open access to care and education as one of the most fundamental rights of all young children, including infants and toddlers.

Many other professional organizations support ACEI in its position on open access to services. In its guidelines for developmentally appropriate practices, the National Association for the Education of Young Children (NAEYC) unequivocally takes the position that all young children deserve access to a quality program (Bredekamp, 1987). The Division for Early Childhood (DEC) of the Council for Exceptional Children (CEC) issued a position paper supporting the right of young children with disabilities to education and care in settings with typically developing children (McLean & Odom, 1988). The Association for Persons with Severe Handicaps (TASH) adopted the position in 1988 that people with disabilities must have opportunities to achieve full integration into society (Meyer, Peck & Brown, 1991).

ACEI also recognizes the need for comprehensive and ongoing screening, monitoring and assessment services for all infants and toddlers and their families. The goal of such services must be to facilitate early identification of children's special needs and ensure provision of appropriate interventions. Early identification activities should be an integral part of a comprehensive early childhood system, birth through age 8, and needed interventions should be embedded within typical child care, education, home and health routines.

Further, ACEI recognizes and supports the legal right of children with special needs and their families to regular child care and education services. The 1991 amendments (P.L. 102-119) to Part H of the Individuals with Disabilities Education Act (IDEA) (P.L. 101-476) require early intervention services to be provided in regular settings with typically developing children, as appropriate for each child. The term "natural environments" is used to refer to regular settings for typically developing age peers.

In 1990, the Americans with Disabilities Act (ADA) was signed into law. The ADA rules went into effect January 26, 1992. All public accommodations are now prohibited from discriminating against individuals because of a disability. Under Title III of the Act, the law specifically includes nursery schools, child care centers and family child care homes in the definition of "public accommodation" (Rab, Wood & Stanga, 1992; Surr, 1992).

ACEI recognizes that increasingly diverse populations of infants and toddlers represent great challenges to child care and education systems and affirms the need for immediate action to support these systems.

The population of infants and toddlers entering or seeking entry into child care and education systems is changing to include special needs and at-risk children. Service providers and decision-makers must respond to these changes if children and families are to reach their full learning and developmental potential (Stevens & Price, 1992). "Special needs" and "at-risk" are popular terms used to describe an extremely heterogeneous population (Hrncir & Eisenhart, 1991). Care must be taken to consider the extreme diversity within a particular special needs or at-risk subgroup. For example, the popular media image of "crack babies," as Griffith (1992) notes, is that they are all severely affected and little can be done for them. In fact, the effects vary dramatically from infant to infant and are moderated or exacerbated considerably by other factors.

The special needs population requires particular attention not only because of its diversity, but also because of the large numbers needing services. As the following statistics illustrate, we clearly need to take immediate action.

■ Each year, some 425,000 infants are born who will manifest a disability within the first four years of life (Garwood, Fewell & Neisworth, 1988). At the end of 1990, only approximately 600,000 children with special needs, birth through 5, were receiving intervention services (Hebbeler, Smith & Black, 1991).

■ Some 350,000 to 375,000 newborns each year have been exposed prenatally to drugs, including alcohol (Pinkerton, 1991; Stevens & Price, 1992). Fetal alcohol syndrome (FAS) is now recognized as the leading known cause of mental retardation in the Western world. Conservative estimates indicate that approximately one in 500 to 600 children in the U. S. are born with FAS and one in 300 to 350 are born with fetal alcohol effects (FAE) (Burgess & Streissguth, 1992; see also, Cohen and Taharally, 1992).

■ Each year, 412,000 infants are born prematurely (Bartel & Thurman, 1992).

■ An estimated 16 percent of all American children (3 to 4 million children) have blood lead levels in the neurotoxic range (Neddleman, 1992).

■ Human immunodeficiency virus (HIV) has become the greatest infectious cause of pediatric mental retardation in the U. S. In October of 1992, the Centers for Disease Control (CDC) reported 3,426 cases of acquired immunodeficiency syndrome (AIDS) among children under the age of 13 and estimated that several times as many children are infected with HIV (Seidel, 1992).

■ An estimated 3,000,000 to 4,000,000 Americans are homeless (Eddowes & Hranitz, 1989; Heflin, 1991). The number of children in the U. S. who are homeless on any given night range from 68,000 to 500,000 (Linehan, 1992).

Much recent rhetoric by politicians and policy-makers centers on ensuring that all children are ready to enter school (e.g., *America 2000*). In a recent survey of U.S. state expenditures, however, half of the states spend less than $25 per child on the care and education of young children and one-third of the states spend less than $17 per child (Adams & Sandfort, 1992). Feeg (1990) reminds us that the U. S. is ranked 18th among industrialized nations in infant mortality and compares poorly in protecting and immunizing well children.

These facts clearly indicate the need for immediate action at national, state and local levels to ensure that additional dollars are made available to support child care, education and health systems in providing high quality, comprehensive services for all children. Such support is critical as these systems begin to upgrade early care and education services for more traditional populations, while simultaneously providing quality services for less familiar, special needs populations.

ACEI affirms the position that child care and education reform movements must be inclusive, addressing the needs of infants and toddlers with special needs and their families within the broader context of society.

Recently, movements to "restructure" or "reform" the education and child care systems have gained much momentum. One such movement is *America 2000* (U. S. Department of Education, 1991), a set of six national education goals developed by President Bush and the nation's governors. The first goal is of particular relevance to infants and toddlers with special needs and their families: "By the year 2000, all children in America will start school ready to learn." While this goal, widely touted as the cornerstone of *America 2000*, clearly focuses attention on the importance of learning during the early years, significant inherent problems remain.

First, children with special needs or disabilities are not specifically mentioned in this or any of the other goals. It is imperative that national programs value

and include the needs of *all* children. The second problem is defining "readiness" according to an expected level of skills and abilities children should possess prior to school entry. Such an approach serves a gatekeeping function of keeping some children out and ignores the central question of how "ready" the education system is for the child (Kelley & Surbeck, 1991; Willer & Bredekamp, 1990). Gatekeeping to exclude children with special needs and their families from the mainstream, whether implemented consciously or unconsciously, is nothing new and is certainly not even remotely related to "restructuring" or "reform." As Bowman (1992) notes:

What is a special-needs child? The usual answer is a child with a disability that prevents him or her from functioning effectively. But is the disability always in the child? I suggest that in most instances, the disability is not in the child, but in the misfit between the child and the environment. (p. 106)

ACEI receives support for this position from DEC, which issued a position statement on the first goal of *America 2000*, and from NAEYC, which endorsed the DEC statement (Holder-Brown & Parette, 1992).

ACEI strongly supports refocusing the reform and restructuring movements to recognize that school success is dependent upon families receiving the comprehensive health, education and social services they need in order to support children's development and learning, beginning with prenatal care. Willer and Bredekamp (1990) and Kelley and Surbeck (1991) argue for a restructured early childhood care and education system that extends well before and beyond the school and classroom to encompass health and human services.

An important step in this direction is the new Family Leave Law, which combines parental leave with disability insurance so that all families at all economic levels can afford to take time off to care for their children (Bond, Galinsky, Lord, Staines & Brown, 1991). New resources must be invested and current ones redirected to ensure that restructuring and reform efforts focus on making the system "ready" to respond to the needs of all children and their families.

QUALITY ASSURANCE

Quality assurance must not be overlooked when attending to the crisis in child care, health care and early childhood education (Daniel, 1990; Kagan, 1988; Willer, 1987). Quality assurance issues for infants and toddlers with special needs and their families must be addressed within the context of ensuring that *all* young children benefit from developmentally appropriate practices. An integrated service system should be designed to support, and not supplant, the role of families.

All young children and their families have a right to expect that child care, health care, and education and intervention systems are designed to enhance and promote their well-being. To ensure that quality services are delivered, some definable, measurable quality indices must be established, validated and adopted by health, child care, education and intervention systems. Such an outcome requires the collaboration of individuals representing multiple agencies and programs, both private and public, as well as consumers. These stakeholders must undertake systematic efforts toward evaluating and developing the context for collaboration, including:

- setting clear and manageable goals
- developing an operational structure that matches the goals
- developing mandates that are facilitative
- arranging for joint leadership
- pooling existing resources and identifying new ones
- establishing processes and policies that are clearly understood. (Kagan, 1991)

ACEI affirms that standards for quality infant and toddler programs must be validated and adopted for all young children, benefiting children, their families and all of society.

Several professional groups support ACEI (ACEI/Gotts, 1988) in advocating for quality assurance standards for child care and early childhood education programs, including NAEYC (Bredekamp, 1987) and the Alliance for Better Child Care (National Association for the Education of Young Children [NAEYC], 1987). Also, the Division for Early Childhood of the Council for Exceptional Children (DEC/CEC) recently published quality indicators for early intervention programs (Division for Early Childhood/CEC, 1993).

The care and education standards promulgated by the early childhood and early intervention communities are similar in philosophy and content. The similarities most likely result from the growing recognition that all children benefit from care environments that are safe, responsive, developmentally appropriate and competency-enhancing. Care environments that meet these and other identified standards should promote children's well-being and, from a transactional/ecological perspective, that of families and society (Bronfenbrenner, 1986; Hamburg, 1991).

A large consensus group comprised of parents, practitioners, policymakers, researchers and advocacy groups from all early childhood communities must collaborate to ensure that appropriate standards for all children are validated and adopted. The accreditation process developed by NAEYC (1986) is certainly a welcome step in this direction.

ACEI recognizes that government regulation through child care licensing is one of the primary policy mechanisms for establishing and overseeing quality care (Kagan, 1988; Phillips, Lande & Goldberg, 1990). The battle continues on a state-by-state basis to establish licensing standards, with many states seeing an erosion in established standards due to nonenforcement or exemption (Lindner, 1986; Willer, 1987). There is no denying that quality early childhood programs require time and money, as well as commitment and broad-based support. Resources must be available to develop and maintain high quality programs that meet the needs of children, parents and staff.

ACEI affirms the position that quality child care and education systems must promote full inclusion.

The most important indicators that must be present in early childhood quality assurance standards include those that address program policies, structures and practices supporting full inclusion of special needs children in settings designed for their age peers without disabilities (Demchak & Drinkwater, 1992; Hanline & Hanson, 1989; Salisbury, 1991). As Campbell (1991) notes, "More than any area of special education, the benefits of noncategorical programming where young children with disabilities are educated with those with typical development have been empirically supported"(p. 473).

Inclusion benefits both children and families. For example, children with and without disabilities benefit developmentally and socially from interaction in a child care environment that individualizes care and promotes ongoing regular contact among children (Demchak & Drinkwater, 1992; Odom & McEvoy, 1988). Families whose children experience inclusion frequently cite the development of empathy, respect for differences and respect for individuals as important outcomes for both themselves and their children.

Campbell (1991) makes the compelling argument that, beyond the cited benefits of inclusion, the real issue is whether we can justify removing children from the normal life experiences to which they are entitled by virtue of being young children. ACEI shares this view, affirming that infants and toddlers with special needs and their families should not be excluded from such experiences or from systems designed to serve all children and families. Developing one quality inclusive system of care, education and intervention can result in improved services for all children and families.

ACEI affirms the position that quality child care, health care and education systems must be integrated and that individualized, or personalized, care and education must be provided all infants and toddlers and their families.

The unique characteristics of all infants and toddlers must be considered in developing quality care, education and intervention programs. As a group, infants and toddlers with special needs are extremely heterogeneous. Individualized care, education and intervention must be provided to capitalize on the unique characteristics of each child and family. In fact, provisions of Part H of IDEA require that intervention for infants and toddlers having known or suspected disabilities include an Individualized Family Service Plan (IFSP) that systematically focuses on the individual family's priorities, resources and concerns (Sexton, 1990).

Kelley and Surbeck (1990) note that individualization, or "personalization," of care is also essential for typically developing infants, toddlers and their families. No accepted, single standard exists regarding the nature of services provided young children prior to school entry. ACEI endorses the principle that services for infants and toddlers with special needs should be designed according to the same standards as those for all other infants and toddlers. Programs adhering to such standards will provide care and education that are individualized, family-directed and culturally normative.

ACEI affirms the position that quality child care and education systems must embed needed interventions for infants and toddlers with special needs within the natural routines, schedules and activities of child care and home settings.

Quality child care and education systems must develop and utilize environments that promote active engagement of children with peers, adults and materials (McWilliam & Bailey, 1992). The learning environment should not be structured by strict schedules or insistence that children remain seated and quiet. Space, equipment, people and materials should be arranged instead to free children to move, choose and busy themselves. As Olds (1979) notes, "For all its manifestations, the environment is the curriculum" (p. 91). The true curriculum for infants and toddlers is everything they experience during the day (Bredekamp, 1987; Hignett, 1988).

Programs serving infants and toddlers with special needs should embed needed interventions within the natural routine or schedule of the child's day (Sexton, 1990). Needed special therapies (e.g., occupational, physical, speech, etc.) should be integrated within caregiving routines. Busenbark and Ward (1992) argue for integrated therapy that:

- lends itself to the inclusion and active involvement of nondisabled peers

Table 1: Core Competencies for Personnel Preparation

- Organize learning environments that are safe, healthy and stimulating.
- Promote all children's physical, intellectual, social, adaptive and communicative competence.
- Select curriculum and teaching/intervention strategies that: a) are developmentally appropriate, b) address all areas of development, c) are responsive to a wide variety of individual needs and d) are based on normal routines.
- Facilitate the success of children in all learning situations.

- Collaborate with families in all aspects of care, education and intervention.
- Ensure that all practices are respectful of and sensitive to cultural diversity.
- Integrate academic and practical experience via field experiences such as practicum, student teaching/internship and technical assistance/support at the job site.
- Maintain a commitment to professionalism via interdisciplinary and interagency teaming, continuing education, and systems change through individual and group advocacy.

- is delivered in the child's natural environment
- affords opportunities for modeling intervention strategies for staff and families during caregiving routines
- promotes focusing on child and family goals that are realistic, appropriate, functional and meaningful
- improves the child's social interaction skills
- builds a strong collaborative partnership among therapist, program staff and parents.

PREPARATION OF PERSONNEL

All disciplines concerned with infants and toddlers and their families agree that overall program quality or developmental appropriateness is determined directly by the knowledge and skills of the individuals caring for and serving this population (Bredekamp, 1987, 1992; Granger, 1989; Klein & Campbell, 1990; Kontos, 1992; Sexton, 1990). Available data indicate, however, enormous personnel problems that demand immediate attention. Granger (1989) reports that the annual personnel turnover rate in child care and early childhood programs not located in public schools is as high as 40 percent. Kontos (1992) also estimates that the annual turnover rate among child care providers is approximately 40 percent. The results of several national surveys (Bailey, Simeonsson, Yoder & Huntington, 1990; Meisels, Harbin, Modigliani & Olson, 1988; U. S. Department of Education, 1990) and state surveys (Hanson & Lovett, 1992; McCollum & Bailey, 1991; Sexton & Snyder, 1991) clearly note that:

- there are critical shortages of early intervention personnel across disciplines
- these critical shortages are predicted to continue, or even worsen, in the future
- there is a dearth of training content at both undergraduate and graduate levels related to working with infants and toddlers who have special needs and their families.

How adequately these and related personnel preparation issues are addressed will determine the future of our youngest children and the education profession (Bredekamp, 1992). A personnel system must be developed that addresses both preservice and inservice education needs.

ACEI promotes collaboration among the fields of early childhood education, child care, early intervention and supporting disciplines in the design and delivery of personnel training.

One key issue in personnel preparation is whether preservice and inservice training programs for early interventionists should be developed and delivered in isolation or in collaboration with general early childhood and care programs. Miller (1992) argues convincingly against educating personnel to work with *either* "regular" *or* "special needs" young children. Concerns over segregated personnel preparation programs have resulted in collaborative efforts among numerous professional groups, such as NAEYC, Association for Teacher Educators (ATE) and DEC, to achieve consensus on personnel preparation issues (Bredekamp, 1992).

ACEI endorses such efforts as absolutely necessary and, in addition, advocates inclusion of related professional groups (e.g., American Occupational Therapy Association and American Speech and Hearing Association) in future efforts. Joint collaboration has the potential to help ensure that full inclusion of infants and toddlers with special needs and their families becomes a reality.

An integrated personnel preparation system is imperative for numerous reasons. First, Part H of IDEA mandates that infants and toddlers with special needs be cared for and served in natural environments available to their typically developing age peers. Therefore, personnel in education and care settings will increasingly educate and care for infants and toddlers with special needs within these more natural and normalized environments. Early interventionists will spend much more of their time providing technical assistance to education and care personnel, collaborating with them on transition and inclusion issues.

IDEA, Part H, also requires that specific early intervention services must be delivered by interdisciplinary teams. Collaboration and joint training must occur across related disciplines such as occupational and physical therapy, audiology, speech and language therapy, social work and psychology. An integrated and collaborative preservice and inservice training system is an efficient, effective mechanism to address shared and related competencies.

Second, a consensus is growing among historically distinct fields that, if quality child care, education and intervention are to be provided all infants, toddlers and their families, an interdisciplinary approach to personnel preparation must build on "core" competencies identified by different professional groups (Burton et al., 1992; Demchak & Drinkwater, 1992; Miller, 1992; NAEYC, 1988). These core competencies should serve as a basis for developing an integrated personnel system. For example, personnel competency domains (Table 1) have been identified by the Council for Early Childhood Professional Recognition in its Child Development Associate (CDA) requirements for infant and toddler caregivers (Council for Early Childhood Professional Recognition, 1992); NAEYC, in its developmentally appropriate practice guidelines (Bredekamp, 1987); and DEC, in its recommendations for certification of early childhood special educators (McCollum, McLean, McCartan & Kaiser, 1989).

There is also growing recognition across fields that inservice or outreach training must receive priority within any personnel preparation system (Bruder & Nikitas, 1992; Granger, 1989; Kontos, 1992; Miller, 1992). Bailey (1989) defines inservice education as the process by which practicing professionals participate in experiences designed to improve or change professional practice. Given the high turnover rates in all areas of child care, education and intervention and the paucity of preservice training programs, inservice or outreach training opportunities must be coordinated, interdisciplinary and immediate. Kontos (1992) presents convincing data that indicate inservice training and technical assistance result in improved child care, as well as a dramatically lower turnover rate for family care workers.

ACEI also recognizes the importance of including administrators in any personnel preparation system. Specific competencies related to integrated early care, education and intervention must be included in preservice and inservice leadership training programs. The extent to which education, care and intervention personnel employ integrated and collaborative practices is directly related to an administrator's ability to identify, nurture and reward such behaviors.

ACEI affirms the right of all infants, toddlers and family members to child care, education and intervention delivered by trained personnel who have appropriate certification and/or licenses and who are adequately and equitably compensated.

One important step in establishing any field as a profession is some means to assess each individual's work performance and to license or credential those deemed competent according to criteria developed by the profession (Radomski, 1986). National surveys across fields, however, clearly indicate the lack of a credentialing or certification system that recognizes and monitors an individual's competency in the education, intervention or care of very young children.

After completing a survey of child care regulations in the U.S., Phillips et al. (1990) concluded:

Among the most disturbing findings in the state-by-state analysis is the lack of attention given to specialized training for child care providers. It is the rare state that requires both pre- and in-service training of center- or home-based staff; many more states fail to require either form of training. (p. 175)

Data reported by NAEYC (1988) indicate that only 24 states and the District of Columbia certify early childhood teachers as distinct from elementary teachers. Only three states define early childhood to be birth through age 8, as does ACEI. Furthermore, in a national survey of personnel standards for Part H of IDEA, Bruder, Klosowski and Daguio (1991) found that few regulatory standards were specific to personnel providing services to infants and toddlers.

ACEI recognizes the importance of formal licensing or credentialing of early childhood educators, care providers and early interventionists for at least two reasons. First, and most important, studies have consistently found developmentally appropriate practices are best predicted by the combination of an individual's formal education and training in child development/early childhood education and his/her exposure to supervised practical experiences (Fischer & Eheart, 1991; Snider & Fu, 1990). Evidence indicates that these same factors also affect the quality of services provided by early interventionists (Kontos & File, 1992).

Second, a credentialing or certification system based on national standards of care, education and intervention for all infants and toddlers, but flexible enough to accommodate the unique needs of different states, could focus the efforts of historically distinct fields to join forces and empower personnel. As Bredekamp (1992) observes:

The most overwhelming barrier to all our work on behalf of children is always financial; we know that we must improve compensation to ensure that we attract and keep the best and brightest in our profession, but we have not figured out how to get the money. (p. 37)

Bellm, Breuning, Lombardi and Whitebook (1992) report that real earnings by child care teachers and family child care providers have actually decreased by nearly one-quarter since the mid-1970s. Historically, professionals have not organized around the issue of compensation, perhaps perpetuating the general perception that child care, education and intervention are basically unskilled labor and that anybody can "watch" children (Modigliani, 1988; Morin, 1989; Phillips et al., 1990). ACEI solicits the support and collaboration of other professional groups to help ensure an integrated system that recognizes and monitors the competencies of personnel via formal credentialing or certification and that equitably rewards individuals accordingly.

CONCLUSIONS

Recent efforts to develop a comprehensive system of intervention for infants and toddlers with special needs and their families have provided opportunities to examine service access and quality issues. The key question in formulating public policy, particularly under Part H of IDEA, is: Should we create or continue a segregated system for early intervention or should we focus on collaborative efforts to support and improve general child care and education systems? It is becoming clear that one inclusive child care and education system is needed. Moreover, a collaborative approach is required if needed special interventions are to be embedded within the system.

The building of such a system entails constructive attention to:

- ensuring access to services for all children
- developing and enforcing quality control assurance standards
- training personnel and administrators to meet the needs of an extremely diverse population in developmentally appropriate ways.

Such a system also requires public policies that provide resources to achieve the collaboration necessary to improve child care and education. Such policies benefit all infants and toddlers and their families, as well as society in general. Now is the time for individuals and groups representing historically distinct areas to join forces with families and decision-makers in creating the best possible system of services and care for our youngest children—our most vulnerable, yet most valuable, resources.

References

Adams, G., & Sandfort, J. R. (1992). State investments in child care and early childhood education. *Young Children, 47*(6), 33-35.

Association for Childhood Education International/E. E. Gotts. (1988). The right to quality child care. Position paper. *Childhood Education, 64*, 268-275.

Bailey, D. B. (1989). Issues and directions in preparing professionals to work with young handicapped children and their faimilies. In J. Gallagher, P. Trohanis, & R. Clifford (Eds.), *Policy implementation and P.L. 99-457: Planning for children with special needs* (pp. 97-132). Baltimore, MD: Paul H. Brookes.

Bailey, D. B., Simeonsson, R. J., Yoder, E. E., & Huntington, G. S. (1990). Preparing professionals to serve infants and toddlers with handicaps and their families: An integrative analysis across eight disciplines. *Exceptional Children, 57*(1), 26-35.

Bartel, N. R., & Thurman, S. K. (1992). Medical treatment and educational problems in children. *Phi Delta Kappan, 74*, 57-61.

Bellm, D., Breuning, G. S., Lombardi, J., & Whitebook, M. (1992). On the horizon: New policy initiatives to enhance child care staff compensation. *Young Children, 47*(5), 39-42.

Bond, J. T., Galinsky, E., Lord, M., Staines, G. L., & Brown, K. R. (1991). Beyond the parental leave debate: The impact of laws in four states. *Young Children, 47*(1), 39-42.

Bowman, B. T. (1992). Who is at risk and why. *Journal of Early Intervention, 16*, 101-108.

Bredekamp, S. (1987). *Developmentally appropriate practice in early childhood programs serving children from birth through age 8.* Washington, DC: National Association for the Education of Young Children.

Bredekamp, S. (1992). The early childhood profession coming together. *Young Children, 47*(6), 36-39.

Bronfenbrenner, U. (1986). Ecology of the family as a context for human development research perspectives. *Developmental Psychology, 22*, 723-742.

Bruder, M. B., Klosowski, S., & Daguio, C. (1991). A review of personnel standards for Part H of P.L. 99-457. *Journal of Early Intervention, 16*, 173-180.

Bruder, M. D., & Nikitas, T. (1992). Changing the professional practice of early interventionists: An inservice model to meet the service needs of Public Law 99-457. *Journal of Early Intervention, 16*, 173-180.

Burgess, D. M., & Streissguth, A. P. (1992). Fetal alcohol syndrome and fetal alcohol effects: Principles for educators. *Phi Delta Kappan, 74*, 24-30.

Burton, C. B., Hains, A. H., Hanline, M. F., McLean, M., & McCormick, K. (1992). Early childhood intervention and education: The urgency of professional unification. *Topics in Early Childhood Special Education, 11*(4), 53-69.

Busenbark, L., & Ward, G. (1992). Service delivery for preschool children with disabilities. *Early Childhood Report, 3*(9), 67.

Campbell, P. H. (1991). An essay on preschool integration. In L. H. Meyer, C. A. Peck, & L. Brown (Eds.), *Critical issues in the lives of people with severe disabilities* (pp. 473-477). Baltimore, MD: Paul H. Brookes.

Cohen, S., & Taharally, C. (1992). Getting Ready for Young Children with Prenatal Drug Exposure. *Childhood Education, 69*, 5-9.

Council for Early Childhood Professional Recognition. (1992). *The child development associate assessment system and competency standards: Infant/toddler caregivers in center-based programs.* Washington, DC: Author.

Daniel, J. (1990). Child care: An endangered industry. *Young Children, 43*(2), 27-32.

Demchak, M. A., & Drinkwater, S. (1992). Preschoolers with disabilities: The case against segregation. *Topics in Early Childhood Special Education, 11*(4), 70-83.

Division for Early Childhood/CEC. (1993). *DEC recommended practices: Indicators of quality in programs for infants and young children with special needs and their families.* Reston, VA: Author.

Eddowes, E. A., & Hranitz, J. R. (1989). Educating children of the homeless. *Childhood Education, 65*, 197-200.

Feeg, V. D. (1990). Health issues in a changing society. In E. Surbeck & M. F. Kelley (Eds.), *Personalizing care with infants, toddlers and families* (pp. 52-61). Wheaton, MD: Association for Childhood Education International.

Fischer, J. L., & Eheart, B. K. (1991). Family day care: A theoretical basis for improving quality. *Early Childhood Research Quarterly, 6*, 549-563.

Gallagher, J. J. (1989). The impact of policies for handicapped children on future early education policy. *Phi Delta Kappan, 71*, p. 121-124.

Garwood, S. G., Fewell, R. R., & Neisworth, J. T. (1988). Public Law 94-142: You can get there from here! *Topics in Early Childhood Special Education, 8*(1), 1-11.

Granger, R. C. (1989). The staffing crisis in early childhood education. *Phi Delta Kappan, 71*, 130-134.

Griffith, D. R. (1992). Prenatal exposure to cocaine and other drugs: Developmental and educational prognoses. *Phi Delta Kappan, 74*, 30-34.

Guralnick, M. J. (1991). The next decade of research on the effectiveness of early intervention. *Exceptional Children, 58*, 174-183.

Hamburg, S. K. (1991). The unfinished agenda must be met. *Young Children, 46*(4), 29-32.

Hanline, M. F., & Hanson, M. J. (1989). Integration considerations for infants and toddlers with multiple disabilities. *Journal of the Association for Persons with Severe Handicaps, 14,* 178-183.

Hanson, M. J., & Lovett, D. (1992). Personnel preparation for early interventionists: A cross-disciplinary survey. *Journal of Early Intervention, 16,* 123-135.

Hebbeler, K. M., Smith, B. J., & Black, T. L. (1991). Federal early childhood special education policy: A model for the improvement of services for children with disabilities. *Exceptional Children, 58,* 104-112.

Heflin, L. J. (1991). *Developing effective programs for special education students who are homeless.* Reston, VA: Clearinghouse on Handicapped and Gifted Children, Council for Exceptional Children.

Hignett, W. F. (1988). Infant/toddler care, yes: But we'd better make it good. *Young Children, 47*(6), 73-77.

Holder-Brown, L., & Parette, H. P., Jr. (1992). Children with disabilities who use assistive technology: Ethical considerations. *Young Children, 47*(6), 73-77.

Hrncir, E. J., & Eisenhart, C. (1991). Use with caution: The "at-risk" label. *Young Children, 46*(2), 23-27.

Kagan, S. L. (1988). Current reforms in early childhood education: Are we addressing the issues? *Young Children, 43*(2), 27-32.

Kagan, S. L. (1989). Early care and education: Beyond the school-house doors. *Phi Delta Kappan, 71,* 107-112.

Kagan, S. L. (1991). *United we stand: Collaboration for child care and early education services.* New York: Teachers College Press.

Kelley, M. F., & Surbeck, E. (1990). Infant day care. In E. Surbeck & M. F. Kelley (Eds.), *Personalizing care with infants, toddlers and families* (pp. 62-70). Wheaton, MD: Association for Childhood Education International.

Kelley, M. F., & Surbeck, E. (1991). *Restructuring early childhood education.* Bloomington, IN: Phi Delta Kappa Educational Foundation.

Klein, H. K., & Campbell, P. (1990). Preparing personnel to serve at-risk and disabled infants, toddlers, and preschoolers. In S. J. Meisels & J. P. Shonkoff (Eds.), *Handbook of early childhood intervention* (pp. 679-699). New York: Cambridge.

Kontos, S. (1992). *Family day care: Out of the shadows and into the limelight.* Washington, DC: National Association for the Education of Young Children.

Kontos, S., & File, N. (1992). Conditions of employment, job satisfaction and job commitment among early intervention personnel. *Journal of Early Intervention, 16,* 155-165.

Lindner, E. W. (1986). Danger: Our national policy of child carelessness. *Young Children, 41*(3), 3-9.

Linehan, M. F. (1992). Children who are homeless: Educational strategies for school personnel. *Phi Delta Kappan, 74,* 61-66.

McCollum, J. A., & Bailey, D. B. (1991). Developing comprehensive personnel systems: Issues and alternatives. *Journal of Early Intervention, 15,* 57-65.

McCollum, J. A., McLean, M., McCartan, K., & Kaiser, C. (1989). Recommendations for certification of early childhood special educators. *Journal of Early Intervention, 13,* 195-211.

McLean, M., & Odom S. (1988). *Least restrictive environment and social interaction.* Reston, VA: Division for Early Childhood, Council for Exceptional Children.

McWilliam, R. A., & Bailey, D. B. (1992). Promoting engagement and mastery. In D. B. Bailey & M. Wolery (Eds.), *Teaching infants and preschoolers with disabilities* (2nd ed.) (pp. 229-255). New York: Macmillan.

Meisels, S. J., Harbin, G., Modigliani, K., & Olson, K. (1988). Formulating optimal state early childhood intervention policies. *Exceptional Children, 55*(2), 159-165.

Meyer, L. H., Peck, C. A., & Brown, L. (1991). *Critical issues in the lives of people with severe disabilities.* Baltimore, MD: Paul H. Brookes.

Miller, P. (1992). Segregated programs of teacher education in early childhood: Immoral and inefficient practice. *Topics in Early Childhood Special Education, 11,* 39-52.

Mitchell, A. (1989). Old baggage, new visions: Shaping policy for early childhood programs. *Phi Delta Kappan, 70,* 665-6723.

Modigliani, K. (1988). Twelve reasons for the low wages in child care. *Young Children, 43*(3), 14-15.

Morin, J. (1989). We can force a solution to the staffing crisis. *Young Children, 44*(6), 18-19.

National Association for the Education of Young Children. (1986). Accreditation: A new tool for early childhood programs. *Young Children, 41*(4), 31-32.

National Association for the Education of Young Children. (1987). Alliance for Better Child Care (ABC). *Young Children, 42*(4), 31-33.

National Association for the Education of Young Children. (1988). Early childhood teacher education. Traditions and trends: An executive summary of colloquium proceedings. *Young Children, 44*(1), 53-57.

Neddleman, H. L. (1992). Childhood exposure to lead: A common cause of school failure. *Phi Delta Kappan, 74,* 35-37.

Odom, S. L., & McEvoy, M. A. (1988). Integration of young children with handicaps and normally developing children. In S. L. Odom & M. B. Karnes (Eds.), *Early intervention for infants and children with handicaps: An empirical base* (pp. 241-268). Baltimore, MD: Paul H. Brookes.

Olds, A. R. (1979). Designing developmentally optimal classrooms for children with special needs. In S. J. Meisels (Ed.), *Special education and development: Perspectives on young children with special needs.* Baltimore, MD: University Park Press.

Phillips, D., Lande, J., & Goldberg, M. (1990). The state of child care regulation: A comparative analysis. *Early Childhood Research Quarterly, 5,* 151-179.

Pinkerton, D. (1991). Substance exposed infants and children. Reston, VA: Clearinghouse on Handicapped and Gifted Children, Council for Exceptional Children.

Rab, V. Y., Wood, K. I., & Stanga, J. (1992). Training child care providers on the impact of the ADA. *Early Childhood Report, 3*(8), 5-8.

Radomski, M. A. (1986). Professionalization of early childhood educators: How far have we progressed? *Young Children, 41*(5), 20-23.

Salisbury, C. L. (1991). Mainstreaming during the early childhood years. *Exceptional Children, 58,* 146-155.

Seidel, J. F. (1992). Children with HIV-related developmental difficulties. *Phi Delta Kappan, 74,* 38-40, 56.

Sexton, D. (1990). Quality integrated programs for infants and toddlers with special needs. In E. Surbeck & M. F. Kelley (Eds.), *Personalizing care with infants, toddlers and families* (pp. 41-50). Wheaton, MD: Association for Childhood Education International.

Sexton, D., & Snyder, P. (1991). *Louisiana personnel preparation consortium project for Part H.* New Orleans, LA: University of New Orleans.

Shuster, C. K., Finn-Stevenson, M., & Ward, P. (1992). Family day care support systems: An emerging infrastructure. *Young Children, 47*(5), 29-35.

Snider, M. H., & Fu, V. R. (1990). The effects of specialized education and job experience on early childhood teachers' knowledge of developmentally appropriate practice. *Early Childhood Research Quarterly, 5,* 68-78.

Stevens, L. J., & Price, M. (1992). Meeting the challenge of educating children at risk. *Phi Delta Kappan, 74,* 18-23.

Surr, J. (1992). Early childhood programs and the Americans with Disabilities Act (ADA). *Young Children, 47*(5), 18-21.

U. S. Department of Education. (1990). *Twelfth annual report to Congress on the implementation of the Education for Handicapped Act.* Washington, DC: Office of Special Education and Rehabilitative Services.

U. S. Department of Education. (1991). *America 2000: An education strategy.* Washington, DC: Author.

Willer, B. (1987). Current reforms in early childhood education: Are we addressing the issues? *Young Children, 42*(6), 41-43.

Willer, B., & Bredekamp, S. (1990). Redefining readiness: An essential requisite for educational reform. *Young Children, 45*(5), 22-24.

Trouble With Testing

What are we really measuring when we test young children? And are the findings worth the frustration?

SUSAN R. ANDERSEN

Susan R. Andersen, a former second-grade teacher, is a consultant in early childhood education at the Iowa Department of Education, Des Moines.

In theory, we give young children standardized tests so we can use the results to improve teaching methods. But most teachers will admit the tests do more to disrupt learning than to benefit teaching.

As a school board member, you're familiar with the public pressure to "improve" test scores, and you probably can cite your district's latest scores, school by school. But you might be unaware of just how much classroom time testing consumes, how frustrating it is for teachers, and how emotionally trying it can be for young students and their families. These effects of standardized tests are not documented; understanding them requires direct observation of the daily reality of the classroom.

Observe, for example, my recent class of 28 second-graders, whose average age is 7 years and 3 months. Among them are Dean, Robin, and Terri—I'll say more about these three later. By the time testing begins, the children and I have had about 30 days together. Our class usually is structured around learning teams, with desks pushed together in islands about the room. The children are learning to question, listen, respond, and cooperate with each other.

But this week is different. We will be taking the mathematics and reading sections of the Iowa Tests of Basic Skills (ITBS). Instead of being in islands, the desks are separated individually; each student will work alone. To 7-year-olds, this is not a trivial change.

To compensate, I plan for morning snacks and double the length of the afternoon "self-selection" period, when the children can choose their own math and science activities. I want them to forget these days.

The district has informed parents of the test dates and asked that children arrive at school promptly with adequate rest. But the parents who read and understand this message are the ones who didn't need to be told. Chances are, it's the other parents—those who had little success at school themselves—who haven't absorbed the message.

A week of tests

Monday, 9 a.m. As the first day of testing begins, everyone is here but Dean, Robin, and Terri. I don't have to wait long for Robin, who runs in, breathless, a few minutes after 9 a.m. She is highly capable, well cared for, and far too pensive for her 7 years. She has self-imposed standards of excellence—and usually attains them.

A few minutes later, Terri walks in. She is a homeless child whose current living conditions are called, in the jargon of the school social worker, "doubling-up." She and her family—recently arrived from out of state—have no home of their own and have moved in with her uncle's family. Her records from previous schools never materialized; the family has obvious health needs and lacks both insurance and employment. Yet Terri's enthusiasm and maturity are high for her age. Her vocabulary includes such words as "unemployment," "welfare," "truck stops," and "migraines."

Twenty minutes later, Dean is still absent. Dean overflows with personality and energy; he struggles to be the best in the class. Weighed against those assets, however, are insecurity and weak academic skills. Dean's family and living conditions are in flux. His personal needs and support systems vary with the day. When Dean enters the classroom, his manner and appearance usually tell me what his life has been like since I said good-bye to him the day before.

These three children are in no way unusual in a class of 28 in a middle-class neighborhood. As their teacher, I must shape the small number of school days we have together into learning experiences that respond to their needs. In my experience, the time we spend on testing is time wasted. But the tests are required, so we begin.

By 9:30, I have explained the testing process and shown the children how to mark the ovals in the answer booklet. I've made sure the children have the correct booklets and have filled in the alphabetized ovals for all the letters of their names—last name, first name, plus more ovals to complete the line. It's a painstaking task.

How do I explain this use of time to the children? I continually encourage and praise them and say this is just one of the jobs we do at school. "Do your best," I tell them, "don't be worried." Time and again, I go to a child's desk, listen to a question, and—yes—help the child believe he or she is succeeding.

Dean finally arrives at 9:45, in the middle of the first test. I have him work quietly on some math puzzles that he enjoys rather than start a test section late and in confusion. He looks very tired.

Robin is smarter than the test. She asks all the logical questions for which there are no answers: Do they have this? Can they do that? Wouldn't this be true if?

I want to tell her, "Yes, Robin, you are right to ask all those questions." Instead, I say, "All we know is what they tell us here. What do you think?"

She marks an answer, and I agree. "That's what I would choose, too. Good thinking." I walk away realizing that the test certainly does not measure Robin's higher-order thinking skills.

Tuesday, 9 a.m. Today Dean is on time. Terri is here. Robin is sick. We begin again. We've completed only one-quarter of the test; the children have a long way to go. Today, because my class is so large, a Chapter 1 teacher is assisting me. Together, we follow the drill: Hand out the correct booklet; turn to the correct page; find the correct starting place; review how to blacken the ovals; and remind students of the test-taking pointers we covered yesterday. "If you're not sure," we tell them, "take your best guess. And when you're done, close your test book and read, or write in your journal."

Five minutes after the test starts, Terri is finished. I go to her desk and ask if she tried to answer all the questions.

"Yes," she said. "They were easy."

"Just let me check and make sure you turned all the pages."

Sure enough, she has filled in an oval for each question. At age 7, she has learned that the smartest person is the first one done. If you don't know the answer, she reasons, why struggle? Just play the game. It's a logical approach, but this time, her analysis has missed the mark, and her test score will fail to register her survival skills.

It's 9:45. Dean has wiggled for 20 minutes, sharpened his pencil, moved his desk, asked to go to the bathroom, lost his lunch ticket, and finally slammed his test book shut. He sighs loudly, feigning relief and accomplishment. I suspect what he really feels is frustration and insecurity.

At 12:30, Robin arrives. She knows we do not give tests in the afternoon. When I talk to Robin's mother by telephone, she suggests the girl was overly worried. We both understand, but neither of us know how to help Robin cope with her high demands on herself and what she perceives to be our expectations.

Wednesday, 9:20. Everyone is here. The tests are becoming routine. The children check their books, check the page, laugh at my jokes about ovals, and ask what the treat is for today. We have almost relaxed. Today there is another math test. Terri and Dean hate math. Robin is quite capable, but works slowly, checking everything.

As my assistant and I pass among the desks, children tug our sleeves, "Is this one right?" Their faces beg for confirmation. We break the test rules, asking the students questions to help them think: "Can you tell me why you chose that answer?"

"Well, because," they begin—and often their eyes brighten and they erase their mark and choose the correct answer. My assistant and I wink at each other and go on, conspirators.

Once again, Terri finishes early. I see her working with the white glue from her desk. With a small dab of glue on each page, she has glued her entire test booklet shut. It's hard not to laugh, imagining how the testing service will deal with this. How will their test appraise Terri's ingenious, mischievous mind?

Dean, meanwhile, has lost all confidence today. He spends most of his time trying to edge closer to John, the best math mind in the class, and copy his answers. Several times I ignore Dean, but finally our eyes meet and I tell him that he is capable by himself. I'm not sure he believes me.

What I want to say is, "Dean, this test is not important to me. You have years to learn this material. I want to help you learn—not frustrate you to the point of giving up. I want you always to be learning, not be discouraged."

At 10:15, it's time for recess. A welcome burst of energy—and the real tests of a child's life. Is there a swing left? Who will play with me? Will I hit the ball? Will anyone make fun of me?

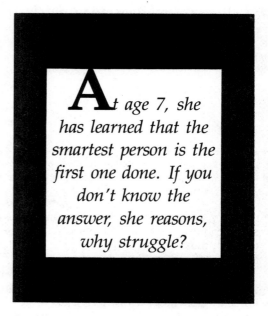

At age 7, she has learned that the smartest person is the first one done. If you don't know the answer, she reasons, why struggle?

Afterward, I wash Martha's skinned knee and apply a bandage. We begin again. The sting of Martha's knee probably won't affect her test score; what will affect it are the 10 times she stops working to check the bandage.

And so the week continues. On Thursday, two students are out with the flu. Robin has to make up the sections of the test from the day she missed. Terri says she has a migraine. Dean arrives late and says he might move again. I buy more treats to celebrate our collective endurance. We have spent the majority of this week on paper-and-pencil assessment—a process that goes against every principle of child development and appropriate practice I learned in college and graduate school.

The aftermath

Within a few weeks, the test results will come back, and Part Two of this insanity will begin. My job then is to enter each child's scores as they fall above and below the line that represents average performance for second-graders. I sit on the floor plotting numbers and ask, Average for whom? For a homeless child, for the child who had no sleep because his dad had an all-night party, for the child who has out-guessed the question, for the child whose knee hurts? How valid are these scores in determining appropriate instructional techniques in my classroom when they ignore such factors?

Perhaps I can compensate in my own class, but the influence of the test scores reaches further than I can. Terri's score will be sent to her next school as a measure of her ability. Dean's score will result in a whipping because his dad thinks Dean didn't try hard enough. And no matter how high her score is, it won't be good enough for Robin, who has been anxious about it for weeks. My school colleagues are anxious, too: This single week of tests will determine placement and funding for our school's Chapter 1 programs for the next school year.

To many adults—even so-called school reformers—one week of ITBS tests (and other tests like it) is only a minor inconvenience that might yield benefits. But during that week, thousands of children throughout the country will pay a real price in lost learning time and fractured self-esteem—and many will pay a further price at home.

Rarely do we interpret the scores to the children; frequently, not even to parents. For many parents, their child's score does not measure just a day, or even a week of their child's work; it mirrors the family's success, the parents' affluence, and the child's future.

And how should they know otherwise? Test scores are usually sent home with no explanation other than a computer statement that goes something like this: "Your son, *Name*, was given the Iowa Tests of Basic Skills. His composite score is the best indicator of his overall achievement. His score shows that he scored better than 3 percent of the pupils in Iowa and that 97 percent scored as well as or better. His overall achievement appears to be low for his grade. The scores of one pupil are often compared with other pupils' scores. Generally, your child's scores are low when described in this way."

All children operate at different developmental levels in different skill areas throughout the year. Children should not be compared to each other. They should be observed and encouraged in their growth, their initiative, and their desire to continue to learn. Instead, by attaching percentage scores to children on the basis of their test scores, we label some 7-year-olds as failures.

In reality, the failure is ours: As a society, we are failing to protect our children from unnecessary stress and unrealistic expectations. Sadly, most parents don't understand how absurd are the blanket judgments we derive from standardized testing—and the significant negative effects on their children. Most educators believe they have no choice in the decision to give an increasing number of standardized tests. The tests are institutionalized; the scores drive too many school initiatives and curriculum decisions to stop using the tests.

And in fact, we're using more tests now than we used to. As teacher educator Vito Perrone pointed out in his 1990 book *A Letter to Teachers*, the average high school graduate in 1990 had taken approximately 19 standardized tests in his or her school career; the average graduate in 1950 had taken only three such tests. It is no wonder professional organizations such as the National Association for the Education of Young Children, the National Council of Teachers of Mathematics, and other groups independently have called for a moratorium on standardized testing of young children before age 8. Instead, they suggest better ways to evaluate and observe young children as they learn.

For example, teachers could make "authentic assessments" of a child's performance, interest, and development by collecting samples of the child's work over time. Compiled into portfolios, these collections could document the child's growth. Items selected by both the student and the teacher would demonstrate the student's progress compared to the student's own potential—which could take into account the home environment and other factors ignored by the standardized tests.

That's one kind of new practice we should try. We must try something: The current process endangers learning—and discourages students, teachers, and parents.

Assessment in Context— Teachers and Children at Work

Tynette W. Hills

Tynette W. Hills, Ed.D., is coordinator of early childhood education, New Jersey State Department of Education. She served on the steering committee for the NAEYC–NAECS/SDE curriculum and assessment guidelines, and wrote on assessment in the NAEYC publication, Reaching Potentials: Appropriate Curriculum and Assessment: Vol. 1 *(Bredekamp & Rosegrant, 1992).*

Jason, age four, newly enrolled in the child care center, seems alternately dependent and aggressive. Long after the first week, he continues to cling to his mother and cry in protest when she leaves for work. Later in the day he may retire to a quiet corner, fingering the stuffed bear he likes to carry with him all the time. He sometimes hits other children to obtain a toy, a trike, or a choice place to build with blocks. When the teacher intervenes Jason sometimes cries or shouts, "I hate this school! I want my mother." He is beginning to show interest in playing near or with a few of the other children, one boy in particular, but his aggressive moves cause potential friends to hesitate and shut him out of their play. Jason's enrollment, coming mid-year, is proving to be disruptive to the group. His mother is concerned because his prior experience in child care was positive. What can be causing his present difficulties, and what can the teachers do to help?

Latisha is a first grader whose teacher has been trying to implement a mandate from the district's central office to adopt an emergent literacy, whole language program. So far the children have been keeping a writing journal, making books that include both their dictation and their own drawings with invented writing, reading big books and related little ones, dramatizing and recounting the stories, and other literacy activities. Latisha's parents, however, are demanding to know when the teacher will teach their daughter to read standard reading-series books and bring home papers with correct spelling. What and how can the teacher communicate about Latisha's progress toward conventional reading and writing?

Roberto, a three-year-old who is very interested in the blocks and accessory toys in his Head Start center, is working hard at a block construction, stacking block after block to build a tower that is teetering and almost sure to collapse. It does. Undaunted, he tries the same approach again and again, reaching as high as he can. The blocks rain down on two children working nearby on a long track for the wooden train. When and how should the teacher intervene?

Felicia's teacher is in the process of evaluating all of her kindergarten children's progress so that she can recommend programs the children should have next year. She has concerns about Felicia, almost six years old, who seems immature for her age, has progressed more slowly than other children in oral language and awareness of its written representations, needs more time and repetition of experiences leading to concept development, and depends more on the teacher and other children than the teacher usually expects. What program will be best for Felicia next year? What program modifications will she need?

Savanna, the supervisor of early childhood education in a local public school system has, with the

From *Young Children*, Vol. Vol. 48, No. 5, July 1993, pp. 20-28. Reprinted by permission of the publisher, the National Association for the Education of Young Children. © 1993 by NAEYC.

school board's and the super-intendent's approval, led the kindergarten/primary teachers in a restructuring of both the curriculum and the assessment system in the district, using as guides the principles of both developmentally appropriate practice (DAP; Bredekamp, 1987) and the guidelines for appropriate curriculum content and assessment (NAEYC & NAECS/SDE, 1991). The teachers and the supervisor are enthusiastic about the changes, although many challenges remain—most recently, the board's concern about accountability: How can they be sure that programs meet the objectives of high standards in learning? Can the teaching staff assure them that teachers' assessment procedures and conclusions about children's progress are unbiased and valid, not skewed by subjectivity?

Assessment and its purposes

Early childhood educators continually face situations like these. All of these situations require an informed professional decision, leading to a plan of action. All of them involve assessment, which is

the process of observing, recording, and otherwise documenting work that children do and how they do it, as a basis for a variety of educational decisions that affect the child. (NAEYC & NAECS\SDE, 1991, p. 21)

In real-life programs for young children, multitudes of educational decisions affect children, either directly or indirectly. To address the problems Jason is having and seemingly creating, Jason's teachers and parents must explore what he is coping with and what they can do to help him. To communicate successfully with Latisha's parents, the teacher must know and articulate the program objectives, have documentation of Latisha's progress, and decide what information is most likely to assuage her parents' concerns and enhance their receptiv-

The purposes for which assessment processes are used in programs for young children:
1. educational planning and communicating with parents;
2. identifying children with special needs; and
3. program evaluation and accountability.

ity to a whole language approach to reading and writing. Roberto's teacher must know his progression in interest, knowledge, and skills in balancing and patterning block structures. She must assess on the spot how best to supervise his play and, if advisable, move to protect his and others' psychological as well as physical safety. Felicia's teacher must draw from her experience with Felicia in the past year to assess Felicia's progress, her strengths, and her needs in order to determine whether Felicia is likely to profit from moving into the regular first grade program, would probably do best in that first grade program with specialized attention to her developmental needs and support of her strengths, or should be referred for screening and possible diagnostic assessment. Savanna and the teachers must collect sufficiently frequent and varied documentation of consistent (i.e., reliable) child performance for the local board of education and demonstrate that the assessment processes measure valid progress, in keeping with program goals and objectives.

The typical situations I have described exemplify the purposes for which assessment processes must be used in programs for young children:

1. educational planning and communicating with parents;

2. identifying children with special needs; and

3. program evaluation and accountability.

Assessment processes require

teachers to discover what children know and can do and where they are in their development and learning as a basis for deciding how they can be assisted in their further growth and learning (Tyler, 1984).

The joint position paper on curriculum content and assessment was issued by NAEYC and NAECS/SDE (1991) in response to a demonstrated need in the profession. Early childhood professionals needed guidance in selecting what to teach and when, and how best to assess children's progress. The guidelines were developed with the review and comments from hundreds of early childhood educators. Together with the DAP publications (NAEYC, 1986; Bredekamp, 1987), the guidelines endorse the integration of curriculum, instruction, and assessment based on what we know about the development, individual differences, and cultural diversity of young children. The guidelines appeal for assessment practices that open educational opportunity to all young children; assure—not delimit—curriculum and learning; and work to the children's benefit.

Early childhood educators are on good theoretical and policy grounds when they feel a sense of urgency about appropriate assessment of the young children they guide and teach. One reason is that in too many instances and over too long a period, assessment has been directed to find out what is wrong, a deficit model that Kenneth Goodman (1992) labels a "disease metaphor." Assessment processes must also document the progress children make, their strengths, and the ways they learn and solve problems.

Urgency is appropriate also because research indicates that after third grade, children perform with marked consistency in school. Although most early childhood educators believe that formal standardized testing of children's achievement should be delayed until third grade (NAEYC, 1988) or later, the critical times for assessing children's progress and needs and designing educational approaches to help them become successful may come earlier (Entwisle, Alexander, Cadigan, & Pallas, 1986). Without well-designed intervention, early attainments may predict limits to later achievement. Developmentally appropriate assessment, then, takes on added importance: It is best practice for children now and best for helping to ensure their optimal opportunity in the future. It can do so, however, only if it accurately reflects children's progress toward objectives of compelling importance to their growth and development and to their learning in areas that their parents and community find valuable.

The real-life context of assessment

The reality of working with young children in child care centers, Head Start programs, kinder- gartens, and primary classes is hard. Garrison Keillor, in a "Prairie Home Companion" broadcast on National Public Radio (November 25, 1989), said, "I believe that sometimes you have to look reality in the eye and deny it!" Some approaches to assessment deny reality. They have been developed and applied without adequate regard for the realities of children's growth, development, and learning; without adequate attention to the circumstances under which early childhood educators work; and without adequate respect for the kinds of information that parents and teachers want.

The reality of children's lives

In real life children are most themselves when they are in familiar environments with adults and children whom they know and trust, engaged in tasks that allow them to use the modalities with which they are most comfortable. In such situations they will most likely demonstrate the knowledge, skills, and attitudes that truly represent their attainments. When we introduce strange people, unfamiliar surroundings, demands for responses to atypical tasks, and constrictions on their usual behaviors, we will likely elicit behaviors that are neither valid nor reliable samples of the children's development and learning.

Young children are rapidly growing and developing, as their language and concept development—and especially their social-personal development—show. Children are engaged in complex developmental processes that come about through the interaction of maturation, experience, and learning: communicating thoughts and feelings to others orally and in writing, reading and understanding the other's communications, understanding and representing patterns and quantitative concepts, negotiating interpersonal differences, and a myriad of other tasks. Annual or interval assessments cannot track such complex developmental processes, which instead require longitudinal approaches—a "kind of history writing" (Sorenson, 1992).

Basing any conclusions, for example, about Jason's developmental status on short-term data collected since he has been in this particular child care center would do a disservice to Jason and to the program staff. By conferring with his parents, teachers could learn that the family has been under stress: His father lost his job and only after six months found another job at lower pay, with no benefits. His mother found employment and placed Jason in a nearby child care center, where he developed warm relationships with teachers and children; but her change to another work location has required Jason's transfer to this new child care center. The number and frequency of changes

In real life children are most themselves when they are in familiar environments with adults and children whom they know and trust, engaged in tasks that allow them to use the modalities with which they are most comfortable. In such situations they will most likely demonstrate the knowledge, skills, and attitudes that truly represent their attainments. When we introduce strange people, unfamiliar surroundings, demands for responses to atypical tasks, and constrictions on their usual behaviors, we will likely elicit behaviors that are neither valid nor reliable samples of the children's development and learning.

in the real context of Jason's daily life demand empathetic responses from his teachers and a temporary suspension of any conclusions about his abilities to respond and cope consistently.

The reality of parents' concerns

Any assessment program must emphasize what parents need to know about the welfare and progress of their children. Parents are the best source of information about the strengths and needs of their own children in the familiar settings of home and community, and they are the ones with the greatest personal stake in their children's status and progress. Although parents, better than anyone else, know their children in the intimate home environment, teachers see the children with other children of similar age and experience and in relation to educational goals and objectives defined by the neighborhood and by the school community.

Parents can contribute invaluable information to teachers about how the children are demonstrating at home what they have learned in the center or at school. Parents' concerns and questions can sensitize teachers to important milestones and outcomes of children's progress: How is my child progressing? What is my child learning? How does my child compare with the expectations for her or him? Parents' concerns extend to areas of accountability for both the program staff and themselves: Is the program of high quality? How are you helping my child? What can I do to help?

Latisha's parents expressed twin concerns: Is their daughter really performing well in language areas, and does the program really ensure that she is learning what will help her become a reader and a writer? In responding to

Questions To Ask in Evaluating a Program's Assessment Procedures*

1. Is the assessment procedure based on the goals and objectives of the specific curriculum used in the program?

2. Are the results of the assessment used to benefit children, i.e., to plan for individual children, improve instruction, identify children's interests and needs, and individualize instruction, rather than label, track, or fail children?

3. Does the assessment procedure address all domains of learning and development—social, emotional, physical, and cognitive—as well as children's feelings and dispositions toward learning?

4. Does assessment provide useful information to teachers to help them do a better job?

5. Does the assessment procedure rely on teachers' regular and periodic observations and record keeping of children's everyday activities and performance so that results reflect children's behavior over time?

6. Does the assessment procedure occur as part of the ongoing life of the classroom rather than in an artificial, contrived context?

7. Is the assessment procedure performance-based, rather than only testing skills in isolation?

8. Does the assessment rely on multiple sources of information about children, such as collections of their work, results of teacher interviews and dialogues, as well as observations?

9. Does the assessment procedure reflect individual, cultural, and linguistic diversity? Is it free of cultural, language, and gender biases?

10. Do children appear comfortable and relaxed during assessment rather than tense or anxious?

11. Does the assessment procedure support parents' confidence in their children and their ability as parents rather than threaten or undermine parents' confidence?

12. Does the assessment examine children's strengths and capabilities rather than just their weaknesses or what they do not know?

13. Is the teacher the primary assessor, and are teachers adequately trained for this role?

14. Does the assessment procedure involve collaboration among teachers, children, administrators, and parents? Is information from parents used in planning instruction and evaluating children's learning? Are parents informed about assessment information?

15. Do children have an opportunity to reflect on and evaluate their own learning?

16. Are children assessed in supportive contexts to determine what they are capable of doing with assistance as well as what they can do independently?

17. Is there a systematic procedure for collecting assessment data that facilitates its use in planning instruction and communicating with parents?

18. Is there a regular procedure for communicating the results of assessment to parents in meaningful language, rather than letter or number grades, that reports children's individual progress?

*Taken from NAEYC & NAECS/SDE, 1991, pp. 34–35.

Early childhood teachers are both the primary assessors and the primary users of assessment information. They must base the what, how, and when of next steps in curriculum and instruction on what they have learned from their assessment of children's performance.

---

their questions, teachers confront the possibility that their program practices may conflict with the parents' beliefs about their own child and what is important in the child's learning. Teachers must then decide what information they can give the parents to reassure them about their child and help them trust the potential efficacy of the language-education program (Powell, 1986).

The reality teachers face in assessing

Early childhood teachers are both the primary assessors and the primary users of assessment information. They must base the what, how, and when of next steps in curriculum and instruction on what they have learned from their assessment of children's performance. Roberto's teacher must draw quickly on what he knows of Roberto's development to pinpoint the best time, if any, to intervene and how best to do it. Felicia's teacher is reflecting about her progress over a long period and considering educational decisions with higher stakes—highly individualized planning and specialized educational placements. Teachers, moreover, must communicate clearly to parents and administrators what they have found, trying to balance the "expert professional" and the supportive roles with parents (Powell, 1986), while confronting the demands of accountability as defined by administrators and policymakers.

Teachers need to know how to integrate instruction and assessment; how to use what they know about young children and their development to design the assess-

ment program; how to analyze and interpret assessment results to know where the children are in their progress toward the goal; how to decide next steps—planning for individual children and communicating with parents; and how to report program accomplishments to administrators. Teachers must fulfill these responsibilities while carrying out a myriad of tasks with a group of children who bring with them a host of personal characteristics

that cry out for notice, endorsement, and help. In Susan Sherwood's first grade class (Sherwood, 1990) were 21 children ranging in IQ from 68 to 137; one reading at eighth grade level, some not reading, and the rest somewhere in between; one diagnosed as learning disabled; one diagnosed as hyperactive; one adept at mathematical problem solving; and one girl, age six, already in puberty. Then Ann was included in the class—Ann who had multiple disabilities from birth trauma—vision impaired, with moderate to severe mental disabilities, but ambulatory and verbal. Sherwood and other hard-pressed teachers need to make assessments in fulfillment of their professional responsibilities, but they need assessment strategies that appropriately sample both children's strengths and their needs, contribute positively to educational planning, and mini-

mally distract them from working with the children.

The reality of administrators and assessment

Administrators are both accountability agents and educational leaders. They face the twin demands of responding to external expectations for outcomes of early childhood programs—children's achievement, program quality, cost effectiveness, and pa-

---

Many administrators have only limited knowledge about early childhood education and limited or outdated knowledge about assessment.

---

rental and policy or school board expectations—while simultaneously providing leadership and support to the teaching staff. When these roles conflict, the knowledge that administrators have and the resources available to them influence which role wins out (Stiggins, 1985). Many administrators have limited knowledge about early childhood education and limited or outdated knowledge about assessment. Such an administrator may have extreme difficulty encouraging or supporting teachers in developmentally appropriate practice, interpreting DAP to parents and the community, and providing leadership to the school board in implementing policy decisions. Administrators in such circumstances should turn to resources for training and information that will make clear the reality of standardized tests and their limitations in assessment, the use of teacher observation and professional judgment as valid and reliable indicators of children's achievements, and the cost *in*effectiveness of mass standardized testing.

As a supervisor, Savanna is confronted with the need to respond to the school board's legitimate concerns for accountability even while she is delighting in the progress that she and the teachers have made in reforming curriculum and educational practices. To respond to the second thoughts some board members have, she must draw on her knowledge of children's language learning; distill the principles of developmentally appropriate instruction, curriculum content, and assessment; and document the children's progress over time, based on teacher observation and recording. In doing so, she will turn to one of the available resources—the teachers who know the children well and, in helping respond to the board's questions, will grow in their ability to analyze and explain the teaching–learning enterprise and its results.

Observation-based assessment

The NAEYC–NAECS/SDE position paper sets forth principles to guide teachers in observing and assessing children. These principles can help teachers make valid decisions about what children need, accumulate adequate information for communicating with parents, and result in worthwhile educational programs for young children.

By emphasizing broad-based, continuing observation and documentation of children's activities, the principles make clear that formal standardized testing, when legitimately used (e.g., to screen for and diagnose special needs or handicapping conditions), can be appropriate but is certainly not sufficient for all of the assessment purposes needed in programs for young children.

In observing the children they teach, teachers may engage in the following activities (and more): "pay attention, be heedful, consider, detect, estimate, examine, investigate, mark, measure, monitor, probe, study, survey, or watch," according to a contemporary thesaurus (Kipfer, 1992, p. 583). Although testing is not specifically listed here, formal standardized tests or teacher-made tests can be observations of children's behavior, perhaps as a way to estimate, mark, or measure. Emphasizing the distinctive qualities of observation-based assessment is therefore important.

Only through observation—attending, heeding, considering, detecting, examining, investigating, monitoring, probing, studying, surveying, and watching—can we know the children. Observation records can document what children know and can do in real-life circumstances and typical learning situations. To contribute well to the assessment process, observation should address the following components (Gordon & Browne, 1985; Hills, 1992):

• **Purpose**—What do we want to know?
• **Focus**—Who or what is being observed? Exhibiting what behaviors? When? Where?

• **Record/documentation**—What information is needed? How will it be recorded? How frequently?
• **Use of the observation**—What does the observed event mean for the child's progress and needs? What next steps should we take to further the child's development?

(For a fuller discussion of these steps and methods of collecting information, see Teale, 1988; Bird, 1992; Goodman, Y.M., 1992; Hills, 1992).

Observation-based assessment emphasizes informal means of collecting assessment data, for example, observing and recording children's behavior in typical classroom situations. These assessment activities, which place minimal constraints on children's usual activities, can include narrative records of what is observed—running records or descriptions, chronicled while the behavior is occurring; anecdotal records, logs, or journals noted after the event; time or event samples focused on behavior of particular interest; and checklists and rating scales of certain behaviors. Gathering such information in the midst of a busy teaching day challenges teachers to learn to take brief notes on conveniently available cards; maintain, for each child, files into which the cards can be dropped; have assistants and volunteers observe; keep journals and write in them briefly but regularly; and use tape and video recorders to capture the action.

Observing and recording do not, by themselves, constitute assessment. Teachers must reflect on *what* they have observed and recorded in relation to program goals and objectives for each child. Observation and recording, followed by reflection—a process that enables teachers to view what is transpiring from an objective plane—help teachers make sound judgments about children's development and learning, while contributing to their growth as teachers (Jaggar, 1985).

Observing and recording do not, by themselves, constitute assessment. Teachers must reflect on *what* they have observed and recorded in relation to program goals and objectives for each child.

Samples of children's work, such as drawings, paintings, block constructions, oral and written language, and storytelling and reading, provide rich documentation of children's learning. A number of scales are available to help teachers objectively assess children's attainments and progress over time (Clay, 1985; Teale, 1988; Chittenden & Courtney, 1989; Engel, 1990; Hills, 1992). Parents find representative samples of their children's work, accompanied by an explanation of the progress represented, to be interesting and compelling ways to understand what is going on. The growing use of portfolio collections of children's work attests to the potential value of this form of documentation (Grace & Shores, 1991).

What assessment can do

The reality is that developmentally appropriate assessment can serve all of its various audiences—parents, administrators, teachers, and children. Parents will be well served when they understand their children's progress toward clear goals and objectives of the program, including children's growth, strengths, and areas they find difficult or challenging. In addition, parents want to know what the teacher is doing about these matters and what they themselves can do to help.

Administrators will be served when assessment information demonstrates that the programs are accomplishing their purposes and the children are indeed developing and learning well.

Teachers will be served when assessment helps them fulfill their professional responsibilities: to determine children's status and progress, to monitor the classroom program's quality, to plan next steps, and to communicate clearly with parents and administrators. Developmentally appropriate assessment is consistent with what most early childhood

Administrators will be served when assessment information demonstrates that the programs are accomplishing their purposes and the children are indeed developing and learning well.

educators believe about young children's learning and development, and it can provide the information that teachers need to teach and guide children well and involve their parents in the process. Bowman (1993) cautions that assessment procedures that are less formal alternatives to testing are difficult to standardize and may be difficult to administer. Teachers may lack the knowledge and skill necessary to interpret the results of such assessment procedures and integrate the results into planning for individual children and groups. Early childhood educators need opportunities for professional development, in-service training, and supportive supervision to learn new duties and respond to new opportunities.

Assessment will serve the best interests of children when it is carried out as an integrated part of an overall program, when it contributes positively to children's self-esteem and developmental progress, and when it recognizes children's individuality and respects their family and community backgrounds. Assessment that will accomplish those ends is continuous, broadly focused on child development and learning, sensitive to children's diversity, integrated into their day-to-day activities, and designed to reap benefits for them, through teachers' knowledgeable planning and teaching and through clear communication between school and home.

References

Bird, L.B. (1992). Getting started with portfolios. In K.S. Goodman, L.B. Bird, & Y.M. Goodman (Eds.), *The whole language catalog supplement on authentic assessment* (p. 128). New York: Macmillan/McGraw-Hill.

Bowman, B. (1993). Early childhood education. In L. Darling-Hammond (Ed.), *Review of research in education* (Vol. 19, pp. 101–134). Washington, DC: American Educational Research Association.

Bredekamp, S. (Ed.). (1987). *Developmentally appropriate practice in early childhood programs serving children from birth through age 8* (exp. ed.). Washington, DC: NAEYC.

Chittenden, E., & Courtney, R. (1989). Assessment of young children's reading: Documentation as an alternative to testing. In D.S. Strickland & L.M. Morrow (Eds.), *Emerging literacy: Young children learn to read and write* (pp. 107–120). Newark, DE: International Reading Association.

Clay, M.M. (1985). *The early detection of reading difficulties* (3rd ed.). Auckland, New Zealand: Octopus, Heinemann.

Engle, B. (1990). An approach to assessment in early literacy. In C. Kamii (Ed.), *Achievement testing in the early grades: The games grown-ups play* (pp. 119–134). Washington, DC: NAEYC.

Entwisle, D.R., Alexander, K.L., Cadigan, D., & Pallas, A. (1986). *American Educational Research Journal, 23*(4), 587–613.

Goodman, K.S. (1992). Myths, metaphors, and misuses: Borrowed metaphors. In K.S. Goodman, L.B. Bird, & Y.M. Goodman (Eds.), *The whole language catalog supplement on authentic assessment* (p. 7). New York: Macmillan/McGraw-Hill.

Goodman, Y.M. (1992). Tools for evaluation. In K.S. Goodman, L.B. Bird, & Y.M. Goodman (Eds.), *The whole language catalog supplement on authentic assessment* (p. 98). New York: Macmillan/McGraw-Hill.

Gordon, A.M., & Browne, K.W. (1985). *Beginnings and beyond: Foundations in early childhood education.* Albany, NY: Delmar.

Grace, C., & Shores, E.F. (1991). *The portfolio and its use: Developmentally appropriate assessment of young children.* Little Rock, AR: Southern Association on Children Under Six.

Hills, T.W. (1992). Reaching potentials through appropriate assessment. In S. Bredekamp & T. Rosegrant (Eds.), *Reaching potentials: Appropriate curriculum and assessment for young children: Vol. 1.* (pp. 43–63). Washington, DC: NAEYC.

Jaggar, A.M. (1985). Introduction and overview. In A.M. Jaggar & M.T. Smith-Burke (Eds.), *Observing the language learner* (pp. 1–7). Newark, DE: International Reading Association.

Kipfer, B.A. (1992). *Roget's 21st century the-*

saurus in dictionary form. New York: Dell.

National Association for the Education of Young Children (NAEYC). (1986). Position statement on developmentally appropriate practice in early childhood programs serving children from birth through age 8. *Young Children, 41*(6), 4–29.

National Association for the Education of Young Children (NAEYC). (1988). Position statement on standardized testing of young children 3 through 8 years of age. *Young Children, 46*(3), 21–38.

National Association for the Education of Young Children & the National Associa-

tion of Early Childhood Specialists in State Departments of Education (NAEYC & NAECS/SDE). (1991). Guidelines for appropriate curriculum content and assessment in programs serving children ages 3 through 8. *Young Children, 46*(3), 21–38.

Powell, D.R. (1986). Parent education and support programs. *Young Children, 41*(3), 47–52.

Sherwood, S.K. (1990). A circle of friends in a first grade classroom. *Educational Leadership, 48*(3), 41.

Sorenson, N.L. (1992). Making evaluation longitudinal: Evaluation as history writ-

ing. In K.S. Goodman, L.B. Bird, & Y.M. Goodman (Eds), *The whole language catalog supplement on authentic assessment* (p. 12). New York: Macmillan/McGraw-Hill.

Stiggins, R.J. (1985). Improving assessment where it means the most: In the classroom. *Educational Leadership, 43*(2), 69–74.

Teale, W.H. (1988). Developmentally appropriate assessment of reading and writing in the early childhood classroom. *The Elementary School Journal, 89*(2), 173–183.

Tyler, S. (1984). Carrying out assessment with young children. In D. Fontana (Ed.), *The education of the young child* (2nd ed.). New York: Basil Blackwell.

The Assessment Portfolio as an Attitude

Cathy Grace and Elizabeth F. Shores

The teacher's use of good judgment is a key to effective assessment of young children. Taking time to think about children and their behavior is very important, whether or not a teacher uses an assessment portfolio. It has been estimated that the average first grade teacher makes about one thousand decisions a day and the average preschool teacher makes twice as many (Jackson, 1968; Murray, 1986). There is little time in the teacher's day to think carefully about individual children and their special needs, yet early childhood professionals must incorporate such "thinking time" into their schedules, not just to plan the next day's activities but to reflect upon the events of the current day. A teacher of three-year-olds once said, "I feel like a detective. There is so much to know and three-year-olds can tell me so little. I would have to guess about everything if I didn't have their behavior to give me clues." This is an example of what can be called *the portfolio attitude.*

Teachers begin to assemble an assessment portfolio by *writing down* these clues, along with their observations, thoughts and questions about individual children. As they collect samples of their pupils' work and observation cards about class and small group games and activities, and as they interview the children to gain more information, teachers assess young children in appropriate ways. The assessment process is a vital part of planning, implementing and maintaining developmentally appropriate practice in the classroom.

In the past, a school might have considered a young child "ready to learn" when he made an acceptable score on a standardized test. Today, however, many school and government officials define "readiness" as the student's being prepared to participate successfully in formal schooling. "Readiness" now has multiple dimensions, the most important being that the child has an orientation toward learning and a certain ability to solve problems. Educators no longer consider first grade the child's first learning experience. Rather, they view first grade as a continuation of the learning process that began at birth.

In response to the shift in public policy, teachers are beginning to use instructional practices that reflect what many have known all the time—that children's concepts of reading and counting, their social skills, and their physical and emotional growth occur over time and in predictable developmental stages. Their innovations in early childhood classrooms are another example of *the portfolio attitude.*

Non-graded primary units are being instituted in public schools and multiage grouping has renewed popularity (Charlesworth, 1989). In 1988 the National Association of State Boards of Education released a report, *Right From the Start,* which set forth recommendations for restructuring schooling for four- through eight-year-olds. The report urged that

> Early childhood units be established in elementary schools to provide a new pedagogy for working with children age 4–8 and a focal point for enhanced services to preschool children and their parents.

All of these events signal the admission by those in education and outside the field that children's learning is a continuous process. Thus, the collection and maintenance of information about the child's learning also should be continuous.

For teachers who always have based instruction and curriculum on their observations of their students, the "fuss about assessment" is bewildering.

For those teachers who have always based the majority of their instructional strategies and curriculum plans on the results of standardized achievement tests, criterion referenced tests based on state-mandated curriculum objectives, or student placement tests such as readiness tests, the "fuss" is intimidating. Some of these teachers are suspicious. Others expect that "this too will pass".

For teachers who are new to the field, the debates over testing, placement and other related issues are confusing and frightening. They may wonder, Who is right? What is right? How do I know if what I choose to do will be the best course of action for the children in my room?

To address the concerns and reactions of these teachers, we should reflect on the old saying that "The more things change, the more they stay the same". In the early history of preschool and primary education, teachers accumulated student work and used it in planning and instruction. Moreover, parents and communities respected the informed judgments of teachers.

Since then, our society has reacted and overreacted to world and national events—Sputnik, *Why Johnny Can't Read* (Flesch, 1955), integration of public schools, shifts in demographics and in family dynamics. Our educational system has felt the turmoil. By the 1970s and 1980s, *what* was taught, *how* it was taught and *when* it would be taught were largely controlled by curriculum guides, standardized tests and state and federal legislation about school assignments and equal educational opportunities. Teachers, once valued as the experts on children's development, seemed to gradually lose the public's respect and, with that, the authority to plan how to meet their students' needs.

With governmental guarantees of equal educational opportunity has come ever-greater government bureaucracy—until many teachers feel their spirits have been broken and the sense of community within many schools and school districts has diminished.

Standardized testing is one dimensional and only depicts the child's brief engagement with an unnatural set of circumstances. Teachers who are new to the profession or not familiar with alternatives to one dimensional testing should seek out teachers who have and are using a variety of strategies to assess children in their classroom; they should read about alternative assessment; they should watch teachers through video taped segments or visit classrooms where continuous assessment is practiced.

Observational skills are learned by observing. Teachers new to implementing the strategy must gain practice, skill and accuracy over time. When implementing portfolios as a strategy for assessment, teachers may want to depend on the collection of work samples to verify their observations. As they become more experienced the means by which data in the portfolios is collected will become more varied.

The early childhood profession has been and will continue to be accountable for the quality of educational programs children attend. As parents and children will be taking a more active role in curricular decisions, teachers will become decision *facilitators*. In this way accountability will be shared by all parties and not be viewed as an unknown that has driven decisions made by school policy makers and frightened some teachers into giving up appropriate teaching practices. *This is an example of the portfolio attitude.*

Today, policymakers, the media and the public all seem very concerned about education, especially early childhood education. President Bush and the nation's governors have set forth the readiness goal. Numerous states are providing new educational opportunities for three- and four-year-olds. Congress has appropriated more money for child care for poor families and for parents seeking job training with the intent of becoming self sufficient. The challenge is to see that these new programs and policies are developmentally appropriate and support the development of all children.

With the advent of school-based management programs, teachers are enjoying a new sense of empowerment and professionalism. They have the opportunity to reclaim their true responsibility. They can again become decision-makers or facilitators, planning appropriate learning experiences and assessment measures for children. The assessment portfolio can help teachers as they recreate their role in society and in the lives of children and families.

Since appropriate assessment is a collaborative process involving children, parents, teachers and the community, the portfolio method promotes a shared approach to making decisions which will affect the child's future and attitude toward learning. True partnerships are formed when parents and teachers work together in determining the best course of action for the young child. Portfolios serve as a departure point for parent and teacher communication to begin and to flourish. Again, *this is an example of the portfolio attitude.*

The time is right to expand the classroom horizon and broaden the child's canvas. The assessment portfolio represents an attitude that frees the teacher so that she may focus on the child and develop an intimate relationship with him—one that will remain long after the paintbrushes are put away.

REFERENCES

Charlesworth, R. (1988). "Behind" before they start? Deciding how to deal with the risk of kindergarten "failure". *Young Children.* 44(3), 5–13.

Flesch, R. F. (1955). *Why Johnny can't read.* New York: Harper.

Jackson, P. (1968). *Life in the classroom.* New York: Holt, Rinehart and Winston.

Murray, F. (1986). *Necessity: The development component in reasoning.* Paper presented at the sixteenth annual meeting, Jean Piaget Society, Philadelphia.

National Association of State Boards of Education. (1988). *Right from the start.* Alexandria, VA: Author.

Guiding Behavior

No subject in early childhood education seems to attract the attention of teachers and parents more than how to guide behavior. New teachers are concerned that they will not be able to keep the children "under control." Mature teachers wrestle with the finer points of how to guide behavior positively and effectively. Parents have strong feelings on the subject of behavior, often based on their own childhood experiences. Teachers spend many hours thinking and talking about the best ways to guide young children's behavior: *What should I do about the child who is out of bounds? What do I say to parents who want their child punished? Is punishment the same as discipline? How do I guide a child who has experienced violence and now acts out violently?*

Early childhood educators have long maintained that discipline means guidance. It is a complex process rather than a single method. First, a teacher must understand typical child development and examine personal attitudes about children. Second, a teacher uses redirection to modify undesirable behavior. Third, modeling and explaining more acceptable, appropriate, or mature behavior are necessary. And fourth, the teacher follows through by teaching children verbal and reasoning skills for better peer interaction. Discipline, in this connotation, means steadily building self-control so children display positive self-esteem and respect for the needs of others. This process gradually moves children toward healthy independence and provides problem-solving skills that they may draw upon in future situations.

The emphasis of this approach to guiding behavior is positive, since punishment is not the goal. A positive approach allows teachers to avoid two extremes; putting pressure on children or giving in to them. Both of these extremes have negative consequences for everyone involved. Children may react to pressure by challenging the teacher's decision. Then, if a teacher gives in, children may lose the continuity necessary in guidance. By teaching children to take responsibility for their own behavior, teachers are expressing respect and kindness. Marianne Modica emphasizes this positive approach to discipline in her article.

The effect of domestic violence or abuse of young children is often inappropriate behavior or lack of control. Traumatic situations can alter children's behavior and lower their self-esteem. In an early childhood setting, it is difficult for these children to cope with others and to express their emotions. Some children who have been affected by trauma may be extremely angry and display unacceptable behaviors. Others may be pessimistic and act out in self-destructive ways. Teachers find that guiding the behavior of children who have suffered trauma is a complicated task. Learning to identify types of abuse and trauma is the first step to supporting young victims. The second step is to learn specific strategies for allowing children to express their feelings while maintaining a firm structure that will help them heal. Several articles in this unit address ways teachers can successfully guide children who endure different types of trauma.

Because the ultimate goal of guiding behavior is self-guidance, teachers will find that the most effective approaches to guiding behavior are based on viewing children as capable and responsible. For those children whose life experiences have been traumatic, the emphasis may need to change in order to strengthen trust and self-respect first. But they must be viewed as capable and responsible, regardless of what occurred in their lives earlier.

Guiding children's behavior actually starts well before

teachers and children interact. It begins by preparing the room and scheduling activities before the children have arrived. Teachers who learn the basics of preplanning find that they spend less time resolving conflicts while they are teaching. Sandra Crosser's article provides a way for teachers to manage the early childhood classroom by anticipating and avoiding behavior problems.

As with all areas of early childhood education, a high-quality, effective plan for guiding behavior does not arrive prepackaged for the teacher's immediate use. Guiding and disciplining are hard work, requiring careful attention to individual children and differing situations. The work is not complete until the teacher examines her or his own sense of control and feelings about children's behavior. Anger and disrespect have no place in a positive environment. When feelings are expressed openly and discussed calmly, teachers create the kind of atmosphere where everyone is able to speak and act responsibly.

Looking Ahead: Challenge Questions

How do early childhood teachers find a balance between classroom chaos and strict control? Which is your tendency, to allow chaos or enforce strict control?

Why do teachers often find classroom discipline to be their greatest challenge?

Should teachers discipline different children differently?

How does trauma, such as war, hurricanes, or domestic violence, affect young children's behavior? When children are affected by violence or abuse, what can teachers do to provide therapeutic experiences for them?

What are the basics of managing an early childhood classroom?

A Positive Approach to Discipline in an Early Childhood Setting

"Sit Down!" shouts Judy, with more than a trace of frustration in her voice. She is trying to maintain control of a group of preschoolers who are none too interested in the lesson she has worked so hard to prepare. "Jonathan, if you won't join the circle you'll have to sit in the time-out chair," she states with determination.

Marianne Modica

Marianne Modica is Program Coordinator for the Calvary Christian Academy and Happy Day Child Care Center in Wayne, NJ.

Jonathan counters with his usual response to adult commands. "No," he says flatly. He, like most two-year-olds, can't be faulted for verbosity. The next move is up to Judy. If she ignores Jonathan, she risks "losing face" in front of the rest of the children. If she follows through with her threat, she must interrupt her lesson and will probably lose control of the group anyway.

Unfortunately, this exhausting game of clashing wills is too frequently played in the early childhood arena. Equally unfortunate is the fact that in this game, nobody wins. Teachers and children alike become angry and frustrated, and the classroom becomes a battleground rather than a nurturing place of growth and development. Why is it that so often we as teachers find classroom discipline to be our greatest challenge?

Discipline can be defined as teaching that corrects, molds, or perfects, and all would agree that it is an important element in any classroom situation. Without it the classroom is un-safe, the children are insecure, and teachers will quickly lose their sanity. Be that as it may, the goal of discipline is not to make the teacher's life easier. The goal of discipline is to guide the behavior of children in such a way that they will internalize our outward expectations and develop the inner controls they need to function as whole and happy individuals.

These goals can easily become muddled when we confuse discipline with punishment. For example, I recently witnessed the following scene while observing a class of three-year-olds. While most of the children were engaged in typical preschool activities, one small child was sitting off to the side in what I quickly ascertained to be the "time-out chair." She was not facing the class, but was seated directly behind the teacher, who was working at a table with another child. The girl was crying pitifully but was obviously being ignored. The teacher saw my concern and proceeded to describe to me, in a loud voice, the child's disruptive behavior. I'm sure this teacher thought she was disciplining her young charge "for her own good." However, little good will result from the way this situation was handled. If we agree with Webster's definition of punishment ("a penalty imposed for a violation; suffering, pain, or loss that serves as retribution"), there can be no doubt that this child was being punished. Perhaps our first task as teaching professionals should be to commit ourselves firmly to the ideal that we are not in the business of punishing children.

Under the umbrella of classroom discipline, there is much room for flexibility and individual differences in teaching style. Some teachers function best in an atmosphere of "controlled chaos." Others prefer a more orderly environment and stick closely to their predetermined schedules. The danger lies in allowing one's personal preference for a discipline style to move too far left or right on the continuum of healthy practice for preschool children. A strict, authoritarian approach to discipline (what I call the "because-I-said-so method") is both an inappropriate and an unrealistic way to handle a class of young children. This method leads children to behave well only to escape punishment, and they will not develop the inner self-control they need. In fact, children who find themselves under this authoritarian style may actually become more aggressive toward other children as a result (Harms, cited in Leeper, Witherspoon, & Day, 1984, p. 444).

At the other end of the spectrum,

and equally inappropriate, is the permissive or "anything-goes" style of discipline. Children neither need nor want to be left to their own devices, and they are not likely to develop inner controls without adult input. Hopefully we will find ourselves somewhere in the middle of these two extremes and will provide developmentally appropriate guidance to the children in our care. Being a teacher means being a model for young children; it is our responsibility to model a reasonable approach to life.

Many discipline problems can be avoided by an awareness of basic classroom management. Things like group size, child-adult ratio, room size, and the availability of materials and equipment are important elements in group interaction and should be considered carefully. More aggressive behavior has been observed in children who are members of larger groups with higher child-adult ratios (McConkie & Hughes, cited in Leeper et al., 1984, p. 446). Likewise, we've all witnessed certain combinations of children that are explosive, and that may need to be gently redirected to more calming activities. Transitional periods between activities are also times of stress for some children. I know a child who needed to be told, "In five minutes I will tell you that in five more minutes it will be cleaning-up time." This may sound elaborate, but with a little extra consideration from a caring teacher, a five-year-old boy was given the tools he needed to cope with an otherwise stressful situation (and I was grateful, since the child is my son!).

Other possible causes of discipline problems in preschoolers are developmentally inappropriate subject matter and unrealistic expectations. Are your children bored during circle time? Is your curriculum uninteresting or too difficult? Have they been sitting still for too long? Expecting children to sit quietly during lessons and activities that they cannot relate to and that do not meet their needs is asking for trouble. Sometimes the fault lies not in the child but in the program itself.

Even the most astute classroom manager and developmentally appropriate teacher sometimes encounters disruptive behavior in preschoolers. Other factors that may affect the children we teach are nutrition, fatigue, and changes in the home life or family structure. A wise teacher will not overlook the obvious when a child's behavior begins to change. Once these influences have been ruled out, we need to take a deeper look into the problem at hand before we can decide how to deal with any discipline concern.

If a child is disruptive and exhibits aggressive or violent behavior consistently, it may be that there is a deeper emotional problem at work, and some type of family counseling may be needed. It is also true that some children develop negative patterns of behavior and learn to draw attention to themselves with this behavior. Often teachers try behavior modification techniques with young children, but, as Lillian Katz warns, it is wise to "Stop, look and listen before you condition" (cited in Leeper, et al., 1984, p. 454). Not every child is an appropriate candidate for this approach, and behavior modification involves more than putting stickers on a chart at the end of the day. If a child has been carefully observed and it is agreed that behavior modification should be attempted, there are many resources available to instruct classroom teachers on the correct way to carry out this plan (see Leeper, et al., 1984; Osborn & Osborn, 1977).

Most disruptive or aggressive behavior in young children can be explained as simply a need to develop skills in social interaction. Teaching young children to relate to others in a positive way is one of our biggest jobs, and if we expect the children who come to us to be already socialized so that we can "teach" them, we are in the wrong profession. There are some basic practices we can follow to help children grow in these important social skills.

First, children need guidance to develop self-expression. When we encourage children to use their words to express anger or frustration, they will be less likely to strike out when these feelings boil over. Say, for instance, Billy knocks down Susie's blocks. Susie can be helped to express her anger in words ("That makes me angry, Billy!") rather than hitting or pushing to show her feelings. By giving children the language they need to express their emotions freely, we are working to build their self-esteem as well, for children will learn that their feelings matter and that they are important enough to be listened to.

Second, teachers can help build self-worth by avoiding the use of labels such as *good* and *bad* when referring to children or their actions. "Great job, Juan" is more desirable than "Good boy, Juan," for Juan will sense that if the teacher thinks he's good today, maybe she will think he's bad tomorrow.

Third, directions and requests can be phrased positively. Rather than "Don't stand on the chair," a child may be told, "Chairs are for sitting on." When we take the time to talk to children and explain our reasoning to them, we are modeling respectful behavior that will go a long way in boosting the self-esteem of our preschoolers.

Perhaps one of the most valuable tools we can give children is the ability to negotiate with their peers. Susanne Wichert explores this idea beautifully in her book *Keeping the Peace*. Wichert believes that children can engage in conflict resolution once we provide them with the tools and practice they need. Suppose two children are fighting over a toy. The first step in the negotiating process is calming the children involved in the conflict and focusing their attention on the problem at hand. This can be done by saying something like "Just a minute, can I help you with this problem?" Then each party involved is given an opportunity to tell his or her side of the story uninterrupted. The next step is to clarify the problem by restating what the children have explained ("So the problem is...right?"). The adult continues to encourage the children to talk to each other as they bargain and ultimately come to a resolution ("I'll let you use the puzzle when I'm done"). How much adult input is actually needed depends on the level of maturity of the children involved. Once resolution has been reached and the children have reconciled, the adult says a few words to the offending party to prevent a recurrence of the behavior ("It's a good idea to ask when you want to use something and someone else is using it"). Finally, the adult affirms the children for the good job they've done in finding a solution. These children have learned to take a

reasonable approach to their problem, and they have successfully negotiated a resolution. Can you think of some adults who would benefit from learning this lesson as well?

So, are your preschoolers driving you to the brink of professional burnout? Remember that they basically want to please us, and they will model our behavior, for better or worse. If we control them by harsh demands and criticism, they will learn to be demanding and critical and will think little of themselves and others. If we raise our voices to them, they will do the same to us and to each other. But if we provide the consistent, car-

ing guidance that young children need and deserve, they will gradually develop the inner discipline and controls that will guide them well in future years.

References

Greenberg, P. (1990, Jan.). Why not academic preschool? (Ideas that work with young children). *Young Children*, 70-80.

Leeper, S. H., Witherspoon, R. L., & Day, B. (1984). *Good schools for young children* (5th ed.). New York: Macmillan.

Osborn, D. K., & Osborn, J. D. (1977). *Discipline and classroom management*. Athens, GA: Education Associates.

Wichert, S. (1989). *Keeping the peace*. Philadelphia: New Society Publishers.

The Tasks of Early Childhood:
The Development of Self-Control —
Part II

Four-year-old Tommy felt mad that Jonah was hogging the big building blocks. He stood nearby, feeling more and more disgruntled. Just a week ago, his teachers had carried out a group discussion about hitting and hurting. No one was supposed to hit, even if you were mad. The group had discussed other ways to express their feelings. They had talked about telling a child what you wanted, or getting a teacher to help you out.

Alice Sterling Honig
and Therese Lansburgh

Alice Sterling Honig teaches at Syracuse University in the Department of Child and Family Studies, College for Human Development, in Syracuse, NY. She is an editorial board member of Day Care & Early Education. *Therese Lansburgh is Chair of the Maryland Committee for Children and an advocate for families and children at the state and national levels.*

But Tommy got so frustrated. Impulsively, he clenched his fist and raised his arm above his head. Ms. Ida glanced over and looked straight at him with a reminding look. "I wasn't going to hit him. I was only just raising my arm, Ms. Ida," Tommy protested. She smiled encouragingly and helped Tommy find another activity to interest him.

Nine-month-old Natalie was restless and whimpering, feeling so hungry she was ready to start hard crying. She needed her bottle and she needed it right away. But Ms. Mollie was not quite ready. She was just finishing a diaper clean-up and was washing her hands. She called softly over to reassure Natalie. Hearing her caregiver's reassuring tones, Natalie brought her fist up to her mouth. She managed to get some fingers into her mouth and suck vigorously. She was able to calm herself and keep in control for a few minutes until her caregiver came over with a bottle of milk and a lap to snuggle Natalie while feeding her.

Three-and-one-half-year-old Deanna was in a crowded shopping mall with her parents. They needed to buy many more items than those on their list, and the shopping trip was growing very long and tiring for their little girl. Papa said, "Deanna, we did not realize that we would need to buy so many extra things, and that our shopping trip would take this long. We're sorry. Thank you for being so patient." The little girl acknowledged her father's courteous explanation and apology and sighed, *"Well, I guess it was necessary."* Her father smiled with pride — at her forbearance and her big vocabulary for such a little girl.

The children described above were practicing a precious skill — the skill of *self-control*. In a time when crime levels are soaring, and many persons heedlessly hurt others horribly with assault, rape, and murder, the personal attributes of self-control are particularly important. The sophisticated conscience of an adult may take years a-building. But the building blocks begin in early childhood. Self-control is a good signpost that moral development is proceeding well for young children.

What Is Self-Control?

Self control in the preschool years is expressed in the ability to:

Trust and cooperate with adults.
Delay the gratification of immediate needs or wants for a little while.
Find internal ways to be more patient without blaming or hurting others.
Channel angry impulses so that words instead of fists are used.
Think about and empathize with upset feelings of others.
Balance rights with responsibilities.
Find ways to cheer up even when things go wrong.
Take turns.
Recognize other's rights as well as one's own.
Find inner ways to keep from whining or falling apart into temper tantrums despite frustrations.
Modify the frequency and intensity of unacceptable actions according to situational needs, even when teachers or parents are not present.

All societies have rules regarding acceptable or unacceptable behavior for children beyond infancy. Parents and other caregivers in the culture teach children what is permitted (toileting on a potty; blowing your nose in a hanky; asking for a turn with a

toy) and what is disapproved (wiping one's nose on one's hand; whacking a peer so you can grab a toy).

When children are very young, adults often maintain strong *external* controls over child behavior. Adults scoop up a toddler who may be ready to bop another baby over the head with a toy. They use scolds, or they distract and refocus the little one. They repeat simple rules over and over. Sometimes they arrange environments to *prevent* conflicts of interest or will when a toddler will get too frustrated and then burst into a temper tantrum or act out angrily. Often *proactive* discipline techniques are used to prevent loss of self-control. For example, a wise parent (knowing that sitting a child in the grocery cart while Papa shops in a crowded store may well end up in a cranky scene, with the child demanding sweets at the checkout counter) often brings along an apple or a few crackers to head off the child's loss of emotional control.

As a preschooler grows, her or his behavior seems to be more and more maintained by *internalized* standards of conduct, particularly when authority figures are not around to say, "No!" Consider the young toddler who moves with fascination toward the wall plug into which a tempting lamp cord is plugged. As she approaches and wants to reach to pull out the cord or poke a finger into the plug, she says to herself, "No, no, no plug" and toddles sadly away. She is well along in the process of developing self-control.

Such behavior begins very early with the help of skilled caregivers who understand the individual differences in children and the seesawing that a child will go through while learning more mature emotional behavior.

Flexibility of Control: Our Goal for Children

Self-control is not easy to learn. Young children have strong needs and few cognitive skills for understanding why they have to wait for a turn or to take others' needs into account.

Sometimes caregivers are so anxious to "civilize" young children that they teach a rote technique like saying, "I'm sorry," without helping a youngster to develop more awareness of others' rights or awareness of the effects of hurtful actions.

Four-year-old Vern had hit a child just a few minutes ago. The teacher had quietly and firmly restated classroom rules about hitting. Now he again raised his fist angrily, about to hit another child. The teacher swiftly moved over and kneeled in front of him, looking him directly in the eye. "Vern, what are you going to do with your hands?" she asked. He was silent. "You were about to hit someone," the teacher said. "That makes me feel angry. We just talked about what hands are for. And hands are not for hitting or hurting someone. Now, you tell me, Vern, what are hands for?" "For hugging ... for playing with toys," Vern answered tentatively. "OK, then, when you feel angry, Vern, what could you do?" the teacher inquired. "I could hug somebody," Vern rejoined. The teacher looked at him. "Vern, I was feeling so angry with you when you went to hit someone that I didn't want to hug you. When you are feeling angry, do you really want to hug someone?" Vern shook his head no. The teacher continued, "When I am angry with you, do I hit you?" Vern said, "No, never." The teacher pursued, "Vern, what *am* I doing with you?" Vern replied, "Talking." "Yes," agreed the teacher, "And what could *you* do when you are feeling angry?" "I could talk," suggested Vern.

Some adults place very high demands for obedience, polite behavior, and neatness on young children, so that the children feel anxious and overcontrolled. Such children may be fearful of using finger paint or playdough because they have been taught that getting messy is something strongly disapproved of by their special adults. Some preschool children have difficulties with constipation because they have been made too fearful about a possible mess in their pants.

On the other hand, some adults bring up little children without the firm guidance, clear rules, and social expectations necessary to assist young children into more socially acceptable interactions. Such children may act rudely, gallop wildly, kick or hit others, and be heedless of other children's or the teacher's needs and rules in the preschool classroom. Neither *overcontrol* nor *undercontrol* is a desirable outcome. Overcontrolled children often act rigid and joyless, not spontaneous. They may be highly anxious, or critical of other children's misbehavior. Undercontrolled children may lash out aggressively or crumple into temper tantrums and whining at the slightest frustration, or they may be easily led into mischief by more dominant peers. *Ego resiliency* refers to flexibility of controls (Honig, 1985), a highly desirable goal for children.

Factors That Influence Self-Control

What factors influence the development of *knowledge* of what is permissible and what is prohibited, of what situations require patience and a willingness to wait? What factors influence children's *ability* to wait, to use words instead of fists, to take others' feelings into consideration, to cooperate instead of defy or cry? Parental child-rearing techniques and the child's cognitive level are probably the most important influences, but other factors come into play, too. Inherited capacities, cultural and religious norms and practices, child-care-setting characteristics, peer interactions (such as bullying or friendliness), and teacher support for prosocial learnings in the classroom are also important influences in shaping children's development of self-control (Honig, 1982).

Babies learn only gradually *what* they must control about their strong emotional responses and *when* and *how* they are expected to control them. Learning self-control begins early. By four months, a baby picked up for nursing may strain and fuss a bit, but she can wait for a few minutes until her caregiver is ready to begin the feeding. She no longer yowls immediately or loudly in response to pangs of hunger when her caregiver has picked her up. She has begun already to learn self-control.

Differences in Temperament

Some children are born more easygoing. Some have a more cheerful mood, and some are more cautious (Thomas and Chess, 1981). Helping easygoing children develop self-control can be easier than working with children whose temperaments are more triggery or impulsive, or who have a low tolerance of any sort of frustration.

Some toddlers have a predisposition to shyness. They stay close to an adult when taking a walk in the neighborhood around the child care center. Others may try to dash madly off down the street. Some are frightened by new experiences, tend to comply with adults, and seem more obedient. Thus, some children may appear self-controlled, but their temperamental fearfulness is what impels their "good" behavior.

Age and Maturity

Just as they differ in the timing and skill with which they develop motoric competence in walking, running, and climbing, children differ in their ability to learn the task of self-control. Some adults have inappropriate expectations about when a child will be able to handle disappointment, anger, frustration, or jealousy more maturely. Children who are expected to develop adult-desired self-control in too many areas too soon, before they are ready, may become overly solemn, sullen, and sneaky, or defiant and noncooperative.

Mastery of Other Emotional Tasks

Children who have developed a basically trusting and secure relationship with their caregivers, who feel that their actions bring results and that they are *willing to try* (Honig and Lansburgh, 1990) are more likely also to develop a sense of personal responsibility for their own actions. Such children learn to influence others in positive ways as friends. They also feel confident enough so that they can have influence over their own internal impulses. Those with little basic trust

in the positive regard of their caregivers or those in whom severe threats and punishments have damaged the will to try may be too discouraged to tackle the work of controlling their impulsive, disapproved behaviors toward others. Grown-ups have dominated them, and they do not see that their own internal efforts at control can be successful.

Parental Methods of Teaching Self-Discipline and Control

Parents and caregivers differ in their ways of socializing and disciplining children. They vary in their ability to "read" a baby's signals. Caregiver beliefs and skills in socializing children are crucial determinants of how successful a young child will be in developing self-control. *Socialization* means learning how to behave in ways approved by your family and culture. For example, during the first year of life, infants gradually learn to obey an adult's firm "no-no" for touching dangerous objects, such as a sharp pair of scissors or an unprotected electrical plug.

Some adults have unrealistic expectations too early that a baby can understand the meaning of "No" or "Quit that!" Often, a baby is bewildered and frightened by the sharp tone and the anger and threat in the adult's voice. Suppose a baby in a high chair is curious about what has happened to the toy he just pushed off the edge of the table top. Where could it be? Curiously the ten-month-old lifts his body to peer over the edge. "Cut that out!" says the caregiver sharply. Startled, the baby bursts into tears. His behavior was interpreted by the adult (unaware of how the baby is figuring this situation out) as deliberate and willful disobedience of the rules for staying in one's seat.

When teachers and parents understand developmentally what task a very young child is trying to accomplish, they may not be so overcontrolling. Finding a positive way to say, "Sit down, honey. Your toy fell down on the floor and I will get it for you. Sit down nice and safe, please!" will be more helpful than undecipherable warnings and prohibitions that cause a baby to freeze but do not lead to either understanding or inner controls.

Some discipline techniques work better than others at helping children develop self-control. Researches have shown that *power-assertive* discipline that involves physical punishment or threats of physical punishment, in particular, leads to defiance and lack of mastery of aggressive actions. Even though they may temporarily stop "misbehaving," these children have been given a strong example of how to lose self-control and to use external power to get others to do what they want!

Some types of discipline have been found far more likely to lead to compliance and self-control. Where *inductive discipline* is used by parents, toddlers begin early to self-monitor and to avoid actions for which they have internalized the rules (Hoffman, 1977). What are inductive methods? They include *reasoning with children* and *explaining the reasons for rules*, rather than using forceful commands, punishments, or threats. Children who have been brought up with parents who use firm rules, give explanations, have high expectations of approved behavior, and are positively and genuinely committed to their child's welfare are more likely to internalize controls. Baumrind (1977) has called this kind of parenting "authoritative" in contrast to either "permissive" or "authoritarian" (dictatorial) disciplining.

Authoritative caregivers are *for* their children. They are warm and nurturant, yet they have high expectations of their children. They are firm in not accepting unacceptable behavior, are effective in disciplining, and explain clearly the reasons why they discipline as they do. Permissive caregivers act in a nonpunitive way, but they let unacceptable behavior go on without dealing with it, and they do not require the child to learn to behave more responsibly and maturely.

Lara came home from the day care and told her mother, "It's OK to hit. You just don't know. It's OK to hit, 'cause when we hit in the day care, Miss Kathy doesn't do anything to anybody."

When adults do not firmly stop bullying or do not notice scapegoating, then they are supporting the continuation of social patterns that do not promote self-control, positive socialization, or optimal peer interactions. Authoritarian patterns are also nonproductive. If a child is required to accept forceful discipline and an adult's authority as absolute, that child can become more nervous, more stressed, and more likely to act out insecurity and resentment by aggressive or aggrieved actions toward others.

Research on Self-Control

Toddlers who have had secure attachments to a nurturant, responsive parent do not fall apart or give up when faced with a difficult tool-using task. Sroufe (1979) found that such toddlers, when faced with challenging tasks, were more able to maintain self-control; they persisted longer without temper tantrums and were more likely to enlist their parents' support in struggling to solve the tool-using tasks which were too hard for them to solve on their own. In contrast, other mothers gave orders but not helpful assistance to their toddlers. They had been insensitive to their children in infancy. These children gave up easily, were unable to maintain self-control, became oppositional, and had more temper tantrums.

The securely attached infants who had exhibited more self-control in the tool-using tasks as toddlers were rated at five years of age, by their preschool teachers as highly ego-resilient, self-reliant, and moderate in self-control. The children who had been insecurely attached in early infancy, and who had had been poor at self-control as toddlers under the stressful task conditions in the laboratory, were rated either as much more undercontrolled or overcontrolled. Thus, research has significantly linked self-control to early patterns of infant-parent attachment.

Longitudinal studies follow chil-

dren over several years. In one such study at the University of Minnesota, 120 children aged three to seven years were given an attractive toy for a short period of time and were then told to stop playing with it (Masters and Binger, 1976). Almost half of the two-year-olds were able to inhibit their impulses when their parents asked them to stop playing with the attractive toy. The percentages of self-control rose dramatically with age, most sharply between two and three years of age. When the children were followed over time, self-control proved to be quite a stable individual characteristic. That is, the children who had good control at age two made greater progress later in self-control.

A talking-clown box was used with 70 four-year-old boys and girls by Patterson and Mischel (1976) to tempt children off-task. The preschoolers were warned that the clown box might tempt them to stop working at their pegboard task, and in that case they would lose an opportunity to play with attractive toys after the pegboard work and would be allowed to play only with broken toys.

Groups of children were taught verbalizations that they could repeat to the clown box in order to help them control the temptation to give up working and thus forfeit the reward they desired. The first group were helped to resist temptation by concentrating on the promised reward. The researcher suggested that they say to themselves, "I want to play with the fun toys and Mr. Clown Box *later*." In the second group the children were to say to themselves, "I'm going to look at my work." Children in a third group were told they could say anything they wanted to themselves to help them avoid looking at the clown box. A nursery rhyme or something else irrelevant was suggested to the fourth group, and the fifth group received no instructions. Children in the first and second groups — those for whom the later reward was emphasized and those who were helped to plan in detail how to ignore Mr. Clown — worked longer at the pegboard task than those children who has less specific plans or no plan. Thus, some self-instructional plans of what to say to yourself are more helpful than others in boosting children's ability to resist temptations that can distract them from their tasks.

At what point, while a child is misbehaving, does a caregiver need to intervene? Some boys in one research study were stopped just before they reached for a forbidden toy. Others were not stopped until after they had touched the toy (Walters, Parke, and Cane, 1965). Adult prevention *prior* to the unacceptable behavior was more effective: The boys in that group demonstrated greater self-control in resisting temptation later when they were left alone with the forbidden toy.

In stress research, self-control has proved to be a factor, along with high self-esteem, problem-solving skills, and higher empathy, that allows children to cope when they live highly stressed lives. Fourth- to sixth-grade urban children who proved resilient despite many stresses were found to have more internalized controls and more realistic expectations for self-control in mastering stressful life conditions (Parker et al., 1990).

Teacher Techniques for Promoting Self-Control

What can caregivers do to promote self-control in early-childhood educational settings? Researches suggest first that a warm, personally attentive, genuinely focused relationship with a child will increase that child's self-esteem and chances of trying harder to control impulses toward disorganization or hurtfulness toward others.

The *teacher is a powerful role model.* If a caregiver shouts, acts very irritated, or blows up at naughtiness, then children are being given a message that it is OK to have a short fuse and lose control.

Teachers can stay near a child who has difficulty in mastering forbidden actions. If an adult is nearby and caring and supportive, the child who may have a strong urge to act out aggressively by sweeping the frustrating puzzle pieces off the table or hitting a

peer will get prompt signals from the teacher. The teacher will keep the classroom and the children safe and secure. The child does not have to explode or act out in anger and fright. A calm, supportive, and alert teacher nearby serves as a beacon of security (Wolfgang, 1977).

Prevention Helps

When children are overtired or teased or feel that others have unfairly received more than their share, they may more easily act out. Teachers need to make sure that fair access to toys and materials is provided. Overcrowding, as when too many children are in a small block corner, can trigger out-of-control use of blocks as pretend guns or throwing toys, which results in hurt children and hurt feelings. Thoughtful planning and judicious use of space as well as resources both help children maintain good self-control in play.

Reasoning with children, as well as providing understandable explanations of regulations, promotes children's development of notions of what is acceptable and what is expected. Such *inductive techniques* promote self-control far more than overcontrolling, critical, or overly permissive methods.

Bibliotherapy is a helpful aid. Teachers need to choose books that tell stories about animals or children who are in difficult, stressful, scary, or frustrating situations where the characters try hard not to use mad feelings or angry outbursts and do try to use more reasonable ways to solve their problems. Children identify with such story characters.

Good plans to remember rules and reasons boost self-control. Teachers can help children think of good plans to help themselves remember rules against hitting. Caregivers can give children words to say that will aid them in controlling impulsivity. One preschooler ran and ran in the long hallways of his center located in a church basement. He would yell out, "Yo-yo, come and play with me," to a four-year-old girl he liked very much. The teacher explained to Yolanda that

she could keep working on her puzzle, and tell her friend, "I'm busy working on my puzzle. You come here and do puzzles with me." This verbal scaffolding helped Yolanda not to dash off and run aimlessly as well as helped lure her playmate into a more constructive activity.

Refocus children on appropriate interactions and activities. If children's play seems to be veering toward a loss of self-control, the caregivers need to step in judiciously and redirect the children. Adults can use firm suggestions. With toddlers, distraction and luring the toddler into more appropriate activities help support positive play while preventing inappropriate behaviors.

If a child has totally lost self-control and is kicking and yelling, a caregiver may need to hold that child firmly so that the child cannot pose a danger to others. The teacher can reassure the child, "I will not let you hurt others or yourself. You can get back into control. I will help you. You are feeling very upset. I will hold you so you feel safe until you can get calm again and get back into control."

Use encouragement and admiration when children are showing good self-control. Specific praise helps. Admire a child who has struggled to use words instead of fists. In the child care setting, express appreciation when children have been patient even though the lunch delivery was delayed. Children need to know that their special persons, their teachers, value their struggles to work toward self-control, an important foundation for classroom cooperation and compliance.

References

Baumrind, D. (1977). Some thoughts about childrearing. In S. Cohen and T. J. Comiskey (eds.), *Child Development: Contemporary perspectives.* Itasca, IL: Peacock.

Hoffman, M. L. (1977). Moral internalization: Current theory and research. In L. Berkowitz (ed.), *Advances in experimental social psychology,* Vol, 10. New York: Academic Press.

Honig, A. S. (1982). Prosocial development in children. *Young Children, 37*(5), 51-62.

Honig, A. S. (1985). Research in review: Compliance, control, and discipline. *Young Children,* Part 1, *40*(2), 50-58; Part 2, *40*(3), 47-52.

Honig, A. S., and Lansburgh, T. (1990). The tasks of early childhood: Part I. The will to try. *Day Care and Early Education, 18*(2), 4-10.

Masters, J.C., and Binger, C.C. (1976, Sept.). *Inhibitive capacity in young children: stability and development.* Paper presented at the annual meeting of the American Psychological Association, New York.

Parker, G. R., Cowen, E. L., Work, W. C., and Wyman, P. A. (1990). Test correlates of

stress affected and stress resilient outcomes among urban children. *Journal of Primary Prevention, 11,* 19-35.

Patterson, C. J., and Mischel, W. (1976). *Self-instructional plans and children's resistance to temptation.* (ERIC Document Reproduction Service No ED 141-679).

Spaner, S. D., and Jordon, T. E. (1973). *Analysis of maternal antecedents to locus of control at age 60 months.* (ERIC Document Reproduction Service No. 087 555).

Sroufe, L. A. (1979). The coherence of individual development. *American Psychologist, 34* 834-841.

Thomas, A., and Chess, S. (1981). The role of temperament in the contribution of children to their own development. In R. M. Lerner and N. A. Busch-Rossnagel (eds.). *Individuals as producers of their own development.* New York: Academic Press.

Walters, R. H., Parke, R. D., and Cane, V. A. (1965). Timing of punishment and the observation of consequences to others as determinants of response inhibition. *Journal of Experimental Child Psychology, 2,* 10-30.

Wolfgang, C. H. (1977). *Helping aggressive and passive preschoolers through play.* Columbus, OH: Merrill.

Helping Children Cope With Violence

Lorraine B. Wallach

Lorraine B. Wallach, M.A., is one of the founders of the Erikson Institute in Chicago and is presently a faculty member there. Her recent work includes staff training around issues of children and violence.

Children who grow up in violent communities are at risk for pathological development because growing up in a constant state of apprehension makes it difficult to establish trust, autonomy, and social competence.

Violence is epidemic in the United States today. The murder rate in this country is the fifth highest in the world. It is 10 times higher than England's and 25 times that of Spain. For many inner-city children, violence has become a way of life. In a study of more than 1,000 children in Chicago, 74% of them had witnessed a murder, shooting, stabbing, or robbery (Kotulak, 1990; Bell, 1991). Almost half (47%) of these incidents involved friends, family members, classmates, or neighbors. Forty-six percent of the children interviewed reported that they had personally experienced at least one violent crime. These figures are similar to those found in other U.S. urban areas, such as Baltimore (Zinsmeister, 1990), Los Angeles County (Pynoos & Eth, 1985), and New Orleans (Osofsky, Wewers, Hann, Fick, & Richters, 1991).

Children are exposed to several kinds of violence, including child abuse and domestic violence. And there are communities where violence is endemic, where gang bangers, drug dealers, petty crimi-

nals, and not-so-petty criminals rule the streets. For children living in these conditions, feelings of being safe and secure do not exist.

Children who are not designated victims of assault can be unintended victims. Shoot-outs between gangs and drive-by shootings result in the wounding, and often killing, of innocent bystanders. In addition, the psychological toll of living under these conditions is immeasurable. The children in these neighborhoods see violence and hear it discussed. They are surrounded by danger and brutality.

Child abuse, other domestic violence, and neighborhood violence can harm development

The effects of this kind of violence on children are widespread and can permeate all areas of development, beginning in infancy and continuing through childhood. The first task a baby faces is the development of trust—trust

in the caregiving environment and eventually in himself. Achieving a sense of trust is compromised by growing up in a violent community. Many families find it difficult to provide infants with support, love, and affection in a consistent and predictable manner when they live in a constant state of apprehension—not knowing when they are going to be victims of violence. Toddlers have difficulty developing a sense of autonomy when their families cannot help them explore their environments because their surroundings are filled with danger. Preschoolers, too, are inhibited from going out into the world. Just at the age when they should be expanding their social contacts and finding out about people beyond the family, they are restricted by the dangers lurking outside. Many children living in high-rise housing projects and other dangerous neighborhoods are cooped up inside all day because it is unsafe to go out-of-doors. The situation is even more tragic when children

From *Young Children*, May 1993, pp. 4-11. © 1993 by The National Association for the Education of Young Children, 1834 Connecticut Avenue, NW, Washington, DC. Reprinted by permission.

experience violence within the family. Where can a child find protection when she is victimized within her own home? Although domestic violence occurs in *every* kind of neighborhood, the effects may be even more damaging when compounded by the harmful effects of growing up in *violent* neighborhoods.

Children who grow up under conditions that do not allow them to develop trust in people and in themselves or learn to handle day-to-day problems in socially acceptable ways are at risk for pathological development; they are at risk for resorting to violent behaviors themselves. The anger that is instilled in children when they are mistreated or when they see their mothers or siblings mistreated is likely to be incorporated into their personality structures. Children learn by identifying with the people they love. They also identify with the people who have power and control. When children see and experience abuse and violence as a way of life, when the people who are responsible for them behave without restraint, the children often learn to behave in the same manner.

Another serious problem for children living in chaotic communities is that the protectors and the dangerous people may be one and the same. The police, who are supposed to be protectors, are often seen as dangerous by community members. In his book *There Are No Children Here,* Alex Kotlowitz (1991) describes how a young man who is idolized by his housing project community be-

It is particularly important for children who come from chaotic environments to have firm but appropriate limits, even though children who feel powerless may try to provoke adults into a battle of wills in an effort to make themselves feel important.

The young child's protectors and the dangerous people in her life may be one and the same.

cause he is successful, has graduated from high school, is not caught up in gangs, and is still his own person is mistakenly killed by the police. What do children think when their idol is gunned down by the people who are supposed to protect them?

Children are confused when they cannot tell the good guys from the bad guys. Their teachers and the media tell them that drug dealers are bad and are the cause of the problems in the community, but the children may know

that cousins or friends or even older brothers are dealing. Some people have likened the inner city, especially housing projects, to war zones; but in a war the enemy is more often than not on the outside, and usually everyone knows who he is.

Children growing up with violence face risks other than becoming violent themselves. Children who live with danger develop defenses against their fears, and these defenses can interfere with their development. When children have to defend themselves constantly from outside or inside dangers, their energies are not available for other, less immediately urgent tasks, such as learning to read and write and do arithmetic and learning about geography and history and science. In addition to not having enough energy to devote to schoolwork, there is evidence that specific cognitive functions such as memory and a sense of time can be affected by experiencing trauma (Terr, 1981).

Boys and girls who are victims of abuse and who see abusive behavior in their families can grow up feeling as if they are responsible for what is happening. Young children cannot always differentiate between what is real and what is part of their inner lives. The literature on divorce has made clear that many children believe that they have caused the breakup of the family, even though it had nothing to do with them (Wallerstein & Kelly, 1980; Hetherton, Cox, & Cox, 1982). Children who feel guilty about the violence in their families often perceive themselves as being bad and worthless. Feelings of worthlessness can lead children to the idea that they

> **When children have to defend themselves constantly from inside and outside dangers, there is little energy for schoolwork. There is also evidence that specific cognitive functions such as memory and a sense of time can be affected.**

are not capable of learning, which leads, in turn, to a lack of motivation to achieve in school.

Children who experience trauma may have difficulty seeing themselves in future roles that are meaningful. Lenore Terr (1983), in her study of the schoolchildren of Chowchilla who were kidnapped in their school bus, found that the views of their future lives were limited and often filled with anticipation of disaster. Children who cannot see a decent future for themselves cannot give their all to the present task of learning and becoming socialized.

Living in unpredictably frightening situations makes children feel as if they have no control over their lives. We know that young children need to feel as if they can direct some parts of their lives,

but children who are victims of violence learn that they have no say in what happens to them. This sense of helplessness interferes with the development of autonomy.

It is difficult for children to keep on growing and maturing when they have been traumatized because an almost universal reaction of children to traumatic occurrences is regression. Children slip back to stages at which they felt more secure. This is particularly true when they have only a tenuous hold on their current status.

What makes some children more resilient than others, and what can we do?

As depressing as all this sounds, however, it does not mean that all children who experience violence are doomed. It is known that some children are more resilient and withstand trauma and stress better than others. If a child has an easy temperament and makes a good fit with his primary caregiver, he or she is more likely to be off to a good start. Some lucky children are born to strong parents who can withstand the ravages of poverty and community violence and still provide some security and hope for their children. Children are shaped not only by their parents' behavior but also by their parents' hopes, expectations, motivations, and view of the future—including their children's future.

It is important to remember that children are malleable, that what happens in the early years is im-

A kindergarten teacher in a Chicago public school was discussing her dilemma concerning two boys in her classroom. All of the children were at their tables, engaged in drawing, when the teacher noticed these boys crawling under the tables, pretending to have guns. When one of the boys saw the teacher watching them, he reassured her, "Don't worry, we're just playing breaking into an apartment." The teacher questioned whether she should let the play continue or offer a more socially acceptable view of behavior. How should she react? A Head Start teacher in the group said that the boy who was taking the lead in this game had been in her class the year before, and that his family's apartment had been burglarized. The boy had been very frightened and, after that experience, had changed from a confident, outgoing youngster to a quiet and withdrawn child. Here it was a year later, and he was just beginning to play out his experience. He was becoming the aggressor in the play instead of the helpless victim. And he was regaining some of his old confidence.

portant, but that many children can overcome the hurts and fears of earlier times. Many can make use of positive experiences that occur both inside and outside their families. Child care centers, recreation programs, and schools can be resources for children and offer them alternative perceptions of themselves, as well as teaching them skills. One of the things that help determine the resiliency of children is the ability to make relationships and to make use of the people in their environments, people who provide to children what they do not get in their families or who supplement what their families cannot offer.

Child care professionals can help offset the negative effects of violence in the lives of young children by providing that supplement. Although teachers, social workers, and human service personnel cannot cure all of the hurts experienced by children today, they can make a difference.

1. **The first thing they need to do is to make sure that their programs provide opportunities for children to develop meaningful relationships with caring and knowledgeable adults.** Teachers and other staff members can offer each child a chance to form an important relationship with one of them, a relationship within which the child can learn that there are people in the world who can be of help. The best thing to offer children at risk is caring people, people who are available both physically and emotionally.

Some years ago the famous Chicago analyst Franz Alexander (1948) coined the term *corrective emotional experience* to explain the curative power of therapy, and that term best describes what child care professionals can do for children at risk. A corrective emotional experience means having a relationship with another person that touches one's deepest core—not a relationship that is superficial or intellectual, but one that engages the emotions. It means having a relationship within which a person can redo old patterns and ties. It means feeling safe enough within a relationship to risk making basic changes in one's psychic structure. Children cannot be forced into these kinds of relationships; they can only be offered the opportunities with the hope that they take advantage of them.

Some children attach easily, and it does not take much effort on the part of the adults for these children to form attachments; these are usually the children who have had a good relationship in their past. Other children have not been lucky enough to have had the kind of relationship that makes them want to seek out others and repeat this satisfying experience; these children need more help in forming ties and trusting alliances. **What can adults do to stimulate relationships with children who do not come easily to this task?** They can look into themselves and see if they are ready for this kind of relationship—a relationship that makes demands on their emotions, their energies, and their time. Relationships with children who have inordinate needs and who do not have past experiences in give-and-take partnerships are not 50–50 propositions; adults must meet these children more than halfway.

2. **Child care professionals can organize their schedules and their time with the children so that they provide as much consistency as possible.** Attachment can be encouraged by reducing the number of people a child encounters during the day and by maximizing the amount of meaningful time and activity the child has with one adult. In this way each child is allowed to form an attachment to one person. There are several models—including therapeutic centers, child-life programs, and primary-care nursing—that use relationship as the principal tool in their interventions. Establishing significant relationships with the children who

A nine-year-old boy in a shelter for battered women told a story about his recurring dream. This is what he said: "I dreamed of someone taking me away. He was dressed like a lady, but he had a moustache. I went inside the house. It was dark. The lights were out, and there were people inside having a party. It was ugly. They were eating worms and they asked me to try one. I took one and threw it away. Then I opened the door, and the light came on in there, and I saw there were no more ghosts, and I saw I was sleeping. When I dream like that, I become afraid."

It was obvious that the boy was expressing his fears, but the exact meaning of the details was not evident—not until one of the child care workers who knew the mother reported that the abusive father was bisexual and brought his male sexual partners to the family's apartment. It then became clear that in addition to struggling with feelings about an abusive father, the boy was also frightened and confused about the meaning of his father's behavior and probably about his own sexual identification. In this case the child was able to tell about a disturbing dream through the telling of a story, and the adults were able to understand it with additional information about his family.

have suffered from trauma is the most important thing that can be done, and it is the basis for all of the work that follows. What is this other work?

3. **Child care professionals must provide structure and very clear expectations and limits.** All children, especially young children, need to know where they stand, but it is particularly important for children who come from chaotic environments to have firm but appropriate limits. It should be noted that they do not take to this kind of structure easily. It is not something they have experienced before, and the newness of it may cause anxiety and tension, just as any new situation does.

Some children see the structure of a new setting as an opportunity to assert themselves and force the adults into power struggles. Children who feel powerless may try to provoke adults into a battle of wills in an effort to make themselves feel important. But even though some of the neediest children may rebel against structure, no matter how benign, it is important to provide it so that the boundaries are clear.

4. **Early childhood professionals should offer children many opportunities to express themselves** within the confines of a comfortable and consistent schedule, with clear expectations about behavior. Children need to air their emotions; they need to tell their stories. They can do this in several activities that can be a part of any good program for children.

Josephine, the child of an abused mother, told a story about a girl with red eyes who bit and scratched her mother because she was angry at her and the devil got into her body. The child care worker listened and accepted her story, thereby accepting the child's feelings. In subsequent sessions, after establishing a more trusting relationship with the child, the worker told her a story about the same little girl who told the devil not to bother her and who talked to her mother about how she was going to try harder to be nicer. By using the same characters and theme, she offered the little girl another way of relating to her mother. At the same time, the mother's worker helped her understand her own anger and supported her in trying to alter her behavior toward her daughter.

Except for life-sustaining activities, play is, of course, the most universal activity of children

Through play, children learn about the physical and social world. As they play, children develop a map of the world, a map that helps them make sense of the complexities that define the world today. Play, in the context of a corrective experience, offers children who live with chaos and violence a chance to redraw their world map.

Play provides an avenue for children to express their feelings. Children who are angry or hurt can take their anger out on toys, dolls, and stuffed animals. Children who feel isolated or lonely can find solace in pretending to live in a world with lots of friends. Children who are frightened can seek safety within a game by pretending to be big and strong. In other words, children

can play out their own scenarios, changing their real life situations to their own design. They can invent happy endings. They can reverse roles and become the big—instead of the small—people. They can become the aggressors rather than the victims.

Play also allows children to repeat some of the bad things in their lives. Some people think that children want to forget the frightening or horrible things that they have experienced and try to put these events out of their minds. Some people think that children's play reflects only happy experiences; and many times it does. But some children gain strength from repeating situations that were overwhelming to them, as a way of trying to come to terms with the experiences.

Traumatic events have a way of staying with us. Sometimes they are repeated in dreams. Adults may review these events by talking about them with their friends

Children may feel guilty about the violence in their families, perceive themselves as being bad and worthless, feel as if they have no control over their lives, and have difficulty seeing themselves in future roles that are meaningful; they often slip back to stages at which they felt more secure.

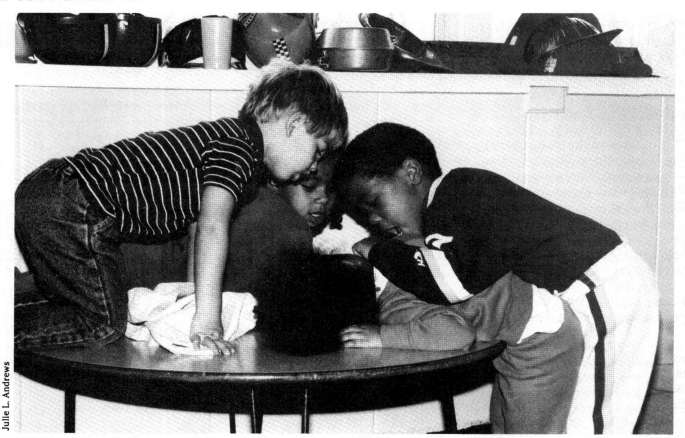

Julie L. Andrews

Children need to tell their stories and play out their own scenarios, perhaps reflecting the reality of their lives, perhaps redesigning them.

and even with strangers. Adults, through discussion—and children, through play—gain control over trauma by repeating it again and again. Repetition allows the trauma victim to absorb the experience little by little, come to grips with what happened, and learn to accept it or live with it.

Expressive art is very therapeutic

In addition to being given many opportunities for dramatic play, children can benefit from a chance to paint and draw. Just as some children make sad or frightening events into happy occasions in their play, others may draw pictures of happy times, even when they are living in far-from-happy circumstances. They draw pictures of nice houses with flowers and trees and sunshine. Others draw pictures that are, or that

represent, disturbing things in their lives. They draw angry or violent pictures and find solace in expressing their feelings through art and conquering their fears by putting them on paper.

Storytelling can bridge to valuable conversation

Storytelling is another way in which children can handle difficult situations and express their inner thoughts. Sharing the telling of stories can be an excellent way to open up communication between adults and children. It can

establish rapport between the two and lay the basis for further discussions of a child's difficulties. It is easier for the adult to understand stories than to interpret drawings or play, and the adult is able to engage a child in a conversation about her or his story.

This does not mean that the stories children tell can be accepted verbatim. Just as play and drawing allow children to express themselves symbolically, so do stories offer them a chance to communicate an idea or feeling without acknowledging its closeness to reality. Adults often can-

The best thing to offer children at risk is caring people, people who are available both physically and emotionally—a relationship that touches one's deepest core.

not understand a child's story without having some outside information about the child's life.

If we understand what children are telling us through their stories, we can help them by participating with them in storytelling. Gardner (1971) used this method in his therapy with children. After the child told a story, Gardner told the same story but with a different, healthier ending. Although teachers are not therapists, they can engage children in joint storytelling sessions and offer alternative endings to the stories told by the children.

Collaboration with families is critically important

Direct work with children is invaluable, but if it can be combined with help for parents, its effectiveness can be increased. Young children are best understood in the context of their families and communities. Professionals need to know the facts about a child's life situation, and that information can be gained from the adults who know the child well.

In addition to obtaining information from parents, the most effective help for a child is in collaboration with help for the family. Because the child is entwined with his family for many years, it is important to make changes in his familial relationships, if possible; even small changes can be important.

It is not possible for teachers and other child specialists to also be social workers and parent therapists. The person who makes contact with a child, however, is often in a good position to establish a working alliance with the child's parents. This alliance can then be used to refer parents to community agencies, clinics, churches, or self-help groups for

---

Not all children who experience violence are doomed.

---

the support, guidance, or therapy that they need. Making a good referral takes skill and patience. It cannot be done quickly, which means that teachers and child care workers must have the time to talk to parents and to make home visits if necessary. They must have time to establish contact with families as an essential part of their work with children who suffer the consequences of violence.

The problems spelled out here are formidable. They will not be easy to solve, but professionals who see children on a daily basis can be an important part of the solution. They cannot cure all of the ills and solve all of the problems that confront children today, but they can offer these chil-

dren a chance to face and accept their feelings and to see alternative ways of relating to others. If child care professionals can help some—not all, but some—children find alternatives to destructive behavior, be it toward themselves or others, they have helped break the cycle of violence.

References

Alexander, F. (1948). *Fundamentals of psychoanalysis.* New York: W.W. Norton.

Bell, C. (1991). Traumatic stress and children in danger. *Journal of Health Care for the Poor and Underserved, 2*(1), 175–188.

Gardner, R. (1971). *Therapeutic communication with children: The mutual storytelling technique.* New York: Science House.

Hetherton, E.M., Cox, M., & Cox, R. (1982). Effects of divorce on parents and children. In M. Lamb (Ed.), *Non-traditional families.* Hillsdale, NJ: Lawrence Erlbaum.

Kotlowitz, A. (1991). *There are no children here.* New York: Doubleday.

Kotulak, R. (1990, September 28). Study finds inner-city kids live with violence. *Chicago Tribune,* pp. 1, 16.

Osofsky, J., Wewers, S., Hann, D., Fick, A., & Richters, J. (1991). *Chronic community violence: What is happening to our children?* Manuscript submitted for publication.

Pynoos, R., & Eth, S. (1985). Children traumatized by witnessing personal violence: Homicide, rape or suicide behavior. In S. Eth & R. Pynoos (Eds.), *Posttraumatic stress disorder in children* (pp. 19–43). Washington, DC: American Psychiatric Press.

Terr, L. (1981). Forbidden games: Posttraumatic child's play. *Journal of American Academy of Child Psychiatry, 20,* 741–760.

Terr, L. (1983). Chowchilla revisited: The effects of psychic trauma four years after a schoolbus kidnapping. *American Journal of Psychiatry, 140,* 1543–1550.

Wallerstein, J.S., & Kelley, J.B. (1980). *Surviving the breakup: How children and parents cope with divorce.* New York: Basic Books.

Zinsmeister, K. (1990, June). Growing up scared. *The Atlantic Monthly,* pp. 49–66.

Supporting Victims of Child Abuse

Classroom teachers have a unique opportunity to identify abused children and to start the healing process that will restore safety to their lives.

Thelma Bear
Sherry Schenk
Lisa Buckner

Thelma Bear coordinates district public school programs for students and works with women survivors of abuse as a psychotherapist in private practice. **Sherry Schenk** works as a school psychologist with elementary and middle school children and has worked with sexually abused children. **Lisa Buckner** has a B.S. in psychology and is a school bus driver. The authors may be reached at Weld County School District Six, 811 Fifteenth St. Greeley, CO 80631.

Our varied roles as therapist, educator, school psychologist, school bus driver, student, and administrator have provided us with the experience and education on which this article is based. This is a new field, an area in which all of us are searching for facts, understanding, and ways to help those who have been and continue to be abused. The combined perspectives we share from personal, professional, and academic experiences have added to our knowledge in ways that have been valuable to us as people who care a great deal about children.

Probably no adult is more trusted by children who have been abused than a beloved and caring teacher. Teachers have an opportunity afforded few adults to identify abused children and to start a process that will restore safety in the child's world. However, many teachers have not been adequately prepared to deal with the complex social issues that have so strongly affected abused children. We want to give teachers a knowledge base about child abuse, describe possible interventions, and communicate an understanding of the emotional issues involved.

The Incidence of Child Abuse

Although the statistics are overwhelming, professionals in the mental health field generally accept that the incidence of child abuse is much greater than that reported.

In 1979, Geiser advised that 200,000 children were sexually abused each

---

Survivors' Voices

Before I started kindergarten, I knew that I could not believe what people said. My father would say, "I know you like this," as he touched me in sexual ways that I did not like or that caused great physical pain. My early years were a real struggle. Because I could not trust what I heard, it was hard to learn sound-letter associations, memorize isolated facts, or learn anything I had heard and not seen.

The messages I received from my perpetrators were intended to prevent my telling what they were doing to me. To keep the horrible secret I learned to be silent, and the silence became my prison. I felt that I was the only child who had ever experienced such bad things. I thought I was so bad that I should separate myself from everyone. It was lonely.

Since I felt I could not talk, I did all kinds of quiet acting out in the hope that someone would notice that something was terribly wrong in my life. My behaviors were either ignored or I was told to behave, to be a good girl. During 3rd and 4th grade, I repeatedly sawed on or cut my wrist with a little knife. I wore bizarre clothing, laughed excessively, and withdrew from others.

Today I am a school psychologist. I have overcome the academic hurdles, but I continue to experience some of the emotional pain of abuse.

—*Sherry Schenk*

The messages about my abuse were also intended to keep me quiet, to protect my perpetrators. I was quiet and shy, but I would also do daring things with little regard for my physical safety. They called me "accident prone." I was told I was crazy and that if I ever told, "someone" would take me away and I would never see anyone in my family again ... or I would be killed. These were terrifying threats to me.

I was a very good student, usually at the top of my class. Looking back now, I was afraid to be anything but perfect. I was afraid of what would happen at home. School became a safe haven, and I worked hard to keep it that way by staying silent about my abuse. I remember more than once trying to get teachers to take me home with them.

I am currently a school bus driver and enjoy daily contact with children in a less-structured environment. When I see symptoms of child abuse, I report what I hear and observe. I would always rather err on the side of the child. I would rather make the report than to ignore what I know.

—*Lisa Buckner*

In 1987, when I was asked to facilitate groups for survivors of abuse at a University Counseling Center, I knew little about the incidence or results of abuse. The frequency of women who had been abused as children was much greater than we had thought. We soon had 4 groups and more than 50 names on a waiting list. I learned about the tremendous cost of keeping the family secret. I learned of the emotional pain that can result from feeling different. As an educator I was appalled at my previous lack of awareness of the consequences of abuse. I vowed to somehow assist in giving a voice to those survivors who can teach us what it was to live with abuse and how to help today's children.

—*Thelma Bear*

Figure 1

	Physical Indicators	**Behavioral Indicators**	
Physical Abuse	■ unexplained bruises (in various stages of healing), welts, human bite marks, bald spots ■ unexplained burns, especially cigarette burns or immersion-burns (glove-like) ■ unexplained fractures, lacerations, or abrasions	■ self-destructive ■ withdrawn and aggressive—behavioral extremes ■ uncomfortable with physical contact ■ arrives at school early or stays late as if afraid	■ chronic runaway (adolescents) ■ complains of soreness or moves uncomfortably ■ wears clothing inappropriate to weather, to cover body
Physical Neglect	■ abandonment ■ unattended medical needs ■ consistent lack of supervision ■ consistent hunger, inappropriate dress, poor hygiene ■ lice, distended stomach, emaciated	■ regularly displays fatigue or listlessness, falls asleep in class ■ steals food, begs from classmates ■ reports that no caretaker is at home	■ frequently absent or tardy ■ self-destructive ■ school dropout (adolescents)
Sexual Abuse	■ torn, stained, or bloodied underclothing ■ pain or itching in genital area ■ difficulty walking or sitting ■ bruises or bleeding in external genitalia ■ venereal disease ■ frequent urinary or yeast infections	■ withdrawn, chronic depression ■ excessive seductiveness ■ role reversal, overly concerned for siblings ■ poor self-esteem, self-devaluation, lack of confidence ■ peer problems, lack of involvement ■ massive weight change	■ suicide attempts (especially adolescents) ■ hysteria, lack of emotional control ■ sudden school difficulties ■ inappropriate sex play or premature understanding of sex ■ threatened by physical contact, closeness ■ promiscuity
Emotional Maltreatment	■ speech disorders ■ delayed physical development ■ substance abuse ■ ulcers, asthma, severe allergies	■ habit disorders (sucking, rocking) ■ antisocial, destructive ■ neurotic traits (sleep disorders, inhibition of play)	■ passive and aggressive—behavioral extremes ■ delinquent behavior (especially adolescents) ■ developmentally delayed

Adapted in part from: D. D. Broadhurst, M. Edmunds, and R. A. MacDicken. (1979). *Early Childhood Programs and the Prevention and Treatment of Child Abuse and Neglect.* The User Manual Series. Washington, D.C.: U.S. Department of Health, Education, and Welfare.

year with victims as young as two months. "Nightline's" Forrest Sawyer (1989) stated that 2 million cases of child abuse are reported in the United States every year. In its newsletter, the National Organization for Victims' Assistance (1989) indicated that 2.2 million children are reported physically or sexually abused each year. Many cases are closed after a cursory investigation; many cases remain unreported.

Of the cases reported, many are young children. Among Blume's (1990) statistics were:

■ 35 percent of all reported child sex abuse cases in 1988 were of girls under 6.

■ Dr. Michael Durfee of the Los Angeles Department of Health Services reported in 1984 that more sexual abuse was reported on 2-year-olds than any other age group; 3- and 4-year-olds were next.

Kantrowitz (1988) gave the following numbers:

■ More than 2 million cases of child abuse were reported in 1986, compared with 669,000 in 1976.

■ More than 1,200 children die each year through child abuse and neglect.

■ Parents who were abused as children were six times more likely to abuse their own children.

Goodwin (1982) reported that:

■ 5 to 20 percent of psychiatric outpatients were women who had experienced incest.

■ 4 out of 10 mothers of children who died of physical abuse were incest victims.

According to Butler (1978), a much greater incidence of incest occurred among affluent, middle-, and upper-class families than was reported. Of reported sexual abuse, she asserted that 75 percent of the incidents were committed by someone the child trusted. Butler (1978) added that:

■ One-half to three-fourths of adult male sexual offenders had been sexually abused.

■ Sexual abuse was one of three reasons children ran away from home.

■ In a questionnaire sent to 1,800 college students, one-third indicated that they had been sexually abused.

Research on child abuse is a fairly

recent development. Only in the last two decades has the subject appeared in professional journals. It is urgent that all personnel in public schools become educated and make every effort to break the continuing cycle of abuse.

Types of Abuse

How is child abuse defined? The Colorado Department of Education (1988) describes four types:

1. *Physical abuse*: nonaccidental physical injury to a child. Examples include slapping, shaking, hitting, kicking, burning, pushing, smothering, restraining (physical or chemical), and torture (may be related to ritualistic abuse and/or satanic worship). A few forms of abuse may be attributed to lack of knowledge on the part of the parent—for instance, neurological damage can result from shaking a child. Physical abuse should be suspected if the following are present: bruises, burns, broken bones, and/or internal injuries. Further, a child who appears fearful or who startles easily may be the victim of abuse.

2. *Emotional maltreatment*: the constant belittling and rejecting of a child, the absence of a positive emotional atmosphere. Examples include verbal abuse, inadequate or inappropriate parenting, and neglect. Any of these can destroy a child's self-esteem and weaken self-concept. The "failure to thrive" syndrome is an example of the results of emotional maltreatment. Delays in emotional development and immature behavior may indicate emotional neglect.

3. *Physical neglect*: failure on the part of the child's caretaker to provide adequate food, clothing, shelter, or supervision. The extreme form of neglect is abandonment of a child with no regard or concern for his or her welfare.

4. *Sexual abuse*: sexual exploitation, molestation, or prostitution of a child (p. 1). Sgroi, Porter, and Blick (1982) define child sexual abuse as a sexual act imposed on a child who lacks the emotional, maturational, and cognitive development to understand what is happening and to protect him- or

Probably no adult is more trusted by children who have been abused than a beloved and caring teacher.

herself. Sexual abuse may be overt or covert. Examples of overt abuse include unwanted touching of any part of the body, such as hugs or kisses presented as innocent signs of affection. More obvious examples include any penetration of the body with objects or body parts. Unexplained infections or diseases and external or internal injuries are symptoms that require investigation for the possibility of sexual abuse.

Covert sexual abuse is more difficult to recognize. Since this type of abuse does not include physical contact, the perpetrator may rationalize the behavior as innocent. Examples may include voyeurism, asking the child to watch inappropriate sexual behaviors, invading the child's privacy, and/or behaving in a seductive manner toward the child.

Most adults who have not been abused would rather not accept the reality of the number of children who have been abused. Many prefer to think of physical injury, terrorizing, and psychological torture as atrocities that only happen to hostages imprisoned in foreign countries. They do not want to accept that these abominations occur to nearly 2.7 million children in this country ("Study Finds ..." 1992). Figure 1 lists physical and behavioral indicators of these four types of abuse.

A Safe Classroom Environment

There is no escape for children caught in a world where silence often seems the only way to survive. And there is no escape from confronting the issues for those who work with children.

Teachers who educate themselves about abuse will find many opportunities to support children who have neither the experience nor the maturity to unravel the turmoil they face.

Although the academic environment is structured for learning, the ability to learn is dependent on a child's arriving at school with basic needs met. Children who have been abused have had the basic requirements for healthy development withheld and violated. Getting physiological needs met, as well as those for safety, belonging, trust, and love, maximizes the child's development as a learner. The classroom teacher has the opportunity to provide an environment where the child can begin to succeed and recognize that he or she is capable and valued.

The most important ingredient in a safe classroom is the teacher's attitude toward students. The most crucial belief a teacher must have is that the child is not to blame. There is nothing that a child can do to prevent or stop the abuse. The discrepancy between the power of a child and that of an adult is too great. However, it is important to remember that these children are strong. They have developed coping mechanisms that have helped them to survive traumatic experiences. An accepting, caring attitude by the teacher will allow the child to trust enough to make the first steps toward developing a saner life.

Each of us needs a personal space into which others do not intrude without permission (Blume 1990). Victimized children have not learned that it is okay to say no, nor do they know how it feels to have personal and physical space honored. The teacher should help an abused child to set healthy boundaries and to know that he or she will be respected. Before the child can believe in his or her ability to set personal boundaries, he or she may need to be taught to trust personal judgments, feelings, and perceptions (Blume 1990).

Part of establishing healthy boundaries is understanding that confidentiality within the school is honored by staff and students. If a student confides in classmates and teachers, the information must be handled with great care in order to protect the vulnerability of the child. At times, the disclosure of information about the abuse may be unintentional. Some of the ways the secret may accidentally be disclosed are observations by the teacher or others, physical injuries or conditions discovered in a doctor's examination, and/or inappropriate sexual behaviors by the child (Sgroi et al. 1982).

To offer support, the teacher must, first, be approachable. If an abused child begins to tell what is happening, positive body language will encourage the child to continue. The teacher must also watch for cues about how to respond. The child may either want to be comforted physically or may not want to be touched. At this point, it is more important to actively listen than to comment or ask questions. Listening to those who will talk is important; however, some students will be unable to share verbally what is happening. In these instances, the teacher must be observant. The indicators listed in Figure 1 may help teachers in attempting to decide if abuse should be suspected.

Drawings, too, may provide clues to students who have been sexually abused. Hillman and Solek-Tefft (1988) list five themes to ask a child about if they are drawn repeatedly: stark sexual images, phallic symbols, general symbols (broken hearts, rain, black skies), self-image distortions, and general confusion (p. 107).

Girls and boys who have been abused attempt both to keep the secret of what is happening and to control the emotional turmoil they feel inside. As a result, the child may act out, or he or she may become the epitome of the "good" child. Both of these behaviors may disguise the problem. A child who behaves as a perfect student may be seen as having no problems, while acting out may cover the real issues, making the child appear to be the problem. Teachers should listen to their gut response to a child, particularly if that feeling is based on a suspicion that something is wrong.

> If an abused student confides in classmates and teachers, the information must be handled with great care to protect the vulnerability of the child.

Occasionally a child will spontaneously disclose an episode of abuse. Although a teacher may doubt the story, it is vitally important to believe the child (Besharov 1990). The child is taking a significant step in trusting the teacher enough to tell what is happening. To betray that trust would repeat the betrayal experienced when an adult abused the child and failed to serve as a protector. Even though the explanation may be fragmented, teachers should listen supportively and ask open-ended questions to fill in gaps. Sometimes after telling the secret, the child may recant the story due to fear, threats, or acceleration of the abuse (Sgroi et al. 1982). Most experts agree that children do not have the ability or knowledge to make up complex lies, especially lies related to adult sexual behavior (Besharov 1990, Conerly 1986, Crewdson 1988).

How to Support an Abused Child

In addition to creating a safe classroom environment, there are other ways teachers can help support an abused child. Most of these behaviors and attitudes are familiar ones.

1. *Expectations.* Teachers can honor the strength and courage of these children by having high expectations for them. Emotionality may interfere with thinking; therefore, it is important to set reasonable goals and to provide the support needed for the child to feel confident in his or her abilities. School can be a place where children rebuild their self-esteem, assert themselves, and see themselves as successful.

2. *Structure.* Abused children may feel powerless to control much in their environment. To cope, they may: (a) refuse to even try to control what happens around them; (b) strive to manipulate everything they can by bossing peers and controlling belongings; and (c) express disproportionate feelings whenever they feel threatened. When these children fly off the handle with little provocation, they may be doing so to try to establish control. To help the child feel a sense of control in a positive manner, teachers should give accurate information and build trust. Allowing expression of feelings when appropriate through art, music, drama, and/or creative writing will also help the child to feel less controlled by pent-up emotion.

3. *Identity.* Children who have been abused in ways that met an adult's needs and denied the child's needs have little sense of personal identity. Teachers can help by pointing out the child's strengths. Statements such as "You are a hard worker," "You are a good friend when you help a classmate with a problem," and "People in this classroom like you because you are fun to be with" will help the child understand how others perceive him or her. Teachers can also help abused children gain a sense of personal identity by asking questions that help them formulate a position on issues, administering interest inventories, and teaching decision-making and problem-solving skills. These skills will assist in interpersonal relationships as well as in self-understanding.

4. *Self-esteem.* Abused children have little self-esteem. Teachers can help them learn that they are valued, accepted, and capable by fostering an environment that honors each child's uniqueness. Valuing differences will enable children to begin to see themselves as having something to contribute that others appreciate.

With each successful completion of a classroom task, the child's sense of competency will be fostered.

5. *Sense of belonging*. Abused children think they did something wrong and that they are bad. Because they have kept a secret from everyone, they assume there is a reason for them to be isolated from others. To facilitate a sense of belonging, the teacher may provide designated places for possessions, display work in the classroom, and make a conscious attempt to include these children in classroom activities. Support through teaching social skills individually, in small group settings, and through cooperative learning will also help abused children practice interacting in a nonthreatening atmosphere.

6. *Social skills*. Because abused children have not learned to listen to their inner selves, they may focus on pleasing and meeting the needs of others while neglecting their own needs. Having been introduced to the adult world through an abusive relationship, the child may have learned inappropriate behaviors and language. The child may feel unworthy to interact on an equal basis with others and may fear rejection. A classroom climate that fosters caring, appreciation for differences, consistent rules and boundaries, and recognition for small successes will nurture a child who has been discounted at home.

7. *Tolerance of differences*. Because each child will respond in a unique way to abuse, classroom behaviors may be variable. Some of the feelings an abused child may experience are anxiety, guilt, embarrassment, depression, anger, and resolution (Hillman and Solek-Tefft 1988). The checklist (fig. 1) may help teachers identify emotions and behaviors that might be explained by abuse. Consultation with a school psychologist, social worker, counselor, or nurse may also help teachers understand unexplainable

> Teachers have the opportunity to give an abused child gifts that cannot be measured in any monetary or quantitative way.

behaviors and emotions of their students.

8. *Consistency*. Teachers can support a child's need for structure by maintaining a consistent daily schedule, by having clear expectations for performance in both behavioral and affective areas, and by allowing the child to provide structure in his or her own way. A child's need for structure can restrict the depth of his or her encounter with the world. Teachers may respond to this need by encouraging risk-taking in ways that will encourage success and personal worth.

Although teachers are not responsible for investigation of child abuse, they are legally obligated to report suspected abuse. When abuse is suspected, the teacher can compare the child's behaviors with those of other students at the same developmental level, review the child's past and present behaviors, and refer to indicators such as those listed in Figure 1. To report any suspicions, the teacher should contact the school district child abuse team or the Department of Social Services. The appropriate agencies will assess the situation and decide how to keep the child safe.

Working with children who have suffered abuse is a skill that every teacher possesses. Given a few guidelines and accurate information, the teacher's natural concern and caring for students will promote the process of healing. Teachers have the opportunity to give an abused child the hope of a childhood, the joy of play, and the sense of being cared for by others. Those are gifts that cannot be measured in any monetary or quantitative way.

References

Besharov, D. (1990). *Recognizing Child Abuse*. New York: The Free Press.

Blume, E. (1990). *Secret Survivors*. New York: The Free Press.

Butler, S. (1978). *Conspiracy of Silence*. San Francisco: New Glide Publications.

Colorado Department of Education (1988). *The School's Role in the Prevention/Intervention of Child Abuse and Neglect*. Denver: Colorado Department of Education.

Conerly, S. (1986). "Assessment of Suspected Child Sexual Abuse." In *Sexual Abuse of Young Children*, edited by K. MacFarlane, pp. 30-51. New York: The Guilford Press.

Crewdson, J. (1988). *By Silence Abused*. New York: Harper & Row.

Geiser, R. (1979). *Hidden Victims: The Sexual Abuse of Children*. Boston: Beacon Press.

Goodwin, J. (1982). *Sexual Abuse: Incest Victims and Their Families*. Boston: John Wright.

Hillman, D., and J. Solek-Tefft. (1988). *Spiders and Flies*. Lexington, Mass.: Lexington Books.

Kantrowitz, B. (December 1988). "A Tale of Abuse." *Newsweek*, pp. 56-59.

National Organization for Victims' Assistance. (March 1989). Newsletter.

Sawyer, F. (Journalist). (1989). *Nightline* television program, ABC.

Sgroi, S., F. Porter, and L. Blick. (1982). "Validation of Child Sexual Abuse." In *Handbook of Clinical Intervention in Child Sexual Abuse*, edited by S. Sgroi, pp. 39-79. Lexington, Mass.: Lexington Books.

"Study Finds Child Care Increasing." (April 1992). *The Greeley Tribune*, p. A-11.

how kids survive
trauma

Waco alerted us to the plight of children who witness horrifying events. What are we doing to help them?

Patricia McCormick

Patricia McCormick, a mother of two who lives in New York City, is a contributing editor of Parents.

One of the most painful realities parents must confront is that we cannot always protect our children from harm. The odds are that our youngsters will never have an experience as frightening as that of the Branch Davidian children in Waco, or as destructive as that of Hurricane Andrew. Nonetheless, as researchers have found, children are trauma's most innocent and vulnerable victims.

Their reactions, experts say, also demonstrate that children perceive and recover from trauma differently from adults. Although traumatized children may experience some of the same physical sensations that affect soldiers in combat, their emotional and psychological adjustment can be primitive and mysterious by comparison.

Researchers, in their treatment of young victims in-cluding the Branch Davidian children, the war-weary children of Cambodia, and the smallest victims of urban violence, have come up with theories that have important implications for children who have been traumatized.

Experts now believe that even very young children can experience posttraumatic-stress syndrome—a disturbing behavioral, physiological, and emotional response to trauma—although their symptoms are distinct from those of adults and often harder to detect. Trauma experts have also identified characteristics that they believe insulate some children from trauma, as well as factors that put other children at greater risk. Most important, experts have developed treatments that give traumatized children and their parents hope.

What is trauma?

"Dreadful things will happen to a child in the course of his life; he'll have to go to the hospital for stitches, or a beloved grandparent may die," says Cynthia Monahon, Psy.D., a clinical child psychologist and the author of *Children and Trauma* (Lexington Books). "But he can usually mobilize his resources to cope with this stress and come away with a sense of having mastered a temporary adversity.

"Trauma, on the other hand, involves an extraordinary occurrence that overwhelms a child's capacity to cope," Monahon says. "The child feels helpless. The suddenness and unpredictability of the event terrorizes him."

Many children experience what experts call "single-event trauma," which is a onetime incident such as being lost in the woods or withstanding a tornado. Experts distinguish between this type of trauma and the sustained, chronic suffering endured by children who witness random urban violence every day or by children who are repeatedly beaten. "The abuse that these latter children sustain is cumulative and more disabling," says Monahon, "and their recovery is more complicated."

No matter what type of trauma a child experiences, the physiological responses are similar. When trauma occurs, centers in the child's brain signal adrenaline, cortisol, and other stress hormones to flood the body. His heart rate and respiration quicken, and blood pressure soars. The pupils dilate, stored sugars pour into the bloodstream, and the muscles tense, according to Bruce Perry, M.D., Ph.D., a leading trauma researcher and head of a team who treated the Branch Davidian children.

Once the trauma ends, the body tries to return to normal. But the brain, trying to make sense of the incomprehensible, keeps replaying the event. In some cases the brain center that triggered the child's alarm response goes into what Perry calls "permanent overdrive," which can last either temporarily or indefinitely.

During this stage, children become excessively vigilant, constantly scanning their environment for signs of danger.

In other instances, the mind tries to short-circuit the relentless flow of stress hormones and alarm signals by going numb, which permits children to gain enough control that they can try to make sense of the experience. "The faces of these children often appear blank, distant, and impassive," says Perry, who is also vice-chairman of research in the department of psychology at Baylor College of Medicine. "But meanwhile their hearts are racing and their brain is screaming 'Danger!'"

This is how the Branch Davidian children responded initially. "They wouldn't appear to react to anything, but their hearts rates were up around 140 beats per minute [compared with the normal range of 70 to 90]," says Perry. "These children were in a persistent state of fear."

The signs of trauma are not always obvious.

Such subtle manifestations of posttraumatic stress are easy for parents to misinterpret, according to Alan M. Delamater, Ph.D., director of clinical psychology at the University of Miami's Mailman Center for Child Development, who has studied the effects of Hurricane Andrew on children and adults. "When your child is destroying her toys, it's easier to notice," says Delamater. "If she is withdrawn, it's easy to miss as a stress reaction."

More-obvious responses are regression or physical symptoms, which many children exhibit after a stressful event. "Children under two will cry more and need to be held more," says Delamater. "Preschoolers may lose toileting skills that they had, go back to sucking their thumbs, or start stuttering.

"School-age children often lose the ability to concentrate on their schoolwork; return to old fears, such as a fear of the dark; or complain of physical pains," Delamater adds. In his studies of families who survived Hurricane Andrew, for example, he found that a third of the children suffered

from headaches, stomachaches, and sleep problems.

Perhaps the key difference between children's and adults' handling of trauma is the ways that they attempt to comprehend it. "Adults use logic to come to terms with what happened to them," says Monahon. "Children often come up with magical and illogical explanations. Usually they find some way to blame themselves."

In a twist that seems doubly cruel, young trauma victims commonly develop a conviction that the traumatic event will recur. "They don't understand that it was a highly improbable event," says Monahon. "A child whose home is washed away in a flood doesn't realize that it was a once-in-a-lifetime occurrence. She may not say anything to anyone, but she wakes up every morning expecting another flood."

Because children have such acute sensory memories, they often suffer vivid and terrifying flashbacks triggered by a sight, smell, or noise. When some Branch Davidian children hear a helicopter overhead, for example, "thoughts of the siege come back, and they experience the same physical sensations and emotional arousal they did when the event was occurring," says Perry.

One of the most distressing results of trauma is that it can leave a child with a sense of hopelessness. James Garbarino, Ph.D., president of the Erikson Institute for Advanced Study in Child Development, in Chicago, has spent seven years studying children who live in war zones in such areas at Mozambique, Cambodia, and Nicaragua. He has found a chilling similarity between these children and those exposed to urban violence. "Trauma can shorten children's expectations of the future," he says. "They engage in what we call 'terminal thinking.' They give up on the future entirely. When you ask a 15-

year-old who experienced chronic traumas as a child what she expects to be at age 30, her answer is 'Dead.'"

Lenore Terr, M.D., a professor of psychiatry at the University of California, San Francisco, studied the children from Chowchilla County who, in 1976, were kidnapped and buried underground for 16 hours in a truck trailor. Terr found that four years later, the children were still suffering from nightmares, feelings of shame, and a deep sense of pessimism about their futures. Many of them doubted that they would live a long life; some even "died" in their dreams.

The resilience of children gives experts hope.

Fortunately, many children rebound from trauma. Individual personality traits may help shield some youngsters, according to researchers. Children who have displayed easygoing

responses to minor stress at an early age are better able to ride out a major trauma, as are children with high self-esteem who see themselves as being in charge of their lives. And the higher a child's IQ, the easier it is for him to cope.

A more important indicator, however, is a child's age and the degree to which he was aware of a threat to his life. A toddler who witnesses a robbery with his mother at his side is more likely to rebound than one who was not with her at the time—although neither child would have a real appreciation of the danger. An older child—with or without his mother—might be more traumatized because of his grasp of the situation.

It is wishful thinking, however, to assume that very young children are insulated by their innocence or limited memory. "They may not have the words to

First-Aid Care for Trauma Victims

Immediately following a trauma, and often for many months afterward, a child will need extra comfort, reassurance, and stability, according to clinical child psychologist Cynthia Monahon, Psy.D. Here are steps that parents can take to minimize trauma's effects:
● Adjust bedtime rituals. Leave the lights on, or play a soothing musical cassette. Help young children relax with such comforting experiences as rocking, cuddling, singing, and hearing familiar stories. Older children may need calming massages at night and storytelling throughout the day. Many children will comfort themselves with a long-outgrown ted-

dy bear or blanket.
● Follow your normal routine. "After experiencing trauma, a child loses his sense of security," says Monahon. "He'll look for signs of normality to undo his sense that life has changed in sinister and frightening ways."
● Treat vivid nightmares or panic attacks with reassurance. Gently guide your child back to the present by using a gentle physical touch to reorient her. Instruct her to breathe deeply or use her senses to help her relax and focus on the here and now. Reassure your child that this scary replay is not real but, rather, a dream or memory that "cannot hurt you now."

Often children will plead to sleep with their parents. One alternative is to create a bed on the floor of your room. Tell your child that he can sleep there for a while and that eventually you will help him return to his own room.
● Allow your child to talk about his experience without having to censor painful details or powerful feelings.
● Provide opportunities and props for your child to play out the trauma. "Children who don't have toy cars and ambulances will latch onto them to re-create a car accident, for example," says Monahon. Provide physical outlets such as sports for kids to run off the tension. —P.M.

describe a traumatic event, but their memories can be disturbingly evident in their play," Monahon says.

Close and loving family relationships can also buffer a child from the effects of catastrophe. "If you have a positive, nurturing family, you have a lot of defenses to begin with," says Garbarino.

Children who have already experienced trauma may have fewer coping mechanisms. "Children dealt many blows of fate can become worn out by repetitive demands for coping," says Monahon. The duration and source of the trauma also affect a child's ability to cope. Traumatic events of long duration often cause greater distress for children than do brief events, according to Monahon. And when traumas stem from intentional, malicious acts of human beings rather than from natural forces or accidents, children suffer more.

Finally, the extent to which the child's family is harmed or his existing social structure is altered influences his ability to recover. "If a child's siblings and other adults remain for his support, he can use them to help himself cope," says Perry. "If they are lost in the trauma or are emotionally

---

How Trauma Affects the Family

Trauma can reverberate powerfully through a family. Perhaps the most profound effect is that it can shatter parents' sense of themselves as their children's protector. Parents often feel frightened, helpless, depressed, or ashamed. Meanwhile, siblings may feel anxious or overlooked.

"Why my child?" Some family members feel a child's pain so acutely that they · develop what experts call "supporter distress," in which they experience feelings similar to the child's. "They ask, 'Why my child?' 'How did we deserve this?' " says clinical child psychologist Cynthia Monahon, Psy.D.

More debilitating is the guilt that many parents suffer. They may obsessively retell the story of the trauma, adding, "If only I had..." Any explanation, "even at the cost of suffering and guilt, may help parents cope with the feelings of helplessness and senselessness that are aroused by the event," says Monahon. Often parents are not even aware of how a trauma has affected them.

The sibling factor. Brothers and sisters may feel abandoned while their sibling is getting so much attention. "Others become alarmed by the changes in their sibling or by their parents' anxiety," says Monahon. "They feel guilty or responsible for not preventing the harm, or believe that they caused it as a result of ordinary anger toward a sibling." Siblings may need counseling.

Because caring for a traumatized child can be terrifying and draining, it is crucial that parents break out of their isolation and get support. —P.M.

---

devastated by it, the child is more likely to suffer long-term effects."

Helping children heal.
Although prompt care and parental reassurance (See "First-Aid Care for Trauma Victims,") helps diminish most early trauma symptoms within six to eight weeks, many children and their families need more sustained help. As part of the healing process, traumatized children need to vent their feelings of outrage and fright. They should also be encouraged to view themselves as survivors rather than victims, Perry states. This can be accomplished by helping kids understand what happened to them and why.

Above all, traumatized children should be viewed not as damaged but as strong. Perry notes that some young survivors become high-achievers, in part because the obstacles that appear so daunting to the average person are nothing compared with what a trauma survivor has endured.

Monahon, who has been saddened by the stories of young trauma survivors and then moved by their resilience, concurs. "I am repeatedly struck by their strength and humanity," she says. "After being subjected to unimaginable horror, these children often come away with a remarkable capacity to feel and reflect."

Even Garbarino, who has seen tiny war victims heal after being raped, maimed, and orphaned, remains optimistic: "I am hopeful that if we can help children process the experience, they need not be emotionally crippled. I've seen how individuals and groups across the world have rallied around traumatized children to rebuild their futures."

Managing the Early Childhood Classroom

Sandra Crosser

Sandra Crosser taught kindergarten and primary children for 12 years. She has operated a private preschool since 1978 and is an assistant professor of education at Ohio Northern University.

Mrs. Green's kindergarten was a zoo. She planned lessons thoroughly and was creative in her choices of age-appropriate activities. She provided a variety of materials and truly cared for the children. Mrs. Green's kindergarten remained a zoo, however. The teachers gossiped about it, the principal thought it might get better in time, the parents blamed it on Rowdy Ralph, and Mrs. Green contemplated the merits of a career as a mortician.

What was it that confounded Mrs. Green's best efforts? What factor could she have neglected? Was she just not cut out to be a teacher?

Successful teachers know that the arrangement and management of the early childhood classroom have a direct effect on the kinds of behaviors children exhibit as they live and work together. The difference between chaos and an orderly atmosphere that facilitates learning depends in great part on how the teacher prepares the environment. That preparation involves what happens before school begins, when children arrive and depart,

First of all, arrange your room to maximize possibilities for satisfying play, optimal supervision, and a safe, orderly environment.

when schedule transitions occur, when children interact freely with equipment and materials, and when conflicts arise. Taken together, "BASIC" classroom management includes carefully preplanning:

Before school begins
Arrival and departure times
Schedule transitions
Interactions with equipment and materials
Conflict management

The practices recommended in this article have been standard among skilled preschool, kindergarten, and first grade teachers for several generations. If any or many of them are new to you, you may want to implement them to create a more effective setting in which young children can learn through play and projects.

Before school begins

Before children are in the classroom, the successful teacher carefully plans the physical arrangement of the room and the routines for using it. The following considerations are important because they can facilitate movement, inhibit rowdiness, enhance safety, and invite meaningful exploration.

Although learning through self-selected play experiences is the cornerstone of developmentally sound early childhood programs, children may occasionally need to come together for large group meetings. Those meetings should be called sparingly and kept short so children are not required to sit and participate for long periods of time.

1. Is there an open area large enough for the entire group to meet together? Can children sit comfortably without being crowded? Is there enough room for large muscle movements? Are there attractive nuisances located so close to the area that children will be distracted during group meetings? Are there electric outlets close enough for using tape recorders and record players? If children are to sit in a circle or other pattern, are there physical indicators such as tape or carpet squares to show

From *Young Children*, Vol. 47, No. 2, January 1992, pp. 23-29. Reprinted by permission of the publisher, the National Association for the Education of Young Children.

children where to sit? If children are expected to bring chairs to group meetings, will they be shown how to carry a chair safely across the room?

2. Does the physical arrangement of work centers allow for quiet areas to be located away from noisier activities? Puzzles, puppets, books, and other quiet activities need to be set apart from the workbench, block, and dramatic play centers. Hollow wooden blocks and housekeeping/dress-up areas facilitate creative interaction when placed close together.

Some centers, such as art, cooking, painting, and water play require frequent cleanups. Are they located near a sink and sponges or paper towels? If no sink is available, can a baby bathtub or bucket of water be substituted?

3. Are centers arranged within the classroom so that they are defined by low boundaries, such as room dividers, shelves, tables, floor mats, or tape? Can the teacher see over and around equipment so that all children are visible at all times?

Are centers arranged to avoid the "hallway effect"? Long, open spaces and runways invite take-off and flight. Room arrangement should suggest walking, rather than running.

4. Are most materials located where children can reach them wihout asking the teacher for help? Can children obtain their own paint shirts, pencils, crayons, paper, yarn, and tissues?

5. Is there a place for everything? Children need the security of organization. Like things belong together, placed low within reach of the shortest arms. Cleanup is easier to manage and safety is easier to maintain when there is one basket for crayons and another for markers, a file box for records, and a rack for scissors. Sectioned cardboard boxes divide kinds and colors of paper. Things to go home belong in each child's mailbox or school bag. Wastepaper baskets

are strategically located where most often needed. Tools hang on pegboard where shapes of hammers and drills indicate placement. Games belong on the game shelf, and building toys each have their own tubs for small pieces. A box of paper sits by the typewriter. Puzzles have individual trays or racks. Dress-up clothes belong on hooks or in a suitcase. A shoe rack holds high heels, and a jewelry box contains gems. Cupboard shelves hold the tea set, and flatware is sorted in a divider tray. There are no toy boxes for indiscriminate dumping (Schilmoeller & Amundrud, 1987). When the child is helped to organize her world, she learns classification skills and a sense of satisfaction from being independent and self-sufficient. An orderly environment can eliminate potential behavior problems.

6. The busier and more involved the children are, the less likely they are to exhibit behavior problems. Is there enough equipment for everyone, but not so much to choose from that the child becomes overwhelmed? Young children can be overstimulated to the point that they move aimlessly from one center to another without becoming involved in any one activity (Shapiro, 1975); therefore, it seems wise to provide basic equipment at first, adding variety and alternatives on a regular basis. The unexpected challenges the child's imagination as the teacher creates variety throughout the school year. For example, one day the water table may contain bubbles and egg beaters. Another day it may have food color and rubber canning rings. Nuts to crack or Cheerios to "cook" offer new

possibilities for the housekeeping corner, keeping children so involved that discipline needs are minimized. Possibilities for enhancing basic equipment are endless.

7. Are routines set? Do children know how to handle routines? What are children expected to do when they take off their coats? How will attendance be taken; can children do it themselves? Is there a routine for giving the teacher messages from home? Is there a set procedure for using the bathroom? Can more than one child go at one time? Is there a sign on the door indicating whether or not the bathroom is in use? How will thirsty children get a drink? What will be the routine if a snack is served? Is there a typical schedule for the day so that children will generally know what happens next? Do we go outdoors to play after snack, or do we have a story? Establishing policies for routines eliminates many possible conflicts and frustrations (Brophy, 1983).

Arrival and departure times

Arrivals. How children's arrival is managed can, and usually does, set the tone for the entire day. The successful teacher meets and greets children as they arrive, whether singly or in a group. Physical presence of the teacher can prevent excessive silliness, tears, and escalating voices. A routine for handling wraps and boots should involve the children in doing as much for themselves as they can without waiting for the teacher's help.

The children need to know what

Thoughtfully established routines are the vaccination against classroom chaos. Too much waiting begets wiggle, giggle, squirm, and poke.

is expected upon entering the classroom. Do they indicate attendance by placing name cards in a basket? Do they hang up school bags? Do they select a free choice activity? Is that choice limited? What should be done with any items brought from home?

Quite frequently young children are expected to wait for everyone to arrive in order for some sort of opening exercise to formally start the day. Perhaps children should not be expected to spend valuable time waiting to start the day's activities. Waiting begets wiggle, giggle, squirm, and poke. If children are encouraged to go right to play upon entering the classroom, many potential discipline problems can simply be avoided.

Departures. Departure, as well as arrival, should follow set routines. Departure routines may begin with a final group meeting to evaluate the day's activities. Plans for making tomorrow even better than today help children see ways to make choices and increase control over their own lives.

The successful teacher remains in control throughout preparation for leave-taking. She plans for quick and easy ways to distribute notices or work to take home. If each child has an individual mailbox or school bag, time waiting for paper-passing can be avoided, along with the disruptive behavior that accompanies that waiting. Thoughtfully established routines are the vaccination against classroom chaos.

Routines might include how many children go to get their coats at one time. When children are moved in herds, stampedes occur.

Early childhood teachers frequently use some sort of good-bye song or poem to end the day pleasantly and calmly when children are all ready to go home. Such practices let children know that the day has officially ended. More important, at the conclusion of the song or poem the teacher is left

with a quiet group of children to whom she can address individual praise, recognition, comments, pats, encouragement, smiles, or winks as they file past and out the door. Kindergarten and first grade children most often end the school day all at the same time with a group dismissal. Day care or preschool dismissals, however, frequently involve individual pickups. In either case, the teacher needs to individually acknowledge the departure of each child. Through thoughtful planning, the teacher can transform the potential hassle of last-minute rush into building one-on-one relationships.

Schedule transitions

Effective classroom managers seem to have a sense of timing very much like a comedian's. They sense when it is time to stop an activity early, when to let things continue longer than usual, and how to move gracefully from one topic to the next. They entice children by subtly capturing their attention, by intriguing them.

Capturing children's attention

Finger plays, rhymes, and action songs can be extremely useful methods of intriguing children who have become inattentive or who need to be brought together for any purpose. For decades, finger plays have been part of the early childhood classroom because they are so useful. Children love the fun and challenge and are curious to see if they can make their fingers do what the teacher's are doing. When the finger play has been completed, children are quiet and ready to listen. The teacher must seize the moment to quickly give directions or move on to the next scheduled activity. The secret is in the timing. If the teacher hesitates for even a moment, attention is once again lost. Short action songs can

be used in the same manner as finger plays. Both can be learned from source books available in libraries or from educational supply houses. The teacher needs to memorize a variety of these transition facilitators in order to have a well-stocked repertoire at her disposal. Children like to repeat rhymes and songs they know, but by adding new ones to the old, teachers keep interest piqued.

Having to stop one activity to move to something else can be very disconcerting for young children. Preparing children for the transition permits them to finish what they are doing, or at least recognize that they will need to stop soon. The teacher might tell children that it is almost cleanup time, or that it will soon be time to stop. Children then are mentally prepared to change gears.

Appropriate signals. Signals can be useful to cue transition times if used sparingly; used too frequently they lose their effectiveness. A designated song played on the piano or record player can signal cleanup time. A bell, a sign, a hand signal, or a flick of the lights can signal time to gather for a story. Signals should be low-key so as not to startle or frighten. A tinkling triangle has the same effect as a loud whistle, without the accompanying shrillness. Shrill or loud noises tend to increase the overall noise level in the classroom, just as an increase in the volume of the teacher's voice tends to increase the volume of the children's voices. Shouting is neither appropriate nor effective. Whispering can be more of an attention-getter than yelling. A low, calm adult voice has a soothing effect, by itself reducing the overall noise level.

Moving groups of children

Frequently, transitions involve moving groups of children some distance. Because small groups tend to move in a more orderly fashion than large groups, the teacher might call for all children with buckle shoes, then tie shoes, then velcro shoes. Eye color, hair color, beginning letters of names, pattern of clothing (plain, striped, solid), color of socks, and other categories are possibilities.

Standing in line and walking in line are regimentations natural to ducks, not children. On occasion, however, children need to move in organized lines for purposes of safety. If children are expected to form a line, they need to know how to do it. Children can line up as a sandwich with two children desig-

---

A teacher can redirect restless energies by stimulating and modeling purposeful play. The teacher's invitation to play "bus" leads to problem-solving: "How can we make seats for the bus?"

---

nated as pieces of bread, and the other children choosing to become good things to eat in between. Pickles, mustard, and bologna must stay in the sandwich. Lining up as a parade or train can also help teach the concept of a line.

Moving the line through hallways can be accomplished by having the first child lead to a stopping place while the remainder of the children pass in front of the teacher. The teacher then designates the next stopping place, and the process is repeated until the group reaches its destination.

When young children walk in strange or potentially dangerous

areas, the teacher must exercise a great degree of care to keep them together and away from traffic or other danger. Partners may be chosen for holding hands as they walk, or children may walk holding individual knots on a long rope. Clothesline rope works well, with knots tied at least fifteen to twenty inches apart so children can walk comfortably.

At journey's end. Upon reaching the destination, children must be told what to do *before* they enter the area. Are they to bounce a ball with a partner in the gym, sit at a table in the art room, or run two times around the yellow line on the playground? If children do not know what to do when they enter a new space, they will explore it on their own, making it difficult for the teacher to maintain a controlled situation. Large, open spaces, such as gyms and playgrounds, invite large muscle movements. Children need to know what they are expected to do, therefore, before they enter such spaces.

Interactions with equipment and materials

Most of the young child's day should be invested in purposeful play. The teacher provides for active engagement with materials and equipment that individual children choose for themselves as they explore their world. The free choice play or work time is a vital part of the early childhood program, but it can become a time for horseplay and haphazard activity if not properly managed. The teacher can, and should, shape interactions with equipment and materials to

• stimulate learning possibilities;
• protect children;
• protect equipment; and
• maintain a peaceful learning environment.

Seven things to think about before school begins:

1. Group time area
2. Location of centers
3. Shapes and boundaries of centers
4. Accessibility of materials
5. Orderly organization of materials and equipment
6. Level of stimulation
7. Routines of classroom life

Questioning and commenting

The skillfully placed question or comment can stimulate learning and deter rowdiness. The teacher needs to move around the room, challenging children to look at different ways of using materials to solve problems (Day, 1975) and acknowledging them for constructive efforts (Katz & Chard, 1989).

"How else could you do it?" "Which container holds the most sand? How can you prove it?" "How did you paint the brown color when we have no brown paint?" "Why do you think your block building fell down? How could you change it next time so it won't fall down?" "I see you are working very hard." The moving teacher manages the early childhood environment through physical presence and by being there to ask the challenging question or make the encouraging comment.

Redirecting play

At times the work/play free choice time reveals children moving aimlessly. Some children have difficulty planning a meaningful activity. At those times, the teacher may observe the need to play *with* children to suggest new play ideas and redirect behavior. In playing with children, the teacher stimulates and models purposeful play without dominating the situation. For example, the teacher may invite a group that has become restless to play "bus" or "restaurant." The teacher asks questions such as, "How can we make seats for the bus?" "Do we need tickets?" "Where is the bus going?" The teacher engages in the play long enough to establish purposefulness, then moves on. Positive redirection can, in this way, replace nagging and similar negative teacher behaviors.

Setting limits with equipment and materials

Some controls need to be placed on use of equipment and materials for safety purposes. The early childhood teacher needs to make rules for the safe use of tools, scissors, blocks, sand, and climbing or swinging apparatus. Children should be expected to follow the rules if they choose to use the equipment. When safety rules are broken, the child needs to be reminded that the teacher is worried about his safety and that repeated misuse will mean that he will no longer be allowed to choose that particular piece of equipment.

Because blocks and dramatic play seem to be favorites of many children, teachers frequently see the need to limit the number of children in each of these areas at one time. A kitchen timer may be used to ensure that each child has a chance to participate. Children can choose centers by placing a name card on a hook or a sign that indicates the maximum number of children to use a center at one time.

Conflict resolution

Preventative classroom management can eliminate many potential discipline problems. Conflict is a natural part of living and working together in groups. It is good that conflicts arise in the early childhood classroom because it is only through facing conflicts that children can learn the skills necessary to resolve real-life problems. Problem and conflict resolution skills are not automatically part of the child's repertoire; they are skills that must be taught and practiced, just as counting or reading skills must be taught and practiced before they become automatic (Brophy, 1985).

Teaching conflict resolution

When conflicts arise, the teacher can facilitate resolution by helping children to identify the choices they have and the variety of behavior options they could employ to resolve the problem. When a child has made an inappropriate choice, the teacher needs to help her examine alternative acceptable choices (McNergney & Haberman, 1988). For example, the child who hits to obtain a desired piece of equipment does need to learn that hitting is an unacceptable way to obtain the goal. Too often, however, the child who hits or exhibits other unacceptable behavior is punished or scolded without being offered follow-up discussion of acceptable behaviors that could replace the inappropriate behavior. The teacher can act as a guide to help the child identify and practice new options (Stocking, Arezzo, & Leavitt, 1979). Teacher and child can role-play new behavior as a replacement for the inappropriate behavior. The teacher may need to play the part of the child, at first, in order to model the new behavior.

Puppet skits presented by the teacher can model common problem situations for group analysis and resolution. The puppets dramatize the conflict. Then the children suggest behavior choices the puppets might employ to resolve the conflict. The puppets then act out the children's suggestions. Finally, children evaluate the effectiveness and appropriateness of each scenario. The same effect can be achieved by parent volunteers or older children acting out skits depicting common conflict situations. Whichever method is used, children are being taught skills in conflict resolution. The teacher guides children to think about their own behavior in an effort to teach socialization and self-discipline.

It's BASIC

When the teacher attends to the BASIC classroom management techniques of preparation—

Before school begins

Arrival and departure times

Schedule transitions

Interactions with equipment and materials

Conflict management

—many potential discipline problems can be avoided. By anticipating possible problems and planning routines and methods to minimize problem times, the teacher can create an orderly classroom environment in which children can learn and work in harmony.

For further reading

Doescher, S. M., & Sugawara, A. I. (1989). Encouraging prosocial behavior in young children. *Childhood Education, 65,* 213–216.

Glasser, W. (1985). Discipline has never been the problem and isn't the problem now. *Theory Into Practice, 24,* 241–246.

Kelman, A. (1990). Choices for children. *Young Children, 45*(3), 42–45.

Nash, B. C. (1981). The effects of classroom spatial organisation on four- and five-year-old children's learning. *British Journal of Educational Psychology, 51,* 144–155.

Neill, S. R. St. J. (1982). Preschool

design and child behavior. *Journal of Child Psychology and Psychiatry, 23,* 309–318.

Ryan, W. P. (1974). Workshops about the physical structure of the classroom: An interesting way to work with teachers. *Journal of School Psychology, 12,* 242–246.

Sargent, B. (1972). *The integrated day in an American school.* Cambridge, MA: National Association of Independent Schools.

Spodek, B., Saracho, O., & Davis, M. (1991). *Foundations of early childhood education.* Englewood Cliffs: Prentice-Hall.

Tegano, D., Sawyers, J., & Moran, J. (1989). Problem-finding and solving in play: The teacher's role. *Childhood Education, 66,* 92–97.

References

Brophy, J. (1983). Classroom organization and management. *The Elementary School Journal, 83,* 265–285.

Brophy, J. (1985). Classroom management as instruction: Socializing self-guidance in students. *Theory into Practice, 24,* 233–240.

Day, B. (1975). *Open learning in early childhood.* New York: Macmillan.

Katz, L., & Chard, S. (1989). *Engaging children's minds: The project approach.* Norwood, NJ: Ablex.

McNergney, R., & Haberman, M. (1988). Research on teaching. *Educational Leadership, 45*(4), 96.

Schilmoeller, G. L., & Amundrud, P. A. (1987, Spring). The effect of furniture arrangement on movement, on-task behavior, and sound in an early childhood setting. *Child and Youth Care Quarterly, 16*(1), 5–20.

Shapiro, S. (1975). Some classroom ABC's: Research takes a closer look. *The Elementary School Journal, 75,* 436–441.

Stocking, S. H., Arezzo, D., & Leavitt, S. (1979). *Helping kids make friends.* Allen, TX: Argus Communications.

Curricular Applications

All articles in this chapter are new for this 1994/95 edition. The lead article, entitled "Curriculum Webs: Weaving Connections from Children to Teachers," builds a strong case for a curriculum that is based on the children's interests and local conditions. For the curriculum to be truly child centered, teachers must get away from using preset themes that are recycled each year and have little if any interest for the children in a particular group during that specific week. The knowledgeable and keenly aware professional will use his or her skills in observing and listening to young children at play, in conversations at snacks and meals, and during routines to develop a curriculum based on individual and local interests that appeal to the children. A teacher who presents to parents a neatly typed list of weekly themes for the year in September has little concern for planning to meet the individual needs and interests of the children in that center or class. The term *child centered* can take on new meaning if teachers use their knowledge of child development while planning the curriculum. Curriculum webs allow the flow of topics, concepts, or ideas explored to have some connection or relevance to the children. Topics for discussion are not chosen because the teacher has always done dinosaurs the third week of March. Neither are they dragged out or squeezed into neat 5-day Monday-through-Friday packages, despite the length of or interest in the topic. The curriculum in a true child-centered program may have activities related to two or more topics, projects, or concepts available simultaneously. Children are free to choose the activities of interest to them on a particular day secure in the knowledge that they will be able to explore initially or revisit at a later time or date something else in the room.

When parents receive little if any explanation as to why a creative-play-based environment is encouraged, but simply observe groups of children playing in various areas with blocks or buttons, they fail to grasp the role of a play-based curriculum. Therefore, professionals in early childhood education have parent education as one of their major tasks. Developing a philosophy and implementing a program that focuses on the developmental needs of young children require, in addition to time and money, a thorough knowledge of how to select play materials and technology for children of differing ages, abilities, and backgrounds. They also require skill in conveying to others goals and objectives and how these will be attained.

One often-misunderstood component of the early childhood curriculum is the development of the creative self. In their article "The Creative Arts Process: What It Is and What It Is Not," Linda Edwards and Martha Nabors present an excellent argument for teachers who are caught by the pressure from parents to send home something every day to hang on the refrigerator door. The idea that creative arts means that everyone in the class must produce a craft project that looks very similar to his or her classmates' but vaguely like the teacher's model is outdated and must be dispelled. The article will be of particular interest to teachers who are struggling to include all types of creative endeavors in their curriculum. Movement, blocks, puppets, clay, and language experiences, as well as the traditional expendable art materials such as paint, paper, and crayons, belong in the creative arts area and should be fostered in the curriculum.

Playing with materials and language is the way the young child conquers the world of objects and symbols and constructs knowledge about their properties. As children grow and begin to communicate through print, they are embarking upon one of the most challenging yet rewarding skills one can develop. Creative writing takes many forms, and, just as learning to talk is a long process, so is learning to write. Elizabeth Sulzby provides suggestions for teachers in her article "I Can Write! Encouraging Emergent Writers." Teachers who are aware of steps children take in emergent literacy recognize the unique skills children bring to the reading process and capitalize upon their eagerness for learning and their insatiable appetite for encouragement while they are learning.

As explained in the overview for Unit 1, the editors, with the assistance of members of the advisory board, develop a list of current topics of interest to professionals in the field of early childhood education and then set about the task of collecting exemplary articles on each topic. Two topics receiving a great deal of interest this year were technology in the early childhood class and respecting diversity in children and families. We are pleased to include an article from a series published in *Child Care Information Exchange*. The series of five articles addresses some of the traditions, unique situations, and family expectations found in Hispanic, African American, American interracial, and Asian families. The study of the educational experiences of African American children is presented in "African American Children" by Ruby Burgess.

Lilian Katz explores a topic many teachers have not considered when planning to meet the needs of the affective or emotional self. Are teachers really helping children develop a positive, healthy self-concept when

they shower them with superficial comments such as "You're terrific" just because they put the blocks back on the shelf, or "What a great friend you are" when a child is observed sitting next to a classmate on a bench? Katz challenges all teachers to closely examine their philosophy on the development of self-concept.

A truly child-centered curriculum in a developmentally appropriate program is constantly changing, just as the children are who attend that program. It is the job of the teachers and caregivers to keep pace with the children's needs and interests as they grown and learn.

Looking Ahead: Challenge Questions

What do young children actually learn by playing? How can play materials be evaluated for their contribution to children's development? What are the developmental characteristics of play?

How are the processes of learning to read and write connected? What can facilitate these processes in the classroom?

How can a healthy, positive self-concept best be developed in young children?

What components of a model technology program in Florida would be beneficial for all preschool children?

List some specific strategies teachers can employ in assisting children from diverse family backgrounds in their classroom.

What learning experiences can be provided outdoors for young children? How can the environment be established for safe and creative play?

Describe the philosophy for developing the creative arts in a developmentally appropriate program. What would be the key components?

How can curriculum webs be built with input from the children?

Curriculum Webs: Weaving Connections From Children to Teachers

Susan Workman and Michael C. Anziano

Susan Workman, Ed.D., is director of the San Juan College Child Development Center, a lab school and child care facility for two- to eight-year-olds. Susan holds a doctorate in early childhood education from Syracuse University.

Michael C. Anziano, Ph.D., is director of early childhood education and associate professor of psychology at San Juan College. Michael's current work involves strategies for early intervention.

In one preschool classroom a group of three- through six-year-old children take turns tracing one another's bodies as they move in a variety of poses. The teacher observes their fascination with posing and extends their interest the following day by placing mirrors in the art area. Several days later, on a walking field trip, children begin to explore the concept of "puddles." The teacher draws their attention to the puddle: "Look in the puddle and tell me what you see." As the children respond she helps them connect their experience with the reflection in the puddle to their experience with mirrors. They return to the classroom and search the art boxes for reflective materials. Aluminum foil on cardboard becomes lakes and puddles, and children explore the idea of reflections in the block corner as they construct houses.

Throughout these activities children are expanding their understanding of the concepts of self, water, and houses. The teacher's skill in extending children's interests and experiences is supported by a webbed curriculum—one that was developed by observing children and documenting their recurring interests and the themes of their activities. The possibilities and connections inherent in the series of related webs this teacher uses provide an unending resource for curriculum development.

Connecting concept webs

Semantic webbing, especially the integration and *connections* among webs, may become the central feature of any curricular approach. Developmentally appropriate activities and outcomes for children result from teachers responding to the children's interests. The preschooler thinks about the world primarily in terms of actions that can be performed, so the choice of concepts must provide for action-oriented, child-initiated plans and activities. In our case, teachers spent an entire semester observing and documenting children's interests. The result was a set of basic concepts—earth, air, water, houses, and self—which could be developed as webs. The child begins with a specific problem, for example, constructing a house. In constructing a house, symbolic media chosen by the child will vary from three-dimensional blocks to paper and pencil, clay, sand, or a computer program (e.g., "Town Builder"). A child could begin with a different problem, such as moving water from one place to another. Each basic concept can be represented by a content web,

From *Young Children*, Vol. 48, No. 20, January 1993, pp. 4-9. Reprinted by permission of the publisher, the National Association for the Education of Young Children. © 1993 by NAEYC.

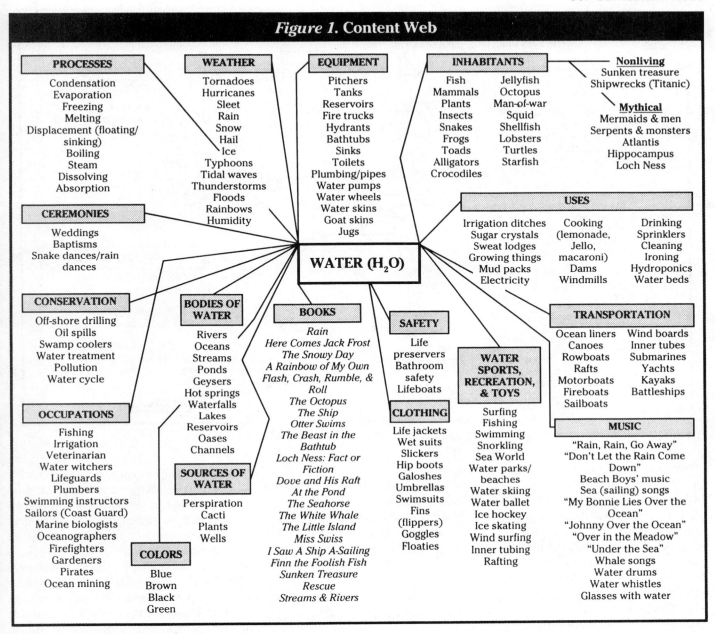

Figure 1. Content Web

PROCESSES
Condensation
Evaporation
Freezing
Melting
Displacement (floating/
    sinking)
Boiling
Steam
Dissolving
Absorption

WEATHER
Tornadoes
Hurricanes
Sleet
Rain
Snow
Hail
Ice
Typhoons
Tidal waves
Thunderstorms
Floods
Rainbows
Humidity

EQUIPMENT
Pitchers
Tanks
Reservoirs
Fire trucks
Hydrants
Bathtubs
Sinks
Toilets
Plumbing/pipes
Water pumps
Water wheels
Water skins
Goat skins
Jugs

INHABITANTS
Fish
Mammals
Plants
Insects
Snakes
Frogs
Toads
Alligators
Crocodiles

Jellyfish
Octopus
Man-of-war
Squid
Shellfish
Lobsters
Turtles
Starfish

Nonliving
Sunken treasure
Shipwrecks (Titanic)

Mythical
Mermaids & men
Serpents & monsters
Atlantis
Hippocampus
Loch Ness

CEREMONIES
Weddings
Baptisms
Snake dances/rain
    dances

USES
Irrigation ditches
Sugar crystals
Sweat lodges
Growing things
Mud packs
Electricity

Cooking
(lemonade,
    Jello,
    macaroni)
Dams
Windmills

Drinking
Sprinklers
Cleaning
Ironing
Hydroponics
Water beds

WATER (H₂O)

CONSERVATION
Off-shore drilling
Oil spills
Swamp coolers
Water treatment
Pollution
Water cycle

**BODIES OF
WATER**
Rivers
Oceans
Streams
Ponds
Geysers
Hot springs
Waterfalls
Lakes
Reservoirs
Oases
Channels

BOOKS
Rain
Here Comes Jack Frost
The Snowy Day
A Rainbow of My Own
*Flash, Crash, Rumble, &
    Roll*
The Octopus
The Ship
Otter Swims
*The Beast in the
    Bathtub*
*Loch Ness: Fact or
    Fiction*
Dove and His Raft
At the Pond
The Seahorse
The White Whale
The Little Island
Miss Swiss
I Saw A Ship A-Sailing
Finn the Foolish Fish
*Sunken Treasure
    Rescue*
Streams & Rivers

SAFETY
Life
preservers
Bathroom
safety
Lifeboats

CLOTHING
Life jackets
Wet suits
Slickers
Hip boots
Galoshes
Umbrellas
Swimsuits
Fins
(flippers)
Goggles
Floaties

**WATER
SPORTS,
RECREATION,
& TOYS**
Surfing
Fishing
Swimming
Snorkling
Sea World
Water parks/
    beaches
Water skiing
Water ballet
Ice hockey
Ice skating
Wind surfing
Inner tubing
Rafting

TRANSPORTATION
Ocean liners
Canoes
Rowboats
Rafts
Motorboats
Fireboats
Sailboats

Wind boards
Inner tubes
Submarines
Yachts
Kayaks
Battleships

MUSIC
"Rain, Rain, Go Away"
"Don't Let the Rain Come
    Down"
Beach Boys' music
Sea (sailing) songs
"My Bonnie Lies Over the
    Ocean"
"Johnny Over the Ocean"
"Over in the Meadow"
"Under the Sea"
Whale songs
Water drums
Water whistles
Glasses with water

OCCUPATIONS
Fishing
Irrigation
Veterinarian
Water witchers
Lifeguards
Plumbers
Swimming instructors
Sailors (Coast Guard)
Marine biologists
Oceanographers
Firefighters
Gardeners
Pirates
Ocean mining

**SOURCES OF
WATER**
Perspiration
Cacti
Plants
Wells

COLORS
Blue
Brown
Black
Green

and Figure 1 illustrates the content web for the concept of water.

By working with several webs simultaneously, children are encouraged to see connections among the concepts. Houses, animals, and babies were three of our initial concept webs. Children began to think in terms of relationships that fostered their understanding that animals—including themselves—live in houses, or that a nest is a particular kind of house that holds babies. Children's ideas about concepts like houses,

earth, air, and water are often derived from the central concept of self, as activities in each web begin with the children's own experience. Figure 2 presents the content web for the concept of self.

The natural interrelations among these webs support the developmental interaction approach of Biber (1977), who, along with others, has advocated for preschool curricula in which cognitive, affective, and social processes are all interdependent. The child's intellectual energy and the

growth of cognitive functions like judging, comparing, reasoning, and problem solving are always interacting with motivational and interpersonal processes. In thinking about concepts like water, earth, and air, the child engages in the environment, transforms materials, and has opportunities to feel competence by observing his effect on materials like water and earth. At the same time social processes are facilitated by opportunities to share, cooperate with others, tutor one's peers, and learn

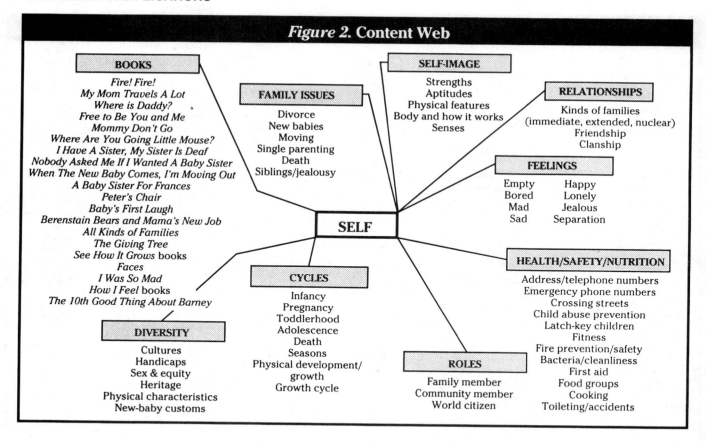

Figure 2. Content Web

BOOKS

Fire! Fire!
My Mom Travels A Lot
Where is Daddy?
Free to Be You and Me
Mommy Don't Go
Where Are You Going Little Mouse?
I Have A Sister, My Sister Is Deaf
Nobody Asked Me If I Wanted A Baby Sister
When The New Baby Comes, I'm Moving Out
A Baby Sister For Frances
Peter's Chair
Baby's First Laugh
Berenstain Bears and Mama's New Job
All Kinds of Families
The Giving Tree
See How It Grows books
Faces
I Was So Mad
How I Feel books
The 10th Good Thing About Barney

FAMILY ISSUES

Divorce
New babies
Moving
Single parenting
Death
Siblings/jealousy

SELF-IMAGE

Strengths
Aptitudes
Physical features
Body and how it works
Senses

RELATIONSHIPS

Kinds of families
(immediate, extended, nuclear)
Friendship
Clanship

SELF

FEELINGS

Empty   Happy
Bored   Lonely
Mad   Jealous
Sad   Separation

HEALTH/SAFETY/NUTRITION

Address/telephone numbers
Emergency phone numbers
Crossing streets
Child abuse prevention
Latch-key children
Fitness
Fire prevention/safety
Bacteria/cleanliness
First aid
Food groups
Cooking
Toileting/accidents

DIVERSITY

Cultures
Handicaps
Sex & equity
Heritage
Physical characteristics
New-baby customs

CYCLES

Infancy
Pregnancy
Toddlerhood
Adolescence
Death
Seasons
Physical development/
growth
Growth cycle

ROLES

Family member
Community member
World citizen

about other cultures. An activity in our earth web, for example, involves small groups of children working together to make a papier maché globe. The globe can be adapted into a piñata and used as part of a Hispanic celebration, such as Cinco de Mayo. Children also interrelate important emotional and affective content through the expression of feelings surrounding a concept like self, which may include discussions or dramatic play involving themes such as a new baby or sibling rivalries. The webbed approach, then, allows for the natural integration of expanding intellectual functions with emotion, attitude, and feeling.

The interrelation of concept webs is an important extension of Levin's (1986) approach. Levin presents some fine examples of a series of activities based on webs such as "rocks" and "gerbils." Our approach focuses on the development of webs and also devotes particular attention to the rela-

tions and connections among various webs. In the next section we describe our approach to curriculum and give examples and applications of these ideas as they are carried out in our laboratory preschool.

Creating a curriculum web

The first step in organizing a webbed curriculum is to identify concepts from children's interests to serve as a starting point. Choose ideas that are small (bread, for example, would be fine; seasons would not) in order to make the task manageable. The concepts should be able to be related to one another. They also should lend themselves to being part of a cycle that can be returned to again and again. "Spring" is difficult to return to, but houses can always be explored. Finally, choose children's ideas that are universal. They are more likely to mesh

with one another, and they facilitate the integration of ideas and customs from diverse cultures. Ongoing concepts in our classrooms are self, houses, air, water, and earth.

Then the fun begins! Groups of four or five staff members brainstorm each topic, listing as many headings and subheadings as their understanding and experience allows. Their observations of children's interests and ideas are critical to a successful, inclusive web. Evaluation is delayed as the collective knowledge of the group is outlined on paper. Each web becomes a source of endless possibilities for active exploration of a concept (see Figure 2). In addition, the relationships among the webs provide flexibility, richness, and depth. Figure 3 illustrates the interactive relationships possible among the basic concepts.

Another critical step in the process is to assure that each web contains possibilities for children to have experiences related to program goals or learner outcome. These goals can be listed and numbered, and the original web can be coded to indicate possibilities for each outcome. Then webs are reorganized according to goals, thus allowing staff to look at a topic from both a concept view and a process view. Figure 4 gives an example of this process, using our program's goals as "learner outcome." It is important to remember, however, that learning is in the hands of the child and may take many directions depending on her developmental level and the individual interests she has.

Curriculum in action

How do teachers and children collaborate to weave the classroom curriculum? This process is an example of the art and the science of good teaching. First, each activity is viewed as a launching pad for extending children's ideas and understanding; for example, a child's interest in houses might extend to houses for dogs, houses for worms (earth), and houses for birds. Each of these options is viable and can serve as a jumping-off place for exploring other concepts. Worms and earth might lead to creating terrariums; terrariums might spark interest in a trip to

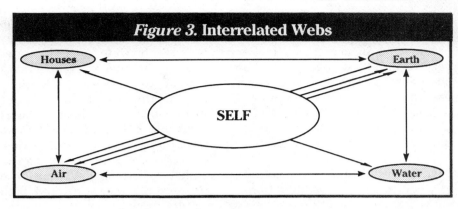

Figure 3. Interrelated Webs

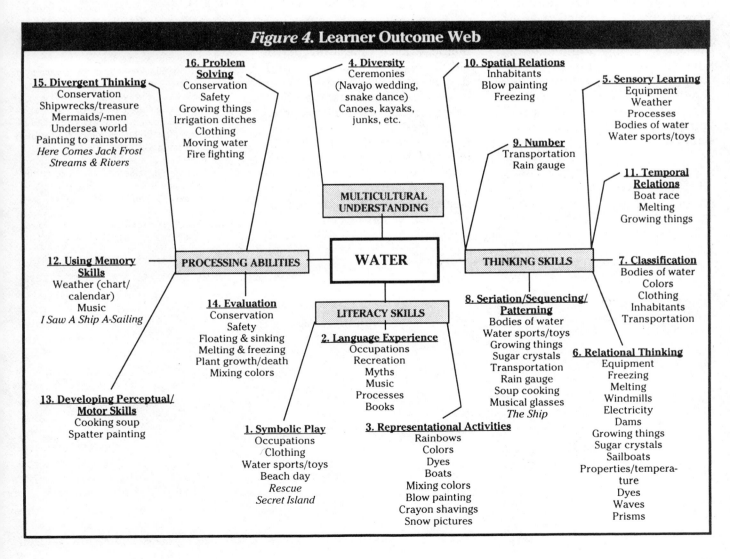

Figure 4. Learner Outcome Web

15. Divergent Thinking
Conservation
Shipwrecks/treasure
Mermaids/-men
Undersea world
Painting to rainstorms
Here Comes Jack Frost
Streams & Rivers

16. Problem Solving
Conservation
Safety
Growing things
Irrigation ditches
Clothing
Moving water
Fire fighting

4. Diversity
Ceremonies
(Navajo wedding,
snake dance)
Canoes, kayaks,
junks, etc.

10. Spatial Relations
Inhabitants
Blow painting
Freezing

5. Sensory Learning
Equipment
Weather
Processes
Bodies of water
Water sports/toys

9. Number
Transportation
Rain gauge

11. Temporal Relations
Boat race
Melting
Growing things

12. Using Memory Skills
Weather (chart/
calendar)
Music
I Saw A Ship A-Sailing

MULTICULTURAL UNDERSTANDING

PROCESSING ABILITIES

WATER

THINKING SKILLS

7. Classification
Bodies of water
Colors
Clothing
Inhabitants
Transportation

14. Evaluation
Conservation
Safety
Floating & sinking
Melting & freezing
Plant growth/death
Mixing colors

LITERACY SKILLS

8. Seriation/Sequencing/ Patterning
Bodies of water
Water sports/toys
Growing things
Sugar crystals
Transportation
Rain gauge
Soup cooking
Musical glasses
The Ship

6. Relational Thinking
Equipment
Freezing
Melting
Windmills
Electricity
Dams
Growing things
Sugar crystals
Sailboats
Properties/tempera-
ture
Dyes
Waves
Prisms

13. Developing Perceptual/ Motor Skills
Cooking soup
Spatter painting

1. Symbolic Play
Occupations
Clothing
Water sports/toys
Beach day
Rescue
Secret Island

2. Language Experience
Occupations
Recreation
Myths
Music
Processes
Books

3. Representational Activities
Rainbows
Colors
Dyes
Boats
Mixing colors
Blow painting
Crayon shavings
Snow pictures

the greenhouse. For another child, or in another classroom, the progression of activities will be very different. At each point the child can be helped to make connections: "Do you remember when . . . ?" "How is this like . . . ?"

Second, webbing assures that both teachers and children see relationships. A cornerstone for curriculum development is the idea of relationships. Relationships are the connections that enable children to organize and make sense of their world, build concepts, and think about things in new ways. The experiences and environments we plan with children, therefore, should be organized in such a way that the connections between ideas and events are apparent to the children—easily grasped and able to be represented from their point of view. This representation—whether through language, drawing, block building, or dramatic play—enables the teacher to observe the connections children are making and plan the best way to extend children's interest and understanding (New, 1990).

Third, these relationships are woven by children and teachers together. Teachers are careful observers of children; they listen and help to clarify children's ideas: "What are your ideas about rain and where it comes from?" "I'm wondering if there's another way to move the water from the water table to the bucket." Teachers extend opportunities for children by helping them make connections to previous experiences: "How is what you see in the puddle like what you saw in the mirror? How is it different?" The teacher's open-ended questions encourage the process of comparing and help children construct notions of similarities and differences. Teachers might share their wonderings—"I wonder if there's a way to make the foil float"—and encourage children's ideas—"How can we find out?" This reflective thinking becomes part of the curriculum development process for teachers and children as they weave a design among the curriculum webs.

The possibilities inherent in a webbed curriculum are virtually limitless. Each time a teacher or child creates an interesting question or sees a relationship that he is interested in pursuing, the follow-up exploration can be documented and added to enrich the repertoire of possibilities for other children and teachers at other times. It becomes possible to document curriculum as it emerges uniquely (see, for example, Jones, 1989) with each group of children and teachers and to add it to the available idea pool for others to use. In this way the curriculum is not a static set of materials but a living, growing resource.

For further reading

National Association for the Education of Young Children & National Association of Early Childhood Specialists in State Departments of Education. (1991). Guidelines for appropriate curriculum content and assessment in programs serving children ages 3 through 8. *Young Children, 46*(3), 21–38.

Workman, S., Bradley, S., Nipper, C., & Workman, D. (1991). *Myself and my surroundings: An early childhood curriculum resource.* Farmington, NM: San Juan College.

References

Biber, B. (1977). A developmental interaction approach: Bank Street College of Education. In M.C. Day & R.K. Parker (Eds.), *The preschool in action* (2nd ed.) (pp. 423–460). Boston: Allyn & Bacon.

Jones, E. (1989, November). *Curriculum can be more than what happens: Three approaches to developing appropriate curriculum for young children.* Paper presented at the annual conference of the National Association for the Education of Young Children, Atlanta, GA.

Levin, D.E. (1986). Weaving curriculum webs: Planning, guiding and recording curriculum activities in the day care classroom. *Day Care and Early Education, 13*(4), 16–19.

New, R. (1990). Excellent early education: A city in Italy has it. *Young Children, 45*(6), 4–10.

The Creative Arts Process:

What It Is and What It Is Not

Linda C. Edwards and Martha L. Nabors

Linda C. Edwards, Ed.D., has been involved in teacher education and the creative arts for more than 20 years. Currently she is program director of early childhood graduate programs at the College of Charleston, South Carolina. She is also the author of Affective Development and the Creative Arts: A Process Approach to Early Childhood Education.

Martha L. Nabors, Ph.D., teaches undergraduate and graduate early childhood and elementary courses at the College of Charleston. She is also on the board of directors of the South Carolina Association on Children Under Six.

Appropriate experiences in the creative arts process for young children depend in part on the knowledge each teacher brings to the encounter. Although most early childhood teachers acknowledge the creative arts as a legitimate and essential component of the curriculum, many still rely on product-oriented activities rather than valuing the *process* of making art. What is and what is not creative arts for young children, and what can we do to ensure that our young children truly experience the creative process when they are involved in the arts?

When we were thinking about this question, an event that happened more than 20 years ago reared its head like a dragon. The author has

since managed to forgive herself because at the time she knew nothing about the importance of the art *process* and was only aware of product-oriented project art. Her teacher-training program had provided enough "cookbook art projects" to last for years.

We invite you to take a look at several early childhood classrooms. Too often teachers forget what it is like to let their imaginations take flight. Children's imaginations soar

automatically; unfortunately, many adults have been "educated out" of being imaginative. The imagination is a powerful tool for getting in touch with the process of creativity, and we encourage you to challenge your imagination as you find pictures in your head to see the following early childhood classrooms.

Toddler room with the yellow door. We are in one of the toddler

Materials such as paint and clay inspire creativity, but most children will be creative only if teachers encourage them to be.

From *Young Children*, Vol. 48, No. 3, March 1993, pp. 77-81. Reprinted by permission of the publisher, the National Association for the Education of Young Children. © 1993 by NAEYC.

rooms. The children are seated at tables. There is a large piece of construction paper in front of each child. The teacher is passing out finger paint. She puts a glob of red finger paint and a glob of blue finger paint on each child's paper. The teacher tells the children that they can put their fingers in the paint and find out how they can move the paint around on the paper. As a last instruction the teacher asks the children to see what happens if their colors get all mixed up.

Toddler room with the blue door. In the toddler room across the hall, the teacher has been reading the story of *Frederick* to the children. *Frederick,* by Leo Lionni, as you may recall, is a little mouse that uses his imagination to gather sunshine and

Creativity is *not* following step-by-step procedures aimed at reproducing the teacher's (or craft book's) ideas.

colors when all the other mice are gathering grain and corn. The mice are gathering things that they will need for the upcoming winter. The teacher and the assistant are passing out colored paper that has been cut into pink and brown circles. Each child also gets a small paper cup and little container of white glue. The teacher shows the children a little mouse that she made by gluing the colored circles onto the paper cup. Then she demonstrates the step-by-step process by which she made her mouse. The assistant moves over to show the children the mouse that she made and tells the children that they, too, can use the circle and cups to make a mouse just like hers and the teacher's. She encourages the children to look carefully at the two little mice and then moves about giving guidance and directions. When several of the toddlers have difficulty getting the circles in the right place on the cup, the teacher and the assistant finish the project for them.

The three-year-old room down the hall. In this three-year-old room, the teacher plays Debussy's *Children's Corner* during center time. The unit for the week is "Butterflies and Other Things That Fly." When it is time for large group, the teacher tells the children that he has a magic wand that can help them move and dance just like butterflies and other things that fly. He tells the children that he will touch their heads with his magic wand and that when he does they will become (pretend) butterflies, or dragonflies, or birds, or even buzzing

bees. The teacher reminds the children that all flying things move differently. "Listen to the music and see how you can fly just like one of the butterflies or other flying things we have been learning about." At that moment he tells the children to stand very still and wait for the touch of the magic wand. He turns up the volume on the record player so that the music is a little louder and moves about, touching the children with his magic wand.

The four-year-old room at the end of the hall. Now let's walk down the

It was time for the annual Christmas program. Because I doubled as the music teacher, my principal appointed me chair of the program committee. I was excited! This was my first year teaching, my first class of five-year-olds, and the principal wanted *me* to be in charge of the Christmas program. I decided that the whole school would do *The Nutcracker Suite,* complete with costumes, music, props, and all the embellishments. I was eager to impress the parents and the other teachers, so I decided to teach my kindergarten girls the ballet, "Waltz of the Flowers," and the kindergarten boys, "Dance of the Toy Soldiers." For weeks I taught these children perfect steps, perfect timing, turn right, stand still, curtsy, and step and turn. At first the children seemed to enjoy it, but as the days and weeks went on, they started resisting going to practice or would actually beg not to have to do "the program" again. On several occasions some complained of being tired and some were discipline problems . . . disrupting, acting out, hitting, and being generally unhappy; however, we did make it to the big night. The parents loved the performance. We all congratulated ourselves on a wonderful program. I remember talking with a first grade teacher about how much the children loved it and what a good time they had. The truth is that the children were exhausted. They were fidgety and irritable, tired and pouty. Some even fell asleep in their chairs during the third grade presentation of the "Dance of the Scarves."

After a long weekend the children returned to school and seemed to be the happy, well-adjusted children they had been before I had had this brilliant idea of performing *The Nutcracker.* Young children, as you know, are so resilient. In the weeks that followed, they didn't want me to play music during center time. I would put on a Hap Palmer album, and they would argue about the right and wrong way to "march around the alphabet." Why would kindergartners turn against the sacred Hap Palmer? They didn't want to hear the music from the ballet. Just the mention of the words *dance* or *costume* or *program* would change them into terrors.

It wasn't until years later that I came to know that I had forced these little children to perform (under the name of "creative arts"— specifically, "dance") in ways that were totally inappropriate for children their age. Not only had I involved these children in inappropriate practice, I had imposed my own ideas of how to be a flower and a toy soldier without regard as to how *they* might interpret or create their own ideas, thoughts, fantasies, or forms of expression.

hall to the fours. The teacher and the children are rehearsing for a play that they will present at the upcoming parent/teacher meeting. The children have been practicing for weeks, and this is the final rehearsal before the big performance. They have memorized all of the lines to one of their favorite stories and are all ready to present *The Three Billy Goats Gruff* to their parents. The dress rehearsal begins, the curtain rises, and these four-year-olds give a perfect performance, complete with correct dialogue, staging, and costumes.

The block room. Now we go into the block room. We see another group of four-year-olds building a bridge with the hardwood blocks. As we listen more closely, we hear the children repeating the words "tramp, tramp, tramp" as they parade up and down their makeshift bridge. Their teacher moves closer to the group and tells them that they sound like the goats in the *Three Billy Goats Gruff.* With that suggestion, one child crawls under the bridge, and the next words we hear are, "Who's that tramping across my bridge?" The teacher suggests using the rug as the green meadow. Then she moves aside. The play continues for the next 20 minutes, during which time the story line is changed several times. At one point the smallest Billy Goat Gruff starts describing how he and his friends can trick the troll with cake and ice cream!

What are the traits of creativity? What is and is not appropriate art for young children? What can we do to facilitate the creative, artistic process in young children?

Let's think about the first two rooms, the toddler room with the finger-paint activity and the toddler room where the children are making a mouse. In the finger-paint activity, the children are experimenting with the finger paint. They may organize the paint in ways that express a thought, experience, or idea. They may find pleasure in using their fingers, hands, or elbows to move the

Ellsabeth Nichols

Expression of inner reality fosters thinking and confidence.

paint all over the paper. They may even end up with a product. This activity enables the children to be involved in a process during which creative impulses can take shape. The teacher has opened the door for these children to become absorbed in what the *process* has to offer rather than in how their *products* will be evaluated. The children have been given permission to respond to internal rather than externally imposed criteria. They are working with the art material in ways that challenge their ideas rather than following step-by-step procedures to represent the teacher's thoughts and ideas.

In the mouse-making activity the creative process is not alive. The children are responding to a dictated step 1, step 2, step 3 procedure that expresses the ideas of the *teacher,* or more likely, of a recipe in a crafts book, not their own childlike ideas of how they can glue shapes to cups to make something *they* have created. Step-by-step procedures that lead children toward a finished product may help children learn to sequence

or follow directions, but we cannot call that creative arts. Having 18 or 20 little cup-and-paper mice that the teacher probably had to finish anyway may give the children something to take home at the end of the day, but projects of this type are really not much better than coloring ditto sheets. Children soon learn to accept the myth that they can never make,

> **Creativity *is* feeling free to be flexible and original, to express one's *own* ideas in one's *own* way.**

in this case, a mouse as "good" as the teacher's.

Paul Torrance (1970), a pioneer in the study of the creative process, identified four characteristics of creativity: **fluency, flexibility, originality,** and **elaboration.** Torrance's findings suggest that creativity is the ability to produce something novel, something with a different stamp on it. The finger-paint activity allows the children to experience *fluency* as their ideas emerge and their thoughts change while they move the colors around the paper. Their paint, fin-

that product must not be the ultimate goal. Older children may need specific procedures for completing a project (e.g., how to make slip to hold clay together), but for young children these techniques should remain closely guarded secrets and should be offered when the child asks for

you see inside of somebody." We should all be able to tell after about one minute in an early childhood classroom if it is a setting that encourages creative arts or if children have been involved in standard "cookbook art." It is easy to see which classrooms are process oriented and which more highly value the product.

How do we encourage the creative process? What are we to do and how are we to do it? We allow children to enjoy the freedom that basic materials provide. We let the *children* select topics and subjects that are important to *them*. We give them time to explore relationships among art materials. We give them permission to arrange art materials into their own designs. **We let them stay with what they are doing until they tell us it's done.**

Let's go back once more to the three-year-old classroom, where we find the teacher with the magic wand and all his "Butterflies and Other Things That Fly." This teacher is wise. He taps the children's imagination as they move about the room in ways that feel good to them. He has given the children freedom to be expressive in personally meaningful ways. He understands that creative experiences must be compatible with children's own basic knowledge of the world and their own basic ways of knowing how butterflies and other things that fly can move about in space. This freedom to respond taps the children's imaginations and allows them to be flexible, fluent, and original. These children are engaged in their own uniqueness.

The children in the block room are tramp, tramp, tramping over the block bridge and grazing on a rug meadow. These children are involved in dramatic play and creative drama,

The process of creating nourishes the child more than the product nourishes the teacher or parent. Do you include expressive rhythms and movement in your program?

gers, and imaginations flow together effortlessly and smoothly. There is fluency in this purposeful activity between the material, the child's body, and the child's ideas. The activity is *flexible* and gives the children freedom to experiment in their own ways with different approaches to the finger paint as they respond to the changing colors and designs. The children certainly show *originality*; they decide what to make and how to make it. They *elaborate* on their painting by adding new colors or more detail or other materials. In the mouse activity, at best the children could elaborate (if their teacher gave them additional materials).

The focus of early childhood art *must* be on the process. We must look at how the children are using the materials. How are the children expressing their originality, and how are they elaborating on their original ideas? It is wonderful when children produce something that is *theirs*, one that they have created and own, but

them and not before (Edwards, 1990). We should assure children that they can combine or dilute colors to discover new colors, that they can create their own images of what something looks like, and that they have access to as many materials (for example, small paper cups) as they might need. Each child deserves the opportunity to at least try out her original ideas. Each child deserves a teacher who honors flexibility and elaboration. Each child must be given the chance to find fluency in the process and originality in the final product. There is no right or wrong in artistic expression for the young child because art comes from within the child, not from without. Creativity cannot be imposed from the outside by a well-meaning teacher or assistant.

Cohen and Gainer (1987), in their wonderful book *Art: Another Language for Learning*, quote a child talking about art. The child, Noel, thoughtfully and analytically says, "Art lets

What can *you* do to encourage each child to paint, color, use clay and blocks, and play and act out familiar stories in his or her spontaneous and unique way?

which are most appropriate for young children. Dramatic play and creative drama in early childhood must not be confused with children's theater. In her book *Creative Drama in the Classroom*, Nellie McCaslin (1980) defines both terms. She describes dramatic play as "the free play of the very young child in which he explores his universe, imitating the actions and character traits of those around him ... it has no beginning and no end, and no development in the dramatic sense." Creative drama is more structured. "It may make use of a story with a beginning, a middle, and an end. ... It is, however, always improvised drama." What have these children (and their teacher) created out of hardwood blocks, an old rug, and the *process approach* to creating art? They have made their bridge, the teacher has suggested that they use the rug for the meadow, and now they are about the serious business of interpreting the story in ways that have meaning and purpose to them. As this process continues, new dialogue evolves and adds a different dimension to the story line; new characters appear; some parts of the story are omitted; and a new, more interesting plot develops. *This* is the creative process. These children are involved in a process of self-expression that encourages movement, gesture, language, communication, originality, flexibility, fluency, and elaboration. The actions, movements, and dialogue are all created by the children. The creativity comes from *within* the child. This is creative art.

As for the children involved in the dress rehearsal, we need only remember the author's first teaching experience to understand how these children must feel. Expecting young children to memorize words and actions and then rigorously follow them is the *product* approach and not the *process* of creativity. It also gives children the clear message that the teacher's way is the right way and the only way to interpret the story. Who's to say that the troll can't be tricked into submission with cake and ice cream? We must allow young children to interpret suggestions, stories,

and events using their own actions and dialogue. The children must decide what actions and words are meaningful to them. These experiences should bring spontaneous responses filled with energy, thought, and feelings of accomplishment, self-satisfaction, and joy!

Morgan is a four-year-old. Her favorite finger play is "Little Cabin in the Woods." She uses the power of her imagination to make her own little rabbit. Now, when Morgan does *her* "Little Cabin in the Woods," what else is happening? The product-centered teacher might see her activity as "just play" or as accomplishment in rote memorization; we know differently. When she is involved in this finger play, Morgan is using her imagination, her intellect, and her cognitive abilities to develop her own thoughts and images of how her little rabbit looks, hops, experiences fear, and comes into the house; and finally, Morgan decides what she will do to comfort her rabbit. She is giving order and structure to her thoughts. She is clarifying concepts such as fear, safety, and security. She is focusing and being sensitive to the stimuli provided by her teacher. She is learning how to solve problems and is gaining an understanding of how the little rabbit used reasoning and logic to get out of a somewhat dangerous situation.

The last line of "Little Cabin in the Woods" reads, "Safely you'll abide." When Morgan and her friends were observed playing in the housekeeping center, their teacher noticed that they were moving blocks from the block center into the housekeeping center. They were using the small rectangle blocks to make little beds. The children then proceeded to repeat the finger play, rock the little rabbits, gather imaginary blankets, and kiss the rabbits. After the line, "Little rabbit come inside," they sang, *"Safely on your side."* The teacher made the perceptive observation that although the children had changed the words, the mood, feeling, and affect were the same: These children were nurturing and taking tender care of an imaginary rabbit. They had sim-

ply substituted "safely on your side" for the more abstract and complicated vocabulary of "safely you'll abide."

The challenge to early childhood educators in the teaching of creative arts for young children is to *provide a variety of meaningful experiences closely related to the knowledge and experiences that children bring to the encounter*. Give young children ample time, space, and permission to be fluent, to flow effortlessly and smoothly into each new creative arts experience. Let them try new ways of experiencing creative arts. Be flexible in your own approaches, and nurture your children's flexibility when you respond to new ideas and new art materials. Value the children's originality, and let them put their own stamp on what they create. Give them permission to engage in elaboration by providing a storehouse of supplies, materials, ideas, and different ways to enter the creative arts process. Young children are great imitators; it is up to us to make sure that they are also creative *instigators*.

For further reading

Clemens, S.G. (1991). Art in the classroom: Making every day special. *Young Children, 46*(2), 4–11.

Early childhood creative arts: Proceedings of the International Early Childhood Creative Arts Conference. (1991). Reston, VA: American Alliance for Health, Physical Education, Recreation and Dance. (available from NAEYC)

Lasky, L., & Mukerji, R. (1980). *Art: Basic for young children*. Washington, DC: NAEYC.

References

Cohen, E.P., & Gainer, R.S. (1987). *Art: Another language for learning*. New York: Schocken.

Edwards, L.C. (1990). *Affective development and the creative arts: A process approach to early childhood education*. Columbus, OH: Merrill-Macmillan.

McCaslin, N. (1980). *Creative drama in the classroom*. New York: Longman.

Torrance, E.P. (1970). *Encouraging creativity in the classroom*. Dubuque, IA: William C. Brown.

I CAN WRITE!

Encouraging Emergent Writers

ELIZABETH SULZBY, PH.D.

Elizabeth Sulzby, Ph.D., has studied young children's writing for over 15 years. She is currently a professor in the Education Studies Program in the School of Education, University of Michigan at Ann Arbor.

Watch young children — infants, toddlers, preschoolers, and kindergartners — when they are around pencils, pens, crayons, or markers. They like to write. As children experiment with writing, they're developing their interest and skills in reading. This early exploration is called emergent literacy — the technical term for the reading and writing young children do before they learn to read and write conventionally.

When children scribble, practice writing letters, or do invented spelling, they make discoveries, learn new skills, and blend earlier abilities with newly mastered forms. The key to fostering writing is accepting and encouraging all children's early experiments with print. At all ages, it's also important to:

■ Keep writing interactions light, playful, and exploratory. Direct "teaching" is rarely effective, and may even harm children's skills or interests.

■ Provide easy access to papers, pencils, markers, paints, books, and other literacy tools.

■ Serve as a model by writing and involving children in your writing.

■ Set limits that protect children's safety but don't unnecessarily hamper their activity.

■ Observe children as they write, and ask them to tell you about their writing.

■ Display children's writing, and provide plenty of opportunities for them to share their creations with the group.

Children's writing development usually emerges in a predictable pattern. The chart on the opposite page outlines skills you can expect to see at particular ages, along with ways you can support children's development. But remember that every child develops at his or her own pace.

▲ **Scribbles are young children's first writing. The circular and angular marks that appear in Louis' scribble form the basis of all letter writing. Be sure to acknowledge and encourage scribbling.**

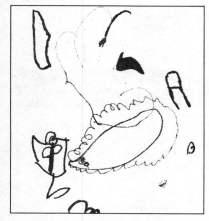

▲ Wanting to write their own names is a powerful motivator for children. Anna's picture includes her initial A. She is learning to tell the difference between drawing and writing, an important developmental step.

▲ Threes and fours often write by making a string of letters about the length of a word, and they may ask you to read it. The letters Christopher chose — C, H, I, T, O — all appear in his name.

▲ Preschoolers often write backward, sometimes switching from backward to forward. Elizabeth's writing shows she understands that words are arranged in one consistent, horizontal direction.

THE ALPHABET: TO TEACH OR NOT TO TEACH

As you know, worksheets and other types of formal lessons aren't beneficial for preschoolers. They tend to be unrelated to children's own interests and usually require a specific right answer. Plus, worksheets encourage children to follow directions passively rather than think creatively. That's why alphabet instruction isn't recommended.

But there's no harm in children learning about the alphabet as long as it's presented appropriately. Also, many children are exposed to the alphabet at home by their parents or educational television. Exploring the alphabet in your program may help keep those children who don't often see the alphabet used at home on a more equal footing.

Your role is to help children become familiar with letters in developmentally appropriate ways. The key is to be sure the activities and materials you use engage children actively, reflect their interests, and are offered as choices rather than requirements. Here are a few appropriate ways to present the alphabet.
● Hang printed alphabet letters on your walls along with children's writing and art.
● Make the alphabet song one of many in your group's repertoire.
● Create letter cards for children to use in open-ended activities. You might also make a few pairs of cards to include in a lotto game.

● Add objects such as magnetized letters and letter-shaped puzzles to your manipulatives area. Look for letter-shaped ice-cube trays and other containers for sand and water play.
● Set out trays of sand, salt, or shaving cream for interested children to practice making letter shapes, numbers, and words.
● Offer a variety of materials such as clay, yarn, and pipe cleaners for children to create three-dimensional shapes and letters.
● Cut letters from sandpaper that children can trace with their fingers.

Thanks to child-development specialist Polly Greenberg, Dr. Elizabeth Sulzby, and Dr. Susan Miller for their thoughts.

PATTERNS OF DEVELOPMENT

Age	Developmental Pattern	How You Can Help
Infants	• Children usually begin to grasp objects at about three to five months. Offer them pens or markers to hold, then gently guide their hands to help them experience marking — the first step in writing. • Older infants — about 6 to 10 months — begin to notice the marks they make and enjoy repeating their motions over and over. Repetition is important for all development, including writing.	• Supervise infants carefully so they don't jab themselves in the eyes or other tender places. Keep the experience warm and playful by talking and singing about what you're doing as you move the baby's hand. • Make a fuss over children's marks! Let them know you value writing and their experiments in literacy.
Ones and Twos	• Most toddlers become skilled scribblers, making repetitive circular or angular marks. They may be fascinated by a variety of marking media, including chalk on a chalkboard or fingers on a frosted windowpane. • Children may say they are "drawing" or "writing." They often use both words to describe the same scribbles, and you might not be able to tell the difference.	• Help children understand that some places — for example, walls — are not okay for writing. Setting appropriate limits is not only necessary, it offers children useful information about how writing is and isn't used. • Invite children to talk about their writing. Then listen to their responses without trying to correct them. Remember, the purpose is to explore children's writing development, not impose adult standards.
Threes and Fours	• Children understand the difference between writing and drawing. Many children begin to explore writing forms and become interested in conventional-looking letters and words. Children may ask for little "lessons" as they practice — "Show me how to make a 'T.'" "Write Keisha!" • Three- and four-year-olds are beginning to understand print's functions as well as its forms, and they often incorporate writing into their play. Children might write pretend telephone messages, create signs to safeguard their block creations, or send letters to faraway friends. • Most threes and fours are interested in any tools that can help them convey messages and explore writing forms.	• Respond to requests for information and provide lots of meaningful opportunities to notice letter shapes, names, and sounds. Let each child decide when, how, and even if he or she wants to explore writing. • Set an example by letting children see you use print in meaningful ways throughout the day. Offer plenty of writing materials. Be sure pens, markers, and many kinds of paper are available at all times. • If possible, add typewriters and computers to your writing-materials supply. Select software programs that allow children to scribble and experiment with language in their own ways.
Fives and Sixes	• Most children who've had rich writing experiences begin to understand the relationship between letters and sounds, and know at least a few specific letter-sound combinations ("b" says "buh"). Their discoveries lead to invented spelling — writing letters to stand for sounds they hear. • Children know a broad range of complex writing skills and can select the ones that meet their current needs. They often combine drawing with writing to create a richer message.	• Let children know you welcome their invented spelling. If they ask for help, you might say the words they want to spell slowly to make it easier for them to hear sounds. Be sure to accept their interpretations. • Writing is an important way to express thoughts, knowledge, and feelings. But it isn't the only way! Encourage children in all their communication efforts.

Taking a Child's Dictation

When it comes to making sense out of print, what could be more helpful to children than seeing their own thoughts written down? That's why dictation — writing children's words exactly as they say them — is so important. It allows children to see the relationship between the words they say and the words that appear on paper. They begin to understand that print is "talk written down."

Dictation makes writing and reading meaningful and compelling to children. By working one on one to record preschoolers' words and stories, you let them know their ideas have value. Plus, because print is permanent, children see that it can be used to help them remember thoughts, feelings, and experiences. They can also see that dictation gives them a way to communicate with people who aren't near enough to hear what they say. By dictating their words, children find they can send messages to people in other rooms, at home, or even to faraway friends and relatives.

Finally, dictation gives you concrete examples to use as you observe children and talk with families about their children's development. Family members also treasure dictation because it offers them a peek into their children's thoughts and feelings while they're in your care.

Dictation Tips
Here are points to keep in mind when doing dictation:
🖎 Use open-ended questions to invite children's dictation, such as "Tell me about that," or "What should I write?"
🖎 Record children's words exactly as they say them.
🖎 Match your writing speed to children's speaking as much as possible. If you can't keep up, ask children to wait a moment so you can write all their words.
🖎 Be patient. Give children plenty of time to compose their ideas and change their minds.

When to Take Dictation
The best way to show children that print is useful is to incorporate it into their everyday activities. When it's used this way, dictation is a meaningful — not isolated — experience.

Help children solve problems. Ask children how they made a collage, designed a block structure, or figured out how to work a new puzzle. Then record their explorations and invite them to illustrate their words. Over time, show children how they can use their dictations to remind them of past ideas and situations that can be helpful in new situations.

Encourage young authors. Listen to the stories children invent during free play, at snacks and meals, and on the playground. Wait for a time when you won't be interrupting and offer to record their stories. You might write them on chart paper, put them on a few sheets in book form, or even type them. However you do it, you'll help validate children's imaginations. Invite your authors to illustrate their stories and share them with the group.

Expand communication. Talk with children about their paintings and drawings to help them further express thoughts and feelings. Maximize children's control over the experience by letting them decide where — and if — you'll write words on their artwork.

Record observations. Science activities provide natural opportunities for dictation. Write children's words on experience-chart paper as they make observations, predictions, and discoveries. Hang the charts in your science area and refer to them as you continue your investigations.

Remember fun experiences. Keep special feelings alive by writing down memories of a shared group experience such as a field trip or celebration. Invite four or five children at a time to dictate their favorite things about the event. Then gather together and read the dictation back to the whole group. (Doing group dictation with a few children at a time ensures that no one has to wait too long for his or her turn.)

Get organized. To plan an event such as a trip to the grocery store or an indoor picnic, gather in a group and make shopping and "things-to-do" lists. Then use your lists to help you get ready and carry out your plans.

Integrating Technology into The Classroom: Lessons from the Project CHILD Experience

Project CHILD, a synthesis of best practices, creates a restructured environment that not only accommodates but embraces technology. Teachers need such realistic yet visionary models and coherent supporting materials, Ms. Butzin avers, if they are to bring about change.

Sarah M. Butzin

Sarah M. Butzin (Florida State University Chapter) is the creator and director of Project CHILD, which was developed at Florida State University, Tallahassee. She is currently vice president for educational research and development at Daniel Memorial Institute, Tallahassee, a nonprofit agency advancing educational programs for children and youth throughout the U.S. and Canada.

For many children traditional American schooling is painful and difficult. Their world outside the classroom is awash in electronic media, while inside the classroom they often find only chalk and paper. Deprived of engaging stimuli, many children quickly lose interest in schooling.

In the past decade, many of the calls for the reform and restructuring of public education have featured technology as a centerpiece. Yet the effective use of technology remains an elusive goal for most teachers. Lack of a sufficient quantity of classroom equipment, lack of training for teachers, and the inherent difficulty of retrofitting technology to the existing structures of education combine to keep computers confined to the back of most classrooms, expensive distractions at best. For most children school continues as it has for generations.

Yet most elementary schools have increasingly sought to bring technology into the educational mix. Virtually every elementary school has some computers.[1] In addition, integrated learning systems (ILSs) have made serious inroads into the schools, with recent sales estimated to be in the billions of dollars.[2] Moreover, many schools are beginning to move both their personal computers and their ILS workstations out of the labs and into the regular classrooms, where children can have daily access to them. The problem is that merely putting computers into the classroom does not mean that they will be used effectively. Until the underlying structural patterns and practices of the traditional elementary school have changed, technology can never achieve its full potential.

A SNAPSHOT OF PROJECT CHILD

In Florida we have undertaken a comprehensive research and development project to explore a new approach to the use of technology in the classroom. It is called Project CHILD (Computers Helping Instruction and Learning Development). Twenty-five schools are currently taking part in this five-year effort, and the results have been very positive. Achievement test scores are up, student attitudes and levels of involvement are high, and teachers and principals champion the program. Indeed, Project CHILD has recently been validated by the Program Effectiveness Panel of the National Diffusion Network.

Project CHILD is a computer-integrated instructional program for grades K–5. It provides a systematic approach for integrating technology into the elementary classroom. Project CHILD is not a software program itself; rather, it is a comprehensive system for effectively using existing hardware and software.

The failure of most attempts to integrate computers into classrooms can be traced to a lack of curriculum materials.

In Project CHILD, classrooms become learning resource rooms for three hours of each day, focused on one of three subject areas: reading, language arts, or math. Children in Project CHILD move from classroom to classroom, working at a variety of learning stations. A typical classroom has a computer station with three to six computers, a teacher station for small-group instruction, stations for hands-on activities, and stations for textbook-based and written work. A wide array of computer software has been correlated with thematic units for each subject area.

From *Phi Delta Kappan*, December 1992, pp. 330-333. Reprinted by permission of *Phi Delta Kappan* and the author.

The structure of the schools taking part in Project CHILD has also been changed to encourage continuous progress. Altogether, six classrooms make up a Project CHILD unit. Students work with the same team of teachers for three years, either in the primary cluster (K–2) or in the intermediate cluster (3–5). Every teacher is a Project CHILD specialist, trained to use technology and hands-on techniques in his or her designated specialty.

Project CHILD materials—a teacher's manual, learning activities guides, and station activities resource books—enable teachers to manage the enhanced classroom environment effectively and to plan enriching learning activities around a common theme. Student record books, called *Passports,* help students learn to set goals and organize their time; they also serve as a way of communicating with parents about their children's activities. A video training program completes the array of Project CHILD materials.

LESSONS FROM PROJECT CHILD

Whether a school uses the Project CHILD program or develops its own, our experience suggests that successful computer integration requires several key components. These relate to the classroom environment, long-term continuous progress, the role of the teacher, student empowerment, curriculum materials, classroom management techniques and materials, multiple assessments, and parent involvement. Project CHILD defines these elements as the "Twenty Essential Components."[3]

Underlying these key components is a philosophical point of view that accommodates a balanced approach to teaching and learning. Traditional schooling has most often taken a didactic approach: the teacher transmits knowledge to the students, who verily that they have learned it by reiterating it on a test. More recently there has been a shift to a constructivist approach: teachers help students to construct their own meaning and to demonstrate their knowledge through performance-based assessment, such as portfolios and projects. Our experience has been that both approaches have their place.

In a typical Project CHILD class period, for example, the teacher might instruct a group (large or small) for a brief lesson and then spend most of the period circulating and guiding students in their work at the various learning stations. While some of that work will include practicing what the teacher has taught, students may also apply and extend what they have learned through collaboration or individual work. Computers can and should be used for both approaches. Instructional software that provides for drill and practice and for learning new information has its place in the software mix along with applications and simulations.

A POSITIVE CLIMATE FOR LEARNING

The classroom should be a stimulating multidimensional environment. Textbooks hands-on activities, computers, and a variety of other technologies should be available and used every day. The ratio of students to computers should be no greater than 7 to 1 if meaningful curriculum integration is to take place. The one-computer classroom is totally ineffective. Except when doing word processing, students in Project CHILD classrooms work with partners at the computers, both to maximize computer time and to encourage collaboration. Project CHILD has three computers in each of the reading and math classrooms and six in the language arts classrooms for classes of up to 30 students each.

Young children with limited reading ability, especially in kindergarten and first grade, need adult assistance at the computer station. Most software requires some set-up in order to find a lesson and get started. Older students or parent volunteers can help out, although our experience has been that designated aides are much more efficient. Without some kind of help, however, the teacher will spend too much time managing operations at the computer station, rather than carrying out the more important role of learning guide and facilitator.

Underlying the classroom environment is a supportive and nurturing ambience. Children must have multiple opportunities for practice and feedback before being assessed and graded. They need opportunities to make mistakes in a risk-free climate. This is where the computer can be a very powerful influence. It is patient, supportive, and fun to use, and it provides immediate feedback.

CONTINUOUS PROGRESS

Learning takes time, and failure is expensive. Traditionally, children who are not ready to move on to the next grade after 180 days of schooling are retained. The failure of this approach, including the high correlation between students who are retained and students who subsequently drop out, has been well documented.[4] Nor are social promotions the answer.

Technology provides another alternative. Most software can be used at a variety of grade levels. One way to take advantage of this capability is to have teachers and students work together for longer periods of time. Project CHILD is structured so that teachers and students stay together for three years: K–2 or 3–5. Students have access to all the software and materials for the full span of ages in each CHILD classroom.

Retentions are discouraged in Project CHILD. Our data show that there were 2% fewer retentions for Project CHILD students across nine schools studied. The schools, now in their fifth year of the program, have virtually eliminated retentions for most grade levels. Teachers report that a student who seemed hopelessly lost one year will suddenly blossom and surge ahead the next year. Making a long-term commitment to students gives them the gift of time.

ENHANCING THE TEACHER'S ROLE

Teachers today are overwhelmed. Asking them to use technology extensively on top of everything else is imposing a burden that few can bear. How can one teacher find the time to learn to integrate effectively the wide array of software that is available in reading, language arts, and mathematics—not to mention science and social studies? Today's model of the teacher as an isolated generalist will be very difficult to maintain in the age of information technology.

The Project CHILD solution is to have teachers specialize and focus on one subject. In this way they can become expert in using and applying software that is more engaging than mere drill-and-practice programs. Teachers in Project CHILD form cluster teams of three specialists—reading, math, and language arts. Each teacher also teaches science and social studies for his or her home-base class.

5. CURRICULAR APPLICATIONS

To avoid fragmentation and encourage coherence, it is important to form collaborative teams that work closely together. This is not an easy or familiar task for many teachers, so they need training and guidance in working together. The Project CHILD program provides a structure for weekly meetings with specific agendas. Teammates also observe in one another's specialty classrooms once during each six-week unit, using a structured observation format.

By observing their own students in their teammates' classrooms, teachers can begin to appreciate the power of the computer and of the hands-on activities that engage children and facilitate learning. Many teachers fear that students working independently will merely goof off when teachers are working with other children. When teachers can concentrate on observing children engaged in independent work, they learn that much of what they believe to be goofing off is actually useful activity. Thus teachers begin the transformation from the "sage on the stage" to the "guide on the side."[5]

With teachers so radically changing their traditional ways of operating, the principal needs to be a sensitive leader who can intervene to help teachers solve scheduling conflicts and resolve other problems that may arise. We are working on advanced training in team-building and conflict resolution as well.

EMPOWERING CHILDREN AND DEVELOPING MATERIALS

Children are whizzes at using computers. They are often far ahead of adults. Technology gives students a chance to be in control, to master tasks that they previously thought impossible. It is not unusual to see a Project CHILD kindergartner not only writing a lengthy story but illustrating and publishing it— all via electronic technology.

To harness technology's ability to empower students, the classroom must provide support in several ways. Frequent and equitable access to the computers is essential, so an adequate ratio of computers to students must be maintained. Beyond this, there must be a systematic method for helping students learn to use the technology for more than fun and games.

In Project CHILD, students learn to set goals, work cooperatively at the computer station, and help one another in

effective ways. This is part of a systematic training program (described below) that helps students learn how to get help if the teacher is unavailable. Students are also encouraged to express their opinions and to engage in self-evaluation of their performance and progress.

The failure of most attempts to integrate computers into classrooms can be traced to a lack of well-developed curriculum materials. Teachers are usually given a software catalog or a guide to various skills that can be "taught" with computers, and then they are turned loose. If they are lucky, teachers might get a few days of training. Under such circumstances, few teachers have the time and expertise to do an adequate job. Schools that are serious about computer integration must provide ample time for curriculum development.

Four people spent a full year developing the Project CHILD integrated curriculum. We laid out a generic elementary school "scope and sequence" in coordinated thematic units and correlated skills and concepts with computer software and hands-on activities. Today, we provide Project CHILD teachers with suggested daily and weekly plans, teaching strategies, activity templates, and task cards. Teachers use this thematic framework to guide their own use of text materials with which they are most familiar.

CLASSROOM MANAGEMENT

Learning centers became popular in the 1960s during the heyday of the "open classroom." They faded into oblivion when the deficiencies in the way they were used became obvious. Most teachers were unable to manage the student movement or tolerate the noise. Keeping track of student progress proved difficult, and students often drifted along aimlessly. The lack of accountability led to the discrediting of the open classroom and the resurgence of the "back to basics" approach to teaching.

Computers in the classroom can lead to many of the same problems if preventive steps are not taken. Many teachers find that a computer in the classroom just creates one more hassle, with students squabbling over whose turn it is, talking animatedly while they work at the computer, and distracting the attention of their classmates from the "real work." It

is little wonder that so few teachers have enthusiastically embraced computers.

Project CHILD corrects the deficiencies of the open classroom by training teachers to use an effective classroom management system. In Project CHILD, students are trained as well. They begin school with a 10-day orientation before work begins on academics. This training guides them in making responsible choices, working cooperatively, seeking and giving help, setting goals, using the computers and other equipment correctly, and keeping records. Students use their *Passports* to guide their movement to and from the various learning stations, to set goals and assess progress toward them, and to track their activities. Teachers use task cards to clearly define activities at each station.

ASSESSMENTS

One of the difficulties associated with using computers intensively is the incompatibility of technology-based learning with current assessment techniques. Teachers fear that their students will not perform well on tests if they spend too much time away from traditional drill work. Even our Project CHILD teachers were under great stress during the first year of the program because they feared that the standardized test scores of their students would fall. The teachers need to learn other ways to assess students beyond the traditional end-of-chapter multiple-choice tests.

Drawing an analogy with learning to ride a bike makes the point clearly. Suppose that, after instruction in identifying the parts of a bike and the appropriate techniques for riding, a group of students using traditional classroom methods spends its practice time reading more about bikes and completing written exercises. A hands-on group, however, spends its practice time taking apart and assembling the pieces of bikes and then riding the bikes. At the end of the unit on bikes, both groups are tested. They must read passages and complete written exercises by bubbling-in answers identifying parts of the bike and techniques for riding. Chances are good that the traditional group will score higher on the test. But which children have learned to ride and repair a bike?

The problem of authentic assessment is one that is still unresolved. In Project

CHILD we encourage teachers to keep portfolios of student work and to use multiple forms of assessment. A team of Project CHILD teachers, along with the district evaluation supervisor for Pasco County, is working to develop multiple assessment materials that match the Project CHILD units. We look forward to the completion of that project. We are also planning to develop software to create student profiles based on key indicators of success in Project CHILD.

INVOLVING PARENTS

Parents want their children to use computers. They like to feel that their children are getting a state-of-the-art education. But they have great anxiety when the children do not bring home lots of worksheets and papers with smiley faces attached. What did you do at school today? We played with computers and games, say the children. Parents then begin to pressure the teachers to get down to basics. Children need to learn to work, they say.

Effective computer integration requires parent education. In Project CHILD we provide a parent orientation class, in which parents learn about Project CHILD and actually go through a simulated classroom experience. Letters to parents explaining the program and the changes they can expect to see from traditional schooling are included in the Project CHILD materials. A parent video provides strategies for supporting children's learning at home.

Parents also review their child's *Passport* at the end of each unit. The students record activities in their *Passports* by topics and skills (e.g., worked on punctuation) rather than by the name of the software or activity (e.g., played *Flippy Frog*). This helps reassure parents that, although the activities may look different from traditional schoolwork, they are indeed academically oriented.

TAKING THE FIRST STEPS

We are all familiar with the shortcomings of American education: lack of appropriate funding, poorly trained teachers clinging to antiquated methods, overcrowded facilities, and growing numbers of poor and neglected children with unmet needs. Project CHILD transforms the current classroom, providing today's teachers with specific strategies and supporting materials to begin the transformation to the future. Teachers do not need to take heroic measures to implement this program. For the program to be successful, they need only follow the guidelines in a variety of areas: classroom organization, implementation of enhanced curricula, the use of multi-dimensional activities, and the training given by Project CHILD trainers.

Project CHILD is designed as a synthesis of best practices. It creates a restructured environment that not only accommodates but embraces technology. By actively involving students in interesting tasks and using highly motivating software that provides immediate feedback and tutorial capabilities, the program increases engaged time-on-task. An increase in engaged time-on-task is strongly associated with increased achievement.[6] By providing teachers with a comprehensive system that includes a well-developed curriculum, classroom management techniques, strategies to foster professional teaming and cooperative learning, and extended time in which to develop a strong relationship with students, the program transforms the teacher's role to that of coach and facilitator.

Schools that are serious about computer integration must be prepared to invest adequately to ensure the success of the program. While the initial investment may be high to fund the purchase of an adequate number of computers and an appropriate array of software, as well as the salary of an aide to assist the youn-

gest children, the payback can be great.

School leaders need the political courage to use limited resources to fund successful models in order to generate public support for continued investment in technology. The beleaguered taxpayers are soon going to expect results for the billions of dollars spent on technology to date. Will educators be able to respond? Our experience with Project CHILD has been that a successful cluster of three or six classrooms can generate considerable support and can attract funding through grants and business partnerships to expand from a single school to neighboring schools. Even non-CHILD teachers begin to adapt some of the strategies of the program.

Change can come only when people see a vision transformed into reality and when they can begin to imagine how it will work for them. Teachers need realistic yet visionary models and coherent supporting materials that can be transferred to today's elementary schools. Project CHILD is a model that can help teachers take their first steps on the bridge to the future.

1. *Microcomputers in Florida Elementary Schools* (Tallahassee: Florida Department of Education, MIS Statistical Brief Series 92–06B, January 1992).
2. Mark Sherry, An EPIE Institute Report: Integrated Instructional Systems," *T.H.E. Journal,* vol. 18, 1990, pp. 86–89.
3. Sarah M. Butzin, *Project CHILD Teacher's Manual* (Tallahassee: Florida Department of Education, 1991).
4. Lorrie A. Shepard and Mary Lee Smith, "Synthesis of Research on Grade Retention," *Educational Leadership,* May 1990, pp. 84–88.
5. Susan Mernit, "The Guide on the Side," *Instructor,* September 1990, pp. 77–90.
6. Janet Graden et al., "Academic Engaged Time and its Relationship to Learning: A Review of the Literature," unpublished paper, ERIC ED 214 930, 1982.

ALL ABOUT ME

*Are We Developing Our
Children's Self-Esteem
or Their Narcissism?*

LILIAN G. KATZ

*Lilian G. Katz is professor of early childhood education
at the University of Illinois, director of the ERIC Clearinghouse on Elementary and Early Childhood Education, and president of the National Association for the
Education of Young Children.*

DEVELOPING AND strengthening young children's
self-esteem typically is listed as a major goal in state
and school district kindergarten curriculum guides. Early
childhood education has long been blessed with a variety of curriculum approaches that emphasize and advocate diverse goals and methods. In spite of this diversity,
the one goal all the approaches agree is important is that
of helping children to "feel good about themselves." The
terms applied to this goal include: self-esteem, self-
regard, self-concept, feelings of self-worth, self-confidence, and often, "feeling good about oneself."

For example, in a 1990 document titled "Early Childhood Education and the Elementary School Principal,"
the National Association of Elementary School Principals
issued "Standards for Quality Programs for Young Children." The first of twelve characteristics given for "quality early childhood programs" is that they "develop a positive self-image."[1]

Many other books, kits, packets, and newsletters urge
teachers to help children gain positive self-concepts.
Here's a typical example of this view:

> . . . the basis for *everything we do* is self-esteem.
> Therefore, if we can do something to give children
> a stronger sense of themselves, starting in
> preschool, they'll be [a lot wiser] in the choices
> they make.[2]

Along similar lines, the prestigious Corporation for
Public Broadcasting issued a twenty-page pamphlet,
directed to teenagers, entitled "Celebrate Yourself. Six
Steps to Building Your Self-Esteem."[3] The first main section, "Learn to Love Yourself Again," asserts that, as
babies, we all loved ourselves, but as we grew up, "we
found that not everyone liked everything we did," so we
"started picking on ourselves." The pamphlet lists six
steps toward self-celebration: The first is "Spot Your Self-
Attacks"; The second step, "See What Makes You Special," includes a recommended "Celebration List," suggesting that the reader compile a 22-item list of all the
"good things about me." The twenty-two items recommended under the heading "My Talents" include: thinking fast, playing trivia, and babysitting. The twelve items
under "My Body" include physical attributes such as
smile, hair, strength, legs, etc. Among eight items under
"My Achievements" are: something special I made; a
grade I got; a compliment I got; an award I won; and so
forth. The third step of the celebration is "Attack your
Self-Attacks." The fourth, "Make Loving Yourself a Habit,"
is illustrated by a cartoon character admiring itself in a
mirror. The final two steps are "Go for the Goal" and
"Lend a Hand to Others." This last step is subtitled "Love
Grows When You Give It Away."

It is perhaps just this kind of literature that accounts
for a large poster I came across in the entrance hall of a
suburban school: Pictures of clapping hands surround
the title, "We Applaud Ourselves." While the sign's prob-
able purpose is to help children "feel good about themselves," it does so by directing their attention inward. The
poster urges self-congratulation; it makes no reference to
other possible ways of earning applause—by consider-

Reprinted with permission from *American Educator,* Summer 1993, pp. 18-23. *American Educator,* the quarterly journal of the
American Federation of Teachers.

ing the feelings or needs of others, for example. Many schools display posters that list the Citizen of the Week, Person of the Week, Super Spellers, Handwriting Awards, and other such honors that seem to encourage showing off.

I also noted a sign over an urban elementary school principal's office that says: "Watch your behavior, you are on display!" Although its purpose may be to encourage appropriate conduct, it does so by directing children's attention to how they *appear* to others rather than to any possible functions of appropriate behavior. What I am suggesting by these examples is, that as commendable as it is for children to have high self-esteem, many of the practices advocated in pursuit of this goal may instead inadvertently develop narcissism in the form of excessive preoccupation with oneself.

It was while observing a first-grade class in an affluent suburb of a large midwestern city that I first became aware of the ways in which self-esteem and narcissism can be confused. Working from dittoed pages prepared by the teacher, each student had produced a booklet called "All about Me." The first page asked for basic information about the child's home and family. The second page was titled "What I like to eat"; the third was called "What I like to watch on TV"; the next was "What I want for a present," and another was "Where I want to go on vacation," and so forth.

On each page, attention was directed toward the child's own inner gratifications. Each topic put the child in the role of consumer—of food, entertainment, gifts, and recreation. Not once was the child asked to assume the role of producer, investigator, initiator, explorer, experimenter, wonderer, or problem-solver.

These booklets, like many others I have encountered around the country, never had pages with titles such as "What I want to know more about," or "What I am curious about," or ". . . want to explore, . . . to find out, . . . to solve, . . . to figure out" or even "to make." Instead of encouraging children to reach out in order to investigate or understand phenomena around them worthy of their attention, the headings of the pages turned their attention inward.

Since first encountering these booklets, I have learned from teachers that the "All about Me" exercise is intended to make children "feel good about themselves" and to motivate them by beginning "where they are." The same intentions, however, could be satisfied in other, better ways. Starting "where children are" can be accomplished by providing topics that (1) encourage children to be curious about others *and* themselves, and, (2) reduce the emphasis on consummatory activities, and (3) at the same time, strengthen the intellectual ethos of the classroom.

Indeed, starting "where the children are" can just as easily be satisfied by pooling class data in a project entitled "All about *Us*." The individual data can be collected, summarized, graphed, compared, and analyzed in a variety of ways that minimize focusing the children's attention exclusively on themselves.

Several years ago, I saw this kind of project put into practice in a rural British infant school. The title of a large display on the bulletin board was: "We Are a Class Full of

Why should children's attention so insistently be turned inward?

Bodies"; just below the main heading was "Here Are the Details." The display space was filled with bar graphs showing birth dates, current weight and height, eye color, number of lost teeth, shoe sizes, etc., in which data from the entire class were pooled. The data started "where the children were." As the children worked in small groups to take measurements, prepare graphs, help one another to post displays of their analyses of the students' individual characteristics, the teacher was able to create an ethos of a community of researchers looking for averages, trends, and ranges.

I observed another example of practices intended to foster self-esteem that may instead contribute to self-preoccupation in a suburban kindergarten in which the comments made by the children about their visit to a dairy farm were displayed on a bulletin board. Each of the forty-seven children's sentences listed on the bulletin board began with the words "I liked. . . ." For example, "I liked the cows," ". . . the milking machine," ". . . the chicks," etc. There were no sentences that began "What surprised me was. . . ," "What I want to know more about is. . . ," or "What I am curious about. . . ."

The children's sentences can be analyzed on many levels. For the purposes of this article, their salient characteristic is the exclusive focus on gratification and the missed opportunity to encourage the natural inclination of children to examine worthwhile phenomena in the world around them. Surely there were features of the farm visit that might have aroused some children's curiosity and sparked further investigations of the real world. Such responses were not solicited and were therefore unlikely to have been appreciated and strengthened.

Another common example of a practice intended to enhance self-esteem but unlikely to do so, was a display of kindergartners' work that consisted of nine large identical paper-doll figures, each having a balloon containing a sentence stem that began "I am special because. . . ." The children completed the sentence with the phrases: ". . . I can color," ". . . I can ride a bike," ". . . I like to play with my friends," ". . . I know how to play," ". . . I am beautiful," ". . . I am learning to read," ". . . I can cut," ". . . everybody makes me happy." These children surely are not likely to believe for very long that they are special because they can color, ride a bike, or like to play. What might these children think when they discover just how trivial these criteria for being special are? The examples described above are not unusual; similar work can be found in schools all over the country.

WHY SHOULD children's attention so insistently be turned inward? Can such superficial flattery really boost self-esteem; and are young children's minds being intellectually engaged by such exercises? Can a child's propensity to explore and investigate worthwhile topics be strengthened by such activities? Is it possible the cumulative effect of such practices, when used frequently, undermines children's perceptions of their teachers as being thoughtful adults, worthy of respect?

Many books and kits for teachers recommend similar exercises that help children "feel good about themselves." One typical example is a booklet with tear-out worksheets called *Building Self-Esteem with Koala-Roo*.[4] One page is bordered by the phrase "YOU ARE SPECIAL!", which appears fourteen times, in capital letters. In the page's upper left-hand corner is a drawing of a smiling koala bear waving one paw, while holding a heart that says "I love you" in the other. The heading on the page is "You Are Special." Below the heading is a line for a child's name following the phrase "You are Special!" again. This is followed by "I am very glad that I have been your X grade teacher." No space is provided for the teacher's own name. This line is followed by text that reads "There's no one else quite like you," "You're one of a kind," "unique," and so forth.

I doubt whether the complete text of the page just described meets the readability index for kindergartners, first graders, or any children young enough to be taken in by such excessive pandering. It would be surprising (and disappointing) if children old enough to read these pages are inspired by their content.

Another example of the genre can be found advertised in a popular teachers' magazine. Titled "Excellence in Early Childhood," the ad promotes a unit of activities called "I Am Special" for 3-, 4- and 5- year-olds. The kit being offered includes a student activity book filled with colorful hands-on projects and illustrated stories, and a teacher guide for twenty-nine lesson plans, stories, and finger plays designed to promote "feeling good abut oneself." In answer to the question of what children will learn from the "I Am Special" kit, the advertisement claims that children "become aware that they are created in a very special and unique way," and "see themselves as good and worthwhile individuals." These illustrations are just two examples from among many similar teaching aids I have seen in early childhood classrooms all over the U.S.

The concept of specialness expressed in these activities seems, by definition, contradictory: If everybody is special, nobody is special. Furthermore, frequent feedback about how special a child is might even raise some doubt along the lines of "Methinks thou dost protest too much"!

In similar fashion, it is not clear whether the traditional "show-and-tell" (or "bring and brag") activity used in traditional early childhood programs does as much to enhance self-esteem as it does to encourage children to be unduly concerned about the impressions they make on others or to learn the techniques of one-upmanship. Many early childhood specialists justify the practice on the grounds that it gives children a chance to practice an early form of public speaking and thereby to strengthen their verbal expressive skills. Some teachers also hope children will sharpen their listening skills as they watch their peers show and tell. However, it is not clear what happens to children who feel that what they have to show and tell cannot compete with their peers' contributions. Furthermore, my observations of such group sessions suggest that more than a few children seem to be tuning out their peers rather than learning to listen to them.

I believe there are other more meaningful and intellectually defensible ways for children to speak to groups of their peers. For example, children can report discoveries and experiences derived from their own efforts, ideas, and real accomplishments.[5]

THE TREND toward overemphasizing self-esteem and self-congratulation may be due to a general desire to correct earlier traditions of eschewing compliments for fear of making children conceited. However, the current practices described above seem to me to be over-corrections of such traditions.

Although there is little doubt that many children arrive at preschool and school with less than optimum self-esteem, telling them otherwise is not likely to have much effect. Feelings cannot be learned from direct instruction. Furthermore, constant messages about how wonderful one is may raise doubts about the credibility of the message and the messenger.

Self-esteem is most likely to be fostered when children have challenging opportunities to build self-confidence and esteem through effort, persistence, and the gradual accrual of skills, knowledge, and appropriate behavior. In addition, adults can show their esteem for children in more significant ways than the awarding of gold stars and happy faces. Esteem is conveyed to children when adults and peers treat them with respect, ask them for their views and preferences (even if they are not acceded to), and provide opportunities for real decisions and choices about those things that matter to the children. Young children's opinions, suggestions, and preferences should be solicited respectfully and considered seriously. To be sure, some children come up with wild or silly notions, and their peers will quickly tell them so. In the course of discussion, however, teachers can gain insight into how children understand the matters at hand and can make sound decisions about which children need their help.

Cheap success in a succession of trivial tasks most likely will not foster self-esteem. Young children are more apt to benefit from real challenge and hard work than from frivolous one-shot activities.

For example, in many early childhood programs, the amount of time and effort given to activities related to holidays seems excessive. Although festive occasions alleviate the routine of daily life, like anything else, they can be overdone. Early childhood educators traditionally have emphasized that play is children's natural way of learning.[6] Indeed, a large body of research and years of practical experience attest to the powerful role of play in all facets of learning in the early years.

It is just as natural, however, for young children to learn through investigation. Children are born natural- and social scientists. Like anthropologists, they devote much time and energy to investigating and making sense of their environments. During the preschool and early school years, teachers can capitalize on this in-born disposition by engaging children in investigations through project work. In-depth investigations of real topics, real environments, events, and objects are worthy of children's attention and understanding.

In the course of such undertakings, children negotiate with their teachers to determine the questions to be answered, the studies to be undertaken, and ways to represent their findings in media such as paintings, drawings, and dramatic play. Project work provides children with ample opportunity for real discussion, decision making, cooperation, initiative, negotiation, compromise, and evaluation of the outcomes of their efforts. In this way, children learn the criteria of self-esteem. This self-esteem can be related to their contribution to the work of the group, to the quality of the effort, and its results.

Most of the tasks offered to young children in early childhood classes allow for individual effort and achievement. However, the interpersonal processes that foster healthy self-esteem require the amount of individual work to be balanced with group work in which each child can contribute to the total group effort through cooperation with other students.

EARLY CHILDHOOD practitioners are right to be diligent in encouraging children through the use of frequent positive feedback. The distinction between praise and flattery is often blurred however. Gushing over a child's fingerpainting may be accepted by the child with pleasure. But, it is difficult to know when frequent praise begins to lose its value and is dismissed by children as empty teacher talk. If children become accustomed to frequent praise, some of them will think its inevitable occasional absence is a rebuke—even when this is not intended. It is difficult for adults to maintain a constant flow of meaningful praise. And, if a child's sense of self-worth can be raised by simple flattery from one person, it just as easily can be deflated by another.

A large body of evidence indicates that children benefit from positive feedback. But, praise and rewards are not the only methods of reinforcement. Another kind of positive feedback is *appreciation.* By appreciation I mean positive reinforcement related explicitly and directly to the *content* of the child's interest and effort. If a child poses a thoughtful question, a teacher might, for example, come to class the next day with a new reference book. Or, she might share with the children ideas generated from reflecting on problems they had raised concerning procedures to try. In these ways, the teacher treats children's concerns with respect, thereby deepening interest in the issues they have raised and providing positive feedback without deflecting children from the content. The important point here is that the teacher shows in a positive way that she appreciates their concerns *without taking their minds off the subjects at hand or directing their attention inwards.* When children see that their concerns and interests are being taken seriously, they are more likely to raise them in the next discussion, and to take their own ideas seriously. Teachers can strengthen children's disposition to wonder, reflect, raise questions, and generate alternative solutions to practical and intellectual problems. Certificates, gold stars, stickers, and trophies also provide children with positive feedback, but the salience of such devices

Cheap success in a succession of trivial tasks most likely will not foster self-esteem.

is likely to deflect the children's and teacher's attention from the content of the work at hand.

Another form of frequent praise stems from teachers' eagerness to reinforce cooperative behavior among young children. Teachers often praise children's efforts by saying such things as "I was really glad when you used your words to get your turn. . . ." or "It made me happy to see you share your wagon with Sally." Such strategies may be helpful when first teaching children how to use verbal strategies for conflict resolution. But, like all strategies, they can be overdone, especially as children reach the preschool years. At issue here is the hypothesis that frequent praise can be taken by children to mean that the praised behavior is not expected—as though the unspoken end of these kinds of elliptical sentences is ". . . because I never expected you to." It may be that children sense our unspoken expectations, and will, indeed, frequently live up to them. Such teacher responses also may imply that the rationale for the desirable behavior is to please the teacher.

It would seem more appropriate for teachers to exercise a quiet and calm authority by stating clearly and respectfully precisely what behavior is expected as occasions arise. Because young children are in the early stages of acquiring interactive and conflict-resolution skills, teachers will have to exercise patience in using this strategy.

ANOTHER APPROACH that teachers might use to make children less dependent upon praise from others is to help them develop and apply their own evaluation criteria.

For example, rather than have children take their work home every day, encourage them to collect it in a special folder or portfolio for a week or so. Then at some point, encourage children to select an item they want to take home and discuss with them the criteria for selection they might apply. The emphasis should not be on whether a child likes a piece of work, or whether it is good or bad. Instead, guide children to think about whether a piece of work includes all they want it to, or whether it is sufficiently clear or accurate, or whether it shows progress compared to the last item they took home, and so forth. At first, parents might be disappointed when the flow of paintings, collages, and worksheets is interrupted; but teachers can help parents to engage their children in fruitful discussion about the criteria of selection used, thus encouraging children to take seriously their own evaluations of their work.

Similarly, when children are engaged with others in project work, they can evaluate the extent to which they have answered the questions they began with, and assess the work accomplished on criteria developed with their teacher concerning the accuracy, completeness, and interest value of their final products.[7] The children should be encouraged to discuss what they might do the next time they undertake an investigation, thus strengthening the propensity to vary their strategies and use their own experience as a source from which to improve their next undertakings. Applying such criteria to their own efforts helps children to become engaged in their work. It also helps them to gain understanding and competence rather than drawing their attention toward themselves or to the image they project to others.

When children are engaged in challenging and significant activities, they are bound to experience some failures, reverses, and rebuffs. Parents and teachers have an important role to play—not in avoiding such events—but in helping children cope constructively when they fail to get what they want—whether it's a turn with a toy or success at a task. In such incidents, the teacher can say something like "I know you're disappointed, but there's tomorrow, and you can try again." As long as the teacher accepts a child's feelings and responds respectfully, the child is more likely to learn from the incident than to be harmed by it. Children are able to cope with rebuffs, disappointments, and failures when adults acknowledge and accept their feelings of discouragement and at the same time tell children they can try again another time.

Another approach is to teach children how to use what they have learned from their own experiences as a source of encouragement. A teacher might, for example, help a child recall an earlier incident when he or she struggled with a task or situation and eventually mastered it.

Learning to deal with setbacks, and maintaining the persistence and optimism necessary for childhood's long and gradual road to mastery: These are the real foundations of lasting self-esteem. Children who are helped to develop these qualities will surely respect themselves—though they probably will have better things to think about.

REFERENCES

[1] National Association of Elementary School Principals. 1990. *Early Childhood Education and the Elementary School Principal. Standards for Quality Programs for Young Children*. Arlington, Va.: NAESP.

[2] Sandy McDaniel quoted in "Political Priority #1: Teaching Kids to Like Themselves," *New Options*, issue no. 27, April 28, 1986.

[3] Corporation for Public Broadcasting. 1991. *Celebrate Yourself. Six Steps to Building Your Self-Esteem*. Washington, D.C.: Corporation for Public Broadcasting.

[4] Femdel, L. and B. Ecker. 1989. *Building Self-Esteem with Koala-Roo*. Glencoe, Ill.: Scott, Foresman and Co.

[5] Katz, L.G. and S.C. Chard. 1989. *Engaging Children's Minds: The Project Approach*. Norwood, N.J.: Ablex Publishing Corp.

[6] Isenberg, J. and N.L. Quisenberry. 1988. *Play: A Necessity for All Children*. A position paper of the Association for Childhood Education International. Wheaton, Md.: Association for Childhood Education International.

[7] Katz and Chard, op. cit.

African American Children

Ruby Burgess

Ruby Burgess is the dean of instruction at Philander Smith College in Little Rock, Arkansas. She is a consultant for the Congress of National Black Churches Carnegie-Project Spirit Curriculum Development Committee and the Smith Day Care Center, Inc. in Macon, Georgia. She serves on the Arkansas Minority Teacher Recruitment Advisory Council and the NAEYC Teacher Education Advisory Panel (NCATE Folio Review Team).

Education in the United States has been characterized by the values of conformity, extreme competition, and high academic achievement — at the cost of social, emotional, and character development. (*Get good grades no matter the cost or method* is the general rule of thumb.) These values, particularly conformity and extreme competition, hinder some children from learning rather than helping them to learn. It has become clearer over the past 25 to 30 years that school systems in the United States are inadequately equipped with the personnel, knowledge, materials, resources, and *know how* to educate children from culturally diverse backgrounds. Yet we know that when children and their teachers share the same cultural background or when the teacher who is in an alien cultural environment is not afraid to express her own culture, the teaching act becomes easier and this environment becomes much more supportive for children.

"Differences in the ways groups think and act are more than a matter of using different words or performing different actions for the same purpose. The behavior of people varies, and the beliefs, values, and assumptions that underlie behavior differ as well. Culture influences both behavior and the

psychological processes on which it rests. Culture forms the prism through which members of a group see the world and create shared meanings." (Bowman, 1989) Therefore, a group's culture is reflected by the group's view of and behavior in educational settings. This brief article is an attempt to increase the sensitivity to and the awareness of parents, directors, and teachers to the cultural perspective of African American children in an early childhood environment and to share some insights about African American culture.

How Children Learn

First, consider how African American children exhibit their culture in educational settings. Classic and current research suggests that African American children:

• are people oriented;

• view things in their entirety;

• prefer inferential reasoning;

• prefer novelty, personal freedom, and distinctiveness;

• are not word dependent but are proficient in both verbal and non-verbal communication;

• prefer oral/aural modalities for learning and communicating;

• use internal cues for problem solving; and

• rely on situational context for interpreting meaning.

From *Child Care Information Exchange,* March/April 1993, pp. 35-38. © 1993 by Exchange Press, Inc. Reprinted with permission from Exchange Press, Inc., P.O. Box 2890, Redmond, WA 98073.

Photograph by Bonnie Neugebauer

Social Orientation

One of the things that we know from the research is that our children, African American children, are highly people oriented. There is a people-to-people orientation in the African American culture that seems to override all the other cultural characteristics. There have been a number of researchers who have clarified this. De Meco in 1983 had African American and European American children look at pictures and pull out pictures they thought meant school. The African American children always chose pictures that had people in them — either teachers or other children. European American children pulled out pictures that focused on the setting — desks, materials, audio visual materials; there were no people in the pictures. There is an object orientation in European Americans as opposed to a people orientation in African Americans.

For African American children the psychological and social environment is as important in the teaching and learning process as is the physical and cognitive environment.

Another study looked at what helped the children develop adaptive behaviors. In the 183 children that Yetal studied, she found that African American

children preferred and used social and people skills in order to do what they were supposed to do and to help them develop adaptive behaviors.

Yet another study looked at how Black children determine what is okay and what is not okay and what they prefer in the way of stimuli. This comes from what they call face and emotions research. Black children were by and large able to determine what people were thinking by looking at their faces first, looking at their emotions. They were also better able to remember. When you asked them about events, they recounted the events based on people's faces and the emotions that were a part of the environment.

Positive development is the process of transforming a child's potential or promising abilities into actual skills or talents. It is a process initiated and sustained by the interaction of the child with his total environment and her "significant others" who are present in that environment. All of these components must work together to maximize the child's development.

It is not feasible to separate and isolate the physical and cognitive environment as early childhood education programs continue to do in order to assess program effectiveness. This is not the most effective way to assess program effectiveness for African American children. Rather, the social, emotional, and psychological nuances of the environment must also be assessed in order to determine their effectiveness for African American children. Rose Marie Duhime tells the story of a kindergarten teacher who said to a child who was African American, "I love you." The child looked at her and said, "I wish you would tell your face."

Program Content

Program content is also an important factor in designing educational settings which will maximize the potential of all children:

"Excellence in education must prepare a student for self knowledge and to become a contributing problem solving member of his or her own community and in the wider world as well. No child can be ignorant of, or lack respect for, his or her own unique cultural group and meet others in the world on an equal footing. We believe that this type of excellence in education is the right of the masses and not merely for a small elite." (The National Alliance of Black School Educators, 1984)

Therefore, two keys to creating educational settings which foster African American children's total development are total environmental evaluation for acceptance of cultural diversity and relevant curriculum content.

The classroom that accommodates and is responsive to the African American child is one that stresses the importance of children working with and getting along with other children, children being responsible for themselves as well as other children, and children respecting themselves as well as other children. Many times early childhood classrooms will have rules about respecting the property of others while never suggesting that children should respect the people in the environment. Conversely, African American culture stresses respect of people over respect of property. The African American value of respecting people over things presupposes that, when one respects another person, he/she will naturally respect the person's property.

Teacher Mindset

Teachers who are responsive to African American children in their classroom are creative, flexible, and innovative. They use every method and technique that they have within their grasp to teach the children. In addition, they create new techniques and methods based upon the children's day-to-day contributions to strengthen the teaching/learning process. These teachers trust their own instincts and internal cues to read and interpret social, psychological, and emotional nuances of the environment in order to determine if they might in some way be an alienating force in the teaching/learning process. They are not bound to a curriculum that is set up by someone else outside of themselves and their children's selves, outside of the environment. They are responsive to the African American child's culture. They are flexible enough to expect and work with the unexpected. Teachers who need to be able to predict everything that is going to happen will be in constant conflict with most children and with African American children in particular. All teachers need systematic retraining to include self-exploration of their own values and self-images.

Affirmation of Culture

African American children need to know who they are, what their culture is; their culture needs to be legitimized.

The curriculum and subject matter in the classroom that is responsive to cultural diversity will be reflective of the cultural background of African American children. It will explore and teach African

Photograph by Bonnie Neugebauer

American history and culture that began in ancient Africa (Kmt) and not "slavery." Materials, children's books, and other resources will reflect African American values and perspectives. The methods and techniques for delivering the content will accommodate various learning styles and ways of interpreting meaning. Activities that require uniqueness, creativity, and innovation will be legitimized by inclusion in the curriculum. Cooperative learning as opposed to competitive learning will also be a legitimate aspect of the curriculum.

And all of us know that for the African American child culture is a real issue. Many African American adults as well as children don't like to express their own culture. They don't like to admit that they are African in origin. They have real problems with it largely due to the total environment of the country, the system, and institutional racism. But we have to legitimize these children and we have to help them understand that they, too, are due respect.

Essential to the curriculum, environment, and teaching/learning process is the emphasis on humanism and the worth and importance of **ALL** people. Unfortunately, this has not been the case in educational programs in the United States. These programs — early childhood through post-graduate — have historically viewed African Americans as commodities, and not human beings (Hale, 1986). African people were brought to the United States as slaves (commodities) for the purpose of increasing the country's economic worth. This image continues to be a significant underlying theme of educational thought, programs, curriculum, and teaching processes.

Excellent early childhood programs will have as their major goal the eradication of the "commodity" image; they will work to wipe this image from the lives of Black children. They will build on diversity and will develop a curriculum that is culturally relevant for all of the children and that focuses on self-awareness and self-esteem. It is in the attitude — an attitude that produces growth and development in all children. Good programs will exercise and develop respect by activities which build upon diversity and maximize the potential of each child to the benefit of the child's own community and people and beyond.

References

Akbar, Na'im. Address Before the National Black Child Development Institute Annual Conference. San Francisco: NBCDI Proceedings, 1975.

Bowman, Barbara T. "Educating Language — Minority Children," in **ERIC Digest**. Urbana, IL: ERIC Publications, 1989.

Hale-Benson, J. E. **Black Children: Their Roots, Culture and Learning Styles** (Revised Edition). Baltimore: John Hopkins University Press, 1988.

Hilliard, Asa. "Equal Education Opportunity and Quality Education," **Anthropology and Education Quarterly**, 92, (1978).

McAdoo, H. P. (editor). **Black Children: Social, Educational, and Parental Environments**. Beverly Hills: Sage Publications, Inc., 1985.

National Alliance of Black School Educators. **Saving the African American Child**, A Report of the National Alliance of Black Academic and Cultural Excellence. Washington, DC: NABSE, 1984.

Shade, Barbara. "Afro-American Cognitive Style: A Variable in School Success," **Review of Educational Research**, 52, 219-224, 1982.

Shade, Barbara. "Afro-American Patterns of Cognition," in **Educational Resources Information Center (ERIC) Document**, #ED223741. Urbana, IL: ERIC Publications, 1982.

Grounds for Play: Sound, Safe, and Sensational

Programs that make a difference in young children's lives do not happen by accident. Rather, these are the result of careful planning, ongoing and systematic evaluation, and the hard work of dedicated professionals. Quality programs are characterized by a developmentally appropriate curriculum, an experienced and informed staff, and a built environment which optimizes children's growth and development through play.*

Pauline Davey Zeece
Susan K. Graul

Pauline Davey Zeece and Susan K. Graul are at the Department of Family and Consumer Sciences, University of Nebraska-Lincoln, Lincoln, NE. This manuscript has been assigned Journal Series No. 10037, Agricultural Research Division, University of Nebraska.

Perceptions of the value of children's play have changed considerably since the beginning of the century (Rubin, Fein, & Vanderberg, 1983). Currently, it is believed that play — both indoor and outdoor — is one of the most effective ways in which chil-

See Bredekamp (1986), Hildebrand (1989), and Weinstein and David (1987).

dren learn about the ever-changing world. It serves vital functions by integrating and balancing all aspects of human functioning (Rogers & Sawyers, 1988). Through play, young children gain mastery over their bodies, discover the world and themselves, acquire new skills, and cope with complex and conflicting emotions (Rubin et al, 1983; Vygotsky, 1976). Bruner (1972; cited in Wasserman, 1992) posits that playful, flexible interactions early in a child's life function as a model for adult problem-solving later on. Thus, it becomes important to understand the characteristics of the built environ-

ment which best facilitate children's play. While increasing attention has focused on children's indoor play, less has been published about optimal outdoor play environments. Ideally, outdoor environments (or playgrounds) serve children best when these are sound, safe, and sensational. This article provides general principles of developmentally appropriate practice and general principles of design for the built environment. In addition, information on careful planning, ongoing mastery, and development of a viable site safety plan is presented. Finally, specific ideas about how to create sensational playgrounds from the unique philosophy and expertise of each program are explored.

Facilitating a Sound Playground Design

General Principles of Developmentally Appropriate Practice

Sound playground design is nested first in the context of developmentally appropriate practice. This means that a playground is conceptualized and planned to meet the needs of children of specific ages. Thus, it is helpful to have an understanding of what the children who will be the primary users of a playground typically do in terms of their physical, motor, social, emotional, and cognitive development. For example, if infants and toddlers are users of a playground, the design should include areas that not only encourage movement, language, and stimulate senses but also protects the children from the elements and older children. The space must provide adequate challenge for different ages, while at the same time encouraging interaction among all users.

A developmentally sound playground provides for individual differences among users. Thus, special needs, special interests, and cultural sensitivity are woven into the design. Shaw (1987) suggests that disabled children are children first and disabled second. Thus, playgrounds for children with special needs should first be considered as places for child's play. He recommends that what makes the solution to a play environment for one group of children different from another lies not in design guidelines, but in the execution of the playground parts. Quality playgrounds integrate design components and playground parts so that these respond to the unique social, cultural, and physical needs of the users and the site's constraints.

General Principles of Design: Children and the Built Environment

David and Weinstein (1987) have identified common features in well-designed child spaces; these may be applied to playground design:

Playgrounds, like all built environments, have both a direct and an indirect symbolic impact on children. Outdoor spaces impact directly on children by facilitating or impeding activities, by creating or limiting opportunities, and by encouraging or discouraging challenges of all kinds (e.g., a playground which provides multi-levels and easy access challenges in healthy ways and encourages; a playground which requires adult input or direction for the majority of activities discourages). All aspects of the outdoor space work together to give children very real messages about what they can and cannot do and what they may and may not attempt.

The indirect, symbolic meaning of a space also impacts on children. While this impact may, in part, be unique to each child, it is generally believed that an inadequate, inappropriate, and uninviting playground indicates to children that (at the very least) activities in that space are not high-priority or highly valued (e.g., unkept, unmanaged, and unplanned outdoor spaces give the message "I don't care — this space is not special," and a playground with no open spaces to run, throw, pedal or just "hang out" limits children's choices and opportunities to try or practice new skills). For some children, the symbolic meaning of the environment may actually impact in part on self-worth (David & Weinstein, 1987). This may also be true for teachers and caregivers working in an inadequate and/or poorly designed space.

Playgrounds create opportunities to optimize child growth across all developmental areas. Fulfilling the need to explore, move, and play within the context of a responsive, interesting outdoor environment optimizes development in all areas (David & Weinstein, 1987). One of the most unfortunate myths about playgrounds is that their primary function is only to facilitate physical and motor development. Developmental progress is an integrated activity; growth (or inhibition of growth) in one area influences all facets of a child's being. Running, climbing, digging, and exploring are typically identified as good activities for outdoor spaces. But in reality, there are very few indoor activities that cannot also happen outside when adults are willing to think creatively and plan innovatively. For example, a walk can be an adventure when it becomes a walk in the rain under a parachute. Well-bundled children can brave freezing temperatures outside long enough to place and retrieve a pan of water for a science experiment about ice. Additionally, social and dramatic play, creative and artistic endeavor, cognitive and linguistic advances happen everyday on playgrounds. It makes sense that these should be optimized by well-planned spaces.

Well-designed playgrounds provide opportunities to develop competence and a positive sense of self. Playground design facilitates the development of young children's competence by providing opportunities to develop mastery and control over the physical environment. Successful manipulation of a space and its components helps a child to feel "I can do this. I'm OK!" (e.g., a playground which is multi-faceted and/or multi-leveled provides children several ways to climb and view the world, thus optimizing their chances of being successful at some point during their exploration of the environment). The layout of a playground builds confidence when environmental cues help children to successfully plan and carry out goal-directed activities (David & Weinstein, 1987; Golbeck, 1985). Children prosper when they can discern (with minimal adult intervention) what activities are appropriate for each area of a playground. Their sense of competence is further enhanced and their development enriched when a playground design unifies all parts of a widely varied, juxtaposed outdoor space (e.g., big vs. little; open vs. closed; single- vs. multiuser) (Shaw, 1987).

Well-designed playgrounds foster a sense of security and trust and create a feeling of belonging. Secure and predictable surroundings are not a luxury, but a prerequisite to learning. A well-designed playground is both predictable and challenging. It gives young children the message that the risks taken are within reasonable limits, that the rules governing space usage and activities result from a thoughtful coordination of the playground's parts, and that learning and exploration begin in well-defined spaces. Knowing what to expect in and from an outdoor space encourages children to seek out the novel and unexpected in appropriate ways. Understanding that a space can remain the same while an activity changes allows children to manipulate their play and to challenge themselves across all areas of their development. Constancy in the overall design of a playground helps children to develop a sense that "This space is mine; I know this space; I belong here."

Maintaining a Safe Outdoors

Safety, security, and liability constitute major factors in determining the quality of children's outdoor play environments. The goals of safety are best balanced with the goals of providing stimulating and challenging environments for children's development and play (Moore, Goltsman, & Iacofano, 1987). Adults ideally work to develop reasonable ways to prevent accidents, while allowing risk to promote developmentally appropriate practice. Mooreland, McIntyre, Iacofano, and Goltsman (1985) outline key components of a *proactive* approach which centers on the prevention (rather than the management) of incidents which threaten child safety on a playground. The key strategies in this approach include evaluating and reporting incidents which threaten safety; developing a coordinated system for adult supervision; creating a program of first-aid preparedness among children and adults (including such things as training in CPR, first aid, and accident prevention); encouraging multilevel communication between parents, teachers, and other playground supervisors; and developing a site safety plan.

Identifying Reporting, and Evaluating Accidents or Playground Safety "Hotspots"

Playground safety is optimized when the adults who monitor their usage are aware of the patterns of past accidents, the presence of current high-risk areas, and the potential for future unique or predictable hazards. An evaluation process can be conceptualized or developed to determine where, when, how, and why accidents occur (Mooreland et al., 1985). To develop a proactive, rather than a reactive, playground safety program, it is valuable to chart accident data over time.

- Where do accidents occur?
- What time of day? Week? Year?
- What season? Weather conditions?
- What happened? To whom? Is this a "repeat" accident for a particular child? A particular-aged child? A child from a specific group or classroom?
- What was done to help the child at the time of the accident? To help onlooking children or adults? To prevent reoccurrence?
- What role did onlookers (children or adults) play before, during, and after the accident?
- How was the accident reported or logged? What formal reports were completed? What program or legal actions were taken?
- How were parents, guardians, staff members, and administrators informed?

It is also useful to monitor safety, as well as accident trends. In this way, risk and safety management strategies can be built on program and playground strengths and weaknesses. The National Council distributes the Safety First Checklist (McIntyre, Goltsman, & Kline, 1989), which contains a comprehensive list of playground safety hazards. This resource can be used not only as a playground-site-inspection system, but also as an objective criterion for evaluating the safeness and suitability of playground sites, surfaces, and equipment.

Awareness of high-risk areas on a playground also contributes to overall safety. For example, the U.S. Consumer Products Safety Commission (CPSC; 1991) has identified falls to surfaces as the single greatest hazard on a playground (accounting for 70 percent of all playground accidents). Likewise, in order of risk or accident potential, merry-go-rounds, slides, swings, seesaws, and climbers have also been identified as high-risk playground sites. These and other related findings, as well as safety recommendations, are summarized in the CPSC handbook.

Developing a Coordinated System for Adult Supervision

Well-designed playgrounds provide many opportunities for adults to supervise children's play. Effective, well-coordinated supervision of playground activities is crucial to safe and successful outdoor play and subsequent learning. Such supervision requires that adults encourage and model safe behavior on a playground. Through wise design, training, and careful attention, adults tell children to "Go for it!" or "Not now, not here!" Thus, the level of adult supervision and allowed risk are closely tied to program philosophy and to each teacher's or caregiver's personal comfort zone. Adults who encourage children to take reasonable chances, but who then visibly cringe, may do as much (or more) damage as those who overprotect youngsters. The key is in the "goodness of fit" between prescribed practice and personal educational goals for children (Wasserman, 1992).

Additionally, a coordinated system of adult supervision requires an adequate adult-child ratio and a realistic spacing of adults on a playground during outdoor play. It is helpful to create designated supervision areas or to divide children into smaller groups when they use a larger playground. Thus, supervision requires that adults watch, act, and react to young children as they play, grow, and learn in the outdoor spaces of a program.

5. CURRICULAR APPLICATIONS

Creating a Program of First-Aid Preparedness Among Children and Adults

Safe behavior can be taught and learned. Even the youngest child can develop a rudimentary familiarity with the safety "rules" associated with an outdoor play area. Safety is enhanced when children are told (and then periodically reminded) about what *can* and *cannot* happen on a playground (e.g., climb here, not there; trikes on the track, not on the stage). Adults optimize playground safety by making such rules clear, short, and developmentally appropriate and consistently enforce them.

First-aid preparedness also mandates concisely stated and often-rehearsed emergency procedures for minor and major accidents associated with outdoor activities (Moore et al., 1987). Parents, teachers, or caregivers should ask themselves the following questions to ensure first-aid preparedness:

• Are first-aid supplies complete? Systematically replaced? Well located?

• Do all staff and children understand emergency routines? Are the routines reviewed regularly? Updated?

• Is there a CPR- and first-aid-trained staff person on the site at all times? Is training updated?

• Do staff talk to children after accidents occur to seek their input and dispel their concerns?

• Are community and program resources utilized to provide safety information to all adults involved with children in a program?

Encouraging Multilevel Communication

Communication is an important part of program quality and playground safety. When adults share insight into and concern about young children, both individual and group needs can be better met in planning and monitoring outdoor activities. Systematic, ongoing dialogue between parents and teachers or caregivers provides a mechanism by which children's safety sense can be monitored.

Likes and dislikes, fears and accomplishments, and understanding and misunderstanding about playground safety rules can be discussed in the context of children's best interests. Goals for culturally sensitive, safe, and stimulating outdoor play can be planned between parents and teachers or caregivers, between teachers or caregivers and children, and among children themselves.

Developing a Viable Site-Safety Plan

A well-constructed site-safety plan is as important as a well-developed curriculum. A site safety plan involves a careful analysis of playground site characteristics. Initially, an assessment of the soil, surface drainage, utility location, visibility, and accessibility of the playground is essential in the development and maintenance of a safe, outdoor play space (Landscape Structures, 1992). An understanding of the human and cultural features, the existing (or potentially accessible) equipment, and the social and geographical setting within the community is an equally useful component of a site analysis. Finally, a site safety plan may include five key criteria for further assessing an optimal outdoor play environment: accessibility, safe challenge, diversity and clarity, graduated challenges, and flexibility and choice (Moore et al., 1987).

Safe playgrounds are *accessible* to both child users and adult supervisors. The comfort level of *all* users contributes to playground safety. When children have spaces where they can play creatively and safely and adults have spaces where they can supervise such activities, everyone prospers. Accessibility enhances usage and promotes the notion that "this is a place where we all belong — where we all live and learn together."

Safe playgrounds facilitate *safe challenge*. The fine line between risk and hazard on a playground rests in safe challenge. Outdoor spaces which allow a child to risk through careful adult planning provide opportunities for children to stretch and grow across

all areas of their development. Safe challenge implies "Try it; I'll help you be successful; it won't be easy, but it will be worth it and wonderful!"

Safe playgrounds provide *diversity and clarity.* Having many things to do and many ways to do the same thing provides a safe focus for children in outdoor spaces. Planned diversity in an outdoor environment reduces inappropriate activities created by boredom (or even curiosity). Clarity in playground design creates subtle direction and gives children a sense of security. This, in turn, promotes exploration and learning.

Safe playgrounds promote *graduated challenges.* Children enter outdoor spaces with a variety of needs. Additionally, as they become familiar with a playground and as they grow and develop over time, their needs change. A safe playground provides spaces which facilitate a mastery of skills in steps and graduated challenges. This also allows children opportunities to regress or to relearn a previously mastered skill. It allows them a way to go back to an area or activity where they have achieved mastery, when a new challenge becomes overwhelming or discouraging.

Safe playgrounds provide *flexibility and choice.* Flexibility in a playground environment can come in the form of multiuse and multilevel spaces. It often evolves from creative pathways, unified (but distinct) parts, and the addition and deletion of equipment. But flexibility is also part of the mindset of the adults who supervise children's outdoor spaces. It is best fostered when children are allowed to redefine space usage (within limits) and encouraged to think of other places and ways to do old favorites and new untried activities.

Creating the Sensational Outdoor Playspace

Sound playgrounds are built on sound child development and design principles. Safe playgrounds are fostered in the context of careful planning and ongoing monitoring of playground characteristics and safety rules and procedures. But sensational playgrounds are created first and foremost deep within the core of the programs which house and support them. The sensational playground is formed from the unique philosophy of each early childhood program. It evolves systematically from a program's beliefs about how young children learn best and how adults and the built environment facilitate this learning. In addition to a unique philosophy which drives its focus, Shaw (1987) suggests that the playground must be given a unique spirit to create a sense of place for all users. Sensational playgrounds feel like special and unique places to all who use them.

Sensational playgrounds evolve from programs where adults recognize and invest in the notion that good playground design comes from an identifiable knowledge base and a specific expertise. Thus, playground designers possess the ability to assess adult, child, and program needs, to translate these needs into spatial and programmatic referents in the context of a unique program philosophy, to analyze site potential and drawbacks, and to maximize resources (usually limited) to create the best possible outdoor space for children and adults. Additionally, sensational playgrounds reside in programs where the final form of the play space is conceptualized, even when the playground is being constructed in painfully slow stages. Thus, although the progress is staged, the final outcome is part of a predictable and unified environmental game plan.

Sensational playgrounds link and unify outdoor environments in effective physical, spatial, and psychological ways. They are characterized by a wealth of spaces that "create a rich landscape that will tolerate and support a wide variety of child-generated activities" (Shaw, 1987, p. 194). They have key places which support a wide array of activities for a wide array of children and an inventive system of parts and pathways which link key activities and areas together.

Finally, sensational playgrounds support the view that learning does not stop at the playground entrance. Rather playgrounds provide a learning link for all areas of a program. Each sensational outdoor space is unique; the children, the adults, the program philosophy, the physical site characteristics, and the program economic constraints are deliberately, skillfully, and carefully integrated into the best possible playground.

Conclusion

Sound, safe, and sensational playgrounds create exciting environments for children to observe, explore, and manipulate their world. With adult help and supervision, children prosper in all developmental domains (i.e., cognitive, social, emotional, and physical) and are able to reach their full potential through an enriched playground setting.

References

Bredekamp, S. (1987). *Developmentally appropriate practice*. Washington, DC: National Association for the Education of Young Children.

Bruner, J. (1972). The nature and uses of immaturity. *American Psychologist. 27*, 687-708.

David, T., & Weinstein, C. (1987). The built environment and children's development. In C. Weinstein & T. David (Eds.), *Spaces for children: The built environment and child development* (pp. 3-20). New York: Plenum Press.

Frost, J., & Klein, B. (1979). Children's play and playgrounds. Boston: Allyn & Bacon.

Golbeck, S. (1985). Spatial cognition as a function of environmental characteristics. In R. Cohen (Ed.), *The development of spatial cognition* (pp. 41-47). Hillsdale, NJ: Erlbaum.

Hildebrand, V. (1988). Management of child development centers. New York: Macmillan.

Landscape Structures, Mexico Forge. (1992). *How to create a successful playground*. Delano, MN: Landscape Structures.

McIntyre, S., Goltsman, S., & Kline, L. (1989). *Safety first checklist: The site inspection system for play equipment*. Berkeley, CA: MIG Communications.

Moore, R., Goltsman, S., & Iacofano, D. (1987). *Play for all guidelines: Planning. design. and management of outdoor play settings for all children*. Berkeley, CA: MIG Communications.

Moreland, G., McIntyre, S., Iacofano, D., & Goltsman, S. (1985). The risky business of children's play: Balancing safety and challenge in programs and environments for all children. *Children's Environment Quarterly, 2*(4), 24-28.

Rogers, C., & Sawyer, J. (1988). *Play in the lives of children*. Washington, DC: National Association for the Education of Young Children.

Rubin, K., Fein, G., & Vanderberg, B. (1983). Play. In E. Hetherington (Ed.), *Handbook of child psychology* (pp. 693-774). New York: Wiley.

Shaw, L. (1987). Designing playgrounds for able and disabled children. In C. Weinstein & T. David (Eds.), *Spaces for children: The built environment and child development* (pp. 187-216). New York: Plenum Press.

U.S. Consumer Product Safety Commission. (1991). *A handbook for public playground safety. Vol. 1: General Guidelines for new and exciting playgrounds: Vol. 2: Technical guidelines for equipment and surfacing*. Berkeley, CA: MIG Communications.

Vygotsky, L. (1976). Play and its role in the mental development of the child. In J. Bruner, A. Jolly, & K. Sylva (Eds.), *Play — its role in development and evolution* (pp. 537-554). New York: Basic Books.

Wasserman, S. (1992). Serious play in the classroom: How messing around can win you the Noble prize. *Childhood Education, 68*, 133-139. Wheaton, MD: Association for Childhood Education International.

Weinstein, C., & David, T. (Eds.). (1987). *Space for children: The built environment and child development*. New York: Plenum Press.

Wortham, S. (1985). A history of outdoor play 1900-1985: Theories of play and play environments. In J. Frost & S. Sunderlin (Eds.), *When children play* (pp. 3-7). Wheaton, MD: Association for Childhood Education International.

Wortham, S., & Wortham, M. (1983). *A place to play: The why and how of building a basic play structure*. Canyon Lake, TX: Matrix Design.

Reflections

For over 60 years, beginning with the Children's Charter from the White House Conference in 1930 and continuing with federal policy statements annually since then, this nation has vowed to improve the amount and quality of child care available to its families. When it comes to fulfillment of policy statements, however, the actual responsibility for the provision of care and education of the nation's children belongs to the 50 states. A sluggish economy, a new federal administration focusing on other national problems, and massive corporate layoffs have combined to steer states away from increasing support for families. Nationwide, close to half of all child care is unregulated, and child-care assistance is unavailable for large portions of the population. At the same time, budget shortfalls in some states will decrease education and social service spending by 10 to 15 percent this year.

Yet, despite these limiting conditions, a few states have made impressive strides in making child care accessible to working families. A look at the progress made in recent years reveals that 10 states do an excellent job of providing quality care and education. Last year, *Working Mother* commissioned a panel to choose the best states for child care. Panel members rated the states on quality (in terms of ratio of children to adults and group size), availability, safety, and commitment to child care. Their results are in the lead article of this unit. We hope *Working Mother* continues to publicize our nation's efforts to support families.

The 1960s were a time of sweeping legislation for assistance of "culturally disadvantaged" families. Concerted efforts were made across the nation to develop comprehensive programs for the children of poverty. Many of these programs devised a balanced curriculum based on the latest information about child development and maturation. Because the latest evidence was that the early years of childhood are the most crucial in educational development, programs included children between the ages of 3 and 5. The goals were to increase children's language and skills, readying them for public school and thereby breaking the downward cycle of poverty.

Among public policy recommendations is a call for full funding of the national Head Start program and similar preschool programs for children of poverty. Under this presidential administration, Head Start's budget has been increased, though the appropriation of money is still problematic. The need for intervention programs has been documented through the years, and Head Start has proven capable of meeting that need.

Since 1965, the design of Head Start has included education, social services, medical and dental services, and nutritional care. From the beginning of Project Head Start, some educators have questioned the lack of quality control in programs for such large groups of disadvantaged children (e.g., Spodek, B., 1965. "Is Massive Intervention the Answer?" *Educational Leadership*, 23:2, p. 109). These concerns are still being expressed, as reported in the article by Mary Jordan.

It is clear from the successful duration of preschool programs like Head Start that intervention programs are a wide investment of the nation's dollars. One additional factor is also clear: These programs are only as effective as the teachers make them. Fortunately, staff development and education are considered a vital part of many child-care programs. This emphasis on increasing the expertise of teachers has led to higher program quality. Unfortunately, despite the emphasis on staff development, the high turnover of child-care teachers lessens the quality of the program. The clear reasons for high turnover are low pay and difficult working conditions. In a concerted effort to combat compensation and benefit problems, the Child Care Employee Project launched the Worthy Wage Campaign three years ago. Camille Colatosti's article highlights the efforts of the campaign to refocus our nation's priorities on the real costs of child care, particularly decent teacher salaries.

Looking Ahead: Challenge Questions

What role should states take in providing child care for working families? What commitments has your state made to provide care for all children who need it?

What are preschool intervention programs? How do they affect the development of young children? Years after children have attended an intervention program, what benefits can be expected?

Describe the curriculum you would choose for an intervention program. Is it identical to or different from the curriculum you would choose for any other early childhood program? Why?

Are child-care teacher salaries and working conditions adequate in your state? If not, who should pay the increased cost of teacher salaries and benefits?

The 10 Best States For Child Care

Our distinguished panel pinpoints the places where working parents can get the best care for their children

Vivian Cadden

Contributing editor Vivian Cadden is a member of the board of the Child Care Action Campaign. Assistant editor Kara Skruck interviewed the working mothers for this article.

As Mona Fukuhara, a real-estate agent and the mother of a six-year-old, can attest, life is simpler for working parents in Hawaii than it is in many other states. She doesn't have to worry about after-school care because the state provides it in every elementary school. Her son enjoys the activities—ranging from judo lessons to crafts—and the snack he gets before she picks him up at 5:30.

After-school care is just one of the many programs Hawaii offers as it moves toward universal care for preschoolers and grade-schoolers. When it comes to child care, this state's aspirations and matter-of-fact assumption that working families must have access to all-day care are impressive.

The nine other states cited here have all, in various ways, made significant strides in the provision of child care. The importance of these efforts cannot be underestimated because it is really the 50 states—their legislatures, their governors and their agencies—that decide how our nation's children will be cared for. It is the states that decide, for example, how many babies one adult can reasonably care for. (Maryland and Massachusetts are the strictest, with only three; Idaho is the most lax, allowing one adult to care for up to 12 infants!)

States also decide whether children should be vaccinated against such dangerous diseases as polio before attending family child care. And they make critical calls about safety—whether a backyard needs to be fenced or how an infant's formula must be stored. Just as important perhaps, each state creates an atmosphere that determines whether the voices of parents, voluntary

organizations, corporations and child advocates are encouraged—or put down and ignored.

That's why WORKING MOTHER has decided to honor the 10 states that do the best job of promoting and expanding quality care for the children within their borders. These states are outstanding because they attend to the health and safety of children and do the best job of trying to make care available to all children who need it.

WORKING MOTHER's 10 Best were chosen in collaboration with Helen Blank, Senior Child Care Associate of the Children's Defense Fund, and Gwen Morgan, senior consultant with Work/Family Directions, and with the help of a distinguished panel of experts. (See "The Judges.")

Because we are talking about the best, you will see many superlatives here: This state has "superior" child care; that state has an "outstanding" referral service or a "unique" program for training teachers. Although such praise is deserved, it is well to keep in mind a few sobering facts:
- It is estimated that at least 40 percent of all care and 75 percent of family child care in this country is entirely unregulated and thus does not need to meet even the most minimal standards of health and safety.
- There is no state that serves all of its children who are eligible for child care assistance.
- In no state is the compensation for providers or staff workers in child care adequate to keep them from leaving in droves.

That said, let us celebrate the 10 states that do the most.

CALIFORNIA

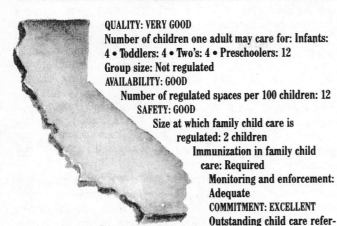

QUALITY: VERY GOOD
Number of children one adult may care for: Infants: 4 • Toddlers: 4 • Two's: 4 • Preschoolers: 12
Group size: Not regulated
AVAILABILITY: GOOD
Number of regulated spaces per 100 children: 12
SAFETY: GOOD
Size at which family child care is regulated: 2 children
Immunization in family child care: Required
Monitoring and enforcement: Adequate
COMMITMENT: EXCELLENT
Outstanding child care referral service that covers entire state; state tax credit for child care costs; statewide network of public and private organizations funding training of providers; family leave law provides 16 weeks for birth/adoption or family illness; state disability insurance that provides 12 weeks of paid leave for workers at firms with 50 or more employees; zoning laws adjusted to encourage family child care.

After Cheryl Escobido, an administrative specialist at an engineering firm in Oakland, had her baby last February, she had no idea how to find child care. "I was completely lost. I didn't even know what types of child care existed," she recalls. Luckily for Escobido, she lives in California, which has a free child care resource and referral network that reaches into every corner of this vast state. She turned to BANANAS, a local agency in the network that helps new parents learn how to choose child care and provides information on licensed providers in their area.

"It was a godsend," says Escobido. "They gave me information about all types of child care to help me choose. They also gave me suggestions on how to interview potential providers—what types of questions to ask. I needed that."

But this state offers more than just help finding child care. California is often cited as a yardstick for other states: It funds a richer variety of child care programs than any other, and it contributes to a public-private partnership to expand the supply and quality of child care. This deep commitment has a long history. During World War II, the federal government funded child care centers so women could work in factories and shipyards. But California was one of the few states to continue funding the centers after the war. "We kept the infrastructure alive in the fifties and sixties so when the great surge of women hit the labor market in the seventies, we were ready for it," says Patty Siegel, executive director of the California Child Care Resource and Referral Network.

And the action hasn't slowed. The Network joined with businesses, foundations and different levels of government to create the California Child Care Initiative, a public-private partnership dedicated to increasing the supply of high-quality child care. For every $2 raised from private firms, foundations and community groups, the state pitches in $1. Already, this effort has recruited and trained more than 3,500 family child care providers, making 14,000 new spaces available for children. This is the kind of program that keeps California out front on child care.

COLORADO

QUALITY: FAIR
Number of children one adult may care for: Infants: 5 • Toddlers: 5 • Two's: 7 • Preschoolers: 10–12
Group size: Regulated for two's and under
AVAILABILITY: GOOD
Number of regulated spaces per 100 children: 11
SAFETY: GOOD
Size at which family child care is regulated: 2 children
Immunization in family child care: Required
Monitoring and enforcement: Adequate
COMMITMENT: EXCELLENT
Particularly strong in creating family child care associations that encourage and train providers; a leader in education and information for new parents; strong alliance with local business groups to improve preschool education and create family-friendly workplaces. ▶

KEY TO THE RATINGS

QUALITY • Number of Children One Adult May Care for: A key indicator of quality in any child care program is the child-to-adult ratio—that is, the number of children a single adult is allowed to care for. For example, a truly high-quality program for infants would not expect one adult to care for more than four babies. As our criteria, we used the standards set by the National Association for the Education of Young Children: Infants (up to one year): 3–4 • Toddlers (one to two years): 3–5 • Two's (two to three years): 4–6 • Preschoolers (three to four years): 7–10.
• Group Size: The maximum number of children that can be in a group. Again, we used NAEYC's recommendations: Infants: 6–8 • Toddlers: 6–12 • Two's: 8–12 • Preschoolers: 14–20.

AVAILABILITY • Number of State-Regulated Spaces: Indicates how many slots per 100 children are available in state-regulated child care centers and family child care homes. Data compiled by Gwen Morgan of Work/Family Directions. (Minnesota ranks highest, with 20 regulated spaces available for every 100 children.)

SAFETY States impose health and safety standards on child care centers, but most children in the U.S. are in family child care. That's why we investigated how well each state regulates family child care.
• Size at Which Family Child Care Is Regulated: When a family child care provider has this number of children (unrelated to her) in her care, she must meet state health and safety standards.
• Immunization: Indicates whether children attending family child care must be immunized for polio, measles, rubella, DPT and mumps.
• Monitoring and Enforcement: How frequently state inspections are mandated and whether there is adequate staff to carry out the inspections and a good system for investigating complaints.

COMMITMENT • Special Efforts: Important ways the state encourages, funds, regulates and otherwise improves the quality, quantity and affordability of child care, such as tax breaks for employers who provide child care, tax credits for parents on child care costs, a parental leave law that makes it easier for parents to care for a newborn or sick child, etc.

An air of excitement pervades the Colorado child care community and it has much to do with the politics of the state. "There is a real sense that we are moving on a lot of fronts and moving together," says Martha Daley, director of the Office of Child Care Initiatives, a Denver advocacy group.

The climate of optimism about child care is a tribute to Governor Roy Romer and his wife, Bea. They have actively worked to improve care for the state's children. Bea Romer chairs First Impressions, the governor's initiative on early childhood that aims to promote public awareness about the crucial first five years of children's lives.

Downtown Denver is the site of one of the most visible achievements of First Impressions—a child care center serving 90 children ranging in age from infancy to five years. The state encouraged 16 businesses, from AT&T to the Denver *Post,* to start the center for their employees' children. Parents will pay tuition, but some scholarships will be available, so that any interested workers, from mail-room clerks to managers, can use the facility. The state was a key investor in the startup and helped find the prime location near major highways, which will make it easy for parents to drop off their children when they go to work. "We hope this will serve as a model for communities throughout the state," says Bea Romer.

Colorado has already worked successfully with other business leaders to expand and improve the quality of child care. The state has long fostered the growth of networks of family child care that fend off the isolation and burnout that cause women to quit. And Colorado Springs is home to Windflower Enterprises, a unique nationally recognized private program that helps to train and support family child care providers.

CONNECTICUT

QUALITY: EXCELLENT
Number of children one adult may care for: Infants: 4 • Toddlers: 4 • Two's: 4 •'
Preschoolers: 10
Group size: Well regulated
AVAILABILITY: VERY GOOD
Number of regulated spots per 100 children: 16
SAFETY: FAIR
Size at which family child care is regulated: 1 child
Immunization in family child care: Not required
Monitoring and enforcement: Adequate
COMMITMENT: VERY GOOD
Ranks high in its expenditures on child care and early-childhood services; leader in the establishment of Family Resource Centers in public schools; family and medical leave of 16 weeks (24 weeks for state employees) for birth/adoption, family illness, personal illness for workers at firms with 75 or more employees.

Lisa Poole is one of the lucky moms to get her four-year-old into one of Connecticut's Family Resource Centers, child care centers that operate out of public schools. Her son, Danny, attends a program at Eastern Point School in Groton, along with 21 other children. There are plenty of activities for these kids, ranging from the water table to books to crafts.

"It's a wonderful program, the best quality," says Poole, an assistant manager at the University of Connecticut's bookstore. And she can afford the program because the state charges sliding-scale fees, based on income. "Often the best-quality care is expensive," Poole says, "and for a while, half my paycheck went for child care. I just couldn't afford it. But now these fees make it feasible for me to work and have my son in a good program."

There are eight centers in Connecticut like the one Danny attends, all started and supported by the state, which hopes to expand them widely. These facilities offer all-day preschool and after-school care for kids up to age 12, as well as family support services, such as books and classes on child rearing. The centers are based on the ideas of one of the nation's leading child-development experts, Edward F. Zigler, director of the Bush Center in Child Development and Social Policy at Yale University, who proposes that public schools around the country offer such services to all working parents.

Family Resource Centers are only one way this innovative state creates, supports and encourages the expansion of high-quality care. Connecticut ranks fourth in the amount of money spent per child on direct child care services. Most recently, the state has embarked on a new program to ensure that all caregivers are properly trained. By 1996, Connecticut hopes to have a system in place to certify every caregiver in early-childhood education. "We hope it will raise the profession of child care to a higher level," says Charisse Hutton, deputy commissioner for the state's department of human resources. "That should translate into better care for kids."

HAWAII

QUALITY: GOOD
Number of children one adult may care for: Infants: 3–4 • Toddlers: 3–6 • Two's: 3–6 • Preschoolers: 8–16
Group size: Regulated
AVAILABILITY: GOOD
Number of regulated spaces per 100 children: 11
SAFETY: GOOD
Size at which family child care is regulated: 3 children
Immunization in family child care: Required
Monitoring and enforcement: Good
COMMITMENT: EXCELLENT
Started the first large-scale experiment in universal child care for working parents. Provides after-school care in every public elementary school.

Care for school-age children is simply not a problem for working parents in Hawaii. "I never have to worry about my son after school," says Mona Fukuhara of Honolulu, whose son Scott is in first grade. She pays $28 a month for a high-quality program right in her son's school. "It makes me feel secure that he's being taken care of so well. If I had to be concerned about what he was doing after school or worry about him getting on a bus to go to another program, I'd be so stressed out at work!"

Scott attends the "A + After School Program," which is available in every public elementary school in Hawaii. Kids can attend every afternoon from two to 5:30, making latchkey children a thing of the past on the islands.

But that's not all Hawaii does. This state has a master plan to eventually provide universal child care for preschool children as well, under its "Open Doors" program. Open Doors is still a model program, serving 1,600 children under the age of five. The lucky parents currently enrolled can pick any licensed child care program and pay a fee based on the family's income. The state pitches in subsidies so that every provider receives the market rate of $350 per child per month. The state already has full-day kindergarten, a boon for working parents and kids alike.

MARYLAND

QUALITY: EXCELLENT
Number of children one adult may care for: Infants: 3 •
Toddlers: 3 • Two's: 6 • Preschoolers: 10
Group size: Well regulated
AVAILABILITY: GOOD
Number of regulated spots per 100 children: 11
SAFETY: VERY GOOD
Size at which family child care is regulated: 1 child
Immunization in family child care: Required
Monitoring and enforcement: Good
COMMITMENT: EXCELLENT
Funds a unique resource and referral service called LOCATE. Family leave law provides state employees with 12 weeks off to care for a newborn or seriously ill child (subject to supervisor's approval). Outstanding public and private cooperation on child care.

If you live in Maryland and need child care, help is only a phone call away. A working mom can call LOCATE, the state's computerized database with information on every licensed child care program in the state. A separate file in the database covers programs for kids with special needs.

Trained counselors answer calls, discuss a parent's needs in terms of location, type of facility, fees and hours. Parents can get the names and phone numbers of caregivers over the phone, or request that a list of 10 possible facilities in their area be mailed to them, along with a pamphlet suggesting the qualities to look for and questions to ask a potential caregiver.

Durlyn Sewell, a case manager for the department of social services in Baltimore, recently learned firsthand just how useful

FLORIDA: A VERY SPECIAL CASE

If there were an award for "The Most Improved State," Florida would win it hands down. "We've always had a great deal of center-based child care here—not all of it good," says Susan Muenchow, executive director of the Florida Children's Forum, which oversees the state's child care referral service. But as of last October, Florida took a giant leap forward to upgrade the quality of care for the most vulnerable children—infants and toddlers. Under previous rules, one adult could care for as many as six infants at once. Under new regulations, one adult can care for no more than four. "It's very exciting. We've convinced the legislature that child care is more than babysitting," says Barbara Weinstein, chief executive officer of Child Care Connection of Broward County.

Over the last five years, Florida has also doubled the money it spends on child care and early-childhood services, established a statewide child care resource and referral network, created more school-age child care and passed laws to upgrade caregivers' training.

Next on the agenda is a big push to expand the supply of licensed family child care, which is greatly underdeveloped in the state. Give Florida a few more years and it may very well make the 10 Best. —V.C.

this service can be. Her children's before- and after-school arrangements fell apart just three days before school started last September. "I never thought I'd call LOCATE myself, but I was hysterical!" she explains. Within a few hours of her call, she had the names of five potential caregivers—and by the first day of school she had signed up with one of them, who happens to live right across the street from her daughters' school.

LOCATE was launched largely because of the efforts made by the Maryland Committee for Children, the state's leading child care advocacy agency and the driving force behind Maryland's initiatives to upgrade and expand child care. Working closely with state agencies, the committee has put together training courses for caregivers, and now holds 437 sessions a year for some 8,800 providers, covering everything from good safety habits to strategies for discipline.

Just as important for the future is the Maryland Child Care Resource Network, a powerful group of corporate, union, foundation and government leaders brought together by the state to expand the supply of child care. So far, the network has set up model programs in three regions in the state—one urban, one suburban and one rural—to identify child care needs, advise parents about their choices and provide assistance to people who want to open child care centers or offer child care in their homes. Millions of private and public dollars have already been dedicated to this ambitious plan to help working parents. "Governor Schaefer is unique," says Sandra Skolnik, executive director of the Maryland Committee for Children. "He believes in his bones in high-quality child care and has been an advocate for it. He truly understands the issue."

MASSACHUSETTS

QUALITY: EXCELLENT
Number of children one adult may care for: Infants: 3 • Toddlers: 3–4
• Two's: 4 • Preschoolers: 10
Group size: Well regulated
AVAILABILITY: VERY GOOD
Number of regulated spaces per 100 children: 15
SAFETY: VERY GOOD
Size at which family child care is regulated: 1 child
Immunization in family child care: Required
Monitoring and enforcement: Good
COMMITMENT: EXCELLENT
Leads the nation in expenditures on child care and early-childhood services; pregnancy-disability and adoption leave that covers employees in businesses of six or more workers for eight weeks and includes benefits; only state to have individual licensing of child care teachers and directors.

Carol Bowen, a marketing consultant in Concord, is grateful for the close attention her state pays to setting high standards in child care. "Susan, my provider, is so conscientious about safety. She never cares for more than two kids under the age of two. She once moved the fire extinguisher from her hallway to the kitchen—a total of three inches—because she learned during a routine inspection that it would be safer in case of a fire. It just makes me feel better knowing that my daughter is in such a safe environment," says Bowen.

Massachusetts—like California—has been a leader in creating quality child care for two decades. It is one of the few states to require every family child care provider—even those who care for only one child besides their own—to obey strict health and safety rules. "That other child may be mine—or yours," says Doug Baird, president of Associated Day Care Services, New England's oldest and largest nonprofit child care agency. It is "unthinkable" that a mother who cares for any child other than her own go unregulated, Baird declares—even though that is exactly the case in most other states.

The high standards not only exist on paper, they are enforced better in this state than in most, despite the state's tight budget. Bowen can recall several surprise state inspections at her daughter's family child care home. The inspectors never found much wrong, but it added to Bowen's peace of mind.

Just as important, Massachusetts has moved to ensure that all child care center teachers, lead teachers and directors are individually certified. This state has adopted a plan to create credentials and a career path for child care workers to help lift their wages and eventually match the salaries of elementary-school teachers. By improving opportunities in the field, the state hopes to curb the high turnover rates that typically plague centers—a move child care experts agree would dramatically improve the quality of care, especially for infants.

MINNESOTA

QUALITY: GOOD
Number of children one adult may care for: Infants: 4 • Toddlers: 4–7 • Two's: 7 • Preschoolers: 10
Group size: Regulated
AVAILABILITY: EXCELLENT
Number of regulated spaces per 100 children: 20
SAFETY: GOOD
Size at which family child care is regulated: 2 children
Immunization in family child care: Required
Monitoring and enforcement: Good
COMMITMENT: EXCELLENT
Preeminent in training for both family child care providers and center staffs; funds grants to family child care providers to improve quality; child care tax credit; six weeks' leave to care for newborn for workers in firms with 21 or more employees; leader in parent education. Climate in this state encourages private businesses to help employees with work/family conflicts. Most notable has been Dayton Hudson Corporation's $2.8 million grant to Child Care Aware, a national campaign to educate the public about the need for high-quality care.

Nowhere in the United States is the probability of finding licensed child care—whether center-based or in a family child care home—greater than in Minnesota. And since Minnesota pays a bonus for its state-assisted children in centers that meet the high standards of the National Association for the Education of Young Children, much of that child care is likely to be superior rather than merely acceptable.

Working parents in Minnesota are also lucky when it comes to after-school care. In this state, every town with a population of 10,000 or more is required to have at least one school with before- and after-school care prorams, which can be used by any resident in the town.

"I'd go nuts without such safe, stable child care," says Barbara Fraley, an account supervisor for an advertising agency in Minneapolis. Both her kindergartner and her third-grader attend the community-sponsored programs, which also run during all school holidays. Fraley pays $230 a month for her third-grader and $350 a month for her kindergartner's before- and after-school programs, but the quality and reliability have won her over. "The kids go on fabulous field trips—to apple orchards, bowling alleys—they've even had a slumber party!"

Parents do get help paying for child care, thanks to state tax breaks for child care expenses. And nowhere but in Minnesota will you find a family leave law that provides workers with 16 hours off from work each year to attend school conferences.

VERMONT

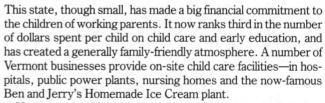

QUALITY: EXCELLENT
Number of children one adult may care for:
Infants: 4 • Toddlers: 4 • Two's: 5 •
Preschoolers: 10
Group size: Well regulated
AVAILABILITY: EXCELLENT
Number of regulated spaces per 100 children: 18
SAFETY: FAIR
Size at which family child care is regulated: No specific size except when there are children from 3 or more families
Immunization in family child care: Required
Monitoring and enforcement: Adequate
COMMITMENT: VERY GOOD
Ranks third in dollars spent per child on early-childhood services; high level of investment in training caregivers; family leave law allows workers in firms with 10 or more employees to take 12 weeks for childbirth.

This state, though small, has made a big financial commitment to the children of working parents. It now ranks third in the number of dollars spent per child on child care and early education, and has created a generally family-friendly atmosphere. A number of Vermont businesses provide on-site child care facilities—in hospitals, public power plants, nursing homes and the now-famous Ben and Jerry's Homemade Ice Cream plant.

Vermont sets high standards for child care centers, a fact many parents appreciate. "I am so glad to know that the staff of my son's center has certain regulations to answer to," says Paula Apfelbach, from Richmond, who takes two-and-a-half-year-old Christopher to Annette's Playschool, a local child care center. "Knowing that the state is sending inspectors gives me extra confidence that Christopher is in good care."

Why is this state so responsive to the needs of working parents? It may be because it has one of the highest female participation rates in the labor force in the United States. "Although wages are low in Vermont, the cost of living, especially housing and heating, is high. The mother with young children really doesn't have a choice about working. The family needs the second income," says Helen Keith, former director of the state's child care programs.

The demand for child care has created an astounding statistic: Every 249th adult Vermonter is a registered child care provider. With their independent Yankee outlook, however, legislators of this state don't impose many regulations on family child care. Vermont does fund programs to train caregivers, and relies on providers with smaller enrollments to meet state rules voluntarily. The state does conduct random unannounced inspections of its larger family child care homes.

Many observers inside and outside the state believe that in

this state, the carrot may work as well as the stick, and that the system is, as Gwen Morgan of Work/Family Directions says, "user-friendly." Many providers take advantage of state-sponsored training programs at local universities and colleges, and parents are well informed about making choices.

WASHINGTON

QUALITY: GOOD
Number of children one adult may care for: Infants: 4 • Toddlers: 7 • Two's: 10 • Preschoolers: 10
Group size: Regulated
AVAILABILITY: GOOD
Number of regulated spaces per 100 children: 10
SAFETY: VERY GOOD
Size at which family child care is regulated: 1 child
Immunization in family child care: Required
Monitoring and enforcement: Good
COMMITMENT: GOOD
Stands eighth in expenditure for direct child care and early-childhood services; outstanding efforts to improve the quality of family child care; significant state investment in Head Start; family leave law allows workers in firms with 100 or more employees to take 12 weeks for childbirth, adoption and child illness; encouragement for business involvement.

Washington has made tremendous strides in child care in the last seven years: Funding for child care slots zoomed from $24 million to $160 million, the number of licensed family child care homes mushroomed from almost 6,000 to 8,200, and the number of child care referral agencies went from practically none to 15, which now cover most of the state.

These efforts make a critical difference to working parents. Sally Reigel, for example, has not only used the state-sponsored referral service to find care for her son, but also gets help paying for it. "Since child care is so expensive, those costs would eat up my salary," says Reigel, who works as an employer specialist with the Child Care Action Council in Olympia.

The state also keeps a watchful eye on the quality of child care. A strong licensing program brought thousands of new family child care providers into compliance with state standards, and Washington has added to its inspection staff to keep pace with this growth. It has also created support for family child care providers, offering them an extensive resource guide that includes activities for children, as well as answers to common questions on health and child development. The guide is considered a model for the profession.

In addition, Washington works closely with employers to encourage them to provide family-friendly benefits such as flextime and child care services, and offers annual Child Care Solutions Awards to exemplary companies. Last year, four employers—two health care facilities, a sporting-goods manufacturer (JanSport) and the University of Washington—were recognized for giving their employees such benefits as on-site child care and flexible work arrangements.

Working parents in the city of Seattle are especially fortunate. In addition to state programs, they also benefit from two local initiatives: In 1986, city voters passed a $5 million bond issue to pay for child care facilities at 14 elementary schools. In 1991, voters approved another levy to raise $1.4 million a year for seven years to expand after-school and low-income child care.

WISCONSIN

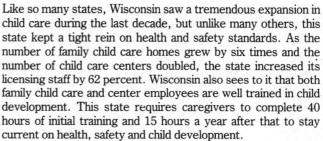

QUALITY: EXCELLENT
Number of children one adult may care for: Infants: 4 • Toddlers: 4 • Two's: 6–8 • Preschoolers: 10–13
Group size: Well regulated
AVAILABILITY: GOOD
Number of regulated spaces per 100 children: 10
SAFETY: GOOD
Size at which family child care is regulated: 4 children
Immunizations in family child care: Required
Monitoring and enforcement: Good
COMMITMENT: EXCELLENT
Requires training for family child care providers and center teachers; has a grant program for school-age child care programs and to help family child care providers get started; family leave law provides time off to care for a newborn or seriously ill family member or the worker herself when employed by a business with 50 or more workers.

Like so many states, Wisconsin saw a tremendous expansion in child care during the last decade, but unlike many others, this state kept a tight rein on health and safety standards. As the number of family child care homes grew by six times and the number of child care centers doubled, the state increased its licensing staff by 62 percent. Wisconsin also sees to it that both family child care and center employees are well trained in child development. This state requires caregivers to complete 40 hours of initial training and 15 hours a year after that to stay current on health, safety and child development.

Laura Koenig, an occupational therapist in Appleton, sees the impact of the state's initiatives on her daughter's care. "Glenna, my provider, gets unannounced visits from the state several times a year. The inspectors watch Glenna with the kids—how she feeds them, diapers them," Koenig says. "They also check out the changing table, making sure it's clean, and the sleeping quarters to see how often the sheets are changed. I make my own unannounced visits, but it's nice to know that inspectors are observing the details that I don't see."

Wisconsin has accomplished this quality control at some cost. During the late 1980s, the state simplified its rules and streamlined its inspection process for family child care. It also started a Child Care Improvement Project, which makes advisers available to help child care providers meet standards.

THE JUDGES: In addition to Helen Blank and Gwen Morgan, the following nationally recognized experts helped choose WORKING MOTHER's 10 Best: Ellen Galinsky, Co-President, Families and Work Institute; Linda Geigle, President, National Association for Family Day Care; Kay Hollestelle, Executive Director, The Children's Foundation; Barbara Reisman, Executive Director, Child Care Action Campaign; Pat Ward, Director, National Council of Jewish Women's National Family Day Care Project; Marcy Whitebook, Executive Director, Child Care Employee Project; Barbara Willer, Director of Public Affairs, National Association for the Education of Young Children.

Head Start's Big Test

Can '60s Success Story Fill '90s Role?

Mary Jordan

Washington Post Staff Writer

Every weekday morning, Erica Robinson steps out of her beaten-up, brick public housing project and into what has long been described as America's smartest social program.

With her great-grandmother holding her hand, Erica, who turned 5 yesterday, climbs the stairs to the Lincoln Heights Head Start center, six rooms of warmth, food and care. Inside, waffles warm children's plates, rainbow-colored carpets layer the floor, a record player spins out "Oh! Susanna," and a teacher readies books and blocks and paints. I'ts a cheerful place that seems a million miles from the ugly graffiti and barred and broken windows outside.

One of more than 720,000 American children enrolled in this program that was born during the 1960s' War on Poverty. Erica may be in the first Head Start class that goes year-round—the first "Clinton" class. Not only is President Clinton seeking $500 million to keep centers open this summer, he is pushing for such a huge school-year expansion that some liken his fervor for Head Start to former president Ronald Reagan's zeal for Star Wars.

While squeezing budgets nearly everywhere else, Clinton is splurging here—seeking to add $8 billion by 1997 to a program that costs $2.8 billion this year.

But as the dollars proposed for Head Start soar, so has criticism of the program. Even advocates are worried about such a huge increase, wondering if the preschool program is ready to grow so fast. And, in Congress, many are now insisting on big changes as Head Start rushes toward becoming the entitlement program of the 1990s.

Two new unpublished inspector general reports obtained by The Washington Post outline many of the chief concerns:

Some of the preschool centers now have trouble spending all their money; others have rotten facilities and management; most have trouble attracting effective teachers.

"I can guarantee that there will be a debate," said Sen. Tom Harkin (D-Iowa), chairman of the Senate Appropriations subcommittee on labor, health and human services and education. Harkin said he supports Head Start but wants it improved.

HEAD START FUNDING

1990	$1.5 billion
1993	$2.8 billion
1997*	$11–12 billion

*Clinton administration proposal

The Washington Post

High on his list of improvements are better wages—teachers average $16,000 a year and aides $8,000—and a program, now mainly for 4-year-olds, that extends to younger children. In light of research showing that the benefits of the preschool program completely fade by the time the child reaches the second grade, Harkin says Head Start's health, social and educational care should not end when disadvantaged children start kindergarten.

"I would not want to spend double [on the program] as it is right now," Harken said in an interview.

The Health and Human Services inspector general's latest reports outline the reasons for Harkin's reservations. Inspectors reviewed the files of 80 centers and 3,200 preschoolers. Among the findings:

- Thirteen percent of the centers couldn't spend all of their budgeted money.
- Half had serious management problems.
- Only 43 percent of the preschoolers had been given all the required immu-

nizations. Nearly 70 percent of the children, for instance, did not receive the full course of polio vaccinations.

- One in four families was not given the basic needs assessments required under the program to determine such simple matters as whether families need medicine and know how to get it.

HHS officials said the records at some centers were in such disarray that many more children than indicated have been tested and vaccinated. But even advocates acknowledge some of the Head Start centers have fundamental flaws, such as having semi-literate instructors teaching children in dreary rooms.

And as reservations grow, even Clinton in recent days has backed off his most ambitious claims for Head Start.

In his State of the Union address on Feb. 17. Clinton said: "We all know that [Head Start] saves money. For every dollar we invest today, we'll save three tomorrow. . . . It is not just the right thing to do, it is the smart thing."

But more recently, on March 11, as scholars challenged him to prove the down the line savings in reduced juvenile delinquency and improvements in other social problems Clinton modified his praise.

"Sure there are serious criticisms," he told a Children's Defense Fund audience. "There are people who say it's not evenly good across the country. That is true. There are people who say it could be managed better. That is true. There are people who say that cognitive improvements don't always last more than two years after children stop attending—depending on where they are. That's true." Clinton concluded by saying that none of this was "an excuse not to fully fund Head Start."

In a recent meeting with Washington Post editors and reporters, HHS Secretary Donna E. Shalala also acknowledged that there was a "serious issue" about whether Head Start could take the "strain" of fast expansion. Nor should we be in the business of just pouring money into the existing program when we know that there are some fundamental problems," she said.

As top White House officials shift the strategy for selling Head Start—away from seeking money for a wildly successful program and toward fixing and expanding a somewhat flawed program—a back-room debate has been ignited. How much of the new money should go to fix the flaws—such as paying higher salaries to attract more qualified teachers—and how much toward expanding? Is any of this spending wise without expensive follow-through programs? Should subsidies be considered for the growing network on non-Head Start preschool programs? And, if long-term success is the aim, would it not make more sense to pump more money into public schools?

"The clock is ticking to the administration's disadvantage," said Douglas J. Besharov, a scholar at the American Enterprise Institute. Because key HHS appointees are not yet in place, the debate is going on without them.

"There are big decisions to make by May 1," Besharov said, nothing the timetable of a congressional vote on funding.

"As far as I can tell, the administration is not a player in the discussions."

Bill Hughey, a director of the United Planning Organization, which runs the Lincoln Heights Head Start center, said that many front line managers are hoping more attention is paid to upgrading the quality of the program. "Because of the struggles we have now with staffing and facilities," he said the program will grow weaker if it expands without increasing teachers salaries and upgrading facilities.

Counting teachers salaries and facilities, the government spends between $3,700 and $4,000 per preschooler.

But many others are worried that no matter how high the per-student investment goes, the biggest problem will still exist: That benefits, from better skills to higher self-esteem, will fade shortly after the preschooler graduates from the program and enters public school. And several billion dollars later, no one will know the difference between the 1 million disadvantaged children who are to enroll in the program this fall and the 1 million preschoolers who do not.

For Erica Robinson, there are no such questions.

She, like many of the 23 other preschoolers at the Lincoln Heights Head Start center, were born into poverty and broken homes and find Head Start a bright place on dim days. Erica's mother left her when she was 3 months old and it is her Head Start teacher, Tamar Chew, who reminds her to drink her juice, brush her teeth, learn new words.

From 9 a.m. until 3 p.m. Erica has the run of the preschool center on 50th Street in Northeast Washington. It is not a perfect place. It shuts down because of water pipe breaks, has a single 20-year-old Cahfone record player and lockers with broken knobs. But Erica has her own blue cot with her name on it for her afternoon nap. The rooms are clean, brimming with books and food. And Chew is always there looking out for those who need glasses or a doctor or a hug.

"Their needs have greatly changed," said Chew, who has been teaching Head Start since Lyndon B. Johnson, who first funded it, was president. "Then the children who came already knew shapes, colors and numbers. They were more mature, more ready to learn."

Now, the teacher said, her students have far greater problems. "We have to spend a lot of time telling them, 'You are important. You are somebody'."

HEART START:
The Emotional Foundations of School Readiness

There is so much we can do to foster children's innate desire to learn. *Heart Start* **is a blueprint for action.**

Why don't all preschoolers flourish equally under your care? Could it be that some simply have no heart for learning? Writing in *Heart Start: The Emotional Foundations of School Readiness* (ZERO TO THREE/National Center for Clinical Infant Programs, 1992), Ernest L. Boyer, president of the Carnegie Foundation for the Advancement of Teaching, had this to say: "Even in preschool, children vary greatly in their readiness to learn. Some are more intellectually curious than others. Some read and speak well, while others have difficulty communicating. Some concentrate more readily than others. Some play and interact successfully with their peers, while others prefer to pick fights or remain alone at the fringe of classroom activity."

Heart Start addresses the variability in children's readiness to learn. Published as three booklets and a one-

page summary of recommendations, Heart Start is a new action initiative of ZERO TO THREE (see box). The goal is to provide four groups of people — parents, caregivers, policy makers, and concerned citizens — with the information they need to ensure that, *before the age of three years*, all children develop the emotional foundation they need for learning.

The Right Heart-Set for Learning

In the past two decades, a great deal has been learned about how children develop. T. Berry Brazelton, M.D., renowned pediatrician and president of ZERO TO THREE at the time the Heart Start initiative was begun, feels strongly that the expectation to succeed or fail is established in infancy. "In our diagnostic work at Children's Hospital in Boston, we can tell by eight months of age whether a baby expects to succeed or to fail by the

way he or she approaches a task." Dr. Brazelton and other experts feel that how children develop depends on the manner and consistency in which they, as infants, are responded to and encouraged.

But what, specifically, do babies need in order to develop the emotional foundation for learning? Heart Start identifies four basic categories of needs: *health, unhurried time, responsive caregiving,* and *safe and supportive environments.* In addition, children with special health needs, or whose families have special problems such as substance abuse or depression, need special help.

How Heart Start Works

Heart Start is an advocacy tool of compelling clarity. It combines non-technical writing and clear examples with detailed recommendations for action. It is written not only for parents, caregivers, and policy makers, but for other citizens as well, including those who are concerned about the nation's economy but may never have recognized the connection between the fiscal health of a nation and the social policies affecting its children and families.

A sampling of Heart Start's recommendations follows, grouped according to the four basic needs of infants and toddlers.

Health: Make affordable, accessible health care available to all, including universal health-care coverage and expanded prevention programs in underserved areas; make child care a health resource by having states require that all child-care providers be trained to recognize apparent health and developmental problems and identify appropriate services.

Unhurried caring: Adopt policies to assure that infants have time with parents and family members, and favorable ratios and continuity in care-child situations; require states to set higher minimum child-care wages, and provide tax benefits to offset the cost to poor families.

Responsive caregiving: Make parenting education and family support programs available, and promote pre- and in-service training to health-care and child-care providers that emphasizes the need for building supportive relationships with parents; institute state and community requirements that child-care providers be trained in infant development at least to the Child Development Associate (CDA) competency standard.

Safe and supportive environments: Provide tax credits and other supports to low-income and single-parent families to defray the costs of child rearing and reduce the child poverty rate; mandate adequate play space in child-care centers and in family child-care settings.

Heart Start: Who Needs It?

In 1989, President Bush and the National Governors' Association set a series of six education goals for the country. The first, called the "readiness goal," has as one objective that all children, by the year 2000, will arrive in school ready to learn. Behind the readiness goal are two concerns. The first is humanitarian: that the individual child who never embraces learning will be deprived of much pride, satisfaction, and stimulation in his or her life. The second is economic: that young men and women who never develop the characteristics they need to learn in school will find it difficult, maybe even impossible, to find productive employment in our increasingly technological society. Clearly, school readiness is important for both

individual and national well-being.

ZERO TO THREE published Heart Start to help the nation reach the readiness goal.

Next Steps

After people understand the need for wise, family-friendly policies, what happens next? Clearly, the interested parties in local communities — elected officials, corporate leaders, community foundation staff, service providers, parents — need to sit down together, discuss the issues raised in Heart Start and examine the extent and quality of their communities' services for infants, toddlers, and their families. To begin this process, ZERO TO THREE is planning to conduct a series of three "Heart Start Days" at

selected localities before the end of 1993. The communities chosen to participate in these "self-assessment" events will be selected from among those around the country that applied to ZERO TO THREE before a deadline of February 1, 1993, for help in organizing a Heart Start Day. (For more information on this initiative, contact Joan Melner at the address given in the box on this page.)

In the end, Heart Start does more than propose a set of new social policies. It calls for a new way of looking at social policy. It asks that from now on, all policy initiatives, both public and private, be held up to this standard: that they improve — or at the very least not worsen — the situation of the nation's youngest children.

ZERO TO THREE

ZERO TO THREE/National Center for Clinical Infant Programs is the only national nonprofit organization dedicated solely to improving the chances for healthy physical, cognitive, and social development of infants, toddlers, and their families. It was founded in 1977 by 12 experts in health, mental health, and human development. They wanted to share with families, caregivers, and especially policy makers the "new" knowledge about how infants and toddlers develop.

Objectives
• To educate the nation about the importance of the first three years of life as well as the importance of prevention and early intervention in helping children grow and develop in healthy ways.
• To determine the best ways to provide services for infants and toddlers and their families, and to promote whatever training is needed to provide them.

Programs
• Training programs and materials that foster an interdisciplinary approach to health and development in the first three years of life.
• Technical assistance at many levels on ways to make services more effective.
• Education of policy makers and the general public about the complex needs of today's infants, toddlers, and families.

Publications/Information
ZERO TO THREE has an extensive list of publications and tapes, some prepared for parents and general readers, others for professionals of many kinds. For a complete listing, or for information on the Heart Start initiative, write to ZERO TO THREE, 2000 14th Street N., Suite 380, Arlington, VA 22201, or call (703) 528-4300.

Child Care Workers Fight For Worthy Wages

Low-pay and difficult working conditions lead 4 out of 10 child care workers to quit or be dismissed within a year of beginning their jobs

Camille Colatosti

Camille Colatosti, co-author of Stopping Sexual Harassment: A Handbook for Union and Workplace Activists, *directs the Working Women's Project in Detroit.*

Why did the child care worker cross the road?" Wendy Shepherd-Bates, an advocate for child care workers, asked her dinner companion. But to Shepherd-Bates' surprise, the waitress answered the question.

"To get to her second job," she said. "I've heard that joke before. I work as a day care teacher during the day. But I wait tables at night to pay my bills."

The waitress's moonlighting isn't uncommon for child care teachers, who, according to the National Committee on Pay Equity, work in the second most underpaid occupation in the U.S.. (Clergy work is the first.) The three million child care workers in the country—96 percent of whom are women—average $9,724 annually. Less than 30 percent receive employer-paid health insurance. Most earn no paid vacation. And fewer than one in five has a retirement plan.

Marcy Whitebook, executive director of the Child Care Employee Project, an advocacy group for day care providers, attributes the low pay to society's view of women's work. "A child care teacher is the quintessential women worker," she explains. "So many people think that child care is not skilled work, that it's just playing with babies all day. More importantly, child care is not something that families have traditionally paid for. It's something women have done while men do the real—paid—work."

But today fewer than 7.5 percent of all U.S. families have a father who goes to work and mother who stays home to care for the children. By 1995, more than two-thirds of preschoolers and over three-fourths of school-age children will have working mothers.

Clearly, someone needs to care for children while parents work. Unfortunately, low-pay and difficult working conditions lead 4 out of 10 child care workers to quit or be dismissed within a year of beginning their jobs. Day care providers complain about the long hours and the high teacher to child ratio at many facilities. Some providers have to care for as many as seven infants at once. To child care activists, the situation is nearing a crisis.

As Wendy Shepherd-Bates explains, "Many well-trained, college-educated people who start careers in child care with hope and enthusiasm eventually leave the field in disgust."

Shepherd-Bates knows this firsthand. She left the profession when the poverty became too much for her. "I made $9,500 a year, worked 80 hours a week, had no benefits, three vacation days, and no sick days," she explains. "I used to eat breakfast and lunch at the center because I couldn't afford food.

"I got home from work one day and looked in the fridge. I had a bottle of pop and half a loaf of bread. That same day, I received a cancellation notice for my auto insurance and a late-payment notice for health insurance. I decided I had to move on. I left the work I loved and became a secretary."

Question Of Quality

Activists argue that the high turnover of child care workers actually hurts children's language and social development. "Now that parents are becoming aware of this, they're beginning to ask questions," says Rosalie Street, executive director of Parent Action, a national parents' rights group.

She likewise notes that the low wages of child care

workers surprise many parents. After all, they feel that they're paying a large sum of money for care.

Day care costs for one child average $3,500. "For a single parent, earning $16,000 a year," says CCEP's Whitebook, "child care costs eat up 25 to 33 percent of her budget." In fact, for many parents, child care is their single biggest household expense, after rent or mortgage payments.

However, some families don't get the chance to worry about day care costs. A shortage of services puts child care beyond their reach. Almost 10 million children under age six lack needed care. Another 10 million under age 11 lack before and after-school programs. In Los Angeles county, for example, 155,000 children compete for 7,000 available openings.

To make matters worse, much of the care that is available isn't regulated. Only 23 states have training requirements for child care teachers.

Non-System System

To educate the public about the problems that child care providers face, and to increase workers' compensation, the Child Care Employee Project launched the Worthy Wage Campaign two years ago. Sponsored by a coalition of 250 child care centers and children's rights groups nationwide, members include the Children's Defense Fund, the National Association for the Education of Young Children, the National Head Start Association, the National Association of Family Day Care, and several labor unions.

The Campaign platform highlights a five-year plan to win paid health insurance for child care providers; to increase wages to $10 an hour, and to make federal reimbursements for parents' child care costs more equitable than they are now. Currently, federal aid applies only to the poorest parents, while the wealthiest earn tax credits. But working-class and middle-income families receive no relief at all.

The Worthy Wage Campaign begins from the premise that, because high quality child care costs more than most parents can afford to pay, the nation as a whole needs to subsidize child care as it does public education.

"We need a national child care program, just as we need national health insurance," says Rosemarie Vardell of United Day Care Services in North Carolina. "We all know about the 37 million people in this country without health insurance. Now we need to talk about the child care workers slaving away for low wages and no recognition. We have to discuss the working mothers struggling to meet their child care bills. And we need to talk about the children who watch their favorite providers leave the field."

While government and corporations currently en-

courage women to enter the labor force, they do little to meet the needs of working women. Only 4,150 U.S. companies, out of six million, offer any form of child care assistance. Much of this is minimal—referral and information services or lunch-time child care seminars.

And only 200 companies and 200 government offices provide on-site or near-site day care facilities. While these centers offer convenience, and peace-of-mind to parents who know they can see their children anytime, they are by no means perfect. Many remain expensive and overcrowded. The center at Queen of Angels/Hollywood Presbyterian Medical Center, for example, costs parents $97.50 per child every 10 days. Able to accommodate only 32 children, it has a waiting list of 30 or more. Likewise, because many continue to compensate teachers poorly, turnover remains high.

Federal child care and developmental block grant programs offer only minimal relief: $925 million in 1993. This amount comes nowhere near the almost $14 billion annually that parents with children under age 15 spend on child care.

To CCEP's Marcy Whitebook, the block grants are really a "mixed bag." It took three years—and a number of trade-offs—to get them through the legislature. Proponents sacrificed the national child care standards that were proposed in early versions of the bill. And, adds Whitebook, "The block grants are a testing ground for parental choice. Parents can use their child care grant for any facility, religious or secular, regardless of whether or not the caregiver is licensed."

Perhaps most important, the money that is available is restricted. California, for example, received $77 million last year in federal child care aid. But only five percent of that could be used for "compensation improvements"—increasing workers' wages.

Worthy Wages

The high point of the Worthy Wage Campaign comes each year in April, on Worthy Wage Day. This year events took place in 40 states. Child care teachers, parents, children and supporters from Anchorage to San Francisco, from Portland, Maine, to Portland, Oregon, marched, rallied, wore "Worthy Wage" buttons and T-shirts to work, sponsored plays and art exhibits, held press conferences, and met with legislators to demand higher pay.

North Carolina coalition members and supporters, for example, mailed mock $10 bills to legislators, demanding government assistance. "Instead of a picture of a president," explains Rosemarie Vardell, "the bills sport a child care emblem. They're blank on the back, so that people can write their own messages."

In Twin Falls, Idaho, children led a parade down Main Street. They held stuffed animals that bore campaign slogans. In Stamford, Connecticut, coalition members held a candlelight vigil for the teachers who left the profession.

Even major sports figures got involved. A Charlotte Hornet basketball player agreed to donate one hour to a day care center. He'll contribute the difference between his hourly wage—close to $2,500—and that of a child care teacher—about $5.35—to the local Worthy Wage Coalition.

Detroit activists convinced the owner of the Tigers baseball team to broadcast 20 statistics about child care teachers—salary, turnover rates, skill level—on the electronic scoreboard during a game.

"The major success of the day," says CCEP's Marcy Whitebook, "was that child care teachers took the lead. This year, finally, they said, 'I deserve to earn a decent living.' I can't tell you what a difficult time it's been convincing people that they can demand more money."

"For the average child care provider," explains Detroit Campaign leader Wendy Shepherd-Bates, "the Worthy Wage Campaign is all about self-esteem. You can't convince others that you deserve higher wages until you convince yourself that your work is worth more. For many teachers, the Campaign itself is threatening. They aren't used to being assertive. Worthy Wage Day helps women find their voices."

Unionization

For Shepherd-Bates, one solution to all the problems that child care workers face involves unionizing. "Why have public school teachers gotten as far as they have?" she asks. "Because they have unions. Now they do work they love—and they make money."

Elda Chesebrough, of the U.S. Coast Guard Child Care Development Center in Connecticut, agrees. "Child care teachers here average $5.35 an hour, without health insurance. If we're lucky, we might get two weeks *unpaid* vacation. Connecticut public school teachers, by contrast, start at $27,000 a year, and average $44,000. It's crazy—especially since studies clearly show that children develop their most important language, learning and social skills before age six."

Currently, only 4 percent of child care workers are unionized compared to 15 percent of women workers nationwide. Unionized child care teachers work primarily in public school systems. Or, they work with Head Start—a federally subsidized pre-school program for high risk children. About one-quarter of Head Start workers belong to unions. Centers in large cities are more likely to be unionized than those in suburban or rural areas. In New York, for example, almost all publicly funded centers are unionized.

Belonging to a union can raise the wages of child care workers by as much as 33 percent. It also brings health insurance, paid vacation, and sick leave. Not surprisingly, unionized workers have the lowest turnover rates of anyone in the field.

No one union has taken responsibility for the industry: the American Federation of State, County and Municipal Employees has unionized some workers in New York; the American Federation of Teachers and the Service Employees International Union have organized in California; and District 65 of the United Auto Workers has organized in Massachusetts, Wisconsin, and Michigan.

As in every field today, winning union elections proves difficult. Dylann Robertson, an infant-toddler caregiver at Waverly Children's Home in Portland, Oregon, puts it this way, "Organizing workers involves answering questions and addressing fears and concerns. This is very time consuming and emotionally taxing."

In Robertson's workplace, a majority of employees supported a recent union drive and signed membership cards with the Oregon Public Employees Union. But when management refused to recognize the union as a legitimate force, many teachers felt discouraged. The National Labor Relations Board is overseeing an election at Waverly, but—because of bureaucratic delays, management intimidation and rapid employee turnover—it's unclear how many union supporters will stick with the job long enough to vote the union in.

Nevertheless, the union drive offers hope to some teachers. Child care provider Susan Sanazaro, for example, loves her work and wants a union so that she can afford to keep her job.

"I wish management could understand," she explains, "that our wish for a union doesn't belie our attachment to Waverly. Many positive relationships exist among workers and management, but rights and obligations need to be codified by a contract and not depend on the good will of an always-fluctuating set of personalities that come and go."

Whitebook likewise believes that unions are important to child care workers, but she wonders if workplace organizing, as it is traditionally defined, is enough. "It's not just a question of redistributing the wealth, because there may not be any wealth there," she explains. "Most child care teachers work in small, isolated centers. They work with a handful of other teachers, and a director who's struggling financially. The real issue involves seeing child care as a form of public education.

"My feeling is that good child care is expensive and we can't shy away from that. As a society, we need to set our priorities and stop exploiting teachers. Employers and government—and not underpaid women workers—need to subsidize the industry."

Credits/ Acknowledgments

Cover design by Charles Vitelli

1. Perspectives
Facing overview—United Nations photo by Jack Ling. 13-17—Photos courtesy of Assessorato Scuole Infanzia e Asili Nido, Comune Reggio Emilia, Italy. 18-21—Photos courtesy of JoAn Vaughan.

2. Child Development and Families
Facing overview—Photo by Elaine M. Ward.

3. Appropriate Educational Practices
Facing overview—The Dushkin Publishing Group, Inc., photo.

4. Guiding Behavior
Facing overview—United Nations photo by Shelley Rotner. 172—Photo by Subjects & Predicates.

5. Curricular Applications
Facing overview—United Nations photo by John Isaac.

6. Reflections
Facing overview—United Nations photo by Christina D. Sagona. 228-233—Illustrations by Martie Holmer.

ANNUAL EDITIONS ARTICLE REVIEW FORM

■ NAME: _____ DATE: _____

■ TITLE AND NUMBER OF ARTICLE: _____

■ BRIEFLY STATE THE MAIN IDEA OF THIS ARTICLE: _____

_____

_____

_____

_____

■ LIST THREE IMPORTANT FACTS THAT THE AUTHOR USES TO SUPPORT THE MAIN IDEA:

_____

_____

_____

_____

_____

■ WHAT INFORMATION OR IDEAS DISCUSSED IN THIS ARTICLE ARE ALSO DISCUSSED IN YOUR
TEXTBOOK OR OTHER READING YOU HAVE DONE? LIST THE TEXTBOOK CHAPTERS AND PAGE
NUMBERS:

_____

_____

_____

_____

_____

_____

■ LIST ANY EXAMPLES OF BIAS OR FAULTY REASONING THAT YOU FOUND IN THE ARTICLE:

_____

_____

_____

_____

■ LIST ANY NEW TERMS/CONCEPTS THAT WERE DISCUSSED IN THE ARTICLE AND WRITE A
SHORT DEFINITION:

_____

_____

_____

_____

_____

*Your instructor may require you to use this Annual Editions Article Review Form in any number of ways:
for articles that are assigned, for extra credit, as a tool to assist in developing assigned papers, or simply
for your own reference. Even if it is not required, we encourage you to photocopy and use this page;
you'll find that reflecting on the articles will greatly enhance the information from your text.

ANNUAL EDITIONS:
EARLY CHILDHOOD EDUCATION 94/95
Article Rating Form

Here is an opportunity for you to have direct input into the next revision of this volume. We would like you to rate each of the 46 articles listed below, using the following scale:

1. **Excellent: should definitely be retained**
2. **Above average: should probably be retained**
3. **Below average: should probably be deleted**
4. **Poor: should definitely be deleted**

Your ratings will play a vital part in the next revision. So please mail this prepaid form to us just as soon as you complete it.
Thanks for your help!

Annual Editions revisions depend on two major opinion sources: one is our Advisory Board, listed in the front of this volume, which works with us in scanning the thousands of articles published in the public press each year; the other is you—the person actually using the book. Please help us and the users of the next edition by completing the prepaid article rating form on this page and returning it to us. Thank you.

Rating	Article	Rating	Article
	1. The World's 5 Best Ideas		24. Preschool Mainstreaming: Attitude Barriers and Strategies for Addressing Them
	2. Fundamentals of the Reggio Emilia Approach to Early Childhood Education		25. A Place for Marie: Guidelines for the Integration Process
	3. Early Childhood Education in China		26. Infants and Toddlers with Special Needs and Their Families
	4. Where Did Our Diversity Come From? A Profile of Early Childhood Care and Education in the U.S.		27. Trouble with Testing
	5. Preventing Early School Failure: What Works?		28. Assessment in Context—Teachers and Children at Work
	6. Television, Kids, and the Real Danny Kaye		29. The Assessment Portfolio as an Attitude
	7. The Crisis of the Absent Father		30. A Positive Approach to Discipline in an Early Childhood Setting
	8. When Parents Accept the Unacceptable		31. The Tasks of Early Childhood: The Development of Self-Control—Part II
	9. Homeless Children: A Special Challenge		32. Helping Children Cope with Violence
	10. Helping Crack-Affected Children Succeed		33. Supporting Victims of Child Abuse
	11. Questions about Serving Children with HIV/AIDS		34. How Kids Survive Trauma
	12. The Amazing Minds of Infants		35. Managing the Early Childhood Classroom
	13. How Boys and Girls Learn Differently		36. Curriculum Webs: Weaving Connections from Children to Teachers
	14. Little Big People		37. The Creative Arts Process: What It Is and What It Is Not
	15. Separation and Divorce: Children Want Their Teachers to Know		38. I Can Write! Encouraging Emergent Writers
	16. "Don't Leave Me": Separation Distress in Infants, Toddlers, and Parents		39. Integrating Technology into the Classroom: Lessons from the Project CHILD Experience
	17. Beyond Parents: Family, Community, and School Involvement		40. All about Me
	18. How Schools Perpetuate Illiteracy		41. African American Children
	19. Recognizing the Essentials of Developmentally Appropriate Practice		42. Grounds for Play: Sound, Safe, and Sensational
	20. Developmental Continuity: From Preschool through Primary Grades		43. The 10 Best States for Child Care
	21. What Good Prekindergarten Programs Look Like		44. Head Start's Big Test
	22. Collaborative Training in the Education of Early Childhood Educators		45. Heart Start: The Emotional Foundations of School Readiness
	23. Preschool Classroom Environments That Promote Communication		46. Child Care Workers Fight for Worthy Wages

(Continued on next page)

ABOUT YOU

Name_____ Date_____

Are you a teacher? ☐ Or student? ☐

Your School Name _____

Department _____

Address _____

City _____ State _____ Zip _____

School Telephone # _____

YOUR COMMENTS ARE IMPORTANT TO US!

Please fill in the following information:

For which course did you use this book? _____

Did you use a text with this Annual Edition? ☐ yes ☐ no

The title of the text? _____

What are your general reactions to the Annual Editions concept?

Have you read any particular articles recently that you think should be included in the next edition?

Are there any articles you feel should be replaced in the next edition? Why?

Are there other areas that you feel would utilize an Annual Edition?

May we contact you for editorial input?

May we quote you from above?

ANNUAL EDITIONS: EARLY CHILDHOOD EDUCATION 94/95

BUSINESS REPLY MAIL

First Class   Permit No. 84   Guilford, CT

Postage will be paid by addressee

The Dushkin Publishing Group, Inc.
Sluice Dock
DPG **Guilford, Connecticut 06437**